LAND O LAKES®

TREASURY OF

COUNTRY

RECIPES

CREDITS:

Published 1992 by
Tormont Publications Inc.
338 Saint Antoine St. East
Montreal, Canada   H2Y 1A3
Tel. (514) 954-1441
Fax (514) 954-1443

Recipes developed and tested by the Land O'Lakes Test Kitchens,
with assistance from Robin Krause and Barbara Strand.

Design, photography and production by Cy DeCosse Incorporated.

Recipes and manuscript © 1987, 1988, 1989 Land O'Lakes, Inc.
Design and photography © 1987, 1988, 1989 Cy DeCosse Incorporated.
All rights reserved.

LAND O LAKES® is a registered Trade Mark of Land O'Lakes, Inc. and
is used under license.

ISBN 2-89429-058-6
Printed in Canada

LAND O LAKES®
TREASURY OF
COUNTRY
RECIPES

TORMONT

LAND O LAKES®
TREASURY OF
COUNTRY RECIPES

The heritage of the country has long been cherished at Land O'Lakes. Founded as a rural dairy cooperative in the early 1920s, Land O'Lakes has maintained a deep understanding and appreciation for the ways of the country.

With this *LAND O LAKES® Treasury of Country Recipes,* the rich heritage of country cooking has been preserved for your eating pleasure. These traditional country-style recipes have been updated yet kept unchanged in their simplicity and hearty goodness.

Home economists in the Land O'Lakes Test Kitchens developed these recipes to showcase the wholesome appeal of country foods while keeping in mind contemporary cooking and eating styles. The recipes were tested extensively to ensure easy preparation and excellent results every time you use them. Beautiful color photos of the completed recipes plus step-by-step photos show you just what to expect.

We hope that you will enjoy using this treasury of great recipes to bring the fresh, wholesome tastes of country cooking home to your family and friends.

Contents

APPETIZERS, SNACKS & BEVERAGES

On a beautiful day, the best place for a party is the porch or patio. The fresh-mown grass and the beds of brightly colored flowers create a lovely backdrop for entertaining, whether it's a birthday celebration, an anniversary or just a long overdue get-together of good neighbors.

Your guests will enjoy the chance to be outdoors. Games for the children. Perhaps a croquet match for the grown-ups. And lots of time to catch up on what's new, what's important in each other's lives.

The occasion calls for your very best nibbles and beverages, from old family favorites to enticing new creations. Start with tall glasses of icy-cold lemonade or fresh fruit juices. Then treat your guests to a bountiful tray of appetizers and snacks. Butter-rich pastry turnovers wrapped around a creamy filling. Crumb-coated chicken bites with a savory sauce for dipping. Fresh vegetable kabobs to admire and devour. A tangy spread to serve with hard rolls or a robust rye bread.

These treats are just as tantalizing when served indoors for a holiday open house or a casual weekend evening in the family room. They're also great take-alongs for someone else's party. But most important, they're good because you made them to share.

Country Chicken Nuggets

30 to 40 nuggets
30 minutes

*Buttery crumb-coated chicken bites
dipped in a sour cream-mustard sauce.*

1 c.	*(250 mL)* corn flake crumbs
1½ tsp.	*(7 mL)* oregano leaves
1½ tsp.	*(7 mL)* thyme leaves
2	whole boneless chicken breasts, skinned, cut into 1" *(2,5 cm)* pieces
½ c.	*(125 mL)* butter or margarine, melted

Sauce

1 c.	*(250 mL)* dairy sour cream
2 tbsp.	*(30 mL)* country-style Dijon mustard
1 tbsp.	*(15 mL)* milk

Heat oven to 425°F *(220°C)*. In small bowl stir together corn flake crumbs, oregano and thyme. Dip chicken pieces in melted butter, then coat with crumb mixture. Place chicken ½" *(1 cm)* apart on 15 × 10 × 1" *(40 × 25 × 2,5 cm)* jelly roll pan. Bake for 10 to 15 min. or until fork tender and crisp. Meanwhile, in small bowl stir together all sauce ingredients. Serve nuggets with sauce.

Tip: Nuggets can be baked ahead of time and reheated at 350°F *(180°C)* for 10 min.

Microwave Directions: In 1-qt. *(1-L)* casserole place chicken pieces. Cover; microwave on HIGH, stirring twice, until fork tender (3 to 4 min.). In small bowl stir together corn flake crumbs, oregano and thyme. In small bowl melt butter on HIGH (70 to 80 sec.). Dip half of chicken pieces in melted butter, then coat with crumb mixture. On 9" *(23 cm)* serving plate place chicken pieces ½" *(1 cm)* apart around outside edge. Cover with paper towel; microwave on HIGH, turning plate ¼ turn after 1 min. of time, until heated through (1½ to 2 min.). Repeat with remaining chicken pieces.

Lemon Vegetable Kabobs

8 servings
30 minutes

This light, nutritious appetizer has a fresh summer taste.

1	whole boneless chicken breast, skinned, cut into 4 × ½" *(10 × 1 cm)* strips
8	cherry tomatoes
1	med. green pepper, cut into 1" *(2,5 cm)* pieces
1 tbsp.	*(15 mL)* chopped fresh parsley
½ tsp.	*(2 mL)* thyme leaves

¼ tsp.	*(1 mL)* salt
	Pinch of pepper
2 tbsp.	*(30 mL)* lemon juice
4	*(½")* *(1 cm)* slices lemon, cut in fourths
8	*(5 to 8")* *(13 × 20 cm)* skewers

In medium bowl stir together all ingredients *except* lemon slices and skewers. Marinate 10 min. Meanwhile, heat broiler. On each skewer place 1 piece lemon. Alternate threading chicken strips and vegetables on each skewer; end with lemon. Brush with marinade; broil 2 to 4" *(5 to 10 cm)* from heat, turning once, until chicken is fork tender (3 to 5 min.).

Tip: Kabobs can be grilled over ash white coals. Grill for 20 to 30 min., turning occasionally, or until chicken is fork tender.

Microwave Directions: Use large size cherry tomatoes and bamboo or wooden skewers. Proceed as directed left *except* cut chicken into 2 × ½" *(5 × 1 cm)* strips. Place filled skewers on microwave-safe roasting rack. Brush with marinade; microwave on HIGH, turning rack ¼ turn and turning kabobs over after 4 min., until chicken is fork tender (7 to 8 min.).

Country Chicken Nuggets (top)
Lemon Vegetable Kabobs (bottom)

30 turnovers
60 minutes

Creamy Chicken-Filled Turnovers

A filled butter pastry that can be made ahead, frozen and baked as needed.

Filling
2 tbsp.	*(30 mL)* butter or margarine
2 tbsp.	*(30 mL)* finely chopped onion
1½ c.	*(375 mL)* cooked, shredded chicken
3 oz.	*(90 g)* cream cheese
¼ tsp.	*(1 mL)* salt
¼ tsp.	*(1 mL)* thyme leaves
¼ tsp.	*(1 mL)* pepper
3 tbsp.	*(45 mL)* white wine or chicken broth

Pastry
1⅓ c.	*(320 mL)* all-purpose flour
½ tsp.	*(2 mL)* salt
½ tsp.	*(2 mL)* paprika
½ c.	*(125 mL)* butter or margarine
2 to 4 tbsp.	*(30 to 60 mL)* cold water

In 10" *(25 cm)* skillet melt butter; add onion. Cook over med. heat until softened (4 to 5 min.). Stir in remaining filling ingredients. Continue cooking, stirring occasionally, until cream cheese is melted and heated through (2 to 3 min.). Set aside. Heat oven to 375°F *(190°C)*. In medium bowl combine all pastry ingredients *except* butter and water. Cut in butter until crumbly. Stir in water; shape into ball. On lightly floured surface roll out dough to ¹⁄₁₆" *(0,1 cm)* thickness. Cut with floured 2½" *(6 cm)* round cookie cutter. Place 1 tsp. *(5 mL)* filling on one half of circle; fold other half over. Press edges with fork to seal. Place on cookie sheets; repeat with remaining pastry and filling. Bake for 15 to 20 min. or until golden brown.

Microwave Directions: Filling: Cut cream cheese into 6 pieces. In 1-qt. *(1-L)* casserole melt butter on HIGH (40 to 50 sec.). Stir in onion; microwave on HIGH until softened (1½ to 1¾ min.). Stir in cream cheese and remaining filling ingredients. Microwave on HIGH, stirring after 1 min., until heated through (2 to 2½ min.). Continue as directed left.

Creamy Chicken-Filled Turnovers

Deviled Chicken (top)
Chicken Wings With Pineapple Sauce (bottom)

30 pieces
(1¾ cups) *(420 mL)*
2 hours 30 minutes

Chicken Wings With Pineapple Sauce

Horseradish adds spark to these tender chicken wings.

Marinade

3 tbsp.	*(45 mL)* cider vinegar
2 tbsp.	*(30 mL)* soy sauce
⅓ c.	*(75 mL)* reserved pineapple juice
2 tbsp.	*(30 mL)* vegetable oil
2 tsp.	*(10 mL)* prepared horseradish
1 tsp.	*(5 mL)* minced fresh garlic

2½ lb. *(1 kg)* chicken wings, cut-up (reserve tips for use in soups)

Sauce

2 (8-oz.)	cans *(500 mL)* crushed pineapple, drained, reserve juice for marinade
½ c.	*(125 mL)* honey
1 tbsp.	*(15 mL)* cornstarch

In large bowl stir together all marinade ingredients and cut-up chicken wings. Marinate at least 1 hr. Heat oven to 425°F *(220°C)*. Place chicken wings and marinade on 15 × 10 × 1" *(40 × 25 × 2,5 cm)* jelly roll pan. Bake, stirring occasionally, for 50 to 60 min. or until browned and fork tender. In 2-qt. *(2 L)* saucepan combine all sauce ingredients. Cook over med. high heat, stirring occasionally, until slightly thickened and heated through (3 to 5 min.).

Microwave Directions: Marinate as directed left. Meanwhile, in small bowl stir together all sauce ingredients. Microwave on HIGH, stirring twice during last half of time, until mixture is slightly thickened and heated through (4½ to 5 min.). Set aside. On 9" *(23 cm)* round serving dish place half of chicken wings spoke fashion, spaced at least ½" *(1 cm)* apart. Cover with waxed paper; microwave on HIGH, turning dish ¼ turn twice, until fork tender (8 to 9 min.). Repeat with remaining wings.

6 servings
45 minutes

Deviled Chicken

*A tangy, buttery appetizer spread that goes well with
French bread or a hearty rye bread.*

2 c.	*(500 mL)* cooked, shredded chicken
½ c.	*(125 mL)* mayonnaise
3 tbsp.	*(45 mL)* butter or margarine, melted
2 tbsp.	*(30 mL)* country-style Dijon mustard pinch of cayenne pepper

1 c.	*(250 mL)* fresh bread crumbs
¼ c.	*(50 mL)* chopped fresh parsley
2 tbsp.	*(30 mL)* butter or margarine, melted

French bread, sliced

Heat oven to 400°F *(200 °C)*. In medium bowl stir together chicken, mayonnaise, 3 tbsp. *(45 mL)* butter, mustard and pepper. Spread into 10" *(25 cm)* quiche pan or 9" *(23 cm)* pie pan. In small bowl stir together bread crumbs, parsley and 2 tbsp. *(30 mL)* butter. Sprinkle over top of chicken mixture. Bake for 20 to 25 min. or until golden brown and heated through. Serve spread on French bread.

Microwave Directions: In small bowl stir together bread crumbs and 2 tbsp. *(30 mL)* melted butter; microwave on HIGH, stirring every 30 seconds, until crumbs are toasted (3 to 4 min.). Stir in parsley; set aside. In 10" *(25 cm)* quiche dish or 9" *(23 cm)* pie plate melt 3 tbsp. *(45 mL)* butter on HIGH (40 to 50 sec.). Stir in chicken, mayonnaise, mustard and pepper. Microwave on MEDIUM (50% power), stirring every 2 min., until heated through (8 to 10 min.). Sprinkle with toasted bread crumbs. Microwave on MEDIUM (50% power) until heated through (1 min.).

Chicken Liver Spread

1¼ cups *(300 mL)*
2 hours, 30 minutes

Serve this flavorful spread with sliced rye bread or wheat crackers.

Spread

3 tbsp.	*(45 mL)* butter or margarine
½ lb.	*(225 g)* chicken livers
1 tsp.	*(5 mL)* minced fresh garlic
2 tbsp.	*(30 mL)* country-style Dijon mustard
¼ tsp.	*(1 mL)* salt
	Pinch of pepper

Frosting

3 oz.	*(90 g)* cream cheese, softened
2 to 3 tbsp.	*(30 to 45 mL)* half-and-half
2 tsp.	*(10 mL)* chopped fresh chives

In 10" *(25 cm)* skillet melt butter; add chicken livers and garlic. Cook over med. high heat, stirring occasionally, until liver is fork tender (6 to 8 min.). Stir in remaining spread ingredients. Continue cooking until heated through (1 to 2 min.). Spoon into blender container or food processor. Blend or process until smooth. Press liver mixture into greased 2 c. *(500 mL)* mold or soup bowl. Chill until firm (1 to 2 hr.). In small bowl stir together all frosting ingredients. Unmold liver spread onto serving plate. Frost and decorate liver spread.

Microwave Directions: Spread: Cut chicken livers in half. In 1-qt. *(1-L)* casserole melt butter on HIGH (40 to 50 sec.). Stir in chicken livers and garlic. Cover; microwave on HIGH, stirring every min., until liver is fork tender (5 to 6 min.). Stir in remaining spread ingredients. Microwave on HIGH until mixture just comes to a boil (45 to 60 sec.). Continue as directed left. Frosting: In small bowl microwave cream cheese on MEDIUM (50% power), stirring once after half the time, until softened (1 to 1¼ min.). Continue as directed left.

To Serve Spread:

1. Unmold liver spread onto serving plate.

2. Frost and decorate liver spread.

Chicken Liver Spread

Garden-Stuffed Mushrooms

20 appetizers
45 minutes

Bacon-Wrapped Chicken Livers

Bacon adds hearty smoked flavor and almonds add crunch to chicken livers.

½ to ¾ lb. *(225 to 350 g)* chicken livers, cut into quarters
20 whole blanched almonds
10 slices bacon, cut in half

Sauce
2 tbsp. *(30 mL)* soy sauce
1 tbsp. *(15 mL)* sherry
1 tsp. *(5 mL)* minced fresh garlic

Heat oven to 400°F *(200°C)*. Place 1 chicken liver and 1 almond on top of ½ slice bacon. Roll up; secure with wooden pick. Repeat with remaining ingredients. In medium bowl stir together sauce ingredients. Add chicken livers; marinate 10 min. Place chicken livers and sauce on 15 × 10 × 1" *(40 × 25 × 2,5 cm)* jelly roll pan. Bake for 10 to 15 min. or until liver is fork tender.

Microwave Directions: On microwave-safe roasting rack microwave bacon on MEDIUM (50% power), turning rack after half the time, until partially cooked (12 to 14 min.). Continue as directed left *except* place wrapped liver pieces on microwave-safe roasting rack. Microwave on HIGH, rearranging pieces after half the time, until liver is fork tender (6 to 8 min.).

16 appetizers
45 minutes

Garden-Stuffed Mushrooms

Carrot and green pepper add color and crunch to these tasty stuffed mushrooms.

½ c. *(125 mL)* dried crumbly style herb seasoned stuffing, crushed
¼ c. *(50 mL)* butter or margarine, melted
¼ c. *(50 mL)* finely chopped carrot
¼ c. *(50 mL)* finely chopped green pepper

Pinch of pepper
2 tbsp. *(30 mL)* finely chopped onion
16 *(2")* *(5 cm)* mushrooms, stems removed

Heat oven to 350°F *(180°C)*. In small bowl stir together all ingredients *except* mushrooms. Stuff each mushroom cap with 1 tbsp. *(15 mL)* filling. Place in buttered 13 × 9" *(33 × 23 cm)* baking pan. Bake for 20 to 25 min. or until tender.

Microwave Directions: Prepare mushrooms as directed left. Place in buttered 12 × 8" *(30 × 20 cm)* baking dish. Cover; microwave on HIGH, turning dish after half the time, until tender (8 to 9 min.).

17

Pepper Swiss Cheese Ball

2 cups *(500 mL)*
20 minutes

Smoked Salmon Cracker Spread

This hearty cracker spread is great for entertaining.

8 oz.	*(250 g)* cream cheese, softened
½ tsp.	*(2 mL)* salt
1 tbsp.	*(15 mL)* lemon juice
2 tsp.	*(10 mL)* finely chopped onion
1 tsp.	*(5 mL)* liquid smoke
½ tsp.	*(2 mL)* prepared horseradish

16-oz. *(439-g)* can salmon, drained, bones removed, flaked

Chopped pecans
Chopped fresh parsley

In small mixer bowl beat cream cheese at med. speed, scraping bowl often, until light and fluffy (2 to 3 min.). Add salt, lemon juice, onion, liquid smoke and horseradish. Continue beating until well mixed (1 to 2 min.).

By hand, stir in salmon. Spoon into serving bowl. If desired, garnish with pecans and parsley. Serve with crackers. Store refrigerated.

1 cheese ball
2 hours

Pepper Swiss Cheese Ball

Pepper complements the nutty flavor of Swiss cheese.

6 oz.	*(170 g)* cream cheese, softened
½ c.	*(125 mL)* dairy sour cream
¼ tsp.	*(1 mL)* garlic salt
1½ c.	*(375 mL) (6 oz.) (170 g)* shredded Swiss cheese

2 tbsp. *(30 mL)* chopped fresh parsley
2 to 3 tbsp. *(30 to 45 mL)* coarsely ground pepper

In small mixer bowl beat cream cheese on med. speed, scraping bowl often, until smooth (1 to 2 min.). Add sour cream and garlic salt; continue beating until

well mixed. By hand, stir in cheese and parsley. Refrigerate at least 2 hr. Shape into flattened cheese ball or log. Roll in pepper to coat. Store refrigerated.

28 appetizers
30 minutes

Cheese & Bacon Pinwheels

Hearty rye bread pairs up with bacon and cheese for a quick, crowd-pleasing appetizer.

1 c.   *(250 mL)* (4 oz.) *(110 g)* shredded Cheddar cheese
¼ c.   *(50 mL)* crisply cooked, crumbled bacon

¼ c.   *(50 mL)* butter or margarine, softened
2 tbsp.   *(30 mL)* sliced ⅛" *(0,2 cm)* green onions
7   slices rye bread, crusts removed

In small bowl stir together all ingredients *except* bread. Flatten each bread slice with rolling pin. Spread each bread slice with 1½ tbsp. *(22 mL)* cheese mixture. Roll up jelly roll fashion beginning with short side. With serrated knife slice each roll into 4 pinwheels; secure each with wooden pick. Place on cookie sheet. Heat broiler. Broil 5" *(13 cm)* from heat for 1½ to 2½ min. or until lightly browned and cheese is melted. Remove from cookie sheet; serve immediately.

To Prepare Pinwheels:

1. Flatten each bread slice with rolling pin.

2. With serrated knife slice each roll into 4 pinwheels; secure each with wooden pick.

Cheese & Bacon Pinwheels

10 to 12 servings
30 minutes

Cheese & Bacon Potato Wedges

A hearty appetizer or late night snack.

24-oz.	*(675-g)* pkg. frozen potato wedges
2 c.	*(500 mL)* (8 oz.) *(250 g)* shredded Cheddar cheese
1 c.	*(250 mL)* crisply cooked, crumbled bacon
¼ c.	*(50 mL)* sliced green onions

Dairy sour cream

Heat oven according to pkg. directions. Place potatoes in single layer on cookie sheet. Bake according to pkg. directions. Immediately sprinkle with cheese, bacon and onions; continue baking for 1 to 2 min. or until cheese is melted. Serve warm. If desired, serve with sour cream.

Microwave Directions: Place potatoes in single layer on large plate or microwave-safe cookie sheet. Microwave on HIGH, rearranging potatoes after half the time, until potatoes are hot (10 to 12 min.). Immediately sprinkle with cheese, bacon and onions. Microwave on HIGH until cheese is melted (1 to 2 min.).

2 cups *(500 mL)*
2 hours 15 minutes

Home-Style Vegetable Dip

Fresh chopped vegetables add a spark of color and flavor to this dip.

1 c.	*(250 mL)* dairy sour cream
½ c.	*(125 mL)* mayonnaise
¼ c.	*(50 mL)* chopped green pepper
2-oz.	*(60-g)* jar diced pimiento, drained
1 tbsp.	*(15 mL)* chopped green onion
1 tsp.	*(5 mL)* seasoned salt

¼ tsp. *(1 mL)* garlic powder

Carrot sticks, broccoli or cauliflower flowerets, celery sticks, pea pods, cherry tomatoes, mushrooms

In medium bowl stir together all ingredients *except* vegetables. Cover; refrigerate at least 2 hr. Serve with vegetables.

Home-Style Vegetable Dip

50 appetizers
45 minutes

Festive Stuffed Pea Pods

*Cheese and coarsely ground pepper add flavor and color
to the cream cheese filling in these extra special appetizers.*

8 oz.   *(250 g)* (approx. 50) pea pods
8 oz.   *(250 g)* cream cheese, softened
½ c.   *(125 mL)* (2 oz.) *(60 g)* shredded Cheddar
           cheese

½ tsp.   *(2 mL)* coarsely ground
           pepper

In 2-qt. *(2-L)* saucepan bring 2 c. *(500 mL)* water to a full boil. Add pea pods; cook 1 min. Drain well; plunge into ice water. Drain well. Cut stems off pea pods. Cut seam on side of pea pod forming pocket; set aside. In small mixer bowl combine cream cheese, Cheddar cheese and pepper. Beat at med. speed, scraping bowl often, until well mixed (1 to 2 min.). Spoon or pipe cheese mixture into pocket of each pea pod. Refrigerate until ready to serve.

To Prepare Stuffed Pea Pods:

1. Cut stems off pea pods. Cut seam on side of pea pod forming pocket; set aside.

2. Spoon or pipe cheese mixture into pocket of each pea pod.

Festive Stuffed Pea Pods

1 cup *(250 mL)*
15 minutes

Buttery Pecan Date Spread

Serve this tasty spread at your next brunch or on bran muffins at breakfast.

⅓ c.   *(75 mL)* butter or margarine, softened
3 oz.   *(90 g)* cream cheese, softened
¼ c.   *(50 mL)* finely chopped dates

¼ c.   *(50 mL)* chopped pecans
1 tbsp.   *(15 mL)* sherry or apple juice

In small mixer bowl combine butter and cream cheese. Beat at med. speed, scraping bowl often, until well mixed (1 to 2 min.). By hand, stir in remaining ingredients. Serve with crackers or nut bread. Store refrigerated.

1¾ cups *(450 mL)*
2 hours

Sunshine Fruit Dip

This sunny fruit dip can be a light refreshing dessert too!

2 c.   *(500 mL)* dairy sour cream
2 tbsp.   *(30 mL)* firmly packed brown sugar
1 tbsp.   *(15 mL)* orange juice

1 tbsp.   *(15 mL)* grated orange peel

Fresh fruit, cut up

In medium bowl stir together all ingredients *except* fruit. Cover; refrigerate at least 2 hr. Serve with fresh fruit.

Sunshine Fruit Dip

6 cups *(1,5 L)*
1 hour 20 minutes

Orange & Cinnamon Spiced Nuts

One taste of these subtly spiced nuts and the dish will soon be empty.

2 c.	*(500 mL)* whole blanched almonds			Pinch of salt
1½ c.	*(375 mL)* pecan halves		2	egg whites
1½ c.	*(375 mL)* filberts		1 tbsp.	*(15 mL)* grated orange peel
1 c.	*(250 mL)* sugar		½ c.	*(125 mL)* butter or margarine
¼ tsp.	*(1 mL)* cinnamon			
¼ tsp.	*(1 mL)* nutmeg			

Heat oven to 325°F *(160°C)*. Spread nuts in 15 × 10 × 1" *(40 × 25 × 2,5 cm)* jelly roll pan. Bake, stirring occasionally, for 20 to 25 min. or until lightly toasted. In small bowl stir together sugar, cinnamon, nutmeg and salt. In small mixer bowl beat egg whites at high speed, scraping bowl often, until soft peaks form (1 to 2 min.). Continue beating, gradually adding sugar mixture, until stiff peaks form (1 to 2 min.). By hand, fold in nuts and orange peel. In same jelly roll pan melt butter in oven (4 to 6 min.). Spread nut mixture over butter. Bake, stirring every 10 min., for 25 to 30 min. or until nuts are brown and no butter remains. Cool completely. Store in airtight container.

Microwave Directions: Spread nuts in 12 × 8" *(30 × 20 cm)* baking dish. Microwave on HIGH, stirring every 2 min., until lightly browned (10 to 12 min.). In small bowl stir together sugar, cinnamon, nutmeg and salt. In small mixer bowl beat egg whites at high speed, scraping bowl often, until soft peaks form (1 to 2 min.). Continue beating, gradually adding sugar mixture, until stiff peaks form (1 to 2 min.). By hand, fold in nuts and orange peel. In same baking dish melt butter on HIGH (70 to 80 sec.). Spread nut mixture over butter. Microwave on HIGH, stirring twice during the time, until nuts are brown and no butter remains (9 to 11 min.). Cool completely. Store in airtight container.

8 cups *(2 L)*
2 hours

Chewy Maple Oat Clusters

A chewy snack for home, work or school.

1½ c.	*(375 mL)* old-fashioned rolled oats		½ c.	*(125 mL)* raisins
1 c.	*(250 mL)* crisp rice cereal		8-oz.	*(225-g)* pkg. diced dried fruit mix
1 c.	*(250 mL)* bran flakes		¼ c.	*(50 mL)* butter or margarine, melted
½ c.	*(125 mL)* pecan halves, cut in half		1½ c.	*(375 mL)* pure maple syrup or maple
½ c.	*(125 mL)* sunflower nuts			flavored syrup

Heat oven to 325°F *(160°C)*. In 13 × 9" *(33 × 23 cm)* baking pan spread rolled oats. Bake, stirring occasionally, for 20 to 30 min. or until light golden brown. Stir in crisp rice cereal, bran flakes, pecans and sunflower nuts. Continue baking for 14 to 16 min. or until lightly toasted. Remove from oven; stir in raisins and dried fruit. In small bowl stir together butter and maple syrup; pour over cereal mixture. Stir to coat well. Continue baking, stirring occasionally, for 45 to 50 min. or until mixture clumps together and is golden brown. Spread on waxed paper. Cool completely; break into pieces.

Microwave Directions: In 12 × 8" *(30 × 20 cm)* baking dish spread rolled oats. Microwave on HIGH, stirring every min., until light golden brown (5 to 8 min.). Stir in crisp rice cereal, bran flakes, pecans and sunflower nuts. Microwave on HIGH, stirring every min., until lightly toasted (2 to 4 min.). Stir in raisins and dried fruit. In small bowl stir together butter and maple syrup; pour over cereal mixture. Stir to coat well. Microwave on HIGH, stirring every 2 min., until mixture clumps together and is golden brown (6 to 8 min.). Spread on waxed paper. Cool completely; break into pieces.

Chewy Maple Oat Clusters (top)
Orange & Cinnamon Spiced Nuts (bottom)

Party Popcorn

12 cups *(3 L)*
15 minutes

Party Popcorn

Four specialty popcorns — great for your next party.

12 c.   *(3 L)* popped popcorn
⅓ c.   *(75 mL)* butter or margarine

In large bowl place popcorn. In 1-qt. *(1-L)* saucepan melt butter over low heat (2 to 3 min.). Follow directions for desired variation. Serve immediately.

Variations:

Tex-Mex Popcorn: Stir ¼ tsp. *(1 mL)* hot pepper sauce into melted butter. Drizzle over popcorn; toss to evenly coat. In small bowl combine 1 tsp. *(5 mL)* chili powder and ¼ tsp. *(1 mL)* garlic salt. Sprinkle over popcorn; toss to evenly coat.

Savory Popcorn: Stir 2 tsp. *(10 mL)* Worcestershire sauce into melted butter. Drizzle over popcorn; toss to evenly coat. In small bowl combine 1 tsp. *(5 mL)* paprika, ½ tsp. *(2 mL)* seasoned salt, ¼ tsp. *(1 mL)* basil leaves, ¼ tsp. *(1 mL)* marjoram leaves, ¼ tsp. *(1 mL)* thyme leaves and ¼ tsp. *(1 mL)* garlic powder. Sprinkle over popcorn; toss to evenly coat.

Parmesan Italian Popcorn: Drizzle melted butter over popcorn; toss to evenly coat. In small bowl combine 2 tbsp. *(30 mL)* grated Parmesan cheese, 1 tsp. *(5 mL)* basil leaves, ½ tsp. *(2 mL)* oregano leaves and ¼ tsp. *(1 mL)* garlic powder. Sprinkle over popcorn; toss to evenly coat.

Praline Pecan Popcorn: Increase butter to ½ c. *(125 mL)*. Stir ½ c. *(125 mL)* firmly packed brown sugar and 1 tsp. *(5 mL)* cinnamon into melted butter. Cook over med. heat, stirring occasionally, until mixture comes to a full boil (3 to 5 min.). Boil, stirring constantly, 7 min. Remove from heat; stir in ⅔ c. *(175 mL)* chopped pecans. Slowly pour over popcorn; stir to evenly coat. Cool 10 min.; break apart.

4 dozen
30 minutes

Crispy Snack Crackers

These savory rye crackers are easy to make and fun to serve for a snack or with soups and salads.

½   loaf (24 slices) cocktail sandwich bread
⅓ c.   *(75 mL)* butter or margarine
1 tbsp.   *(15 mL)* sesame seed
½ tsp.   *(2 mL)* thyme leaves

Pinch of pepper
½ tsp.   *(2 mL)* minced fresh garlic

Heat oven to 350°F *(180°C)*. Cut each bread slice in half diagonally. In 15 × 10 × 1" *(40 × 25 × 2,5 cm)* jelly roll pan melt butter in oven (3 to 5 min.). Stir in remaining ingredients *except* bread slices. Place bread slices in butter mixture; turn to coat. Bake 10 min.; stir crackers.

Continue baking for 5 to 10 min. or until crackers are crisp.

Tip: Cocktail sandwich bread can be cut out with small (2") *(5 cm)* cookie cutters.

Old-Fashioned Hot Buttered Rum (right)
Orange Mint Coffee (left)

16 servings
15 minutes

Old-Fashioned Hot Buttered Rum

Chase away those winter chills with this traditional hot beverage.

1 c.   *(250 mL)* sugar
1 c.   *(250 mL)* firmly packed brown sugar
1 c.   *(250 mL)* butter
2 c.   *(500 mL)* vanilla ice cream, softened

Rum or rum extract
Boiling water
Nutmeg

In 2-qt. *(2-L)* saucepan combine sugar, brown sugar and butter. Cook over low heat, stirring occasionally, until butter is melted (6 to 8 min.). In large mixer bowl combine cooked mixture with ice cream; beat at med. speed, scraping bowl often, until smooth (1 to 2 min.).

Store refrigerated up to 2 weeks or frozen up to 1 month. For each serving, fill mug with ¼ c. *(50 mL)* mixture, 1 oz. *(30 mL)* rum or ¼ tsp. *(1 mL)* rum extract and ¾ c. *(200 mL)* boiling water; sprinkle with nutmeg.

6 servings
3 hours

Orange Mint Coffee

Poured over mint and orange, this pleasing coffee is delicious, iced or hot.

Iced Coffee
6   sprigs fresh mint
6   orange slices
10 c.   *(2,5 L)* fresh brewed coffee
2½ c.   *(625 mL)* vanilla ice cream

For Iced Coffee: Place mint and orange slices into large heat-proof pitcher; add fresh brewed coffee. Let cool 1 hr. Cover; refrigerate until chilled (about 2 hr.). Into each of 6 glasses scoop ½ c. *(125 mL)* ice cream; pour chilled coffee over ice cream.

Hot Coffee
6   sprigs fresh mint
6   orange slices
10 c.   *(2,5 L)* fresh brewed coffee
        Sweetened whipped cream

For Hot Coffee: Place 1 sprig of mint and 1 orange slice in each of 6 cups. Pour fresh brewed coffee into each cup. Serve with sweetened whipped cream. If desired, refill cups with additional coffee.

1½ quarts *(1,5 L)*
4 hours, 45 minutes

Hot Spiced Punch

Serve this spicy punch with a spoon so no one misses
the raisins and almonds at the bottom of the cup.

4 c.	*(1 L)* apple cider		1	cinnamon stick
2 c.	*(500 mL)* grape juice or dry red wine		⅔ c.	*(150 mL)* raisins
2 tbsp.	*(30 mL)* chopped crystallized ginger		⅔ c.	*(150 mL)* slivered almonds
8	whole cloves			
6	strips 3 × ½" *(7 × 1 cm)* orange peel			

In 3-qt. *(3-L)* saucepan combine all ingredients *except* raisins and almonds. Let stand at room temperature for 4 hr. Cook over med. heat until mixture just comes to a boil (15 to 20 min.). Reduce heat to low; simmer for 15 min. Strain; discard spice mixture. Return to saucepan. Add raisins and almonds. Continue cooking over low heat until raisins are tender (10 to 15 min.). Serve hot with a spoon in each mug.

1 gallon *(4 L)*
20 minutes

Sunny Apple Cider

A traditional cold weather chaser with a splash of orange juice.

1 gal.   *(4 L)* apple cider
6-oz.   *(180-mL)* can frozen orange juice
         concentrate
3   whole cloves
2   cinnamon sticks

In Dutch oven combine all ingredients. Cook over med. heat until heated through and flavors are blended (about 15 min.).

Tip: To keep cider warm, hold in crockery cooker on low temperature.

Hot Spiced Punch (left)
Sunny Apple Cider (right)

Rich n' Creamy Hot Chocolate (top)
Old-Fashioned Creamy Eggnog (bottom)

8 cups *(2 L)*
30 minutes

Rich n' Creamy Hot Chocolate

Enjoy a heartwarming mugful of this rich, creamy all-time favorite.

½ c.	*(125 mL)* semi-sweet real chocolate chips
½ c.	*(125 mL)* sugar
½ c.	*(125 mL)* water
	Pinch of salt
5½ c.	*(1,4 L)* milk
2 c.	*(500 mL)* whipping cream
2 tsp.	*(10 mL)* vanilla

Liqueurs
Sweetened whipped cream
Grated chocolate
Grated lemon peel
Grated orange peel
Cinnamon
Nutmeg

In 3-qt. *(3-L)* saucepan melt chocolate chips over low heat, stirring constantly. Stir in sugar, water and salt. Cook over med. heat, stirring constantly with wire whisk, until mixture comes to a full boil (4 to 5 min.). Boil, stirring constantly, 2 min. Stir in milk and whipping cream. Continue cooking over med. heat, stirring occasionally, until heated through (12 to 15 min.). DO NOT BOIL. Add vanilla. Beat with wire whisk or rotary beater until frothy. Pour into mugs. If desired, add 1 to 2 tbsp. *(15 to 30 mL)* liqueur to each serving. Top each serving with a dollop of sweetened whipped cream. If desired, garnish with one of the following: grated chocolate, grated lemon peel, grated orange peel, cinnamon or nutmeg.

Microwave Directions: In 3-qt. *(3-L)* bowl combine chocolate chips, sugar, water and salt. Microwave on HIGH, stirring every min., until chocolate chips are melted and mixture comes to a full boil (3 to 4 min.). Microwave on HIGH 2 min. Stir in milk and whipping cream. Microwave on HIGH, stirring after half the time, until heated through (8 to 10 min.). DO NOT BOIL. Add vanilla. Beat with wire whisk or rotary beater until frothy. Pour into mugs. If desired, add 1 to 2 tbsp. *(15 to 30 mL)* liqueur to each serving. Top each serving with a dollop of sweetened whipped cream. If desired, garnish with one of the following: grated chocolate, grated lemon peel, grated orange peel, cinnamon or nutmeg.

5 cups *(1,3 L)*
25 minutes

Old-Fashioned Creamy Eggnog

Fresh cream makes this warmed eggnog extra rich — perfect for holiday gatherings!

½ c.	*(125 mL)* powdered sugar
4	eggs
¼ tsp.	*(1 mL)* salt
½ tsp.	*(2 mL)* vanilla
4 c.	*(1 L)* whipping cream or milk

Rum
Sweetened whipped cream
Nutmeg

In 5-c. *(1,3-L)* blender container combine powdered sugar, eggs, salt and vanilla. Cover; blend at high speed until well blended (15 to 20 sec.). In 2-qt. *(2-L)* saucepan place 2 c. *(500 mL)* whipping cream. Cook over med. heat until thermometer reaches 140°F *(60°C)* (5 to 6 min.). While blending at med. speed, slowly add warm whipping cream to egg mixture. Continue blending until frothy (15 to 20 sec.).* In same 2-qt. *(2-L)* saucepan stir together egg mixture and remaining 2 c. *(500 mL)* whipping cream. Cook over med. heat, stirring occasionally, until thermometer reaches 140°F *(60°C)* (5 to 6 min.). If desired, add 1 to 2 tbsp. *(15 to 30 mL)* rum to each serving; top with sweetened whipped cream and nutmeg.

*Mixture can be stored refrigerated 2 to 3 days.

1 gallon *(4 L)*
15 minutes

Lime Cream Cooler

A creamy, refreshing punch that's just right for your next special party.

4 c.	(1 qt.) *(1 L)* vanilla ice cream, slightly softened
4 c.	(1 qt.) *(1 L)* lime sherbet, slightly softened
4 c.	*(1 L)* milk

6-oz.	*(180-mL)* can frozen lemonade concentrate
6-oz.	*(180-mL)* can frozen limeade concentrate
2 c.	*(500 mL)* water
4 c.	*(1 L)* ginger ale

In large punch bowl stir together ice cream, sherbet and milk. In 1-qt. *(1-L)* pitcher stir together lemonade concentrate, limeade concentrate and water. Pour over ice cream mixture. Add ginger ale; stir until slightly mixed.

4¾ cups *(1,2 L)*
15 minutes

Ice Cream Parlor Chocolate Malt

A traditional malt with four mouth-watering variations.

¾ c.	*(175 mL)* milk
¼ c.	*(50 mL)* natural instant malted milk
4 c.	(1 qt.) *(1 L)* chocolate ice cream

In 5-c. *(1,3-L)* blender container combine milk and instant malted milk. Blend at med. speed, stopping blender frequently to scrape sides, until instant malted milk is dissolved (30 to 40 sec.). Add ice cream; continue blending, stopping blender frequently to scrape sides, until smooth (30 to 40 sec.). Serve immediately.

Variations:

Chocolate Raspberry: Prepare chocolate malt as directed above. By hand, stir in 1 c. *(250 mL)* sweetened raspberries.

Chocolate Mint Cookie Malt: Prepare chocolate malt as directed above. Blend in 12 crushed chocolate mint sandwich cookies.

Peanut Butter Chocolate Malt: Prepare chocolate malt as directed above. Blend in 1 c. *(250 mL)* peanut butter.

Chocolate Almond Malt: Prepare chocolate malt as directed above. Blend in 1 tsp. *(5 mL)* almond extract. By hand, stir in 1 c. *(250 mL)* mini semi-sweet chocolate chips.

Lime Cream Cooler (right)
Ice Cream Parlor Chocolate Malt (left)

3 quarts *(3 L)*
10 minutes

Apple Orchard Punch

This quick and easy punch would be delightful at a country wedding or any celebration.

32-oz.	*(1-L)* bottle apple juice, chilled
12-oz.	*(341-mL)* can frozen cranberry cocktail concentrate
1 c.	*(250 mL)* orange juice

1½ qt.	(6 c.) *(1,5 L)* ginger ale or champagne, chilled
1	red apple, do not core

In large punch bowl combine apple juice, cranberry cocktail concentrate and orange juice. Stir to dissolve. Slowly add ginger ale or champagne. Vertically, thinly slice apple forming whole apple slices. Float apple slices on top of punch.

1½ quarts *(1,5 L)*
40 minutes

Sparkling Pink Lemonade

Spending a hot day on the front porch is just not the same without homemade lemonade — especially when it's sparkling pink!

1½ c.	*(375 mL)* sugar
1½ c.	*(375 mL)* (6 lemons) freshly squeezed lemon juice
1 qt.	(4 c.) *(1 L)* club soda, chilled*

4 tsp.	*(20 mL)* grenadine syrup**
	6" *(15 cm)* wooden skewers
	Fresh fruit pieces (strawberries, melon balls, pineapple chunks, etc.)

In 2-qt. *(2-L)* pitcher combine sugar and lemon juice. Stir well; refrigerate at least 30 min. Just before serving, add club soda. Stir in grenadine syrup.

*1 qt. (4 c.) *(1 L)* water can be substituted for club soda.

On 6" *(15 cm)* wooden skewers, thread fruit pieces to make kabobs. Place kabobs in glasses; add ice. Pour in lemonade.

**4 to 6 drops red food coloring can be substituted for grenadine syrup.

Apple Orchard Punch

BREADS

Bread baking in the oven. It fills the air with an aroma so tantalizing that you can hardly wait for your first taste. Finally, the bread has cooled enough to eat. The butter begins to melt as you spread it on the warm, thick slice of bread. Topped with your favorite strawberry jam, it's every bit as good as dessert.

Fresh bread has an appeal that's hard to match. Spicy-sweet muffins warm from the oven. Homemade doughnuts and crisp, flaky pastries. They're made to be enjoyed around the kitchen table for a leisurely weekend breakfast or when friends stop by to catch up on the news of your household.

For lunch and dinner, too, homemade bread adds so much. Moist and tender cornbread, served with honey butter, to enjoy with hearty soup. Big, flaky buttermilk biscuits for a country-style supper. And loaves of hearty wheat bread, so good for sandwiches.

Homemade bread keeps the house full of good smells and tastes. And it's possibly the most welcome gift you can give to those who gather in your kitchen.

6 servings
30 minutes

Honey-Moist Cornbread

Moist and tender cornbread, even better served with butter.

1 c.	*(250 mL)* all-purpose flour		1 c.	*(250 mL)* whipping cream
1 c.	*(250 mL)* yellow cornmeal		¼ c.	*(50 mL)* vegetable oil
¼ c.	*(50 mL)* sugar		¼ c.	*(50 mL)* honey
1 tbsp.	*(15 mL)* baking powder		2	eggs, slightly beaten
½ tsp.	*(3 mL)* salt			

Heat oven to 400°F *(200°C)*. In medium bowl stir together flour, cornmeal, sugar, baking powder and salt. Stir in remaining ingredients just until moistened. Pour into greased 9" *(23 cm)* sq. baking pan. Bake for 20 to 25 min. or until wooden pick inserted in center comes out clean.

Microwave Directions: Mix cornbread as directed left. Pour into greased 6-c. *(1,5-L)* microwave ring mold. Microwave on HIGH, turning dish every 3 min., until cornbread pulls away from sides of pan and is dry on top (7 to 9 min.). Let stand 3 min.

8 biscuits
25 minutes

Flaky Buttermilk Biscuits

Warm, flaky, melt-in-your-mouth biscuits.

2 c.	*(500 mL)* all-purpose flour		⅔ c.	*(150 mL)* shortening
4 tsp.	*(20 mL)* baking powder		¾ c.	*(180 mL)* buttermilk
½ tsp.	*(3 mL)* salt			

Heat oven to 425°F *(220°C)*. In large bowl combine flour, baking powder and salt. Cut in shortening until crumbly. Stir in buttermilk just until moistened. Turn dough onto lightly floured surface; knead until smooth (1 min.). Roll out dough to ¾" *(2 cm)* thickness. Cut into 8 (2") *(5 cm)* biscuits; place 1" *(2,5 cm)* apart on cookie sheet. Bake for 10 to 14 min. or until lightly browned.

Honey-Moist Cornbread (left)
Flaky Buttermilk Biscuits (right)

1 dozen
35 minutes

Parmesan Butter Pan Biscuits

Parmesan and basil make the difference
in these country-style pan biscuits.

⅓ c.	*(80 mL)* butter or margarine		3½ tsp.	*(20 mL)* baking powder
2¼ c.	*(525 mL)* all-purpose flour		1 tsp.	*(5 mL)* basil leaves
2 tbsp.	*(30 mL)* grated Parmesan cheese		1 tbsp.	*(15 mL)* chopped fresh parsley
1 tbsp.	*(15 mL)* sugar		1 c.	*(250 mL)* milk

Heat oven to 400°F *(200°C)*. In 9" *(23 cm)* sq. baking pan melt butter in oven (3 to 5 min.). Meanwhile, in medium bowl combine all ingredients *except* milk. Stir in milk just until moistened. Turn dough onto lightly floured surface; knead 10 times or until smooth.

Roll dough into 12 × 4" *(30 × 10 cm)* rectangle. Cut into 12 (1") *(2,5 cm)* strips. Dip each strip into melted butter. Place in same pan. Bake for 20 to 25 min. or until lightly browned.

To Prepare Biscuits:

1. Roll dough into 12 × 4" *(30 × 10 cm)* rectangle. Cut into 12 (1") *(2,5 cm)* strips.

2. Dip each strip into melted butter. Place in same pan.

Parmesan Butter Pan Biscuits

Nutmeg Streusel Muffins

1 dozen
30 minutes

Nutmeg Streusel Muffins

Enjoy these nutmeg muffins fresh from the oven.

Streusel Mixture

1⅓ c.	(325 mL) all-purpose flour
1 c.	(250 mL) firmly packed brown sugar
½ c.	(125 mL) butter or margarine, softened

Muffins

⅔ c.	(150 mL) all-purpose flour
1½ tsp.	(10 mL) baking powder
1½ tsp.	(10 mL) nutmeg
½ tsp.	(3 mL) baking soda
½ tsp.	(3 mL) salt
⅔ c.	(150 mL) buttermilk
1	egg

Heat oven to 400°F *(200°C)*. In large bowl combine 1⅓ c. *(325 mL)* flour and brown sugar; cut in butter until crumbly. Reserve ½ c. *(125 mL)* for streusel topping. In same bowl add all muffin ingredients to streusel mixture. Stir just until moistened. Spoon into greased 12 c. muffin pan. Sprinkle with reserved streusel mixture. Bake for 18 to 22 min. or until lightly browned. Let stand 5 min.; remove from pan.

Microwave Directions: Mix muffins as directed left. Spoon ⅓ of batter into 6 c. paper-lined muffin pan, filling ½ full. Microwave on HIGH 1 min. Sprinkle with ⅓ of streusel mixture; turn. Microwave on HIGH until muffins are dry on top (1½ to 2½ min.). Repeat with remaining batter.   18 muffins.

---

1 dozen
30 minutes

Spiced Pumpkin Muffins

During the fall harvest enjoy tender pumpkin muffins subtly spiced with cinnamon and ginger.

2 c.	(500 mL) all-purpose flour
⅔ c.	(175 mL) firmly packed brown sugar
⅓ c.	(75 mL) sugar
1 tbsp.	(15 mL) baking powder
1 tsp.	(5 mL) salt
1 tsp.	(5 mL) cinnamon
¼ tsp.	(1 mL) baking soda
¼ tsp.	(1 mL) ginger
½ c.	(125 mL) butter or margarine, melted
½ c.	(125 mL) cooked pumpkin
⅓ c.	(75 mL) buttermilk
2	eggs, slightly beaten

Heat oven to 400°F *(200°C)*. In large bowl stir together all ingredients *except* butter, pumpkin, buttermilk and eggs. In medium bowl stir together remaining ingredients. Add to flour mixture; stir just until moistened. Spoon batter into greased 12 c. muffin pan. Bake for 15 to 20 min. or until lightly browned. Let stand 5 min.; remove from pan.

Microwave Directions: Mix muffins as directed left. Spoon ⅓ of batter into 6 c. paper-lined muffin pan, filling ½ full. Microwave on HIGH, turning after half the time, until muffins are dry on top (2½ to 3½ min.). Repeat with remaining batter.   18 muffins.

Cheddar Dill Scones

The irresistible aroma of this quick bread will fill the kitchen and tempt the appetite.

2½ c.	*(600 mL)* all-purpose flour
1 c.	*(250 mL)* (4 oz.) *(110 g)* shredded Cheddar cheese
¼ c.	*(50 mL)* chopped fresh parsley
1 tbsp.	*(15 mL)* baking powder
2 tsp.	*(10 mL)* dill weed
½ tsp.	*(2 mL)* salt
¾ c.	*(175 mL)* butter or margarine
2	eggs, slightly beaten
½ c.	*(120 mL)* half-and-half

Heat oven to 400°F *(200°C)*. In medium bowl combine all ingredients *except* butter, eggs and half-and-half. Cut in butter until crumbly. Stir in eggs and half-and-half just until moistened. Turn dough onto lightly floured surface; knead until smooth (1 min.). Divide dough in half; roll each half into 8" *(20 cm)* circle. Cut each circle into 8 pie-shaped wedges. Place 1" *(2,5 cm)* apart on cookie sheets. Bake for 15 to 20 min. or until lightly browned.

To Prepare Cheddar Dill Scones:

1. Stir in eggs and half-and-half just until moistened. Turn dough onto lightly floured surface; knead until smooth (1 min.).

2. Divide dough in half; roll each half into 8" *(20 cm)* circle. Cut each circle into 8 pie-shaped wedges.

Cheddar Dill Scones

Tender Popovers

Popovers that pop up and over the pan to provide old-fashioned goodness.

3	eggs, room temperature
1¼ c.	*(300 mL)* milk, room temperature
1¼ c.	*(300 mL)* all-purpose flour
¼ tsp.	*(1 mL)* salt

Heat oven to 450°F *(230°C)*. In small mixer bowl beat eggs at med. speed, scraping bowl often, until light yellow (1 to 2 min.). Add milk; continue beating for 1 min. to incorporate air. By hand, stir in remaining ingredients. Pour batter into greased 6 c. popover pan or 6 custard cups. Bake for 15 min.; reduce temperature to 350°F *(180°C)*. *Do not open oven door.* Bake for 25 to 30 min. or until golden brown. Insert knife in popovers to allow steam to escape. Serve immediately.

Tip: Eggs and milk should be at room temperature (72°F) *(22°C)* to help ensure successful popovers.

To Prepare Popovers:

1. Pour batter into greased 6 c. popover pan or 6 custard cups.

2. Insert knife in popovers to allow steam to escape.

Tender Popovers

M

Crackling Bacon Corn Cakes

6 corn cakes
25 minutes

Crackling Bacon Corn Cakes

Savory griddle cakes that taste great with sausage, eggs and maple syrup.

6	slices bacon, cut into ½" *(1 cm)* pieces
⅓ c.	*(75 mL)* chopped onion
1 c.	*(250 mL)* all-purpose flour
2 tbsp.	*(30 mL)* chopped fresh chives
1 tsp.	*(5 mL)* baking powder
½ tsp.	*(3 mL)* salt
	Pinch of cayenne pepper
⅔ c.	*(175 mL)* milk

1	egg, slightly beaten
1 tbsp.	*(15 mL)* vegetable oil
8-oz.	*(227-mL)* can whole kernel corn, drained
½ c.	*(125 mL) (2 oz.) (60 g)* shredded Monterey Jack cheese
	Maple syrup or maple flavored syrup, warmed

In 10" *(25 cm)* skillet cook bacon and onion over med. high heat until bacon is browned (7 to 9 min.). Meanwhile, in medium bowl combine flour, chives, baking powder, salt and cayenne pepper. Stir in milk, egg and oil just until moistened. Stir in bacon and onion and remaining ingredients *except* maple syrup.

Heat griddle to 350°F *(180°C)* or until drops of water sizzle. For each corn cake pour ⅓ c. *(75 mL)* batter onto greased griddle. Cook until corn cakes are golden brown (3 to 4 min. on each side). Serve warm with maple syrup.

2 loaves
1 hour 30 minutes

Zucchini Harvest Bread

Cinnamon fills the air with its tantalizing aroma as this quick bread bakes.

3 c.	*(725 mL)* all-purpose flour
1½ c.	*(350 mL)* sugar
½ c.	*(125 mL)* firmly packed brown sugar
1 c.	*(250 mL)* butter or margarine, softened
3	eggs
1 tbsp.	*(15 mL)* cinnamon
1 tsp.	*(5 mL)* salt
1 tsp.	*(5 mL)* baking soda

¼ tsp.	*(1 mL)* baking powder
¼ tsp.	*(1 mL)* nutmeg
¼ tsp.	*(1 mL)* cloves
1 tbsp.	*(15 mL)* vanilla
2 c.	*(475 mL) (2 med.)* unpeeled, shredded zucchini
½ c.	*(125 mL)* chopped walnuts

Heat oven to 350°F *(180°C)*. In large mixer bowl combine all ingredients *except* zucchini and walnuts. Beat at low speed, scraping bowl often, until well mixed (2 to 3 min.). By hand, stir in zucchini and nuts. Spread

into 2 greased 8 × 4" *(20 × 10 cm)* loaf pans. Bake for 50 to 65 min. or until wooden pick inserted in center comes out clean. Cool 10 min.; remove from pans. Cool completely; store refrigerated.

4 cracker breads
45 minutes

Crispy Cracker Bread

While soup is simmering, prepare this thin, crisp bread.

¼-oz.	*(7-g)* pkg. active dry yeast
1 c.	*(250 mL)* warm water (105° to 115°F) *(40° to 46°C)*
2 tsp.	*(10 mL)* sugar
1 tsp.	*(5 mL)* salt
3 tbsp.	*(45 mL)* butter or margarine, melted

2½ to 3 c.	*(600 to 725 mL)* all-purpose flour
1	egg, slightly beaten
	Coarse salt*
	Coarse pepper*
	Sesame seed

Heat oven to 400°F *(200°C)*. In large bowl dissolve yeast in warm water. Stir in sugar, 1 tsp. *(5 mL)* salt and butter. Gradually stir in flour, 1 c. *(250 mL)* at a time, using enough flour to make dough easy to handle. Turn dough onto lightly floured surface; knead until smooth (5 min.). Divide dough into 4 equal portions; shape into balls. Let rest 10 min.; roll each ball into 12" *(30 cm)* circle. Place on greased cookie sheets. Brush with

beaten egg; sprinkle with salt, pepper or sesame seed. Bake for 10 to 15 min. or until lightly browned. Cool completely on wire rack. (Bread will be irregular in shape and browning.) To serve, break into pieces.

*Table salt and pepper can be substituted for coarse salt and coarse pepper.

To Prepare Crispy Cracker Bread:

1. Divide dough into 4 equal portions; shape into balls. Let rest 10 min.; roll each ball into 12" *(30 cm)* circle.

2. Place on greased cookie sheets. Brush with beaten egg; sprinkle with salt, pepper or sesame seed.

Crispy Cracker Bread

Pan-Toasted Garlic Bread

Bread is toasted with garlic butter and topped with a sprinkling of Mozzarella cheese.

⅓ c.   *(75 mL)* butter or margarine
⅛ tsp.   *(0,5 mL)* cayenne pepper
1 tsp.   *(5 mL)* minced fresh garlic

6   (1") *(2,5 cm)* slices French bread
½ c.   *(125 mL)* (2 oz.) *(60 g)* shredded
    Mozzarella cheese

In 10" *(25 cm)* skillet melt butter until sizzling. Stir in cayenne pepper and garlic. Dip both sides of *each* bread slice in melted butter; place in same skillet. Cook over med. heat, watching closely, until bread is lightly browned (2 to 3 min.). Reduce heat to low. Turn bread slices over; sprinkle each slice with about 1 tbsp. *(15 mL)* cheese. Cover; continue cooking until cheese is melted (1 to 2 min.). Serve immediately.

To Prepare Pan-Toasted Garlic Bread:

1. Dip both sides of *each* bread slice in melted butter; place in same skillet. Cook over med. heat, watching closely, until bread is lightly browned (2 to 3 min.). Reduce heat to low.

2. Turn bread slices over; sprinkle each slice with about 1 tbsp. *(15 mL)* cheese. Cover; continue cooking until cheese is melted (1 to 2 min.).

Pan-Toasted Garlic Bread

Homemade Bread

Serve this delicious bread warm from the oven and smothered with butter.

2 c.	*(500 mL)* milk
1 tbsp.	*(15 mL)* butter or margarine
¼-oz.	*(7-g)* pkg. active dry yeast
¼ c.	*(50 mL)* warm water (105° to 115°F) *(40° to 46°C)*

5½ to 6½ c.	*(1,4 to 1,6 L)* all-purpose flour
2 tbsp.	*(30 mL)* sugar
2 tsp.	*(10 mL)* salt
	Butter or margarine, softened

In 1-qt. *(1-L)* saucepan scald milk; stir in butter until melted. Cool to lukewarm (105° to 115°F) *(40° to 46°C)*. In large mixer bowl dissolve yeast in warm water. Add milk mixture, 3 c. *(750 mL)* flour, sugar and salt to yeast. Beat at med. speed, scraping bowl often, until smooth (1 to 2 min.). By hand, stir in enough remaining flour to make dough easy to handle. Turn dough onto lightly floured surface; knead until smooth and elastic (about 10 min.). Place in greased bowl; turn greased side up.

Cover; let rise in warm place until double in size (about 1½ hr.). Dough is ready if indentation remains when touched. Punch down dough; divide in half. Shape each half into loaf. Place loaves in 2 greased 9 × 5" *(23 × 13 cm)* loaf pans. Cover; let rise until double in size (about 1 hr.). Heat oven to 400°F *(200°C)*. Bake for 25 to 35 min. or until loaves sound hollow when tapped. Remove from pans immediately. If desired, brush tops of loaves with butter.

Hearty Honey Wheat Bread

This whole grain bread fills the kitchen with its tempting aroma.

1 c.	*(250 mL)* milk
3 tbsp.	*(50 mL)* butter or margarine
2	(¼-oz.) *(7-g)* pkg. active dry yeast
1 c.	*(250 mL)* warm water (105° to 115°F) *(40° to 46°C)*
4¾ to 5¾ c.	*(1,2 to 1,6 L)* all-purpose flour

2 c.	*(500 mL)* whole wheat flour
⅓ c.	*(75 mL)* honey
2	eggs
1 tbsp.	*(15 mL)* salt
1 tsp.	*(5 mL)* sugar
	Butter or margarine, softened

In 1-qt. *(1-L)* saucepan combine milk and butter. Cook over med. heat until butter is melted (3 to 4 min.). Cool to lukewarm (105° to 115°F) *(40° to 46°C)*. In large mixer bowl dissolve yeast in warm water. Add milk mixture, 2 c. *(500 mL)* flour, whole wheat flour, honey, eggs, salt and sugar to yeast. Beat at med. speed, scraping bowl often, until smooth (1 to 2 min.). By hand, stir in enough remaining flour to make dough easy to handle. Turn dough onto lightly floured surface; knead until smooth and elastic (about 10 min.). Place in greased bowl; turn greased side up. Cover; let rise in warm place until double in size (about 1½ hr.). Dough is ready if indentation remains when touched. Punch down dough; divide in half. Shape each half into loaf. Place loaves in 2 greased 9 × 5" *(23 × 13 cm)* loaf pans. Cover; let rise until double in size (about 1½ hr.). Heat oven to 350°F *(180°C)*. Bake for 25 to 35 min. or until loaves sound hollow when tapped. Remove from pans immediately. If desired, brush tops of loaves with butter.

Homemade Bread (right)
Hearty Honey Wheat Bread (left)

Oatmeal Molasses Rolls

4 dozen
3 hours

Grandma's Dinner Rolls

Old-fashioned goodness, perfect for any occasion.

2 c.	*(500 mL)* boiling water	½ c.	*(125 mL)* sugar
½ c.	*(125 mL)* butter or margarine, softened	3	eggs
2	(¼-oz.) *(7-g)* pkg. active dry yeast	1½ tsp.	*(7 mL)* salt
½ c.	*(125 mL)* warm water (105° to 115°F) *(40° to 46°C)*		Butter or margarine, softened
9 to 10 c.	*(2,2 to 2,5 L)* all-purpose flour		

In medium bowl stir together boiling water and butter until butter is melted. Cool to warm (105° to 115°F) *(40° to 46°C)*. In large mixer bowl dissolve yeast in warm water. Add butter mixture, 3 c. *(750 mL)* flour, sugar, eggs and salt to yeast. Beat at med. speed, scraping bowl often, until smooth (1 to 2 min.). By hand, stir in enough remaining flour to make dough easy to handle. Turn dough onto lightly floured surface; knead until smooth and elastic (about 10 min.). Place in greased bowl, turn greased side up. Cover; let rise in warm place until double in size (about 1 hr.). Dough is ready if indentation remains when touched. Punch down dough; divide in half. With floured hands shape each half into 24 rounds. Place in 2 greased 13 × 9" *(33 × 23 cm)* baking pans. Cover; let rise until double in size (about 1 hr.). Heat oven to 400°F *(200°C)*. Bake for 20 to 25 min. or until golden brown. If desired, brush tops of rolls with butter.

3 dozen
3 hours

Oatmeal Molasses Rolls

Homemade dinner rolls that are tender and slightly sweet.

2 c.	*(500 mL)* old-fashioned rolled oats	1 c.	*(250 mL)* firmly packed brown sugar
1½ c.	*(375 mL)* boiling water	⅓ c.	*(75 mL)* light molasses
¼ c.	*(50 mL)* butter or margarine	2	eggs
2	(¼-oz.) *(7-g)* pkg. active dry yeast	1½ tsp.	*(7 mL)* salt
½ c.	*(125 mL)* warm water (105° to 115°F) *(40° to 46°C)*		Butter or margarine, softened
6¼ to 7¼ c.	*(1,5 to 1,8 L)* all-purpose flour		

In medium bowl stir together oats, boiling water and butter until butter is melted. Cool to warm (105° to 115°F) *(40° to 46°C)*. In large mixer bowl dissolve yeast in warm water. Add oat mixture, 2 c. *(500 mL)* flour, brown sugar, molasses, eggs and salt to yeast. Beat at med. speed, scraping bowl often, until smooth (1 to 2 min.). By hand, stir in enough remaining flour to make dough easy to handle. Turn dough onto lightly floured surface; knead until smooth and elastic (about 10 min.). Place in greased bowl, turn greased side up. Cover; let rise in warm place until double in size (about 1½ hr.). Dough is ready if indentation remains when touched. Punch down dough; divide in half. With floured hands shape each half into 18 rounds. Place in 2 greased 13 × 9" *(33 × 23 cm)* baking pans. Cover; let rise until double in size (about 1 hr.). Heat oven to 375°F *(190°C)*. Bake for 20 to 25 min. or until golden brown. If desired, brush tops of rolls with butter.

Double Caramel-Raisin Rolls

All-time favorite caramel rolls or the goodness of frosted orange rolls — both from the same recipe.

Dough*

4½ to 5 c.	*(1,2 to 1,3 L)* all-purpose flour
⅓ c.	*(75 mL)* sugar
1 c.	*(250 mL)* warm milk (120° to 130°F) *(49° to 54°C)*
½ c.	*(125 mL)* butter or margarine, melted
¼-oz.	*(7-g)* pkg. active dry yeast
2	eggs
½ tsp.	*(2 mL)* salt
¾ c.	*(200 mL)* raisins

Filling

1¼ c.	*(300 mL)* firmly packed brown sugar
⅔ c.	*(175 mL)* butter or margarine, melted
3 tbsp.	*(50 mL)* light corn syrup
1½ tsp.	*(10 mL)* cinnamon

In large mixer bowl combine 2 c. *(500 mL)* flour, sugar, milk, ½ c. *(125 mL)* butter, yeast, eggs and salt. Beat at med. speed, scraping bowl often, until smooth (1 to 2 min.). By hand, stir in raisins and enough remaining flour to make dough easy to handle. Turn dough onto lightly floured surface; knead until smooth and elastic (3 to 5 min.). Place in greased bowl; turn greased side up. Cover; let rise in warm place until double in size (about 1 to 1½ hr.). Dough is ready if indentation remains when touched. Punch down dough. In medium bowl stir together all filling ingredients *except* cinnamon. Spread ½ of filling on bottom of greased 13 × 9" *(33 × 23 cm)* baking pan. Stir cinnamon into remaining filling. On lightly floured surface roll dough into 18 × 9" *(45 × 23 cm)* rectangle; spread with remaining filling. Roll up jelly roll fashion beginning with 18" *(45 cm)* side. Pinch edge of dough into roll to seal well. Cut into 1" *(2,5 cm)* slices; place slices in prepared pan. Cover; let rise until double in size (about 1 hr.). Heat oven to 375°F *(190°C)*. Bake for 25 to 30 min. or until golden brown. Immediately invert pan onto serving platter; remove pan.

Glazed Orange Rolls: Prepare dough as directed left except omit raisins. Omit filling. To prepare orange filling: In small bowl stir together ⅓ c. *(75 mL)* melted butter, ¾ c. *(200 mL)* sugar, 1 tbsp. *(15 mL)* light corn syrup and 1 tbsp. *(15 mL)* grated orange peel. On lightly floured surface roll dough into 18 × 9" *(45 × 23 cm)* rectangle; spread with orange filling. Roll up jelly roll fashion beginning with 18" *(45 cm)* side. Pinch edge of dough into roll to seal well. Cut into 1" *(2,5 cm)* slices; place slices in greased 13 × 9" *(33 × 23 cm)* baking pan. Cover; let rise until double in size (about 1 hr.). Heat oven to 375°F *(190°C)*. Bake for 25 to 30 min. or until golden brown. Immediately invert pan onto wire rack; remove pan. Invert rolls onto serving platter (top sides up). To prepare glaze: In small bowl stir together 2 c. *(500 mL)* powdered sugar, ¼ c. *(50 mL)* orange juice and 1 tsp. *(5 mL)* grated orange peel. Glaze top of warm rolls.

*2 (1-lb.) *(450-g)* loaves frozen bread dough can be substituted for dough recipe. Let frozen dough thaw according to pkg. directions. If preparing Double Caramel-Raisin Rolls, knead ¾ c. *(200 mL)* raisins into dough. Prepare filling and continue as directed left.

Double Caramel-Raisin Rolls

10 servings
3 hours

Glazed Lemon Daisy Bread

Take some time to shape this tender bread to look like a daisy.

Dough

½ c.	*(125 mL)* sugar
½ c.	*(125 mL)* butter or margarine
¾ c.	*(175 mL)* milk
¼-oz.	*(7-g)* pkg. active dry yeast
4¼ to 4¾ c.	*(1 to 1,2 L)* all-purpose flour
3	eggs
½ tsp.	*(3 mL)* salt
1 tbsp.	*(15 mL)* grated lemon peel
1 tsp.	*(5 mL)* vanilla

Filling

¼ c.	*(50 mL)* butter or margarine, softened
½ tsp.	*(3 mL)* ground cloves

Glaze

½ c.	*(125 mL)* sugar
½ c.	*(125 mL)* dairy sour cream
¼ c.	*(50 mL)* butter or margarine
2 tbsp.	*(30 mL)* lemon juice

In 1-qt. *(1-L)* saucepan combine ½ c. *(125 mL)* sugar, ½ c. *(125 mL)* butter and milk. Cook over med. heat until butter is melted (3 to 5 min.). Pour into large bowl; cool to warm (105° to 115°F) *(40° to 46°C)*. Stir in yeast until dissolved. Add 3 c. *(725 mL)* flour and remaining dough ingredients; stir until well mixed. Stir in remaining flour, ½ c. *(125 mL)* at a time, until soft dough forms. Turn dough onto lightly floured surface; knead until smooth and elastic (3 to 5 min.). Place in greased bowl; turn greased side up. Cover; let rise in warm place until doubled in size (1 to 1½ hr.). Dough is ready if indentation remains when touched. Punch down dough; let rest 10 min. On lightly floured surface roll dough into 18" *(45 cm)* circle. Spread with softened ¼ c. *(50 mL)* butter;

sprinkle with cloves. Place beverage tumbler in center; make 4 cuts at equal intervals from outside of circle to beverage tumbler. Cut each wedge into 5 wedges. Twist every two wedges together tightly, making 10 twists; pinch ends of twists together. Coil twists toward center, making daisy design; remove beverage tumbler. Coil one twist for center. Place on greased large cookie sheet; reshape design, if necessary. Cover; let rise about 45 min. Heat oven to 350°F *(180°C)*. Bake for 20 to 30 min. or until golden brown. In 2-qt. *(2-L)* saucepan combine all glaze ingredients. Cook over med. heat, stirring occasionally, until mixture comes to a full boil (5 to 6 min.); boil 3 min. Pour warm glaze over warm bread.

To Prepare Bread:

1. Place beverage tumbler in center; make 4 cuts at equal intervals from outside of circle to beverage tumbler. Cut each wedge into 5 wedges. Twist every two wedges together tightly, making 10 twists; pinch ends of twists together.

2. Coil twists toward center, making daisy design; remove beverage tumbler. Coil one twist for center.

Glazed Lemon Daisy Bread

1 coffee cake
3 hours 40 minutes

Raisin n' Nut Pull-Apart Coffee Cake

Perfect for a potluck or family gathering,
this old-fashioned pull-apart sweetbread will serve a crowd.

1 c.	*(250 mL)* milk		½ tsp.	*(3 mL)* salt
¼ c.	*(50 mL)* butter or margarine		1 c.	*(250 mL)* sugar
¼-oz.	*(7-g)* pkg. active dry yeast		½ c.	*(125 mL)* chopped pecans
¼ c.	*(50 mL)* warm water (105° to 115°F) *(40° to 46°C)*		1½ tsp.	*(7 mL)* cinnamon
3½ to 4 c.	*(750 mL to 1 L)* all-purpose flour		½ c.	*(125 mL)* butter or margarine, melted
¼ c.	*(50 mL)* sugar		½ c.	*(125 mL)* golden raisins
1	egg			

In 1-qt. *(1-L)* saucepan scald milk; stir in ¼ c. *(50 mL)* butter until melted. Cool to warm (105° to 115°F) *(40° to 46°C)*. In large mixer bowl dissolve yeast in warm water. Add cooled milk mixture, 2 c. *(500 mL)* flour, ¼ c. *(50 mL)* sugar, egg and salt. Beat at med. speed, scraping bowl often, until smooth (1 to 2 min.). By hand, stir in enough remaining flour to make dough easy to handle. Turn dough onto lightly floured surface; knead until smooth and elastic (about 10 min.). Place in greased bowl, turn greased side up. Cover; let rise in warm place until double in size (about 1½ hr.). Dough is ready if indentation remains when touched. Punch down dough; divide in half. With floured hands shape each half into 24 balls. In small bowl stir together 1 c. *(250 mL)* sugar, pecans and cinnamon. Dip balls first in melted butter, then in sugar mixture. Place 24 balls in bottom of greased 10" *(25 cm)* tube pan or Bundt pan. (If removable bottom tube pan, line with aluminum foil.) Sprinkle with raisins. Top with remaining 24 balls. Cover; let rise until double in size (about 45 min.). Heat oven to 375°F *(190°C)*. Bake for 35 to 40 min. or until coffee cake sounds hollow when tapped. (Cover with aluminum foil if coffee cake browns too quickly.) Immediately invert pan on heat-proof serving plate. Let pan stand 1 min. to allow sugar mixture to drizzle over cake. Remove pan; serve warm.

To Prepare Coffee Cake:

1. With floured hands shape each half into 24 balls. In small bowl stir together 1 c. *(250 mL)* sugar, pecans and cinnamon. Dip balls first in melted butter, then in sugar mixture. Place 24 balls in bottom of greased 10" *(25 cm)* tube pan or Bundt pan.

2. Immediately invert pan on heat-proof serving plate. Let pan stand 1 min. to allow sugar mixture to drizzle over cake. Remove pan; serve warm.

Raisin n' Nut Pull-Apart Coffee Cake

Honey-Glazed Raised Donuts

*These old-fashioned donuts satisfy hungry appetites
with their hearty yeast bread-like texture and allspice flavor.*

Donuts

1 c.	*(250 mL)* sugar
⅔ c.	*(150 mL)* butter or margarine, cut into pieces
1½ c.	*(375 mL)* milk
1 tbsp.	*(15 mL)* allspice
1½ tsp.	*(7 mL)* salt
½ c.	*(125 mL)* warm water (105° to 115°F) *(40° to 46°C)*
3	(¼-oz.) *(7-g)* pkg. active dry yeast
4	eggs
7 to 8 c.	*(1,8 L to 2 L)* all-purpose flour

Vegetable oil

Glaze

2½ c.	*(625 mL)* powdered sugar
¼ c.	*(50 mL)* water
2 tbsp.	*(30 mL)* honey

In 2-qt. *(2-L)* saucepan combine sugar, butter, milk, allspice and salt. Cook over med. heat until butter melts (3 to 4 min.). Cool to warm (105° to 115°F) *(40° to 46°C)*. Meanwhile, in large mixer bowl combine ½ c. *(125 mL)* water and yeast. Add milk mixture, eggs and 4 c. *(1 L)* flour. Beat at low speed, scraping bowl often, until moistened. Increase to med. speed; continue beating 3 min. By hand, stir in enough remaining flour to form a soft dough. Turn dough onto lightly floured surface; knead until smooth and elastic (5 to 10 min.). Place in greased bowl; turn greased side up. Cover; let rise in warm place until double in size (1 to 1½ hr.). Dough is ready if indentation remains when touched. Punch down dough; divide in half. On lightly floured surface roll each half to ½" *(1 cm)* thickness. With lightly floured 3" *(7,5 cm)* donut cutter cut out donuts. Place donuts on greased cookie sheets. Cover; let rise in warm place until double in size (30 to 45 min.). Heat 3" *(7,5 cm)* oil in deep fat fryer or Dutch oven to 375°F *(190°C)*. Place donuts into hot oil. Fry until golden brown (30 to 45 sec. on each side). Remove from oil; drain on paper towels. In small bowl stir together all glaze ingredients. Dip warm donuts in glaze; place on waxed paper. Serve warm.

Tip: To reheat donuts in microwave, microwave one donut on HIGH 5 to 6 seconds.

To Prepare Honey-Glazed Raised Donuts:

1. Heat 3" *(7,5 cm)* oil in deep fat fryer or Dutch oven to 375°F *(190°C)*. Place donuts into hot oil. Fry until golden brown (30 to 45 sec. on each side).

2. Dip warm donuts in glaze; place on waxed paper.

Honey-Glazed Raised Donuts

Bake Shop Krispies

2 dozen
3 hours 20 minutes

Bake Shop Krispies

A homemade recipe for a bake shop favorite — also known as elephant ears.

Dough

3¾ to 4¼ c.	*(950 mL to 1 L)*	all-purpose flour
¼-oz.	*(7-g)*	pkg. active dry yeast
¼ c.	*(50 mL)*	sugar
1¼ c.	*(300 mL)*	milk
¼ c.	*(50 mL)*	butter or margarine
1 tsp.	*(5 mL)*	salt
1		egg

Filling

1 c.	*(250 mL)*	sugar
¼ c.	*(50 mL)*	butter or margarine, melted
½ tsp.	*(3 mL)*	cinnamon

Topping

¼ c.	*(50 mL)*	butter or margarine, melted
1 c.	*(250 mL)*	sugar
1 tsp.	*(5 mL)*	cinnamon
½ c.	*(125 mL)*	chopped pecans

In large mixer bowl combine 2 c. *(500 mL)* flour and yeast. In 1-qt. *(1-L)* saucepan combine ¼ c. *(50 mL)* sugar, milk, ¼ c. *(50 mL)* butter and salt. Cook over med. heat, stirring constantly, until warm (115° to 120°F) *(46° to 49°C)*. Add to flour mixture; add egg. Beat at low speed, scraping bowl often, until well mixed (1 to 2 min.). Beat at high speed, scraping bowl often, 3 min. By hand, stir in enough remaining flour to make dough easy to handle. Turn dough onto lightly floured surface; knead until smooth and elastic (about 5 min.). Place in greased bowl; turn greased side up. Cover; let rise in warm place until double in size (about 1½ hr.). Dough is ready if indentation remains when touched. Punch down dough; divide in half. Roll each half into 12" *(30 cm)* sq. In medium bowl stir together filling ingredients. Spread half over each 12" *(30 cm)* sq. Roll each 12" *(30 cm)* sq. up jelly roll fashion; pinch to seal seams

well. Cut each into 12 rolls. Place on greased cookie sheets 3 to 4" *(7 to 10 cm)* apart (about 6 rolls per cookie sheet). Cover with waxed paper. With rolling pin flatten each roll to about 3" *(7 cm)* in diameter. Do not remove waxed paper; let rise in warm place 30 min. Heat oven to 400°F *(200°C)*. With rolling pin flatten to ⅛" *(0,2 cm)* thickness; remove waxed paper. Brush rolls with ¼ c. *(50 mL)* melted butter. In small bowl stir together 1 c. *(250 mL)* sugar and 1 tsp. *(5 mL)* cinnamon; sprinkle over rolls. Sprinkle pecans over rolls. Cover with waxed paper; roll flat. Remove waxed paper. Bake for 8 to 12 min. or until golden brown. Remove from pan immediately.

Orange Krispies: Omit cinnamon in filling. Add 1 tbsp. *(15 mL)* grated orange peel to filling. *Omit cinnamon and pecans in topping.* Add ½ c. *(125 mL)* sliced almonds and 1 tsp. *(5 mL)* grated orange peel to topping.

To Prepare Krispies:

1. Place on greased cookie sheets 3 to 4" *(7 to 10 cm)* apart (about 6 rolls per cookie sheet). Cover with waxed paper. With rolling pin flatten each roll to about 3" *(7 cm)* in diameter.

2. Sprinkle pecans over rolls. Cover with waxed paper; roll flat. Remove waxed paper.

To Prepare Dough:

How to: Prepare Yeast Bread

1. Use a thermometer to assure the correct water temperature for the yeast. Water should be 105° to 115°F *(40° to 46°C)*.

2. Add just enough flour to make dough easy to handle. Dough should leave the side of the bowl almost clean when the correct amount has been mixed in.

3. Knead dough on a lightly floured surface. Add more flour as needed until dough no longer sticks.

4. To knead, fold dough toward you; with heels of hands push dough away, using a rocking motion. Turn dough a quarter turn and repeat. Continue repeating until dough is smooth and elastic.

5. Let dough rise in a warm (80° to 85°F) *(25° to 30°C)* place until double in size. Dough is ready if indentation remains when poked.

6. To release large air bubbles, punch down dough with fist. Shape dough as directed.

To Shape a Loaf:

1. Roll into an 18 × 9" *(45 × 23 cm)* rectangle. Fold 9" *(23 cm)* sides crosswise into thirds, overlapping ends.

2. Roll up tightly, beginning at one of the open ends. Pinch end of dough into roll to seal well.

3. Press each end with the side of your hand to seal, then fold the end underneath. Place loaves, seam sides down, in greased loaf pans. Let rise until double in size.

To Bake and Store Bread:

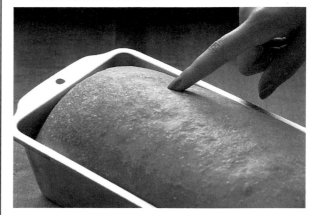

1. Bake as directed. Bread is done when loaf sounds hollow when tapped.

2. Remove from pans immediately. If desired, brush tops of loaves with butter.

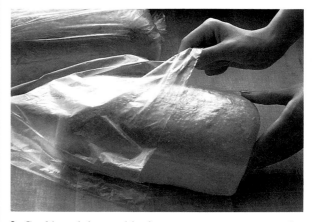

3. Cool bread thoroughly. Store at room temperature in tightly sealed plastic bags for up to 1 week or freeze for up to 3 months.

SOUPS & STEWS

No special invitation is necessary when you share the hospitality of homemade soup. The savory aroma of a long-simmering soup or stew is invitation enough. Neither dainty nor elegant, your own made-from-scratch soups and stews will bring back memories of those marvelous kettles of goodness that bubbled on the back of Grandma's stove.

She always seemed to know how to add a pinch of this or that to create steaming mixtures that were unbelievably delicious. Like a spicy, tomato-rich stew, thick with beans and beef and pork sausage, just right for those cool fall days. Creamy chowder made with new red potatoes. Chicken noodle soup with those long flat noodles that were so much fun to slurp, even if it did bring a gentle scolding.

Soups, stews and chowders — so simple and nourishing — are among the classics of country cooking. Served for lunch or supper any time of the year, they satisfy the soul and the appetite in wonderfully familiar ways.

Hearty Bacon Potato Chowder

6 servings
40 minutes

A rich, hearty and simple soup welcome at almost any occasion.

8	slices bacon, cut into 1" *(2,5 cm)* pieces
2 c.	*(500 mL)* (6 med.) cubed ½" *(1 cm)* new red potatoes
1 c.	*(250 mL)* (2 med.) chopped onions
1 c.	*(250 mL)* dairy sour cream
1¼ c.	*(300 mL)* milk

10¾-oz.	*(284-mL)* can condensed cream of chicken soup
8-oz.	*(199-mL)* can whole kernel corn, drained
¼ tsp.	*(1 mL)* pepper
¼ tsp.	*(1 mL)* thyme leaves

In 3-qt. *(3-L)* saucepan cook bacon over med. heat for 5 min.; add potatoes and onions. Continue cooking, stirring occasionally, until potatoes are tender (15 to 20 min.). Add remaining ingredients. Continue cooking, stirring occasionally, until heated through (10 to 12 min.).

Microwave Directions: In 3-qt. *(3-L)* casserole combine bacon, potatoes and onions. Cover; microwave on HIGH, stirring after half the time, until potatoes are tender (12 to 18 min.). Stir in remaining ingredients. Cover; microwave on HIGH until heated through (2 to 4 min.).

Seashore Chowder

4 servings
50 minutes

Feel free to use all oysters or all clams in this chowder from the sea.

6	slices bacon, cut into 1" *(2,5 cm)* pieces
2 c.	*(500 mL)* (6 med.) cubed ½" *(1 cm)* new red potatoes
½ c.	*(125 mL)* (1 med.) chopped onion
½ c.	*(125 mL)* chopped celery
3 tbsp.	*(45 mL)* butter or margarine
3 tbsp.	*(45 mL)* all-purpose flour

3 c.	*(750 mL)* milk
8-oz.	*(227-g)* can oysters, drained, rinsed
6½-oz.	*(184-g)* can clams, drained, rinsed
2 tsp.	*(10 mL)* basil leaves
	Pinch of cayenne pepper
¼ c.	*(50 mL)* chopped fresh parsley

In 3-qt. *(3-L)* saucepan cook bacon over med. heat for 5 min.; add potatoes, onion and celery. Continue cooking, stirring occasionally, until potatoes are tender (15 to 20 min.). Remove from pan; set aside. In same pan melt butter; stir in flour until smooth and bubbly (1 min.). Add potato mixture and remaining ingredients *except* parsley. Cook over med. heat, stirring occasionally, until heated through (10 to 15 min.). Stir in parsley.

Microwave Directions: In 4-qt. *(4-L)* casserole combine bacon, potatoes, onion and celery. Cover; microwave on HIGH, stirring after half the time, until potatoes are tender (12 to 18 min.). Cut up butter; stir into vegetable mixture. Stir in flour until smooth. Stir in remaining ingredients *except* oysters, clams and parsley. Cover; microwave on HIGH, stirring after half the time, until slightly thickened (6 to 10 min.). Stir in remaining ingredients. Cover; microwave on HIGH until heated through (1 to 2 min.).

Hearty Bacon Potato Chowder

4 servings
30 minutes

Creamy Spinach & Carrot Soup

Subtly spiced with nutmeg and orange, this soup is colorful and delicious.

3 tbsp.	*(45 mL)* butter or margarine
1 c.	*(250 mL)* (2 med.) chopped onions
2 tbsp.	*(30 mL)* all-purpose flour
1 c.	*(250 mL)* half-and-half
10¾-oz.	*(284-mL)* can chicken broth
1 c.	*(250 mL)* (2 med.) shredded carrots
10-oz.	*(300-g)* pkg. frozen chopped spinach, thawed, drained

¼ tsp.	*(1 mL)* salt
¼ tsp.	*(1 mL)* pepper
	Pinch of nutmeg

Zest or strip of orange peel

In 2-qt. *(2-L)* saucepan melt butter; add onions. Cook over med. heat, stirring occasionally, until onions are tender (5 to 6 min.). Stir in flour until smooth and bubbly (1 min.). Stir in half-and-half and chicken broth. Add remaining ingredients *except* orange peel. Continue cooking over low heat, stirring occasionally, until soup is heated through (12 to 15 min.). Garnish with zest or strip of orange peel.

Microwave Directions: In 2½-qt. *(2,5-L)* casserole combine butter and onions. Microwave on HIGH, stirring after half the time, until onions are tender (2½ to 3 min.). Stir in flour until smooth. Microwave on HIGH until bubbly (30 to 45 sec.). Stir in half-and-half and chicken broth. Add remaining ingredients *except* orange peel. Cover; microwave on HIGH, stirring after half the time, until soup is heated through (8 to 10 min.). Garnish with zest or strip of orange peel.

To Make Strip of Orange Peel:

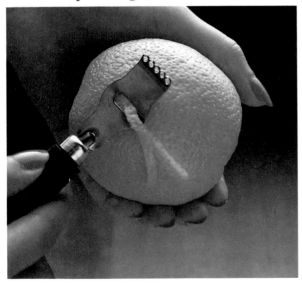

1. Using a citrus stripper, cut strips of peel from orange.

2. Or, cut a piece of peel from orange using a vegetable peeler. Scrape away any of the white pith on back of peel. Cut peel into fine strips with a sharp knife.

Creamy Spinach & Carrot Soup

Northwoods Wild Rice Soup

8 servings
60 minutes

The nutty flavor of wild rice rounds out this popular midwestern cream soup.

3 c.	*(750 mL)* cooked wild rice
2 c.	*(500 mL)* cubed 1" *(2,5 cm)* cooked chicken or turkey
1 c.	*(250 mL)* cubed ½" *(1 cm)* cooked ham
1 c.	*(250 mL)* (2 med.) shredded carrots
1 c.	*(250 mL)* (2 stalks) sliced ½" *(1 cm)* celery
1 qt.	(4 c.) *(1 L)* half-and-half

1 c.	*(250 mL)* chicken broth
¼ c.	*(50 mL)* sherry or chicken broth
1	med. onion, chopped
½ tsp.	*(2 mL)* salt
¼ tsp.	*(1 mL)* pepper
¼ c.	*(50 mL)* all-purpose flour
3 tbsp.	*(45 mL)* butter or margarine, melted

In Dutch oven combine all ingredients *except* flour and butter. Cook over med. heat, stirring occasionally, until heated through (15 to 20 min.). In small bowl stir together flour and butter; stir into hot soup. Continue cooking, stirring occasionally, until thickened (5 to 8 min.).

Microwave Directions: In 4-qt. *(4-L)* casserole combine all ingredients *except* flour and butter. Cover; microwave on HIGH, stirring after half the time, until heated through (13 to 15 min.). In small bowl stir together flour and butter; stir into hot soup. Microwave on HIGH, stirring after half the time, until thickened (5 to 8 min.). Let stand 5 min.

Open Hearth Split Pea Soup

6 servings
2 hours 30 minutes

Homemade split pea soup, made with smoked ham, warms the heart and body.

1 lb.	*(450 g)* (2¼ c.) *(550 mL)* dried green split peas
1½ c.	*(375 mL)* (3 stalks) chopped celery
1 c.	*(250 mL)* (2 med.) chopped onions

9 c.	*(2,3 L)* water
1 to 1½ lb.	*(450 to 675 g)* smoked ham hocks
5	sprigs fresh parsley
	Salt and pepper

In Dutch oven combine all ingredients *except* salt and pepper. Cook over med. heat until mixture comes to a full boil. Cover; reduce heat to low. Continue cooking, stirring occasionally, 1½ hr. Remove cover; continue cooking until soup is thickened (30 to 60 min.). Remove ham hocks; when cool enough to handle, cut off meat. Discard bones; return meat to soup. Season to taste.

Microwave Directions: In 4-qt. *(4-L)* casserole combine all ingredients *except* salt and pepper. Cover; microwave on HIGH, stirring after half the time, until soup is thickened (40 to 60 min.). Remove ham hocks; when cool enough to handle, cut off meat. Discard bones; return meat to soup. Season to taste.

Northwoods Wild Rice Soup

Garden Zucchini Bisque

4 servings
30 minutes

Rich and creamy with the delicate flavors of garden zucchini and mushrooms.

2 tbsp.   *(30 mL)* butter or margarine
2 c.   *(500 mL)* (2 med.) sliced ⅛" *(0,2 cm)* zucchini
1 c.   *(250 mL)* sliced ¼" *(0,5 cm)* fresh mushrooms
½ c.   *(125 mL)* (1 med.) chopped onion

¼ c.   *(50 mL)* chopped fresh parsley
3 tbsp.   *(45 mL)* butter or margarine
3 tbsp.   *(45 mL)* all-purpose flour
10¾-oz.   *(284-mL)* can chicken broth
¾ c.   *(200 mL)* whipping cream
          Pinch of pepper

In 3-qt. *(3-L)* saucepan melt 2 tbsp. *(30 mL)* butter; add zucchini, mushrooms, onion and parsley. Cook over med. heat, stirring occasionally, until vegetables are crisply tender (6 to 8 min.). Meanwhile, in 2-qt. *(2-L)* saucepan melt 3 tbsp. *(45 mL)* butter over med. heat; stir in flour until smooth and bubbly (1 min.). Add chicken broth; continue cooking, stirring occasionally, until soup is thickened (5 to 7 min.). Stir in cream, pepper and zucchini mixture. Continue cooking until heated through (5 to 6 min.).

Microwave Directions: In 3-qt. *(3-L)* casserole melt 2 tbsp. *(30 mL)* butter on HIGH (30 to 40 sec.). Stir in zucchini, mushrooms, onion and parsley. Cover; microwave on HIGH until vegetables are crisply tender (2½ to 3½ min.). Cut up 3 tbsp. *(45 mL)* butter; stir into vegetable mixture until melted. Stir in flour until smooth; microwave on HIGH until bubbly (1 to 1½ min.). Stir in remaining ingredients. Cover; microwave on HIGH, stirring after half the time, until slightly thickened and heated through (6 to 9 min.).

Tomato Barley Soup

6 servings
60 minutes

Fill your kitchen with the aroma of garlic, onions and vegetables.

1 c.   *(250 mL)* (2 med.) chopped onions
1 c.   *(250 mL)* (2 med.) sliced ¼" *(0,5 cm)* carrots
1 c.   *(250 mL)* (2 stalks) sliced ¼" *(0,5 cm)* celery
2 tbsp.   *(30 mL)* vegetable oil
2 tsp.   *(10 mL)* minced fresh garlic

¼ c.   *(50 mL)* pearled barley
2½ c.   *(625 mL)* water
2 c.   *(500 mL)* (2 med.) cubed 1" *(2,5 cm)* ripe tomatoes
14½-oz.   *(398-mL)* can whole tomatoes
10¾-oz.   *(284-mL)* can chicken broth
¼ tsp.   *(1 mL)* pepper

In 2-qt. *(2-L)* saucepan combine onions, carrots, celery, oil and garlic. Cook over med. heat, stirring occasionally, until vegetables are crisply tender (8 to 10 min.). Meanwhile, in 3-qt. *(3-L)* saucepan combine remaining ingredients. Cook until mixture comes to a full boil. Add vegetable mixture. Return to boil; reduce heat to low. Cover; cook until barley is tender (35 to 40 min.).

Microwave Directions: In 3-qt. *(3-L)* casserole combine onions, carrots, celery, oil and garlic. Cover; microwave on HIGH, stirring after half the time, until vegetables are crisply tender (3 to 4 min.). Add remaining ingredients. Cover; microwave on HIGH, stirring after half the time, until barley is tender (18 to 25 min.). Let stand 5 min.

Garden Zucchini Bisque

Hearty Minestrone Soup

Homemade Chicken Broth

5 cups *(1,3 L)*
4 hours

Save the backs, wings and necks from chickens until you have 3 to 4 lb.;
then, prepare your own flavorful, economical chicken broth.

3 to 4 lb.	*(1,3 to 1,8 kg)* chicken backs, wings, necks
8 c.	*(2 L)* water
2	med. onions, cut into eighths
2	stalks celery with leaves, cut into thirds

2	carrots, cut into thirds
1	bay leaf
½ tsp.	*(2 mL)* salt
¼ tsp.	*(1 mL)* pepper

In large kettle or stockpot combine all ingredients. Cover; cook over high heat until mixture comes to a full boil (15 to 20 min.). Reduce heat to med. low; continue cooking 3 to 4 hr. Strain; skim fat. Stock can be refrigerated 2 to 3 days or frozen 3 to 4 months.

Microwave Directions: In 5-qt. *(5-L)* casserole combine all ingredients. Cover; microwave on HIGH until mixture comes to a full boil (25 to 30 min.). Stir. Cover; reduce power to MEDIUM (50% power). Microwave until carrots are crisply tender (30 to 40 min.). Let stand 5 min. Strain; skim fat. Store as directed left.

Hearty Minestrone Soup

14 (1 cup) *(250 mL)* servings
2 hours

Vegetables, fresh from the garden, make this soup extra special.

1½ lb.	*(675 g)* cubed 1" *(2,5 cm)* beef stew meat
8 c.	*(2 L)* water
2 tsp.	*(10 mL)* salt
1½ c.	*(375 mL)* (3 med.) chopped onions
1 c.	*(250 mL)* (2 med.) sliced ¼" *(0,5 cm)* carrots
1 c.	*(250 mL)* (2 stalks) chopped celery
½ c.	*(125 mL)* butter or margarine
1 tbsp.	*(15 mL)* chopped fresh parsley

1 tsp.	*(5 mL)* minced fresh garlic
2 c.	*(500 mL)* (2 med.) chopped ripe tomatoes
2 c.	*(500 mL)* (2 med.) cubed ½" *(1 cm)* potatoes
1 c.	*(250 mL)* (1 med.) unpeeled, sliced ¼" *(0,5 cm)* zucchini
½ c.	*(125 mL)* uncooked long grain rice
15-oz.	*(398-mL)* can kidney beans, drained
	Salt and pepper

In Dutch oven combine beef, water and salt. Cover; cook over med. heat until mixture comes to a full boil (10 to 12 min.). Reduce heat to low; continue cooking until beef is fork tender (about 1 hr.). Meanwhile, in 10" *(25 cm)* skillet combine onions, carrots, celery, butter, parsley and garlic. Cook over med. heat, stirring occasionally, until vegetables are crisply tender (5 to 6 min.). Add vegetable mixture to beef along with remaining ingredients *except* kidney beans. Cook over med. heat until mixture comes to a full boil (10 to 12 min.); reduce heat to low. Cover; continue cooking until vegetables are crisply tender (20 to 30 min.). Stir in kidney beans. Continue cooking until heated through (2 to 3 min.). Season to taste.

Microwave Directions: In 5-qt. *(5-L)* casserole combine beef, water and salt. Cover; microwave on HIGH until beef is fork tender (30 to 40 min.). Add rice. Cover; microwave on HIGH until rice is tender (12 to 15 min.). Let stand covered. Meanwhile, in 3-qt. *(3-L)* casserole melt butter on HIGH (70 to 80 sec.). Stir in remaining ingredients *except* tomatoes and kidney beans. Cover; microwave on HIGH until vegetables are crisply tender (5 to 8 min.). Add vegetable mixture to beef mixture. Cover; microwave on HIGH until vegetables are fork tender (10 to 12 min.). Add kidney beans. Cover; microwave on HIGH until heated through (8 to 10 min.). Stir in tomatoes. Let stand covered 5 min. Season to taste.

Crock of Savory Vegetable Stew

Crock of Savory Vegetable Stew

6 servings
60 minutes

Full of hearty ingredients and sweet savory spices.

2 c.	*(500 mL)* (4 med.) sliced ¼" *(0,5 cm)* carrots
1 c.	*(250 mL)* (2 med.) chopped onions
1 c.	*(250 mL)* (2 stalks) sliced ½" *(1 cm)* celery
1 lb.	*(450 g)* pork sausage links, cut into 2" *(5 cm)* pieces
4 c.	*(1 L)* shredded cabbage
½ c.	*(125 mL)* chopped fresh parsley
1 c.	*(250 mL)* apple juice
15-oz.	*(398-mL)* can tomato sauce
14½-oz.	*(398-mL)* can whole tomatoes
10¾-oz.	*(284-mL)* can tomato soup
1	bay leaf
½ tsp.	*(2 mL)* salt
½ tsp.	*(2 mL)* thyme leaves
¼ tsp.	*(1 mL)* pepper

In 2-qt. *(2-L)* saucepan combine carrots, onions, celery and sausage. Cook over med. heat, stirring occasionally, until sausage is browned and vegetables are crisply tender (8 to 12 min.). Pour off fat. Meanwhile, in 3-qt. *(3-L)* saucepan combine remaining ingredients. Cook over low heat, stirring occasionally, until heated through (12 to 15 min.). Stir in cooked sausage and vegetables. Continue cooking, stirring occasionally, until stew is thickened (20 to 30 min.).

Microwave Directions: In 3-qt. *(3-L)* casserole combine carrots, onions, celery and sausage. Cover; microwave on HIGH, stirring after half the time, until sausage is done and vegetables are crisply tender (4 to 8 min.). Stir in remaining ingredients. Cover; microwave on HIGH, stirring after half the time, until slightly thickened and heated through (10 to 15 min.).

Farmhouse Chicken Noodle Stew

6 servings
60 minutes

A marvelous heart-warming stew.

3 to 3½ lb.	*(1,3 to 1,6 kg)* frying chicken, cut into 8 pieces
6 c.	*(1,5 L)* hot water
2 c.	*(500 mL)* (4 stalks) sliced ¼" *(0,5 cm)* celery
1 c.	*(250 mL)* (2 med.) chopped onions
½ c.	*(125 mL)* chopped fresh parsley
3	med. carrots, cut into 1" *(2,5 cm)* pieces
2	bay leaves
1 tbsp.	*(15 mL)* basil leaves
1 tsp.	*(5 mL)* thyme leaves
1 tsp.	*(5 mL)* marjoram leaves
1 tsp.	*(5 mL)* salt
½ tsp.	*(2 mL)* pepper
12-oz.	*(340-g)* pkg. frozen egg noodles*

In Dutch oven cover chicken with water. Cover; cook over med. high heat for 10 min. Meanwhile, prepare vegetables. Add vegetables and remaining ingredients *except* noodles. Cover; cook over med. high heat for 20 min. or until chicken is fork tender. Remove chicken pieces; add noodles. Return to a full boil, skimming off fat during cooking. (Some herbs will be removed.) Meanwhile, remove chicken from bone. Reduce heat to low. Add chicken. Cook until noodles are tender (20 to 25 min.).

*2 c. *(500 mL)* uncooked med. egg noodles can be substituted for frozen egg noodles.

Microwave Directions: In 6-qt. *(6-L)* casserole combine 4 c. *(1 L)* water and remaining ingredients *except* noodles. Cover; microwave on HIGH, stirring after half the time, until chicken is fork tender (25 to 35 min.). Remove chicken from broth; skim off fat. Add noodles and 2 c. *(500 mL)* water; continue microwaving on HIGH (8 to 10 min.). Meanwhile, remove chicken from bone. Add chicken to noodle mixture. Cover; microwave on HIGH, stirring after half the time, until noodles are tender (18 to 20 min.).

8 servings
2 hours

Chicken Stew with Dumplings

A great Saturday night supper with tender homemade dumplings.

Stew

2½ to 3 lb. *(1,1 to 1,3 kg)* chicken thighs
5 c.   *(1,3 L)* water
4   new red potatoes, cut into sixths
3   carrots, cut into quarters
2   stalks celery, sliced ¼" *(0,5 cm)*
1   med. onion, cut into eighths
10-oz.   *(350-g)* pkg. frozen peas
½ tsp.   *(2 mL)* salt
              Pinch of pepper

Dumplings

1½ c.   *(375 mL)* all-purpose flour
2 tsp.   *(10 mL)* baking powder
¾ tsp.   *(3 mL)* salt
3 tbsp.   *(45 mL)* butter or margarine, softened
¾ c.   *(200 mL)* milk
¼ c.   *(50 mL)* chopped fresh parsley

In Dutch oven place chicken; cover with water. Cover; cook over med. heat until fork tender (50 to 60 min.). Remove chicken from broth; skim fat. Remove chicken from bones; return to broth. Add remaining stew ingredients. Cover; cook over med. heat until vegetables are fork tender (15 to 20 min.). In large bowl stir together flour, baking powder and salt. Cut in butter until mixture is crumbly. Stir in milk and parsley. Drop dumplings by rounded tablespoonfuls into hot stew. Cook, uncovered, 10 min. Cover; continue cooking until dumplings are tender (8 to 10 min.).

Microwave Directions: *Cut carrots into ¼" (0,5 cm) slices. Reduce baking powder to 1¾ tsp. (7 mL), butter to 1½ tbsp. (20 mL) and milk to ½ c. (125 mL) plus*

1 tbsp. (15 mL). In 5-qt. *(5-L)* casserole place chicken; cover with water. Cover; microwave on HIGH until water comes to a full boil (16 to 18 min.). Rearrange chicken. Reduce power to MEDIUM (50% power); microwave 10 min. Remove chicken from broth; skim fat. Remove chicken from bones; return to broth. Add remaining stew ingredients *except* peas. Cover; microwave on HIGH 8 min. Reduce power to MEDIUM (50% power); microwave until vegetables are crisply tender (7 to 9 min.). Meanwhile, prepare dumplings as directed left. Add peas to stew. Microwave on HIGH until mixture comes to a full boil (3 to 4 min.). Drop dumplings by tablespoonfuls into hot stew. Cover; microwave on HIGH, turning dish ¼ turn after half the time, until dumplings are tender (4 to 5 min.).

To Prepare Dumplings:

1. Drop dumplings by rounded tablespoonfuls into hot stew.

2. Cook, uncovered, 10 min. Cover; continue cooking until dumplings are tender (8 to 10 min.).

Chicken Stew With Dumplings

Country-Style French Onion Soup

The light chicken broth and Dijon mustard bring out the mellow, rich flavor of onions.

Soup

2 tbsp.	*(30 mL)* butter or margarine
4 c.	*(1 L)* (4 med.) sliced ⅛" *(0,2 cm)* onions
½ tsp.	*(2 mL)* minced fresh garlic
¼ c.	*(50 mL)* chopped fresh parsley
2 c.	*(500 mL)* water
10¾-oz.	*(284-mL)* can chicken broth
2 tbsp.	*(30 mL)* country-style Dijon mustard
1 tsp.	*(5 mL)* basil leaves
¼ tsp.	*(1 mL)* thyme leaves
¼ tsp.	*(1 mL)* pepper

Croutons

¼ c.	*(50 mL)* butter or margarine
1 tsp.	*(5 mL)* basil leaves
½ tsp.	*(2 mL)* minced fresh garlic
3 c.	*(750 mL)* cubed 1" *(2,5 cm)* rye bread
6	(1 oz.) *(30 g)* slices Mozzarella cheese

Heat oven to 400°F *(200°C)*. In 3-qt. *(3-L)* saucepan melt 2 tbsp. *(30 mL)* butter; add onions and ½ tsp. *(2 mL)* garlic. Cook over med. heat, stirring occasionally, until onions are tender (7 to 10 min.). Add remaining soup ingredients; continue cooking until heated through (12 to 15 min.). Meanwhile, in 13 × 9" *(33 × 23 cm)* baking pan melt ¼ c. *(50 mL)* butter in oven (4 to 6 min.). Stir in basil and ½ tsp. *(2 mL)* garlic. Add bread cubes; toss to coat. Bake for 10 to 15 min., stirring occasionally, until toasted. Pour soup in oven-proof bowls; place 1 cheese slice in each bowl. Bake for 7 to 10 min. or until cheese is lightly browned. Serve with rye croutons.

Microwave Directions: In 4-qt. *(4-L)* casserole combine 2 tbsp. *(30 mL)* butter, onions and ½ tsp. *(2 mL)* garlic. Cover; microwave on HIGH, stirring after half the time, until onions are tender (5 to 6 min.). Add remaining soup ingredients. Cover; microwave on HIGH, stirring after half the time, until heated through (8 to 10 min.). Let stand 5 min. In 10" *(25 cm)* pie plate melt ¼ c. *(50 mL)* butter on HIGH (50 to 60 sec.). Stir in basil and ½ tsp. *(2 mL)* garlic. Add bread cubes; toss to coat. Microwave on HIGH, stirring every 2 min., until dry to the touch (4 to 5 min.). Pour soup in bowls; place 1 cheese slice in each bowl. Microwave on HIGH until cheese is melted (30 to 45 sec.). Serve with rye croutons.

Country-Style French Onion Soup

Savory Turkey Tomato Stew

4 to 6 servings
60 minutes

Savory Turkey Tomato Stew

Italian sausage adds extra flavor to this garden fresh stew.

1 tbsp.	*(15 mL)* vegetable oil		1 tsp.	*(5 mL)* basil leaves
2 tsp.	*(10 mL)* minced fresh garlic		1 tsp.	*(5 mL)* oregano leaves
1 lb.	*(450 g)* Italian sausage links, casing removed, cut into 1" *(2,5 cm)* pieces		½ tsp.	*(2 mL)* salt
			¼ tsp.	*(1 mL)* cracked pepper
2 c.	*(500 mL)* cooked, cubed 1" *(2,5 cm)* turkey		2	med. ripe tomatoes, cut into 2" *(5 cm)* pieces
2½ c.	*(625 mL)* chicken broth		2	med. green peppers, cut into 1" *(2,5 cm)* pieces
2	med. onions, cut into eighths			
6-oz.	*(156-mL)* can tomato paste			

In Dutch oven heat oil; add garlic. Cook over med. high heat 2 min. Add sausage pieces. Continue cooking, stirring occasionally, until lightly browned (4 to 7 min.). Drain fat. Reduce heat to med.; stir in remaining ingredients *except* tomatoes and green peppers. Cover; cook, stirring occasionally, until heated through (15 to 20 min.). Remove from heat; stir in tomatoes and green peppers. Cover; let stand 5 min. or until heated through.

Microwave Directions: Omit oil. In 2½-qt. *(2,5-L)* casserole stir together garlic and sausage pieces. Cover; microwave on HIGH, stirring after half the time, until sausage is no longer pink (5 to 8 min.). Drain fat. Add remaining ingredients *except* tomatoes and green peppers. Cover; microwave on HIGH, stirring twice during last half of time, until heated through (12 to 13 min.). Stir in tomatoes and green peppers. Cover; microwave on HIGH until heated through (1 min.). Let stand 5 min.

6 servings
60 minutes

Chili Spiced Beef & Bean Stew

*It's not chili or spaghetti but a spicy rich stew
with ground beef and pork sausage.*

1 c.	*(250 mL)* (2 med.) chopped onions		2 tbsp.	*(30 mL)* chili powder
1 lb.	*(450 g)* ground beef		1 tbsp.	*(15 mL)* basil leaves
1 lb.	*(450 g)* pork sausage		1 tsp.	*(5 mL)* oregano leaves
1 c.	*(250 mL)* water		1 tsp.	*(5 mL)* pepper
28-oz.	*(796-mL)* can whole tomatoes		½ tsp.	*(2 mL)* salt
16-oz.	*(450-mL)* can kidney beans		3 tbsp.	*(45 mL)* country-style Dijon mustard
15-oz.	*(425-mL)* can tomato sauce		8 oz.	*(225 g)* uncooked spaghetti
12-oz.	*(340 mL)* can tomato paste			

In 10" *(25 cm)* skillet cook onions, beef and sausage over med. heat until meat is browned (10 to 12 min.); pour off fat. Meanwhile, in Dutch oven combine remaining ingredients *except* spaghetti. Cook over med. heat, stirring occasionally, for 15 min. Reduce heat to low; add browned meat. Cook, stirring occasionally, until stew is thickened (20 to 30 min.). Meanwhile, cook spaghetti according to pkg. directions. Serve stew over spaghetti.

Microwave Directions: In 4-qt. *(4-L)* casserole combine onions, crumbled ground beef and sausage. Cover; microwave on HIGH, stirring after half the time, until no longer pink (5 to 8 min.). Pour off fat. In same casserole combine meat and remaining ingredients *except* spaghetti. Cover; microwave on HIGH, stirring after half the time, until heated through (15 to 20 min.). Meanwhile, cook spaghetti according to pkg. directions. Serve stew over spaghetti.

How To: Prepare Soups & Stews

Tomato Barley Soup, p. 84; Seashore Chowder, p. 78

To Identify Clear Soups:

Stock: The liquid in which meat, fish or vegetables are slowly cooked together; often used as a base for other soups.

Broth: Stock that is ladled and served.

Bouillon: Clarified, strained and seasoned broth. A plain, clear soup. Also available in dried cubes or granules that are dissolved in hot water.

Consommé: Stock or broth reduced to half by boiling, thus intensifying flavor.

To Identify Hearty Soups:

Cream: Thickened with flour, egg yolk, rice or vegetables. Milk, cream or broth are used for the liquid.

Bisque: Cream soup with shellfish, vegetable puree or bits of solid food added.

Pureed: Similar to bisque or cream soup. Pureed vegetables are used as the thickening agent.

Chowder: Contains pieces of ingredients and is typically seafood or vegetable-based.

Stew: A combination of meat and vegetables cooked by simmering in a liquid.

To Make Better Soups & Stews:

To extract the most flavor from meats and vegetables in soups and stews, start with cold water.

Raw, uncooked bones with meat and marrow provide the most intense meat flavor.

Fresh aromatic vegetables such as onion, garlic, celery and carrot enrich the broth flavor.

Herbs such as parsley, bay leaf, thyme, basil and peppercorns add flavor and distinction to soups and stews.

Stewing is a good method for tenderizing inexpensive or tougher cuts of meat while producing good flavor.

To Store Soups & Stews:

Cool soups and stews quickly; store in airtight containers.

Bean soups and broth-type soups with meat and vegetables can be frozen for up to three months.

When planning to freeze stews, do not thicken with flour or starch when preparing; thicken when reheating.

Cream-based soups such as chowders and creamed vegetable soups or those containing cheese or eggs do not freeze well.

To Skim Fat:

It is common to remove fat using a large (metal) spoon. Here are other methods:

1. Chill soup or stew for several hours until fat has solidified on top. Remove solid fat layer and discard.

2. Cool soup or stew to lukewarm and add ice cubes. The fat will solidify around the ice cubes; remove ice cubes and fat with slotted spoon and discard.

3. Several paper towels can be used to absorb the fat from the top of the soup or stew.

4. A meat baster can be used to suction off the fat.

POULTRY

A special holiday or a family celebration. It's a time to put aside the demands of daily life, to gather loved ones who share in the joys of the occasion. And one of the time-honored traditions of a special event at home is the bounty of foods that welcomes family and friends to the dining room table.

When the guest list is a long one, holiday hospitality often begins with a turkey — plump, golden brown and trimmed with dishes that have become an expected part of the feast. Bread stuffing studded with apples and raisins. Baked sweet potatoes. Cranberry sauce with just a hint of orange. A basket of homemade dinner rolls. A big bowl of green vegetables, steaming hot and glistening with butter. And so much more!

A smaller gathering might call for chicken, rubbed with herbs and roasted, or chicken breasts simmered in a savory sauce or perhaps chicken fried crispy in the cast-iron skillet.

With special occasion cooking, there's the satisfaction of preparing a truly delectable feast of foods that are spectacular to see and a pleasure to eat. But even more rewarding is the chance to share this time with those most dear to you.

6 servings
3 hours

Roasted Chicken With Garden Vegetables

Reminiscent of Sunday pot roast and vegetables,
but oh-so-good with chicken and herbs.

4 to 5 lb.	*(1,8 to 2,3 kg)* whole roasting chicken	2 tsp.	*(10 mL)* minced fresh garlic
½ c.	*(125 mL)* butter or margarine, softened	6	new red potatoes, cut in half
2 tsp.	*(10 mL)* rosemary leaves, crushed	6	carrots, cut in half crosswise
½ tsp.	*(2 mL)* salt	2	med. onions, cut into quarters
¼ tsp.	*(1 mL)* pepper	2 tbsp.	*(30 mL)* chopped fresh parsley

Heat oven to 350°F *(180°C)*. Secure wings to body of chicken. In small bowl stir together butter, rosemary, salt, pepper and garlic. Rub chicken with half of butter mixture. Place chicken on rack in roasting pan. Place potatoes, carrots and onions on bottom of pan around chicken. Dollop remaining butter mixture evenly over vegetables. Bake, basting chicken and vegetables occasionally, for 2 to 2½ hr. or until chicken is fork tender. Sprinkle with parsley.

Microwave Directions: Cut carrots into 2" *(5 cm)* pieces. In small bowl stir together butter, rosemary, salt, pepper and garlic. In 5-qt. *(5-L)* casserole place chicken, breast side down. Rub chicken with small amount of butter mixture. Cover; microwave on HIGH 5 min. Reduce power to MEDIUM (50% power); microwave 20 min. Drain off fat and juice. Turn chicken, breast side up. Place carrots around chicken. Spread chicken and carrots with half of butter mixture. Cover; microwave on MEDIUM (50% power), turning dish ¼ turn after half the time, 10 min. Rearrange carrots. Place potatoes and onions on top of carrots. Spread vegetables with remaining butter mixture. Cover; microwave on HIGH, turning dish ¼ turn every 5 min., or until chicken is fork tender (15 to 17 min.). Tent with aluminum foil; let stand 5 min. Sprinkle with parsley.

4 servings
2 hours 30 minutes

Herb Butter Roasted Chicken

Rosemary, fresh parsley and garlic create a savory roasted chicken.

4 to 5 lb.	*(1,8 to 2,3 kg)* whole roasting chicken	1 tsp.	*(5 mL)* salt
¼ c.	*(50 mL)* butter or margarine, softened	¼ tsp.	*(1 mL)* pepper
1 tsp.	*(5 mL)* rosemary leaves, crushed	2 tbsp.	*(30 mL)* chopped fresh parsley
		1 tsp.	*(5 mL)* minced fresh garlic

Heat oven to 350°F *(180°C)*. Secure wings to body of chicken. In small bowl stir together remaining ingredients. Rub chicken with butter mixture. Place on rack in roasting pan. Bake for 2 to 2½ hr. or until fork tender.

Microwave Directions: Secure wings to body of chicken. In small bowl stir together remaining ingredients and ½ tsp. *(2 mL)* paprika. Rub chicken with half of butter mixture. Place chicken, breast side down, on microwave-safe roasting rack. Cover; microwave on HIGH 5 min. Reduce power to MEDIUM (50% power); microwave, turning rack ¼ turn after half the time, 30 min. Turn chicken, breast side up. Spread chicken with remaining butter mixture. Cover; microwave on MEDIUM (50% power); turning rack ¼ turn after half the time, until fork tender (25 to 35 min.). Tent with aluminum foil; let stand 5 to 10 min.

Roasted Chicken With Garden Vegetables

Red Apple Glazed Chicken

Spiced apples create a unique spiced chicken.

Stuffing

16-oz.	*(454-mL)* jar spiced apple rings, *reserve juice*
1½ c.	*(375 mL)* dried bread cubes
1 c.	*(250 mL)* (2 stalks) sliced ½" *(1 cm)* celery
¼ c.	*(50 mL)* chopped onion
¼ c.	*(50 mL)* butter or margarine, melted
2 tbsp.	*(30 mL) reserved* spiced apple juice or water
½ tsp.	*(2 mL)* salt
	Pinch of pepper
	Pinch of allspice

4 to 5 lb.	*(1,8 to 2,3 kg)* whole roasting chicken

Glaze

¼ c.	*(50 mL) reserved* spiced apple juice
2 tbsp.	*(30 mL)* light corn syrup
2 tbsp.	*(30 mL)* water

Heat oven to 350°F *(180°C)*. Cut 5 spiced apple rings into eighths; reserve remaining apple rings. In medium bowl stir together cut-up apples and remaining stuffing ingredients. Stuff chicken; secure wings to body of chicken. Place chicken on rack in roasting pan. In 1-qt. *(1-L)* saucepan stir together all glaze ingredients. Cook over med. high heat, stirring occasionally, until heated through (5 to 6 min.). Spoon glaze over chicken. Bake, basting occasionally, for 1 hr. If needed, add ¼ c. *(50 mL)* water to basting juices. Loosely cover chicken with aluminum foil. Continue baking, basting occasionally, for 1 to 1½ hr. or until chicken is fork tender. Garnish with reserved apple rings.

Microwave Directions: Cut 5 spiced apple rings into eighths; reserve remaining apple rings. In medium bowl stir together cut-up apples and remaining stuffing ingredients. Stuff chicken; secure wings to body of chicken. In small bowl combine all glaze ingredients. Microwave on HIGH until heated through (45 to 60 sec.). Place chicken, breast side down, on microwave-safe roasting rack. Spoon half of glaze over chicken. Cover; microwave on HIGH 5 min. Reduce power to MEDIUM (50% power); microwave, turning rack ¼ turn after half the time, 25 min. Turn chicken, breast side up. Spoon remaining glaze over chicken. Cover; microwave on MEDIUM (50% power), turning rack ¼ turn after half the time, until chicken is fork tender (22 to 24 min.). Tent with aluminum foil; let stand 5 to 10 min. Garnish with reserved apple rings.

Red Apple Glazed Chicken

Country-Style Chicken Kiev

4 servings
2 hours

Preparation takes a little more time for this old favorite, but the taste is well worth the effort!

Filling

¼ c.	*(50 mL)*	butter or margarine, softened
2 tbsp.	*(30 mL)*	chopped green onion
1 tbsp.	*(15 mL)*	minced fresh garlic
¼ tsp.	*(1 mL)*	salt
		Pinch of cracked pepper

Chicken

4		whole boneless chicken breasts, skinned
¼ c.	*(50 mL)*	butter or margarine
⅔ c.	*(175 mL)*	crushed buttery crackers
¼ c.	*(50 mL)*	chopped fresh parsley
¼ tsp.	*(1 mL)*	salt
¼ tsp.	*(1 mL)*	thyme leaves
		Pinch of cracked pepper

In medium bowl stir together all filling ingredients. Divide into 4 equal portions. Freeze portions at least 30 min. Heat oven to 350°F *(180°C)*. Flatten each chicken breast to about ¼" *(0,5 cm)* thickness by pounding between sheets of waxed paper. Place 1 portion of frozen filling onto each flattened breast. Roll and tuck in edges of chicken; secure with wooden picks. In 9" *(23 cm)* sq.

baking pan melt ¼ c. *(50 mL)* butter in oven (4 to 6 min.). Combine remaining chicken ingredients. Dip rolled chicken in melted butter, then coat with crumb mixture. Place chicken in same pan; sprinkle with remaining crumb mixture. Bake for 55 to 65 min. or until fork tender. Remove wooden picks before serving.

To Roll Chicken Breasts:

1. Flatten each chicken breast to about ¼" *(0,5 cm)* thickness by pounding between sheets of waxed paper.

2. Place 1 portion of frozen filling onto each flattened breast. Roll and tuck in edges of chicken; secure with wooden picks.

Country-Style Chicken Kiev

Cheesy Tomato Basil Chicken Breasts

6 servings
1 hour 15 minutes

Cheesy Tomato Basil Chicken Breasts

Fresh tomatoes, basil and Mozzarella cheese make chicken extra special.

Sauce

3 tbsp.	*(45 mL)* butter or margarine
2 c.	*(500 mL)* (2 med.) cubed 1" *(2,5 cm)* ripe tomatoes
⅓ c.	*(75 mL)* chopped onion
6-oz.	*(156-mL)* can tomato paste
1 tbsp.	*(15 mL)* basil leaves
½ tsp.	*(2 mL)* salt
¼ tsp.	*(1 mL)* pepper
2 tsp.	*(10 mL)* minced fresh garlic
3	whole boneless chicken breasts, skinned, cut in half

Topping

1 c.	*(250 mL)* fresh bread crumbs
¼ c.	*(50 mL)* chopped fresh parsley
2 tbsp.	*(30 mL)* butter or margarine, melted
6 oz.	*(180 g)* Mozzarella cheese, cut into strips

Heat oven to 350°F *(180°C)*. In 13 × 9" *(33 × 23 cm)* baking pan melt 3 tbsp. *(45 mL)* butter in oven (4 to 6 min.). Meanwhile, in medium bowl stir together remaining sauce ingredients *except* chicken; set aside. Place chicken in baking pan, turning to coat with butter. Spoon sauce mixture over chicken. Bake for 30 to 40 min. or until chicken is no longer pink. Meanwhile, in small bowl stir together all topping ingredients *except* cheese. Place cheese strips over chicken; sprinkle with topping mixture. Continue baking 5 to 10 min. or until chicken is fork tender and bread crumbs are browned.

Microwave Directions: Topping: In small bowl melt 2 tbsp. *(30 mL)* butter on HIGH (40 to 50 sec.). Stir in bread crumbs. Microwave on HIGH, stirring every 30 sec., until crumbs are toasted (3 to 4 min.). Stir in parsley; set aside. In 9" sq. *(23 cm)* baking dish melt 3 tbsp. *(45 mL)* butter on HIGH (40 to 50 sec.). Arrange chicken pieces in dish, turning to coat with butter. In medium bowl stir together remaining sauce ingredients. Spread over chicken. Cover with waxed paper; microwave on HIGH, turning dish ¼ turn twice during last half of time, until chicken is fork tender (16 to 20 min.). Place cheese strips over chicken. Cover; microwave on HIGH until cheese melts (2 to 2½ min.). Sprinkle toasted bread crumbs over cheese. Microwave on HIGH to heat crumbs (1 min.).

4 to 6 servings (1⅓ cups *[325 mL]* dip)
1 hour 15 minutes

Picnic Drumsticks

Onion crispy drumsticks are served hot or cold with a fresh sour cream-cucumber dip.

Chicken

⅓ c.	*(75 mL)* butter or margarine
⅓ c.	*(75 mL)* crushed saltine crackers
2 tbsp.	*(30 mL)* onion soup mix
8	chicken legs

Dip

1 c.	*(250 mL)* (1 med.) peeled, chopped cucumber
1 c.	*(250 mL)* dairy sour cream
1½ tsp.	*(7 mL)* chopped fresh chives
½ tsp.	*(2 mL)* salt
½ tsp.	*(2 mL)* dill weed

Heat oven to 350°F *(180°C)*. In 13 × 9" *(33 × 23 cm)* baking pan melt butter in oven (5 to 7 min.). Stir together crushed crackers and onion soup mix. Dip chicken legs into melted butter, then coat with crumb mixture. In same pan place chicken legs; sprinkle with remaining crumb mixture. Bake for 45 to 55 min. or until fork tender. Meanwhile, in medium bowl stir together all dip ingredients. Cover; refrigerate at least 1 hr. Serve chicken hot or cold with dip.

6 servings
1 hour 45 minutes

Sour Cream Onion-Chive Chicken

Succulent onion-flavored chicken is topped with a creamy, flavorful sauce.

Coating

2 c.	*(500 mL)* fresh bread crumbs
½ tsp.	*(2 mL)* salt
¼ tsp.	*(1 mL)* cracked pepper
¼ tsp.	*(1 mL)* onion powder
¼ tsp.	*(1 mL)* paprika
½ c.	*(125 mL)* butter or margarine, melted
2½ to 3½ lb.	*(1,2 to 1,6 kg)* frying chicken, cut into 8 pieces
3	med. onions, cut in half

Sauce

1 tbsp.	*(15 mL)* all-purpose flour
1 c.	*(250 mL)* dairy sour cream
¼ tsp.	*(1 mL)* cracked pepper
	Milk
2 tbsp.	*(30 mL)* chopped fresh chives

Heat oven to 350°F *(180°C)*. Combine all coating ingredients *except* butter. Dip chicken in melted butter; coat with crumb mixture. *Reserve remaining crumbs and butter.* In 13 × 9" *(33 × 23 cm)* baking pan place chicken; add onions. Sprinkle remaining crumbs over onions; drizzle with remaining butter. Bake, basting occasionally, for 60 to 70 min. or until fork tender. Remove chicken to platter; keep warm. To make sauce, scrape baking pan; pour pan drippings into 2-qt. *(2-L)* saucepan. Stir in flour. Cook over med. high heat, stirring occasionally, until bubbly (1 min.). Reduce heat to med. Stir in sour cream and pepper. Continue cooking, stirring occasionally, until heated through (1 to 2 min.). If needed, add milk until desired consistency is reached. Serve sauce over chicken and onions. Sprinkle with chives.

Microwave Directions: Divide butter. In 1-qt. *(1-L)* casserole melt ¼ c. *(50 mL)* butter on HIGH (50 to 60 sec.). Stir in coating ingredients. Microwave on HIGH, stirring twice, until crumbs are toasted (4 to 5 min.). Set aside. In 12 × 8" *(30 × 20 cm)* baking dish melt remaining ¼ c. *(50 mL)* butter on HIGH (50 to 60 sec.). Arrange chicken in dish, placing thickest part to outside edge, turning to coat with butter. Place onions over chicken. Cover; microwave on HIGH, turning dish ¼ turn twice during time, until fork tender (21 to 23 min.). Remove chicken to platter; keep warm. Scrape drippings into small bowl. Stir in flour. Microwave on HIGH until bubbly (1 to 1¼ min.). Stir in sour cream and pepper. Reduce power to MEDIUM (50% power); microwave until sauce is heated through (3 to 4 min.). If needed, add milk until desired consistency is reached. Return chicken and onions to baking dish. Pour sauce over chicken and onions. Sprinkle toasted bread crumbs on top. Microwave on HIGH to heat crumbs (2½ to 3 min.). Sprinkle with chives.

Sour Cream Onion-Chive Chicken

Chicken Vegetable Bundles

6 servings
1 hour 15 minutes

*Cut into these tasty chicken breasts for a colorful show of carrot and zucchini,
seasoned just right with rosemary.*

3	whole boneless chicken breasts, skinned, cut in half
3 tbsp.	*(45 mL)* butter or margarine, melted
2	med. carrots, cut into 4 × ⅛ × ⅛" *(10 × 0,2 × 0,2 cm)* strips
1	med. zucchini, cut into 4 × ⅛ × ⅛" *(10 × 0,2 × 0,2 cm)* strips
½ tsp.	*(2 mL)* salt
¼ tsp.	*(1 mL)* rosemary leaves, crushed
¼ tsp.	*(1 mL)* pepper

6	slices bacon
¼ c.	*(50 mL)* brandy or chicken broth
¼ c.	*(50 mL)* chicken broth

Sauce

¼ c.	*(50 mL) reserved* pan drippings or chicken broth
½ c.	*(125 mL)* dairy sour cream
1 tbsp.	*(15 mL)* all-purpose flour

Heat oven to 350°F *(180°C)*. Flatten each chicken breast half to about ¼" *(0,5 cm)* thickness by pounding between sheets of waxed paper; set aside. In medium bowl combine butter, carrots, zucchini, salt, rosemary and pepper. Divide mixture evenly between each flattened chicken breast. Roll up chicken breasts. Wrap 1 bacon slice around each chicken bundle; secure with wooden picks. In 13 × 9" *(33 × 23 cm)* baking pan place chicken bundles. In small bowl stir together brandy and chicken broth. Pour over chicken. Bake, basting occasionally, for 35 to 40 min. or until chicken is fork tender. Place chicken bundles on platter; keep warm. *Reserve pan juices.* In 1-qt. *(1-L)* saucepan combine reserved pan juices plus enough chicken broth to equal ¼ c. *(50 mL)*. In small bowl stir together sour cream and flour. Stir into pan juice mixture. Cook over med. heat, stirring occasionally, until thickened (2 to 4 min.). DO NOT BOIL. Serve over chicken bundles.

To Prepare Chicken Breasts:

1. Flatten each chicken breast half to about ¼" *(0,5 cm)* thickness by pounding between sheets of waxed paper; set aside.

2. Divide mixture evenly between each flattened chicken breast. Roll up chicken breasts. Wrap 1 bacon slice around each chicken bundle; secure with wooden picks.

Chicken Vegetable Bundles

Pineapple-Tarragon Chicken Breasts

Pineapple-Tarragon Chicken Breasts

6 servings
60 minutes

Tarragon and the sweet tang of pineapple
complement each other in this delicious chicken.

Sauce

6-oz.	*(180-mL)* can frozen pineapple juice concentrate, thawed
¼ c.	*(50 mL)* honey
1 tsp.	*(5 mL)* tarragon leaves
½ tsp.	*(2 mL)* salt
	Pinch of pepper
6	split chicken breasts

Prepare grill placing coals to one side; heat until coals are ash white. Make aluminum foil drip pan; place opposite coals. In 1-qt. *(1-L)* saucepan stir together all sauce ingredients. Cook over med. heat, stirring occasionally, until heated through (3 to 5 min.). Place chicken breasts on grill over drip pan. Baste with sauce. Grill, turning and basting occasionally with sauce, for 25 to 35 min. or until fork tender. To serve, cook remaining sauce over med. heat, stirring occasionally, until heated through (3 to 5 min.). Serve sauce over chicken.

Tip: 6-oz. *(180-mL)* can frozen orange juice concentrate, thawed, can be substituted for pineapple juice concentrate.

Microwave Directions: In small bowl stir together all sauce ingredients. Microwave on HIGH, stirring after 1 min., until heated through (1½ to 1¾ min.). In 12 × 8" *(30 × 20 cm)* baking dish place chicken breasts. Sprinkle chicken with paprika. Spoon half of sauce over chicken. Cover; microwave on HIGH, rearranging pieces and spooning remaining sauce over chicken after half the time, until fork tender (19 to 21 min.). Serve sauce over chicken.

Chicken Breasts Southwestern

4 servings
1 hour 20 minutes

Green chilies and salsa add south-of-the-border flavor
to grilled chicken breasts.

Marinade

⅔ c.	*(175 mL)* vegetable oil
⅓ c.	*(75 mL)* lime juice
2 tbsp.	*(30 mL)* chopped green chilies
1 tsp.	*(5 mL)* minced fresh garlic
2	whole boneless chicken breasts, skinned, halved
8	slices 2 × 1 × ¼" *(5 × 2,5 × 0,5 cm)* Cheddar cheese
	Salsa

In 9" *(23 cm)* sq. baking pan stir together all marinade ingredients. Add chicken breasts; marinate, turning once, in refrigerator at least 45 min. Meanwhile, prepare grill placing coals to one side; heat until coals are ash white. Make aluminum foil drip pan; place opposite coals. Remove chicken from marinade; drain. Grill chicken 7 min.; turn. Continue grilling until fork tender (6 to 8 min.). Top each chicken breast with 2 slices cheese. Continue grilling until cheese begins to melt (1 to 2 min.). Serve with salsa.

Garlic Broiled Chicken

6 servings
60 minutes

Company's Coming Kabobs

These kabobs can be assembled ahead of time, covered and refrigerated until the party starts!

4	whole boneless chicken breasts, skinned, cut into 1" *(2,5 cm)* pieces

Sauce

⅔ c.	*(175 mL) reserved* pineapple juice
¼ c.	*(50 mL)* honey
½ tsp.	*(2 mL)* salt
¼ tsp	*(1 mL)* pepper
¼ tsp.	*(1 mL)* ginger

Kabobs

2	med. green peppers, cut into 2" *(5 cm)* pieces
12	cherry tomatoes
2	med. onions, cut into eighths
15¼-oz.	*(398-mL)* can pineapple chunks, drained, *reserve juice*
6	(12") *(30 cm)* metal skewers

In medium bowl place chicken pieces. In 2-qt. *(2-L)* saucepan stir together all sauce ingredients. Cook over med. heat, stirring occasionally, until honey is melted (2 to 3 min.). Pour over chicken pieces; marinate, stirring occasionally, 20 min. Drain; *reserve marinade*. Prepare grill placing coals to one side; heat until coals are ash white. Make aluminum foil drip pan; place opposite coals. To assemble kabobs on metal skewers, alternate chicken pieces, green peppers, cherry tomatoes, onions and pineapple chunks. Place kabobs on grill over drip pan. Grill, turning and basting occasionally, until chicken is fork tender (8 to 12 min.). In 1-qt. *(1-L)* saucepan cook remaining marinade over med. heat, stirring occasionally, until mixture comes to a full boil (2 to 3 min.). Just before serving, spoon marinade over kabobs.

Microwave Directions: *Use 6 (12") (30 cm) wooden skewers. Use large cherry tomatoes.* In medium bowl place chicken pieces. In small bowl stir together all sauce ingredients. Microwave on HIGH, stirring after half the time, until honey is melted (1½ to 2 min.). Pour over chicken pieces; marinate, stirring occasionally, 20 min. Drain; *reserve marinade*. To assemble kabobs on wooden skewers, alternate chicken pieces, green peppers, large cherry tomatoes, onions and pineapple chunks. Place kabobs on microwave-safe roasting rack. Microwave on HIGH, turning rack ¼ turn after half the time, 7 min. Rearrange and turn kabobs over; baste. Microwave on HIGH, turning rack ¼ turn after half the time, until chicken is fork tender (3 to 5 min.). Microwave reserved marinade on HIGH, stirring after half the time, until mixture comes to a full boil (2 to 2½ min.). Just before serving, spoon marinade over kabobs.

4 to 6 servings
60 minutes

Garlic Broiled Chicken

The garlic in this recipe mellows during broiling, creating a rich aroma and flavor.

¼ c.	*(50 mL)* butter or margarine, melted
¼ tsp.	*(1 mL)* pepper
3 tbsp.	*(45 mL)* minced fresh garlic
2 tbsp.	*(30 mL)* soy sauce
2½ to 3½ lb.	*(1,2 to 1,6 kg)* whole frying chicken, cut in half

¼ c.	*(50 mL)* chopped fresh parsley
	Cooked rice

In small bowl stir together butter, pepper, garlic and soy sauce. Heat broiler. Place chicken on greased broiler pan. Broil chicken 6 to 8" *(15 to 20 cm)* from heat, turning every 10 min. and brushing with butter mixture during last 10 min., for 30 to 35 min. or until fork tender. Just before serving, brush with butter mixture and sprinkle with parsley. Serve with cooked rice.

8 servings
1 hour 15 minutes

Hot Chicken Salad Casserole

A popular casserole that uses your leftover chicken or turkey.

4 c.	*(1 L)* cooked, cubed 2" *(5 cm)* chicken or turkey	2-oz.	*(60-g)* jar chopped pimiento, drained
2 c.	*(500 mL)* cooked rice	3	hard cooked eggs, chopped
1 c.	*(250 mL)* (2 stalks) chopped celery	2 tbsp.	*(30 mL)* chopped green pepper
½ c.	*(125 mL)* slivered almonds	2 tbsp.	*(30 mL)* chopped onion
¾ c.	*(200 mL)* mayonnaise	¼ tsp.	*(1 mL)* salt
10¾-oz.	*(284-mL)* can condensed cream of chicken soup	1 tbsp.	*(15 mL)* lemon juice
		½ c.	*(125 mL)* crushed potato chips

Heat oven to 350°F *(180°C)*. In large bowl stir together all ingredients *except* potato chips. Spread into greased 13 × 9" *(33 × 23 cm)* baking pan. Sprinkle with chips. Bake for 40 to 50 min. or until heated through.

Microwave Directions: Prepare as directed left *except* spread into 12 × 8" *(30 × 20 cm)* baking dish. Microwave on HIGH, stirring every 4 min., until heated through (14 to 15 min.). Sprinkle with chips. Microwave on HIGH to heat chips (1 to 1½ min.).

6 servings
60 minutes

Biscuit-Topped Spinach Chicken Pie

Tender buttermilk biscuits top this savory spinach and chicken pie.

Filling

2 c.	*(500 mL)* cooked, shredded chicken
½ c.	*(125 mL)* (1 med.) chopped onion
10-oz.	*(300-g)* pkg. frozen chopped spinach, thawed, drained
2-oz.	*(60-g)* jar chopped pimiento, drained
1 c.	*(250 mL)* dairy sour cream
1	egg, slightly beaten
½ tsp.	*(2 mL)* salt
¼ tsp.	*(1 mL)* pepper
	Pinch of nutmeg
1 tsp.	*(5 mL)* minced fresh garlic

Biscuits

1⅔ c.	*(425 mL)* all-purpose flour
¼ c.	*(50 mL)* butter or margarine, melted
¾ c.	*(200 mL)* buttermilk*
2 tsp.	*(10 mL)* baking powder
½ tsp.	*(2 mL)* salt

Heat oven to 375°F *(190°C)*. In large bowl stir together all filling ingredients. Spread in greased 9" *(23 cm)* pie pan; set aside. In medium bowl stir together all biscuit ingredients. Drop dough by tablespoonfuls onto spinach mixture. Bake for 30 to 40 min. or until biscuits are golden brown and pie is heated through.

*1 tbsp. *(15 mL)* vinegar plus enough milk to equal 1 c. *(250 mL)* can be substituted for 1 c. *(250 mL)* buttermilk.

Biscuit-Topped Spinach Chicken Pie

4 to 6 servings
1 hour 30 minutes

Deep Dish Chicken Pot Pie

*This special pot pie crust — butter flaky and
mouth-watering good — will make memories.*

Crust

2 c.	*(500 mL)* all-purpose flour
¼ tsp.	*(1 mL)* salt
⅔ c.	*(175 mL)* butter or margarine
¼ c.	*(50 mL)* cold water

Filling

2½ c.	*(625 mL)* cooked, cubed 1" *(2,5 cm)* chicken
2 c.	*(500 mL)* fresh or frozen peas
¼ c.	*(50 mL)* finely chopped onion
3	med. sliced 1" *(2,5 cm)* carrots
2	med. potatoes, peeled, cubed 1" *(2,5 cm)*

Sauce

3 tbsp.	*(45 mL)* butter or margarine
3 tbsp.	*(45 mL)* all-purpose flour
1 c.	*(250 mL)* half-and-half
½ c.	*(125 mL)* chicken broth
½ tsp.	*(2 mL)* salt
¼ tsp.	*(1 mL)* pepper

Milk

Heat oven to 375°F *(190°C)*. In large bowl stir together 2 c. *(500 mL)* flour and ¼ tsp. *(1 mL)* salt. Cut in ⅔ c. *(175 mL)* butter until crumbly; with fork mix in water. Divide dough into ⅔ and ⅓ portions. Set aside ⅓ dough. Roll ⅔ dough into 14" *(35 cm)* circle ⅛" *(0,2 cm)* thick. Gently fit into 3-qt. *(3-L)* deep dish casserole; set aside. In large bowl combine all filling ingredients; set aside. In 2-qt. *(2-L)* saucepan melt 3 tbsp. *(45 mL)* butter; stir in 3 tbsp. *(45 mL)* flour. Cook over med. high heat, stirring occasionally, until hot and bubbly (3 to 4 min.). Whisk in half-and-half, chicken broth, ½ tsp. *(2 mL)*

salt and pepper. Continue cooking, stirring occasionally, until sauce thickens (3 to 5 min.). Stir hot sauce into filling; spoon into prepared pie crust. Roll reserved ⅓ dough into 10" *(25 cm)* circle ⅛" *(0,2 cm)* thick. Place on top of pie. Flute edges to seal. Make 3 small slits in top crust; lightly brush top crust with milk. Bake for 50 to 60 min. or until golden brown.

Tip: 12 × 8" *(30 × 20 cm)* baking pan can be used for 3-qt. *(3-L)* casserole. Roll ⅔ dough into 18 × 14" *(45 × 35 cm)* rectangle. Roll reserved ⅓ dough into 13 × 9" *(33 × 23 cm)* rectangle.

To Prepare Crust:

1. Cut in ⅔ c. *(175 mL)* butter until crumbly.

2. Flute edges to seal.

Deep Dish Chicken Pot Pie

Beer Batter Fried Chicken

4 to 6 servings
60 minutes

Beer Batter Fried Chicken

*Chili powder is the secret ingredient in this special deep-fried chicken;
the sour cream-green onion sauce adds cool refreshment.*

2½ to 3½ lb. *(1,2 to 1,6 kg)* chicken,
        cut into 8 pieces
4 c. *(1 L)* water

        Vegetable oil

Batter
1 c. *(250 mL)* all-purpose flour
1½ tsp. *(7 mL)* baking powder
1 tsp. *(5 mL)* salt
2 tbsp. *(30 mL)* chili powder

1 tsp. *(5 mL)* cumin
½ tsp. *(2 mL)* cayenne pepper
½ tsp. *(2 mL)* pepper
1 egg white
¾ c. *(200 mL)* beer

Sauce
¼ c. *(50 mL)* chopped green onions
1 c. *(250 mL)* dairy sour cream

In Dutch oven combine chicken and water. Cover; cook over med. high heat, stirring occasionally, until water comes to a full boil (20 to 25 min.). Reduce heat to med. Cook for 20 min. Drain; pat dry. In deep-fryer or 3-qt. *(3-L)* saucepan heat 2'' *(5 cm)* of oil to 375°F *(190°C)*. In medium bowl combine all batter ingredients *except* egg white and beer. In small mixer bowl beat egg white at med. speed until stiff (2 to 3 min.); set aside. Stir beer into flour mixture; fold in egg white. Dip chicken into batter; place in hot oil. Fry until golden brown (2 to 3 min. on each side). Remove from oil; drain on paper towels. Repeat with remaining chicken. In small bowl stir together green onions and sour cream. Serve sauce with chicken.

Country Oven-Fried Chicken

4 to 6 servings
1 hour 30 minutes

Thyme and rosemary add extra flavor to this easy oven-fried chicken.

⅓ c.	*(75 mL)* butter or margarine, melted
⅓ c.	*(75 mL)* all-purpose flour
¾ tsp.	*(3 mL)* salt
½ tsp.	*(2 mL)* pepper
¼ tsp.	*(1 mL)* thyme leaves

¼ tsp.	*(1 mL)* rosemary leaves, crushed
¼ tsp.	*(1 mL)* paprika
2½ to 3½ lb.	*(1,2 to 1,6 kg)* chicken, cut into 8 pieces

Heat oven to 375°F *(190°C)*. In roasting pan melt butter in oven (4 to 6 min.). Meanwhile, combine remaining ingredients *except* chicken. Dip chicken in melted butter, then coat with flour mixture. In same pan place chicken, skin side down. Bake for 25 to 30 min.; turn chicken over. Continue baking for 30 to 35 min. or until fork tender.

Microwave Directions: Reduce butter to ¼ c. *(50 mL)*. *Eliminate flour.* Increase paprika to ¾ tsp. *(3 mL)*. In 12 × 8" *(30 × 20 cm)* baking dish melt butter on HIGH (50 to 60 sec.). Arrange chicken in dish, placing thickest part to outside edge, turning to coat with butter. In small bowl stir together salt, pepper, thyme, rosemary and paprika. Sprinkle over chicken. Cover; microwave on HIGH, turning dish ¼ turn twice during last half of time, until fork tender (18 to 25 min.).

Country Chicken Piccata

4 servings
30 minutes

Lemons and green onions give a delicate taste to this elegant chicken dish.

¼ c.	*(50 mL)* milk
1	egg, slightly beaten
⅓ c.	*(75 mL)* all-purpose flour
⅓ c.	*(75 mL)* crushed corn flakes
¼ tsp.	*(1 mL)* salt
	Pinch of pepper
2	whole boneless chicken breasts, skinned, halved
6 tbsp.	*(90 mL)* butter or margarine

1 tsp.	*(5 mL)* minced fresh garlic
2 tbsp.	*(30 mL)* lemon juice
1 c.	*(250 mL)* sliced 1" *(2,5 cm)* green onions
1 c.	*(250 mL)* fresh mushrooms, halved
	Lemon slices
	Fresh parsley

In small bowl combine milk and egg. Combine flour, crushed corn flakes, salt and pepper. Flatten each chicken breast half to about ¼" *(0,5 cm)* thickness by pounding between sheets of waxed paper. Dip chicken into milk mixture, then into flour mixture, turning to coat. In 10" *(25 cm)* skillet melt 4 tbsp. *(60 mL)* butter. Add garlic and chicken. Cook over med. heat, turning occasionally, until golden brown (5 to 6 min.). Place chicken on serving platter; keep warm. Add remaining 2 tbsp. *(30 mL)* butter to drippings in pan. Stir until butter melts; stir in lemon juice. Add green onions and mushrooms. Continue cooking, stirring occasionally, until heated through (2 to 4 min.). Spoon over chicken. Garnish with lemon slices and parsley.

Country Chicken Piccata

Apple n' Cabbage Chicken

6 servings
60 minutes

Cabbage, apples and caraway seed blend with chicken for a succulent harvest time meal.

8	slices bacon, cut into 1" *(2,5 cm)* pieces
1 c.	*(250 mL)* (2 med.) chopped onions
½ c.	*(125 mL)* sliced ½" *(1 cm)* celery
2 tbsp.	*(30 mL)* butter or margarine
2½ to 3 lb.	*(1,2 to 1,4 kg)* (8) chicken thighs
⅓ c.	*(75 mL)* apple juice

1½ tsp.	*(7 mL)* caraway seed
1 tsp.	*(5 mL)* salt
¼ tsp.	*(1 mL)* pepper
1	small head cabbage, cut into eight wedges
2	med. tart red apples, cut into sixths

In Dutch oven cook bacon over med. high heat until softened (5 to 7 min.). Add onion and celery; continue cooking until vegetables are tender (2 to 3 min.). With slotted spoon remove bacon mixture from pan; set aside. Add butter to same pan; heat until sizzling. Place half of chicken in pan. Continue cooking, stirring occasionally, until chicken is lightly browned (5 to 8 min.). Remove from pan; set aside. Repeat with remaining chicken. Reduce heat to med.; return chicken and bacon mixture to pan. Add remaining ingredients *except* cabbage and apples. Place cabbage on top of chicken to steam. Cover; continue cooking, basting occasionally, until chicken is fork tender and cabbage is crisply tender (15 to 20 min.). Top with apples. Cover; continue cooking until apples are crisply tender (10 to 15 min.).

Microwave Directions: In 12 × 8" *(30 × 20 cm)* baking dish place bacon pieces. Cover; microwave on HIGH until softened (8 to 9 min.). Stir in onions and celery. Cover; microwave on HIGH, stirring after half the time, until vegetables are tender (2 to 3 min.). With slotted spoon remove bacon mixture from dish; set aside. Add butter to same dish; melt butter on HIGH (40 to 50 sec.). Arrange chicken thighs in dish, turning to coat with butter; spoon bacon mixture over chicken. Cover; microwave on HIGH, rearranging chicken pieces after half the time, until chicken is fork tender (8 to 10 min.). Place cabbage on top of chicken. Add remaining ingredients *except* apples. Cover with vented plastic wrap; microwave on HIGH until cabbage is partially cooked (4 min.). Baste cabbage. Place apple pieces over cabbage. Cover; microwave on HIGH, turning dish ¼ turn after half the time, until cabbage and apples are crisply tender (5 to 6 min.).

Apple n' Cabbage Chicken

Chicken Breasts & Zucchini With Garlic Cream

4 servings
45 minutes

Chicken Breasts & Zucchini With Garlic Cream

*The subtle flavor of chicken partners perfectly with zucchini
and a rich cream cheese garlic sauce.*

¼ c.   *(50 mL)* butter or margarine
3   whole, boneless chicken breasts,
           skinned, halved
3 c.   *(750 mL)* (3 med.) sliced
           ⅛" *(0,2 cm)* zucchini
⅓ c.   *(75 mL)* sliced ¼" *(0,5 cm)* green onions

Garlic Cream
2 tbsp.   *(30 mL)* butter or margarine
½ tsp.   *(2 mL)* minced fresh garlic
3 tbsp.   *(45 mL)* all-purpose flour
3-oz.   *(90-g)* pkg. cream cheese
10¾-oz.   *(284-mL)* can chicken broth
½ tsp.   *(2 mL)* pepper

           Cooked rice

In 10" *(25 cm)* skillet melt ¼ c. *(50 mL)* butter until sizzling; add chicken breasts. Cook over med. high heat, turning once, until chicken is browned and fork tender (12 to 15 min.). Add zucchini and onions. Continue cooking, stirring occasionally, until zucchini is crisply tender (5 to 7 min.). Meanwhile, in 2-qt. *(2-L)* saucepan melt 2 tbsp. *(30 mL)* butter until sizzling; add garlic. Cook over med. heat, stirring occasionally, for 1 min. Add flour; continue cooking until smooth and bubbly (1 min.). Add remaining garlic cream ingredients *except* rice. Continue cooking, stirring occasionally, until sauce is thickened (5 to 7 min.). Serve zucchini and chicken over rice; pour sauce over chicken.

Microwave Directions: Increase flour to ¼ c. *(50 mL)* In 12 × 8" *(30 × 20 cm)* baking dish melt butter on HIGH *(30 to 45 sec.)*. Place chicken in dish; turn chicken to coat. Cover; microwave on HIGH, rearranging after half the time, until chicken is no longer pink (5 to 8 min.). Add zucchini and onions. Cover; microwave on HIGH until zucchini is crisply tender (5 to 6 min.). With slotted spoon remove chicken and vegetables to serving plate; keep warm. Stir 2 tbsp. *(30 mL)* butter, garlic, ¼ c. *(50 mL)* flour, cream cheese, chicken broth and pepper into pan juices. Microwave on HIGH, stirring every 2 min., until sauce is thickened (4 to 6 min.). Serve zucchini and chicken over rice; pour sauce over chicken.

6 servings
60 minutes

Corn on the Cob n' Chicken Dinner

Chosen for the cover photo, this colorful one-dish meal is finger-licking good.

3 tbsp.   *(45 mL)* butter or margarine
3 lb.   *(1,4 kg)* chicken legs
2 tsp.   *(10 mL)* minced fresh garlic
¼ c.   *(50 mL)* water
3   ears fresh or frozen corn on the cob,
             husked, cut into thirds

1 tsp.   *(5 mL)* tarragon leaves
½ tsp.   *(2 mL)* salt
¼ tsp.   *(1 mL)* pepper
2   med. zucchini, cut into 2" *(5 cm)* pieces
2   med. ripe tomatoes, cut into
            1" *(2,5 cm)* pieces

In Dutch oven melt butter; add chicken and garlic. Cook over high heat, stirring occasionally, until chicken is golden brown (10 to 15 min.). Reduce heat to med. Add remaining ingredients *except* zucchini and tomatoes.

Cover; cook until chicken is fork tender (20 to 25 min.). Place zucchini on top of chicken and corn mixture. Cover; steam 3 to 6 min. Add tomatoes. Cover; let stand 5 min.

4 servings
2 hours

Cornish Hens With Herb-Buttered Vegetables

Garden vegetables make these oven-baked Cornish hens extra special.

4	Cornish game hens	1 tsp.	*(5 mL)* salt
8	small carrots	½ tsp.	*(2 mL)* sage leaves, crushed
8	small patty pan squash*	¼ tsp.	*(1 mL)* pepper
8	small new red potatoes	2 tsp.	*(10 mL)* minced fresh garlic
⅓ c.	*(75 mL)* butter or margarine, melted		

Heat oven to 375°F *(190°C)*. Place hens, breast side up, on rack in large roasting pan. Arrange carrots, squash and potatoes around hens. In small bowl stir together remaining ingredients. Spoon over hens and vegetables. Cover; bake, basting occasionally, for 1 hr. Remove cover; continue baking for 30 to 45 min. or until hens are fork tender.

*Yellow summer squash or zucchini can be substituted for patty pan squash; add during last half hour of baking time.

---

4 servings
2 hours 15 minutes

Apricot-Glazed Cornish Hens

Apricots and marjoram add spark to these stuffed Cornish hens.

Stuffing

2 c.	*(500 mL)* dried bread cubes
½ c.	*(125 mL)* sliced ¼" *(0,5 cm)* celery
¼ c.	*(50 mL)* chopped onion
½ tsp.	*(2 mL)* salt
¼ tsp.	*(1 mL)* pepper
¼ tsp.	*(1 mL)* marjoram leaves
½ c.	*(125 mL)* apricot preserves
¼ c.	*(50 mL)* butter or margarine
2 to 3 tbsp.	*(30 to 45 mL)* white wine or chicken broth

4	Cornish game hens

Sauce

½ c.	*(125 mL)* apricot preserves
½ c.	*(125 mL)* butter or margarine
½ tsp.	*(2 mL)* marjoram leaves

Heat oven to 375°F *(190°C)*. In medium bowl stir together all stuffing ingredients *except* preserves, butter and wine. In 1-qt. *(1-L)* saucepan melt ½ c. *(125 mL)* apricot preserves and ¼ c. *(50 mL)* butter. Stir into stuffing; add 2 to 3 tbsp. *(30 to 45 mL)* wine to moisten stuffing. Stuff hens with stuffing; secure opening with wooden picks. Tuck under wings of hens. Place hens, breast side up, in roasting pan. Bake for 1 hr.

Meanwhile, in same saucepan combine all sauce ingredients. Cook over med. heat, stirring occasionally, until melted (2 to 3 min.). Brush hens with half of sauce. Continue baking, uncovered, for 40 to 50 min. or until hens are fork tender. Loosely cover with aluminum foil if browning too quickly. Serve with remaining sauce.

Apricot-Glazed Cornish Hens

Turkey Breast With Sausage-Raisin Stuffing

Sausage, combined with raisins and pecans, delights the senses when roasted with turkey.

12 oz.	*(340 g)* pork sausage	1	med. onion, chopped
2 c.	*(500 mL)* dried bread cubes	½ tsp.	*(2 mL)* salt
1 c.	*(250 mL)* (2 stalks) sliced ½" *(1 cm)* celery	¼ tsp.	*(1 mL)* sage leaves, crushed Pinch of pepper
1 c.	*(250 mL)* pecan halves		
½ c.	*(125 mL)* raisins	5 to 7 lb.	*(2,3 to 3,2 kg)* bone-in turkey breast
¼ c.	*(50 mL)* butter or margarine, melted	3 tbsp.	*(45 mL)* butter or margarine, melted
⅓ c.	*(75 mL)* chicken broth		

Heat oven to 350°F *(180°C)*. In 10" *(25 cm)* skillet brown sausage over med. heat; drain off fat. In large bowl stir together browned sausage and remaining ingredients *except* turkey breast and 3 tbsp. *(45 mL)* butter. Gently loosen skin from turkey in neck area to make a large area to stuff. Stuff with sausage mixture; secure skin flap with wooden picks. Place remaining sausage mixture in 1-qt. *(1-L)* covered casserole; refrigerate. During last 30 min. of turkey breast baking time, bake remaining stuffing for 25 to 30 min. or until heated through. Place stuffed turkey breast, breast side up, on rack in roasting pan. Brush with melted 3 tbsp. *(45 mL)* butter. Bake, basting occasionally, for 2 to 2½ hr. or until meat thermometer reaches 170° to 175°F *(77° to 80°C)* and turkey breast is fork tender. Let stand 10 min.

Microwave Directions: *Reduce ¼ c. (50 mL) butter to 3 tbsp. (45 mL).* In 2-qt. *(2-L)* casserole microwave sausage on HIGH, stirring twice during last half of time, until sausage is cooked through (4½ to 5 min.). Stir in remaining ingredients *except* turkey breast and 3 tbsp. *(45 mL)* butter. Stuff as directed left. Place remaining sausage mixture in same 2-qt. *(2-L)* covered casserole; refrigerate. Place turkey breast, breast side down, in 12 × 8" *(30 × 20 cm)* baking dish. Brush with melted 3 tbsp. *(45 mL)* butter. *Sprinkle with paprika.* Cover with vented plastic wrap; microwave on HIGH 10 min. Reduce power to MEDIUM (50% power); microwave, turning dish ¼ turn after half the time, 25 min. Turn turkey breast, breast side up. Baste. *Sprinkle with paprika.* Cover; microwave on MEDIUM (50% power), turning dish ¼ turn after half the time, until meat thermometer reaches 170° to 175°F *(77° to 80°C)* and turkey breast is fork tender (22 to 25 min.). Place turkey breast on serving platter. Tent with aluminum foil; let stand 5 to 10 min. Meanwhile, microwave remaining stuffing on HIGH, stirring after half the time, until heated through (5½ to 6½ min.).

To Stuff Turkey Breast:

1. Gently loosen skin from turkey in neck area to make a large area to stuff.

2. Stuff with sausage mixture; secure skin flap with wooden picks.

Turkey Breast With Sausage-Raisin Stuffing

Hearty Cheese, Turkey & Zucchini Supper

4 servings
30 minutes

Hearty Cheese, Turkey & Zucchini Supper

Rich Cheddar cheese sauce smothers turkey and zucchini served over English muffins.

Cheese Sauce

2 tbsp.	*(30 mL)* butter or margarine
1 tbsp.	*(15 mL)* all-purpose flour
¼ tsp.	*(1 mL)* salt
¼ tsp.	*(1 mL)* dry mustard
¼ tsp.	*(1 mL)* pepper
1 c.	*(250 mL)* milk
1 c.	*(250 mL) (4 oz.) (110 g)* shredded Cheddar cheese

1 tbsp.	*(15 mL)* chopped fresh chives
2 tbsp.	*(30 mL)* butter or margarine
1	med. zucchini, sliced ¼" *(0,5 cm)*
1 tsp.	*(5 mL)* basil leaves
4	English muffins, split, toasted
8	*(1 oz.) (30 g)* slices cooked turkey

In 2-qt. *(2-L)* saucepan melt 2 tbsp. *(30 mL)* butter; stir in flour, salt, mustard and pepper. Cook over low heat, stirring constantly, until smooth and bubbly (1 min.). Add milk. Continue cooking over low heat, stirring constantly, until mixture thickens and comes to a full boil (4 to 5 min.). Boil 1 min. Remove from heat. Stir in cheese and chives until cheese is melted; keep warm.

In 10" *(25 cm)* skillet melt 2 tbsp. *(30 mL)* butter; stir in zucchini and basil. Cook over med. high heat, stirring occasionally, until crisply tender (3 to 5 min.). Place toasted English muffin halves on serving plate; top each half with 1 slice turkey, ⅛ zucchini mixture and cheese sauce.

4 servings
30 minutes

Baked Broccoli & Turkey With Cheddar Sauce

Cheese sauce with a splash of lemon brings out extra flavor in this easy-to-prepare casserole.

8	*(1 oz.) (30 g)* slices cooked turkey breast
8-oz.	*(240-g)* pkg. individually frozen broccoli spears
½	med. red onion, sliced ⅛" *(0,2 cm)*
3 tbsp.	*(45 mL)* butter or margarine
2 tbsp.	*(30 mL)* all-purpose flour

1 c.	*(250 mL)* half-and-half or milk
½ tsp.	*(2 mL)* salt
¼ tsp.	*(1 mL)* pepper
1 tsp.	*(5 mL)* lemon juice
1 c.	*(250 mL) (4 oz.) (110 g)* shredded Cheddar cheese

Heat oven to 350°F *(180°C)*. Place turkey on bottom of greased 9" *(23 cm)* sq. baking pan; top with broccoli and onion. Set aside. In 2-qt. *(2-L)* saucepan melt butter over med. heat; stir in flour until smooth and bubbly (1 min.). Stir in remaining ingredients *except* cheese. Continue cooking, stirring occasionally, until thickened (2 to 3 min.). Remove from heat; stir in cheese until melted. Pour over broccoli and onion. Bake for 15 to 20 min. or until heated through.

Microwave Directions: Place turkey on bottom of greased 9" *(23 cm)* round baking dish; top with broccoli and onion. Cover with plastic wrap; microwave on HIGH until heated through (4 to 6 min.). Drain off excess moisture; set aside. In medium bowl melt butter on HIGH (50 to 60 sec.). Stir in flour. Microwave on HIGH until bubbly (45 to 60 sec.). Stir in remaining ingredients *except* cheese. Microwave on HIGH, stirring after half the time, until thickened (2 to 3 min.). Stir in cheese until melted. Pour over broccoli and onion. Cover with plastic wrap; microwave on HIGH until heated through (2 to 3 min.).

Spinach-Stuffed Turkey Breast

6 servings
2 hours 30 minutes

Spinach and bacon stuffing flavor this delightful grilled turkey.

Stuffing

1 c.	*(250 mL)* dried bread cubes
1 c.	*(250 mL)* (2 stalks) sliced ½" *(1 cm)* celery
⅓ c.	*(75 mL)* butter or margarine, melted
¼ c.	*(50 mL)* white wine or chicken broth
10-oz.	*(300-g)* pkg. frozen chopped spinach, thawed, drained

6	slices crisply cooked bacon, cut into 1" *(2,5 cm)* pieces
1	med. onion, chopped
½ tsp.	*(2 mL)* salt
¼ tsp.	*(1 mL)* cracked pepper
5 to 7 lb.	*(2,3 to 3,2 kg)* bone-in turkey breast
2 tbsp.	*(30 mL)* butter or margarine, softened

Prepare grill placing coals to one side; heat until coals are ash white. Make aluminum foil drip pan; place opposite coals. In large bowl stir together all stuffing ingredients. Turn turkey, breast side down. To make a large area to stuff, gently loosen skin from meat in neck cavity. Stuff with stuffing. (Extra stuffing may be placed in aluminum foil pan, covered and heated during last 30 min. of grilling.) Secure skin over stuffing with wooden picks. Lightly rub turkey breast with butter. Place on grill over drip pan. Grill 1½ to 2 hr. or until meat thermometer reaches 180° to 185°F *(82° to 85°C)* and turkey is fork tender.

Turkey Legs With Barbecue Sauce

6 servings
2 hours 30 minutes

A spicy, chunky tomato sauce adds special flavor to these hearty turkey legs.

6	*(¾ to 1 lb.) (335 to 450 g)* turkey legs
4 to 6 c.	*(1 to 1,5 L)* water

Sauce

¼ c.	*(50 mL)* firmly packed brown sugar
1 c.	*(250 mL)* (1 med.) cubed ½" *(1 cm)* ripe tomato
½ c.	*(125 mL)* (1 med.) chopped onion

¼ c.	*(50 mL)* country-style Dijon mustard
¼ c.	*(50 mL)* red wine vinegar or cider vinegar
¼ c.	*(50 mL)* tomato juice
6-oz.	*(156-mL)* can tomato paste
½ tsp.	*(2 mL)* salt
¼ tsp.	*(1 mL)* cracked pepper
1 tbsp.	*(15 mL)* minced fresh garlic

In Dutch oven combine turkey legs and water. Cover; cook over med. heat, stirring occasionally, until turkey legs are just fork tender (40 to 60 min.). Drain; pat dry. Prepare grill placing coals to one side; heat until coals are ash white. Make aluminum foil drip pan; place opposite coals. Place turkey legs on grill over drip pan. Grill, turning occasionally, until fork tender and heated through (40 to 50 min.). Meanwhile, in 2-qt. *(2-L)* saucepan stir together all sauce ingredients. Cook over low heat, stirring occasionally, until heated through (10 to 15 min.). Baste turkey legs with sauce during last 15 min. Serve with remaining warm sauce.

Spinach-Stuffed Turkey Breast

Grilled Turkey & Vegetable Kabobs

6 servings
3 hours 45 minutes

Grilled Turkey & Vegetable Kabobs

A homemade teriyaki sauce adds flavor to these "grilled to perfection" kabobs.

Marinade

⅓ c.	*(75 mL)*	lemon juice
¼ c.	*(50 mL)*	soy sauce
¼ c.	*(50 mL)*	vegetable oil
2 tbsp.	*(30 mL)*	firmly packed brown sugar
½ tsp.	*(2 mL)*	ginger
¼ tsp.	*(1 mL)*	pepper
3 tbsp.	*(45 mL)*	catsup
1 tsp.	*(5 mL)*	minced fresh garlic

In medium bowl combine all marinade ingredients. Stir in turkey pieces. Cover; refrigerate, stirring occasionally, 3 to 4 hr. Drain; *reserve marinade*. Prepare grill placing coals to one side; heat until coals are ash white. Make aluminum foil drip pan; place opposite coals. To

Kabobs

1½ lb.	*(675 g)*	fresh turkey breast, skinned, boned, cut into 1½ × 1" *(3,5 × 2,5 cm)* pieces
12		med. fresh mushrooms
2		med. red onions, each cut into 6 wedges
1		green pepper, cut into 12 pieces
12		cherry tomatoes
6		*(12")* *(30 cm)* metal skewers

assemble kabobs on metal skewers, alternate turkey pieces, mushrooms, onions, green pepper and cherry tomatoes. Brush kabobs with marinade. Place kabobs on grill over drip pan. Grill, turning and basting occasionally, until turkey is fork tender (15 to 20 min.).

3 hours

Turkey on the Grill

Juicy, tender turkey, cooked outdoors, is the center of a perfect summer meal.

Kettle or Covered Grill

Thaw and prepare 10 to 12 lb. *(4,5 to 5,4 kg)* turkey for roasting as directed on pkg.; do not stuff. Season cavity with salt and brush skin with melted butter or margarine. Prepare grill placing coals to one side; heat until coals are ash white. Make aluminum foil drip pan; place opposite coals. Place top grilling rack over coals and drip pan. Place prepared turkey on grill over drip pan. Open bottom vents directly under coals. Cover grill, positioning top vent directly over side of grill with turkey. Adjust vent as necessary to keep a consistently hot fire. Add coals to fire as necessary. Grill turkey 11 to 20 min. per lb. *(450 g)*, turning half way through the time. Turkey is done when thermometer inserted in thigh muscle reaches 180° to 185°F *(82° to 85°C)*.

Gas Grill

Thaw and prepare 10 to 12 lb. *(4,5 to 5,4 g)* turkey for roasting as directed on pkg.; do not stuff. Season cavity with salt and brush skin with melted butter or margarine. If dual control gas grill is used, make aluminum foil drip pan; place over coals on one side of grill, then heat other side 10 to 15 min. on high. If single control gas grill is used, make aluminum foil drip pan; place over one half of coals to block out direct heat, then heat grill 10 to 15 min. on high. Reduce heat to med. Replace top rack; place turkey on rack directly above drip pan. Grill turkey on med. heat 11 to 20 min. per lb. *(450 g)*, turning half way through the time. Turkey is done when thermometer inserted in thigh muscle reaches 180° to 185°F *(82° to 85°C)*.

Roasted Turkey

The perfect oven-roasted turkey!

To Prepare:

1. Thaw turkey in original plastic wrapper according to chart below.

2. Remove turkey from plastic bag. Remove neck and giblets from cavities.

3. Rinse turkey thoroughly in cold water and drain well.

4. Stuff neck and body cavities lightly (about ¾ c. *(200 mL)* of stuffing per pound *(450 g)* of turkey).

5. Fold neck skin to back of bird and secure. Fold wing tips under back or tie to body. Tuck tail into body cavity. Tie legs together.

6. If using a standard meat thermometer, insert into thigh muscle next to body, not touching bone. Turkey is done when meat thermometer reaches 180° to 185°F *(82° to 85°C)*.

Approximate Thawing Times

Weight	In Cold Water*	In Refrigerator
10 - 14 pounds *(4,5 to 6,5 kg)*	5 - 6 hours	2 - 3 days
14 - 18 pounds *(6,5 to 8 kg)*	6 - 7 hours	2 - 3 days
18 - 22 pounds *(8 to 10 kg)*	7 - 8 hours	3 - 4 days

*Change water frequently to keep cold.

Keep thawed turkey refrigerated. Do not stuff until ready to roast. Roast within 24 hours after thawing. Refreezing is not recommended.

To Roast:

1. Place turkey, breast up, in shallow pan and brush with melted butter.

2. Roast turkey in 325°F *(160°C)* oven according to chart below. If roasting turkey unstuffed, subtract 3 minutes per pound *(450 g)*.

3. Giblets, *except* liver, may be simmered in salted water for 2 to 2½ hours; add liver for last half hour. Use cooked, chopped giblets in gravy or dressing.

Approximate Roasting Times

Weight	325°F *(160°C)* Oven In Shallow Open Pan	325°F *(160°C)* Oven In Loose Foil Tent
10 - 14 pounds *(4,5 to 6,5 kg)*	3 - 4½ hours	3½ - 5 hours
14 - 18 pounds *(6,5 to 8 kg)*	4 - 5 hours	4½ - 5½ hours
18 - 22 pounds *(8 to 10 kg)*	4½ - 6 hours	5 - 6½ hours

Roasting time will be shorter or longer than indicated on the chart if the turkey is warmer or colder than refrigerator temperature.

Roasted Turkey

9 cups *(2,3 L)*
20 minutes

Spiced Fruit & Bread Stuffing

Dried fruit adds new flavor to homemade stuffing.

4 c.	*(1 L)* dried bread cubes	2	med. onions, chopped
2 c.	*(500 mL)* (4 stalks) sliced ½" *(1 cm)* celery	1 tsp.	*(5 mL)* salt
½ c.	*(125 mL)* butter or margarine, melted	¼ tsp.	*(1 mL)* pepper
½ c.	*(125 mL)* sherry or chicken broth	¼ tsp.	*(1 mL)* ground cloves
8-oz.	*(230-g)* pkg. whole, mixed dried fruit, cut in half	¼ tsp.	*(1 mL)* ginger

In large bowl stir together all ingredients. Use to stuff 12 to 14 lb. *(5,4 to 6,5 kg)* turkey.

Tip: Prepare half of recipe to stuff 4 to 5 lb. *(1,8 to 2,3 kg)* roasting chicken, duck or goose.

9 cups *(2,3 L)*
20 minutes

Bread Sage Stuffing

Traditional old-fashioned sage stuffing with ideas for new variations.

4 c.	*(1 L)* dried bread cubes	2	med. onions, chopped
2 c.	*(500 mL)* (4 stalks) sliced ½" *(1 cm)* celery	1 tbsp.	*(15 mL)* sage leaves, crushed
½ c.	*(125 mL)* butter or margarine, melted	1 tsp.	*(5 mL)* salt
½ c.	*(125 mL)* chicken broth		Pinch of pepper

In large bowl stir together all ingredients. Use to stuff 12 to 14 lb. *(5,4 to 6,5 kg)* turkey.

Tip: Prepare half of recipe to stuff 4 to 5 lb. *(1,8 to 2,3 kg)* roasting chicken, duck or goose.

Variations:

Oyster Stuffing — Add 2 c. *(500 mL)* rinsed, drained oysters. Reduce salt to ½ tsp. *(2 mL).*

Raisin-Nut Stuffing — Add 1 c. *(250 mL)* whole pecans or walnuts and 1 c. *(250 mL)* raisins.

Bread Sage Stuffing (top)
Spiced Fruit & Bread Stuffing (bottom)

Bacon Rice Stuffing

8 cups *(2 L)*
30 minutes

Bacon Rice Stuffing

A moist rice stuffing with a smoky bacon flavor which makes your chicken,
duck or goose just a little more special.

4 c.	*(1 L)* cooked long grain rice*	1	med. onion, chopped
2 c.	*(500 mL)* (4 stalks) sliced ½" *(1 cm)* celery	1 lb.	*(450 g)* crisply cooked bacon, cut into 1" *(2,5 cm)* pieces
¼ c.	*(50 mL)* chopped fresh parsley	¼ tsp.	*(1 mL)* salt
⅓ c.	*(75 mL)* butter or margarine, melted	¼ tsp.	*(1 mL)* pepper
¼ c.	*(50 mL)* white wine or chicken broth		

In large bowl stir together all ingredients. Use to stuff 12 to 14 lb. *(5,4 to 6,5 kg)* turkey.

*Cooked wild rice can be substituted for all or part of long grain rice.

Tip: Prepare half of recipe to stuff 4 to 5 lb. *(1,8 to 2,3 kg)* roasting chicken, duck or goose.

6½ cups *(1,6 L)*
30 minutes

Cornbread Stuffing

Cornbread and bacon are mixed for a one-of-a-kind country-style stuffing.

4 c.	*(1 L)* crumbled cornbread*	1	med. onion, chopped
2 c.	*(500 mL)* (4 stalks) sliced ½" *(1 cm)* celery	1 tsp.	*(5 mL)* salt
¼ c.	*(50 mL)* butter or margarine, melted	¼ tsp.	*(1 mL)* pepper
¼ c.	*(50 mL)* chicken broth	3 tbsp.	*(45 mL)* reserved bacon drippings
8	slices crisply cooked bacon, crumbled, reserve drippings		

In large bowl stir together all ingredients. Use to stuff 12 to 14 lb. *(5,4 to 6,5 kg)* turkey.

*9" *(23 cm)* sq. baking pan of cornbread will make 4 c. *(1 L)* crumbled cornbread.

Tip: Prepare half of recipe to stuff 4 to 5 lb. *(1,8 to 2,3 kg)* roasting chicken, duck or goose.

2 cups *(500 mL)*
20 minutes

Creamy Mustard n' Green Onion Sauce

This creamy, smooth and tangy sauce livens up chicken.

3 tbsp.	*(45 mL)* butter or margarine
2 tbsp.	*(30 mL)* all-purpose flour
⅓ c.	*(75 mL)* chopped green onions
¾ c.	*(200 mL)* chicken broth

¼ tsp.	*(1 mL)* salt
	Pinch of pepper
1 tbsp.	*(15 mL)* country-style Dijon mustard
1 c.	*(250 mL)* plain yogurt

In 2-qt. *(2-L)* saucepan melt butter over med. high heat. Stir in flour; continue cooking until bubbly (1 min.). Reduce heat to med. Stir in remaining ingredients *except* yogurt. Continue cooking, stirring occasionally, until sauce thickens (3 to 5 min.). Stir in yogurt. Continue cooking, stirring occasionally, until heated through (3 to 5 min.).

Microwave Directions: In small bowl melt butter on HIGH (40 to 50 sec.). Stir in remaining ingredients *except* yogurt. Microwave on HIGH, stirring twice during last half of time, until sauce thickens (2 to 2½ min.). Beat yogurt with wire whisk; stir into sauce mixture. Microwave on HIGH, stirring every 30 sec., until heated through (1¼ to 1½ min.).

1½ cups *(375 mL)*
15 minutes

Sour Cream White Wine Sauce

An easy sauce to quickly dress up baked chicken breasts.

3 tbsp.	*(45 mL)* butter or margarine
1 tbsp.	*(15 mL)* minced fresh garlic
2 tbsp.	*(30 mL)* all-purpose flour
¼ c.	*(50 mL)* chopped fresh parsley
½ c.	*(125 mL)* chicken broth

¼ c.	*(50 mL)* white wine
¼ tsp.	*(1 mL)* salt
	Pinch of pepper
1 c.	*(250 mL)* dairy sour cream

In 2-qt. *(2-L)* saucepan melt butter until sizzling; stir in garlic. Cook over med. high heat 1 min. Stir in flour; continue cooking until bubbly (1 min.). Reduce heat to med. Stir in remaining ingredients *except* sour cream. Cook, stirring occasionally, until sauce thickens (1 to 2 min.). Stir in sour cream. Continue cooking, stirring occasionally, until heated through (3 to 5 min.).

Microwave Directions: In small bowl melt butter on HIGH (40 to 50 sec.). Stir in garlic and flour. Microwave on HIGH 1 min. Stir in remaining ingredients *except* sour cream. Microwave on HIGH, stirring twice during last half of time, until sauce thickens (2 to 2½ min.). Stir in sour cream. Microwave on MEDIUM (50% power), stirring every min., until heated through (4 to 5 min.).

Creamy Mustard n' Green Onion Sauce

Herb Wine Marinade

¾ cup *(200 mL)*
60 minutes

Tarragon, rosemary and thyme are the flavorful herbs in this marinade.

⅔ c.   *(175 mL)* white wine
1 tsp.   *(5 mL)* tarragon leaves
¼ tsp.   *(1 mL)* rosemary leaves, crushed

¼ tsp.   *(1 mL)* thyme leaves
2 tbsp.   *(30 mL)* vegetable oil
1 tbsp.   *(15 mL)* minced fresh garlic

In medium bowl combine all marinade ingredients. Use to marinate 2½ to 3 lb. *(1 to 1,4 kg)* of chicken pieces. Cook as desired, basting occasionally with marinade.

Tip: If desired, use to marinate 2 to 3 lb. *(900 g to 1,4 kg)* of beef or pork.

Lemon Parsley Marinade

1¼ cup *(300 mL)*
60 minutes

This marinade brings a refreshing, light lemon flavor to chicken.

¼ c.   *(50 mL)* chopped fresh parsley
½ c.   *(125 mL)* chicken broth
½ c.   *(125 mL)* lemon juice

4   slices lemon, halved
¼ tsp.   *(1 mL)* pepper
3 tbsp.   *(45 mL)* vegetable oil

In medium bowl combine all marinade ingredients. Use to marinate 2½ to 3 lb. *(1 to 1,4 kg)* of chicken pieces.

Cook as desired, basting occasionally with marinade.

Lemon Parsley Marinade (top)
Herb Wine Marinade (bottom)

Brown Turkey Gravy

3 cups *(750 mL)*
15 minutes

Brown Turkey Gravy

This gravy method works for chicken, beef or pork gravy too.

Chicken broth or water
½ c.   *(125 mL)* water
¼ c.   *(50 mL)* all-purpose flour

Salt
Cracked pepper

Deglaze pan by stirring ¼ c. *(50 mL)* water into pan with drippings. Heat, stirring and scraping pan, 2 to 3 min. Strain pan juices into 4-c. *(1-L)* measure; remove excess fat, *reserving 3 tbsp.* (45 mL) *fat.* Add enough chicken broth or water to equal 3 c. *(750 mL)* liquid. In 3-qt. *(3-L)* saucepan combine 3 c. *(750 mL)* pan juice mixture and 3 tbsp. *(45 mL)* reserved fat; cook over med. heat until mixture comes to a full boil (3 to 5 min.). Meanwhile, in jar with lid combine ½ c. *(125 mL)* water and flour; shake well to mix. Slowly stir into hot pan juice mixture. Continue cooking, stirring constantly, until mixture comes to a full boil; boil 1 min. Season to taste.

Microwave Directions: Deglaze pan as directed left. Strain pan juices into 8-c. *(2-L)* measure; remove excess fat, *reserving 3 tbsp.* (45 mL) *fat.* Add enough chicken broth or water to equal 3 c. *(750 mL)* liquid; add reserved 3 tbsp. *(45 mL)* fat. Microwave on HIGH until mixture comes to a full boil (3 to 5 min.). Meanwhile, in jar with lid combine ½ c. *(125 mL)* water and flour; shake well to mix. Slowly stir into hot pan juice mixture. Microwave on HIGH, stirring twice during time, until mixture comes to a full boil (3½ to 4½ min.). Season to taste.

2 cups *(500 mL)*
15 minutes

Grandma's Cream Gravy

Smooth creamy gravy, just like Grandma makes.

Milk
3 tbsp.   *(45 mL)* all-purpose flour
Salt
Cracked pepper

Deglaze pan by stirring ¼ c. *(50 mL)* water into pan with drippings. Heat, stirring and scraping pan, 2 to 3 min. Strain pan juices into 2-c. *(500-mL)* measure; remove excess fat, *reserving 2 tbsp.* (30 mL) *fat.* Add enough milk to equal 2 c. *(500 mL)* liquid; set aside. In 2-qt. *(2-L)* saucepan cook reserved 2 tbsp. *(30 mL)* fat over med. heat until bubbly (1 to 1½ min.). Stir in flour. Continue cooking, stirring constantly, for 1 min. Stir in pan juice mixture. Continue cooking, stirring constantly, until thickened (3 to 5 min.). Season to taste.

Microwave Directions: Deglaze pan as directed left. Strain pan juices into 2 c. *(500 mL)* measure; remove excess fat, *reserving 2 tbsp.* (30 mL) *fat.* Add enough milk to equal 2 c. *(500 mL)* liquid; set aside. In 4-c. *(1-L)* glass measure combine reserved 2 tbsp. *(30 mL)* fat and flour. Microwave on HIGH until bubbly (1 to 1½ min.). Stir in pan juice mixture. Microwave on HIGH, stirring twice during last half of time, until thickened (3½ to 4½ min.). Season to taste.

How To: Buy, Store & Thaw Poultry

TO BUY: Poultry is popular today, not only because it is nutritious and low in fat, but also because of its delicate flavor that blends well with herbs and spices. In addition, it is an economical buy at the supermarket.

When purchasing poultry, look for a plump-bodied, blemish-free, smooth-skinned bird.

Chickens: Allow about ½ pound *(225 g)* chicken per serving. Whole chickens are usually the best buy — the bigger the bird, the more meat in proportion to bone. Chicken can also be purchased in a variety of cuts. Some of the different types and cuts of chicken you will find are:

Whole Roasting Chickens (A) are larger and older birds. They weigh between 3½ to 5 pounds *(1,5 to 2,3 kg)* and are excellent for stuffing and roasting.

Broilers—Fryers (B) are the most common type of chicken. The birds are young and weigh between 2 to 3½ pounds *(900 g to 1,5 kg)*.

Cornish Game Hens (C) are the smallest and youngest of the chicken family, weighing about 1 to 1½ pounds *(450 to 675 g)*. They are usually found in the grocer's freezer case.

Quartered Chickens (D) are cut into four pieces with wing attached to breast and leg attached to thigh.

Chicken Pieces consist of a whole chicken cut into eight pieces — two legs, two thighs, two wings and the breast split into two pieces. Sometimes the back and giblets are included.

Chicken Breasts (E) can be purchased whole, with or without ribs attached; split, with or without the ribs; or boneless.

Chicken Thighs, Legs and Wings (F) come in a variety of package sizes and should be purchased according to number of servings needed.

Turkeys: Allow about ½ to ¾ pound *(225 to 350 g)* turkey per serving. The best buy in yield of meat per pound *(450 g)* is in the 16 to 24-pound *(7 to 10-kg)* range. Turkey can also be purchased in a variety of cuts.

Whole Roasting Turkeys (A) weigh between 10 and 26 pounds *(4,5 to 12 kg)* and are excellent for stuffing and roasting.

Turkey Breasts (B) can be whole or cut in half, with or without bones attached.

Turkey Legs and Wings (C) come in a variety of package sizes and should be purchased according to number of servings needed.

TO STORE: Proper storage of poultry is essential to maintain flavor and quality. Poultry may be kept safely in the refrigerator for up to two days and in the freezer for six months. Wash poultry in cold water, pat dry and wrap in plastic wrap or aluminum foil for refrigeration. If stored in freezer, wash in cold water, pat dry and wrap in freezer paper, aluminum foil or plastic freezer bags. The freezer temperature should be 0°F *(-18°C)* or less.

TO THAW FROZEN POULTRY: The safest way to thaw poultry is in the refrigerator. Thawing a whole 4-pound *(1,8-kg)* bird takes 12 to 16 hours. Thawing a cut-up chicken takes 4 to 9 hours. If desired, poultry can be thawed in cold water. In large bowl, cover poultry with cold water; *change water frequently to keep water cold.*

Microwave Thawing Chart for Poultry

Poultry	Defrost or Low (30%) Power
Boneless Chicken Breasts	9 to 13 min./lb. *(450 g)*
Chicken Pieces	4 to 8 min./lb. *(450 g)*
Chicken Quarters	5 to 9 min./lb. *(450 g)*
Cornish Game Hens	8 to 11 min./lb. *(450 g)*
Duckling	7 to 10 min./lb. *(450 g)*
Turkey Pieces	7 to 9 min./lb. *(450 g)*
Turkey Halves	5 to 8 min./lb. *(450 g)*
Whole Chickens	5 to 9 min./lb. *(450 g)*

Rearrange poultry frequently during thawing time.

How To: Cut Up & Bone Chicken

To Cut Up a Whole Chicken:

1. Pull leg away from body of chicken to find joint that connects thigh to backbone. With sharp knife, cut leg and thigh from body by cutting through joint.

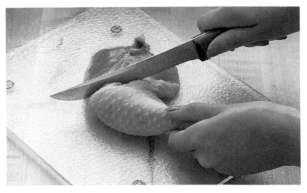

2. To separate thigh and leg, bend to find joint. Cut through joint to separate.

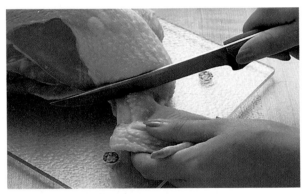

3. Pull wing away from body of chicken to find joint that connects wing to body. Cut wing from body by cutting through joint, rolling knife to let blade follow through at the curve of the joint.

4. Stand bird upright on neck end. Cut along each side of the backbone through the rib joints to separate backbone.

5. Hold breast, skin side down and neck end at top. Cut through cartilage at V of neck. Bend back both sides to pull and pop out the bone and cartilage. Pull out bone and cartilage.

6. Cut breast into halves.

To Bone Chicken Breast:

1. Place whole chicken breast, skin side down, on cutting surface. With sharp knife, cut through white gristle at the end of the bone at the center of the breast.

2. Bend breast halves back to pop out bone. Loosen and remove bone.

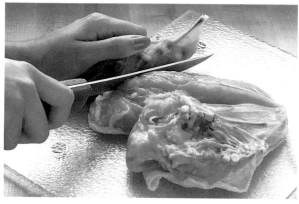

3. On one side of breast, cut rib bones away from breast. While cutting, gently pull the meat away from the rib bones. Cut through shoulder joint to remove entire rib cage. Repeat on other side.

4. Turn breast over and cut away wishbone. With knife, loosen and pull out white tendons.

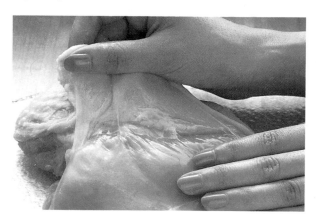

5. If desired, remove skin by pulling skin away from meat.

To Coat Chicken Pieces:

How To: Coat & Stuff Poultry

One method of coating chicken pieces is to combine all the dry coating ingredients in a plastic food bag and the wet ingredients in a pie plate. Dip the chicken into the wet ingredients and then place one to two pieces into the plastic food bag, shaking to coat.

Another method is to use two pie plates, one for dry ingredients and one for wet ingredients. Dip chicken pieces into wet ingredients and then roll in dry ingredients to coat.

To Stuff Poultry:

Neck and body cavities and the area underneath the breast skin can all be stuffed. Stuff cavities lightly, leaving space for stuffing to expand. Use about ¾ c. *(200 mL)* stuffing per pound *(450 g)* of poultry. Spoon stuffing into cavities, filling about ¾ full.

Tip: When stuffing poultry, be sure stuffing mixture is cool. Always stuff the bird *just before baking;* never

To stuff under breast skin, loosen skin with a spoon and fill out area between skin and breast with stuffing.

stuff it the night before to avoid an increased chance of bacterial growth.

How To: Carve Poultry

To Carve Poultry:

1. Separate Leg: To remove entire leg — drumstick and thigh — hold drumstick firmly with fingers and pull away from body. At the same time, cut through skin between leg and body. With skin cut, entire leg will pull freely from body.

2. Remove Leg: Press leg away from body. The joint connecting leg to backbone will often snap free or may be severed easily with knife point. Cut dark meat completely from body by following body contour carefully with knife.

3. Slicing Dark Meat: Place leg on separate plate and cut through connecting joint. Both pieces may be individually sliced. Hold drumstick with napkin and tilt to convenient angle, slice toward plate.

4. Slicing Thigh: To slice thigh meat, hold firmly on plate with fork. Cut even slices parallel to the bone. Dark meat slices may be arranged neatly on a plate. Repeating this process with the other leg will provide ample meat.

5. Preparing Breast: In preparing the breast for easy slicing, place knife parallel and as close to wing as possible. Make a deep cut into the breast, cutting right to the bone. This is your base cut. All breast slices will stop at this vertical cut.

6. Carving Breast: After base cut, begin to slice breast. Start halfway up the side, carving down, ending at base cut. Start each new slice slightly higher up on breast. Keep slices thin and even.

MEATS

There's a closeness, a coziness that surrounds a table when friends and family gather for a meal. It might be a special occasion with a bowl of flowers centered on your best lace tablecloth and each place set with beautiful china and stemware. Maybe it's a casual evening around the picnic table or an informal supper at the kitchen table.

The setting you create is simply the stage for your warmth and hospitality. But don't be surprised if your friendly kitchen is the place to congregate before mealtime. One of your dear friends just may be tempted to peek into the oven to see how that delicious ham is coming along. Or sneak a taste of your beef stroganoff bubbling on the stovetop. And chances are, you'll get lots of offers to help with last-minute preparation — like stirring the barbecued pork or checking the roast in the oven.

There's something about a good home-cooked meal, served with love, that seems to bring out the best in all of us. Good conversation. Joy and laughter. And a feeling that all is well in the world.

Grandma's Sunday Roast

6 servings
2 hours

A special family recipe that makes any day of the week a Sunday.

3 to 4 lb. *(1,4 to 1,8 kg)* beef rump roast
3   med. onions, quartered
1   bay leaf
1 tsp.   *(5 mL)* salt
1 tsp.   *(5 mL)* pepper

1 tsp.   *(5 mL)* minced fresh garlic
1 c.   *(250 mL)* water
6   carrots, cut in half crosswise
6   med. potatoes, quartered

Heat oven to 350°F *(180°C)*. Place roast on rack in roasting pan. Add remaining ingredients *except* water, carrots and potatoes. Pour water over roast. Cover; bake for 45 min. Uncover; arrange carrots and potatoes around meat. Baste with pan juices. Cover; bake, basting occasionally, for 60 to 70 min. or until vegetables are fork

tender and meat thermometer reaches 160°F *(71°C)* (Medium). Serve with pan juices.

Beef	Internal Cooking Temperature
Rare	140°F *(60°C)*
Medium	160°F *(71°C)*
Well	170°F *(76°C)*

Peppery Beef Roast

6 servings
1 hour 30 minutes

*The aroma of garlic and pepper will fill the kitchen
when you prepare this succulent roast.*

3 to 4 lb. *(1,4 to 1,8 kg)* rolled beef
           rump roast
¼ c.   *(50 mL)* vegetable oil

1 tbsp.   *(15 mL)* minced fresh garlic
1 tbsp.   *(15 mL)* fresh cracked pepper

Heat oven to 325°F *(160°C)* Place roast on rack in roasting pan. In small bowl stir together remaining ingredients. Spoon oil mixture over roast. Bake for 70 to 90 min. or until meat thermometer reaches 160°F *(71°C)* (Medium).

Beef	Internal Cooking Temperature
Rare	140°F *(60°C)*
Medium	160°F *(71°C)*
Well	170°F *(76°C)*

Grandma's Sunday Roast

Brisket With Stone-Ground Mustard

6 to 8 servings
3 hours 30 minutes

A tantalizing sauce of sweet, sour and spice is served over tender, boiled brisket.

Brisket

3 to 4 lb.	*(1,4 to 1,8 kg)* beef brisket
6 c.	*(1,5 L)* water
¼ c.	*(50 mL)* chopped fresh parsley
4	stalks celery, cut into 1" *(2,5 cm)* pieces
4	med. carrots, cut into 1" *(2,5 cm)* pieces
2	med. onions, cut into 1½" *(3,5 cm)* pieces
1 tsp.	*(5 mL)* salt
1 tsp.	*(5 mL)* coarsely ground pepper
1 tsp.	*(5 mL)* thyme leaves
2	bay leaves

Sauce

3 tbsp.	*(45 mL)* all-purpose flour
½ c.	*(125 mL)* country-style Dijon mustard
½ c.	*(125 mL)* currant jelly
½ c.	*(125 mL)* whipping cream
1 tsp.	*(5 mL)* Worcestershire sauce

In Dutch oven place brisket; cover with water. Add remaining brisket ingredients; bring to a full boil. Cover; cook over med. low heat for 2½ to 3 hr. or until brisket is fork tender. Remove bay leaves. Place brisket and vegetables on serving platter; *reserve broth*. In same pan or 2-qt. *(2-L)* saucepan place 1½ c. *(375 mL)* reserved broth; whisk in flour. Cook over med. heat, stirring occasionally, until smooth and bubbly (2 to 3 min.). Stir in remaining sauce ingredients. Continue cooking, stirring occasionally, until sauce is thickened (4 to 5 min.). Serve over carved brisket and vegetables.

Winter Warm-Up Beef Simmer

8 servings
4 hours 30 minutes

While this rich, hearty supper simmers, enjoy the brisk autumn air or the first snowflakes of the season.

1 c.	*(250 mL)* (2 med.) chopped onions
6	slices bacon, cut into ½" *(1 cm)* pieces
3 lb.	*(1,4 kg)* beef chuck roast, trimmed, cut into 2½" *(6 cm)* pieces
8	med. red potatoes, halved
3	med. carrots, cut into 1" *(2,5 cm)* pieces
3	med. onions, halved
8-oz.	*(227-g)* pkg. fresh mushrooms, halved
½ c.	*(125 mL)* chopped fresh parsley

1 c.	*(250 mL)* apple juice
10½-oz.	*(284-mL)* can beef broth
6-oz.	*(156-mL)* can tomato paste
½ tsp.	*(2 mL)* salt
½ tsp.	*(2 mL)* pepper
½ tsp.	*(2 mL)* thyme leaves
1 tsp.	*(5 mL)* minced fresh garlic
2	bay leaves

Heat oven to 325°F *(160°C)*. In Dutch oven place onions, bacon and roast. Cook over med. high heat, stirring occasionally, until bacon and roast are browned (8 to 10 min.). Stir in vegetables. Stir in remaining ingredients. Cover; bake for 1½ hr. Uncover; continue baking, stirring occasionally, for 2 to 2½ hr. or until roast is fork tender.

Winter Warm-Up Beef Simmer

Spinach-Stuffed Steaks or Burgers

Home cooking like this brings out the best of steaks or hamburgers.

Stuffing

10-oz.	*(300-g)* pkg. frozen spinach, thawed, drained
¼ tsp.	*(1 mL)* salt
¼ tsp.	*(1 mL)* pepper
½ tsp.	*(2 mL)* minced fresh garlic
2	(¾-lb.) *(340-g)* steaks (strip, porterhouse, T-bone) OR 1½ lb. *(675 g)* ground beef
6	slices bacon, cut into ½" *(1 cm)* pieces
2 tbsp.	*(30 mL)* butter or margarine

Sauce

1 tbsp.	*(15 mL)* all-purpose flour
1 c.	*(250 mL)* water
¼ tsp.	*(1 mL)* salt
2 tbsp.	*(30 mL)* tomato paste
½ tsp.	*(2 mL)* minced fresh garlic

In small bowl stir together all stuffing ingredients; set aside. To prepare steaks, trim excess fat from steaks. Split each steak from outer edges toward bone, making a pocket. Divide spinach mixture; fill each pocket. To prepare hamburgers, divide ground beef into 4 equal portions. Form into oblong (4 × 3") *(10 × 7,5 cm)* patties. Make indentation in middle of each pattie. Divide spinach mixture; fill each indentation. In 10" *(25 cm)* skillet cook bacon and butter over med. high heat until browned (5 min.). Place steaks or hamburgers in same skillet. Cook over med. high heat, turning once, until desired doneness (7 to 9 min. for medium steaks or 10 to 15 min. for medium hamburgers). Place meat on platter; keep warm while preparing sauce. Pour off fat, leaving bacon and brown particles in pan. Reduce heat to med.; stir in flour. Cook, stirring occasionally, until mixture is smooth and bubbly (1 min.). Stir in remaining sauce ingredients. Continue cooking, stirring occasionally, until thickened (4 to 5 min.). Serve over steaks or hamburgers.

To Stuff Steaks:

1. Split each steak from outer edges toward bone, making a pocket.

2. Divide spinach mixture; fill each pocket.

Spinach-Stuffed Burgers

Ranch Steak Platter

4 servings
35 minutes

Ranch Steak Platter

Feed your family this hearty steak platter.

Marinade

½ tsp.	*(2 mL)* salt
½ tsp.	*(2 mL)* oregano leaves
½ tsp.	*(2 mL)* pepper
2 tbsp.	*(30 mL)* cider vinegar
2 tbsp.	*(30 mL)* vegetable oil
1 tbsp.	*(15 mL)* country-style Dijon mustard
1 tsp.	*(5 mL)* minced fresh garlic

Steak

1½ lb.	*(675 g)* sirloin steak
2	med. carrots, cut into 1" *(2,5 cm)* pieces
1	med. onion, sliced ¼" *(0,5 cm)*
2	med. tomatoes, cut into 2" *(5 cm)* pieces
1	med. green pepper, cut into 1" *(2,5 cm)* strips

In 10" *(25 cm)* skillet stir together all marinade ingredients. Coat both sides of steak with marinade; place in same skillet. Place carrots and onion around steak in marinade mixture. Cover; cook over med. high heat, turning once, until browned (10 to 12 min.). Reduce heat to med. Add remaining ingredients. Cover; cook, stirring occasionally, until vegetables are crisply tender and meat reaches desired doneness (5 to 7 min. for medium).

Microwave Directions: Cut steak in half. In 2-qt. *(2-L)* casserole stir together all marinade ingredients. Coat both sides of steak with marinade; place in same casserole. Place carrots and onion around steak in marinade mixture. Cover; microwave on HIGH, turning steak over after half the time (8 to 10 min.). Add remaining ingredients. Cover; microwave on HIGH until vegetables are crisply tender and meat reaches desired doneness (5 to 7 min. for medium).

4 servings
35 minutes

Beef Stroganoff With Pearl Onions

Cream cheese makes this stroganoff extra creamy and rich.

3 tbsp.	*(45 mL)* butter or margarine
1½ lb.	*(675 g)* sirloin steak, cut into 1½" *(3,5 cm)* pieces
½ tsp.	*(2 mL)* salt
½ tsp.	*(2 mL)* pepper
2 tbsp.	*(30 mL)* all-purpose flour
2 c.	*(500 mL)* half-and-half
3 oz.	*(90 g)* cream cheese, softened
2 tbsp.	*(30 mL)* tomato paste

2 c.	*(500 mL)* *(½ lb.)* *(225 g)* fresh mushrooms, halved
1 c.	*(250 mL)* frozen pearl onions, thawed, drained
¼ c.	*(50 mL)* chopped fresh parsley
1 tsp.	*(5 mL)* marjoram leaves
	Cooked egg noodles

In 10" *(25 cm)* skillet melt butter until sizzling. Add steak, salt and pepper. Cook over med. high heat, stirring occasionally, until browned (5 min.). Stir in flour to coat steak; add half-and-half, cream cheese and tomato paste. Reduce heat to med. Cook, stirring occasionally, until sauce is thickened (7 to 9 min.). Stir in remaining ingredients *except* noodles. Continue cooking, stirring occasionally, until mushrooms are tender (3 to 4 min.). Serve over noodles.

Microwave Directions: In 3-qt. *(3-L)* casserole melt butter on HIGH (30 to 40 sec.). Stir in steak, salt and pepper. Cover; microwave on HIGH, stirring after half the time, just until steak is no longer pink (3 to 4 min.). Stir in flour, half-and-half, cream cheese and tomato paste. Microwave on HIGH, stirring after half the time, until sauce is thickened (4 to 6 min.). Stir in remaining ingredients *except* noodles. Microwave on HIGH until mushrooms are tender (2½ to 3½ min.). Serve over noodles.

4 servings
30 minutes

Marinated Beef & Broccoli Supper

Sirloin steak is tenderized in a light, lemon-ginger marinade.

¼ c.	*(50 mL)* butter or margarine
3 c.	*(750 mL)* broccoli flowerets
1	med. onion, sliced ⅛"*(0,2 cm)*
¾ tsp.	*(3 mL)* ginger
¼ tsp.	*(1 mL)* salt
¼ tsp.	*(1 mL)* pepper
1 tbsp.	*(15 mL)* lemon juice
1 tbsp.	*(15 mL)* Worcestershire sauce

1 tsp.	*(5 mL)* minced fresh garlic
1 lb.	*(450 g)* beef sirloin steak, cut into 3 × ½" *(7,5 × 1 cm)* strips
2	med. ripe tomatoes, cut into 1" *(2,5 cm)* pieces
	Cooked rice

In 10" *(25 cm)* skillet melt butter until sizzling. Add broccoli and onion. Cook over med. heat, stirring occasionally, until crisply tender (5 to 6 min.). Meanwhile, in medium bowl stir together remaining ingredients *except* steak, tomatoes and rice. Add sirloin strips; let stand 5 min. Add sirloin and marinade to vegetable mixture. Continue cooking, stirring occasionally, until meat is browned (6 to 8 min.). Stir in tomatoes. Cover; let stand 2 min. or until heated through. Serve meat and vegetables with juices over rice.

Microwave Directions: In 2-qt. *(2-L)* casserole melt butter on HIGH (40 to 50 sec.). Stir in broccoli and onion. Cover; microwave on HIGH until crisply tender (2 min.). Meanwhile, in medium bowl stir together remaining ingredients *except* steak, tomatoes and rice. Add sirloin strips; let stand 5 min. Add sirloin and marinade to vegetable mixture. Cover; microwave on HIGH, stirring after half the time, until meat is no longer pink (3 to 5 min.). Stir in tomatoes. Cover; let stand 5 min. Serve meat and vegetables with juices over rice.

6 servings
1 day

Sweet & Tangy Family Steak

The marinade enhances both the subtle flavor and the tenderness of this popular cut of meat.

Marinade

½ c.	*(125 mL)* catsup
¼ c.	*(50 mL)* country-style Dijon mustard
2 tbsp.	*(30 mL)* firmly packed brown sugar
1 tbsp.	*(15 mL)* cider vinegar
1 tsp.	*(5 mL)* minced fresh garlic

½ tsp.	*(2 mL)* fresh cracked pepper
¼ tsp.	*(1 mL)* salt
1½ lb.	*(675 g)* beef top round steak, cut 1" *(2,5 cm)* thick

In medium bowl stir together all marinade ingredients. Pierce steak with fork; place steak in plastic food bag. Pour in marinade; seal bag. Place in 9" *(23 cm)* sq. pan. Refrigerate 24 hr. Heat broiler. Drain steak; *reserve marinade.* Place steak on greased broiler pan. Broil 4 to 5" *(10 to 12,5 cm)* from heat for 5 to 6 min. Turn steak over, brush with marinade; continue broiling 4 to 5 min. or until desired doneness. In 1-qt. *(1-L)* saucepan cook remaining marinade over med. heat until heated through (2 to 4 min.). To serve, cut steak, on the diagonal, into thin slices. Serve with hot marinade.

Grilling Directions: Marinate steak as directed left. Prepare grill placing coals to one side; heat until coals are ash white. Make aluminum foil drip pan; place opposite coals. Place steak on grill over drip pan. Grill 5 to 8 min. Turn steak over, brush with marinade; continue grilling 5 to 8 min. or until desired doneness. In 1-qt. *(1-L)* saucepan cook remaining marinade over med. heat until heated through (2 to 4 min.). To serve, cut steak, on the diagonal, into thin slices. Serve with hot marinade.

Marinated Beef & Broccoli Supper

Cheddar Cheese-Pecan Rolled Flank Steak

Slice into this tender, marinated flank steak and discover a moist, flavorful stuffing.

Marinade

1 c.	*(250 mL)* (2 med.) chopped onions
2 c.	*(500 mL)* pineapple juice
1 tsp.	*(5 mL)* salt
1 tsp.	*(5 mL)* thyme leaves
½ tsp.	*(2 mL)* pepper
½ tsp.	*(2 mL)* rosemary leaves, crushed
2 tbsp.	*(30 mL)* Worcestershire sauce
1½ to 2 lb.	*(675 to 900 g)* beef flank steak

Stuffing

1½ c.	*(375 mL)* fresh bread crumbs
1½ c.	*(375 mL)* (6 oz.) *(170 g)* shredded Cheddar cheese
½ c.	*(125 mL)* chopped pecans
¼ c.	*(50 mL)* chopped onion
¼ c.	*(50 mL)* chopped fresh parsley
½ tsp.	*(2 mL)* minced fresh garlic

In medium bowl stir together all marinade ingredients *except* steak. With mallet, pound steak to ¼" *(0,5 cm)* thickness. Place steak in plastic food bag. Pour marinade into bag; seal tightly. Place bag in 13 × 9" *(33 × 23 cm)* baking pan. Refrigerate, turning twice, 24 hr. Heat oven to 400°F *(200°C)*. Remove steak from marinade; *reserve marinade*. In medium bowl combine all stuffing ingredients. Place stuffing mixture over entire surface of steak; pressing slightly. Tightly roll up steak, jelly roll fashion. Tie with string to secure filling inside roll. Line 13 × 9" *(33 × 23 cm)* baking pan with heavy-duty aluminum foil.

Place steak in prepared pan; baste with reserved marinade. Bake, basting with marinade every 15 min., for 50 to 60 min. or until meat thermometer reaches 160°F *(71°C)* (Medium). Just before serving, baste with marinade.

Beef	Internal Cooking Temperature
Rare	140°F *(60°C)*
Medium	160°F *(71°C)*
Well	170°F *(76°C)*

To Prepare Steak:

1. Place stuffing mixture over entire surface of steak; pressing slightly.

2. Tightly roll up steak, jelly roll fashion. Tie with string to secure filling inside roll.

Cheddar Cheese-Pecan Rolled Flank Steak

Tenderloin of Beef With Blue Cheese

6 to 8 servings
1 hour 15 minutes

Tenderloin of Beef With Blue Cheese

This rich, noble beef tenderloin is full of character.

Beef

¼ c.	*(50 mL)* butter or margarine
½ tsp.	*(2 mL)* coarsely ground pepper
1 tsp.	*(5 mL)* minced fresh garlic
2 to 3 lb.	*(900 to 1,4 kg)* beef tenderloin, trimmed, tied

Sauce

2 tbsp.	*(30 mL)* butter or margarine
4-oz.	*(110-g)* pkg. crumbled blue cheese
1 c.	*(250 mL)* beef broth
¼ c.	*(50 mL)* Madeira wine
2 c.	*(500 mL) (8 oz.) (225 g)* sliced ¼" *(0,5 cm)* fresh mushrooms
½ c.	*(125 mL)* chopped pecans, toasted
½ c.	*(125 mL)* pine nuts or sliced almonds, toasted
⅓ c.	*(75 mL)* sliced ¼" *(0,5 cm)* green onions

Heat oven to 400°F *(200°C)*. In 10" *(25 cm)* skillet melt ¼ c. *(50 mL)* butter until sizzling; stir in pepper and garlic. Place tenderloin in same skillet. Cook over med. high heat until browned on all sides (7 to 9 min.). Remove from pan; *reserve pan juices and browned particles in skillet.* Line 13 × 9" *(33 × 23 cm)* baking pan with aluminum foil; place tenderloin in pan. Bake for 35 to 50 min. or until meat thermometer reaches 160°F *(71°C)* (Medium). Meanwhile, melt 2 tbsp. *(30 mL)* butter in same skillet with reserved pan juices and browned particles until sizzling; stir in blue cheese. Cook over med. heat, stirring occasionally, until cheese is melted (4 to

to 5 min.). Stir in beef broth and wine; add mushrooms. Continue cooking, stirring occasionally, until mushrooms are tender (4 to 5 min.). Stir in remaining sauce ingredients. Serve over carved tenderloin.

Beef	Internal Cooking Temperature
Rare	140°F *(60°C)*
Medium	160°F *(71°C)*
Well	170°F *(76°C)*

4 servings
2 hours

Grilled Steak With Herb Peppercorn Butter

Grilled steak is elegantly served with a wonderful herb butter that melts over the steak to provide superb flavor.

¼ c.	*(50 mL)* dry white wine
1 tbsp.	*(15 mL)* minced fresh shallots
1 tbsp.	*(15 mL)* chopped fresh chives
1 tsp.	*(5 mL)* chopped fresh tarragon
½ tsp.	*(2 mL)* coarsely ground pepper

¼ tsp.	*(1 mL)* salt
½ c.	*(125 mL)* butter, softened
4	beef porterhouse or T-bone steaks

In 1-qt. *(1-L)* saucepan stir together all ingredients *except* butter and steaks. Cook over med. heat, stirring occasionally, until all liquid has evaporated (5 to 6 min.). Set aside; cool completely. In small bowl stir together butter and cooled herbs. Place mixture on waxed paper; shape into 4" *(10 cm)* log. Refrigerate until serving

time. Meanwhile, grill or broil steaks to desired doneness. Place ½" *(1 cm)* slice herb butter on each grilled or broiled steak. Serve as butter is melting over steaks.

Tip: Remaining herb butter can be used to season cooked vegetables or to serve with breads.

Prairie Pot Roast With Dill

6 to 8 servings
3 hours 30 minutes

Prairie Pot Roast With Dill

A Sunday evening family favorite, served with a dill sour cream gravy.

Roast

2 tbsp.	*(30 mL)* vegetable oil
2 tbsp.	*(30 mL)* cider vinegar
1 tsp.	*(5 mL)* salt
1 tsp.	*(5 mL)* dill seed
½ tsp.	*(2 mL)* pepper
3 to 4 lb.	*(1,4 to 1,8 kg)* beef chuck roast
6 to 8	med. new red potatoes, cut into 1" *(2,5 cm)* pieces
4 to 6	med. carrots, cut into 1½" *(3,5 cm)* pieces
2	leeks, quartered, sliced lengthwise into 2" *(5 cm)* pieces*
¼ c.	*(50 mL)* water
1	bay leaf

Gravy

¼ c.	*(50 mL)* all-purpose flour
½ tsp.	*(2 mL)* salt
½ tsp.	*(2 mL)* dill weed
1 c.	*(250 mL)* dairy sour cream

Heat oven to 350°F *(180°C)*. In 13 × 9" *(33 × 23 cm)* baking pan combine oil, vinegar, 1 tsp. *(5 mL)* salt, dill seed and pepper; add roast. Turn to coat all sides of roast with herbs and oil. Let stand 15 min. Meanwhile, in large roasting pan place potatoes, carrots and leeks. Place roast and herb and oil mixture in roasting pan with vegetables; add water and bay leaf. Cover; bake, basting occasionally, for 2½ to 3 hr. or until roast is fork tender. Remove bay leaf. Place roast and vegetables on serving platter; *reserve pan juices*. In 2-qt. *(2-L)* saucepan place 1½ c. *(375 mL)* reserved pan juices. Whisk in flour, ½ tsp. *(2 mL)* salt and dill weed. Cook over med. heat, stirring occasionally, until smooth and bubbly (1 min.). Stir in sour cream; continue cooking, stirring occasionally, until gravy is thickened (4 to 5 min.). Serve over carved roast and vegetables.

*2 large onions, cut into 2" *(5 cm)* pieces can be substituted for 2 leeks.

6 to 8 servings
1 day

Roasted Beef With Horseradish Cream

Marinating and slow cooking make this pot roast tender and flavorful.

Marinade

¼ c.	*(50 mL)* vegetable oil
2 tbsp.	*(30 mL)* cider vinegar
1 tsp.	*(5 mL)* salt
1 tsp.	*(5 mL)* pepper
1 tbsp.	*(15 mL)* prepared horseradish
1 tsp.	*(5 mL)* minced fresh garlic
¼ c.	*(50 mL)* chopped fresh parsley
3 to 4 lb.	*(1,4 to 1,8 kg)* beef chuck roast

Horseradish Cream

½ c.	*(125 mL)* dairy sour cream
½ c.	*(125 mL)* mayonnaise
¼ tsp.	*(1 mL)* salt
¼ tsp.	*(1 mL)* pepper
1 tbsp.	*(15 mL)* prepared horseradish
1 tsp.	*(5 mL)* lemon juice
1 tsp.	*(5 mL)* country-style Dijon mustard
¼ c.	*(50 mL)* chopped fresh parsley

In Dutch oven stir together all marinade ingredients *except* parsley and roast; stir in parsley. Place roast in marinade; turn to coat all sides with marinade. Cover; refrigerate overnight. Heat oven to 350°F *(180°C)*. Bake roast in marinade for 1½ to 2 hr. or until roast is fork tender. Meanwhile, in small bowl stir together all horseradish cream ingredients *except* parsley. Stir in parsley. Cover; refrigerate until ready to serve. Serve over carved roast.

Peppery Steak With Pan Fries & Gravy

Peppery Steak With Pan Fries & Gravy

4 servings
40 minutes

Honest, wonderful home-cooked fare that is sure to become a family favorite.

Potatoes

¼ c.   *(50 mL)* butter or margarine
6   med. new red potatoes, cut into wedges
¼ tsp. *(1 mL)* salt
¼ tsp. *(1 mL)* pepper

Steak

⅓ c.   *(75 mL)* all-purpose flour
¼ tsp. *(1 mL)* salt
            Pinch of pepper
4   beef cubed steaks

Gravy

1 tbsp. *(15 mL)* butter or margarine
1 tbsp. *(15 mL)* all-purpose flour
1 c.   *(250 mL)* milk
¼ tsp.   *(1 mL)* salt
             Pinch of pepper

In 10" *(25 cm)* skillet melt ¼ c. *(50 mL)* butter until sizzling. Add remaining potato ingredients. Cook over med. high heat, turning occasionally, until golden brown (10 to 15 min.). Place potatoes on platter; keep warm while preparing steaks and gravy. In 9" *(23 cm)* pie pan stir together all steak ingredients *except* steaks. Coat both sides of steaks with flour mixture. Place 2 steaks in same skillet. Cook over med. high heat until brown and crispy (3 min. on each side). Remove steaks to platter with potatoes. Cook remaining steaks. Reduce heat to med. In same skillet with drippings and brown particles melt 1 tbsp. *(15 mL)* butter; stir in 1 tbsp. *(15 mL)* flour. Cook, stirring occasionally, until smooth and bubbly (1 min.). Stir in remaining gravy ingredients. Continue cooking, stirring occasionally, until gravy thickens (4 to 5 min.). Serve over steaks and potatoes.

Microwave Directions: In 13 × 9" *(33 × 23 cm)* baking dish melt ¼ c. *(50 mL)* butter on HIGH (50 to 60 sec.). Stir in remaining potato ingredients. Cover; microwave on HIGH, stirring after half the time, until potatoes are tender (8 to 11 min.). Place potatoes on platter; keep warm while preparing steaks and gravy. Omit ⅓ c. *(75 mL)* flour. Place steaks in same dish; sprinkle with salt and pepper. Cover; microwave on HIGH, turning steaks over after half the time, until meat is no longer pink. Remove steaks to platter with potatoes. Omit 1 tbsp. *(15 mL)* butter; increase flour to 3 tbsp. *(45 mL)* Stir 3 tbsp. *(45 mL)* flour into pan juices. Microwave on HIGH until bubbly (1 to 1½ min.). Stir in remaining gravy ingredients. Cover; microwave on HIGH, stirring after half the time, until gravy thickens (3 to 5 min.). Serve over steaks and potatoes.

Meatballs With Garden Tomato Sauce

4 servings
60 minutes

This recipe is sure to bring back memories of childhood.

Meatballs

1 lb.	*(450 g)* ground beef
½ c.	*(125 mL)* uncooked long grain rice
½ c.	*(125 mL)* water
½ tsp.	*(2 mL)* salt
½ tsp.	*(2 mL)* basil leaves
½ tsp.	*(2 mL)* pepper

Sauce

1 c.	*(250 mL)* water
3	med. tomatoes, cut into 1" *(2,5 cm)* pieces
2	stalks celery, sliced ½" *(1 cm)*
1	med. onion, cut into ½" *(1 cm)* pieces
6-oz.	*(156-mL)* can tomato paste
½ tsp.	*(2 mL)* salt
¼ tsp.	*(1 mL)* pepper
1 tsp.	*(5 mL)* minced fresh garlic

Heat oven to 375°F *(190°C)*. In medium bowl stir together all meatball ingredients. Form mixture into 12 meatballs; place in 12 × 8" *(30 × 20 cm)* baking pan. In medium bowl stir together all sauce ingredients; pour over meatballs. Cover; bake for 45 to 50 min. or until rice is tender.

Microwave Directions: Prepare meatballs as directed left. Place meatballs in 12 × 8" *(30 × 20 cm)* baking dish. In medium bowl stir together all sauce ingredients; pour over meatballs. Cover with plastic wrap; microwave on HIGH, stirring and rearranging meatballs after half the time, until rice is tender (25 to 35 min.). Let stand 5 min.

Herb-Spiced Meat Loaf

6 to 8 servings
1 hour 30 minutes

This spicy meat loaf makes a hearty and very special, old-fashioned meal.

1½ c.	*(375 mL)* fresh bread crumbs
½ c.	*(125 mL)* finely chopped onion
½ c.	*(125 mL)* finely chopped red or green pepper
½ c.	*(125 mL)* tomato sauce
1 lb.	*(450 g)* regular ground beef*
1 lb.	*(450 g)* ground pork
6-oz.	*(156-mL)* can tomato paste
2	eggs, slightly beaten
2 tbsp.	*(30 mL)* chopped fresh parsley

1 tbsp.	*(15 mL)* sage leaves, rubbed
1 tsp.	*(5 mL)* salt
½ tsp.	*(2 mL)* pepper
½ tsp.	*(2 mL)* thyme leaves
1 tbsp.	*(15 mL)* lemon juice
1 tsp.	*(5 mL)* minced fresh garlic
½ c.	*(125 mL)* whipping cream
1 tbsp.	*(15 mL)* all-purpose flour
½ tsp.	*(2 mL)* thyme leaves

Heat oven to 350°F *(180°C)*. In large bowl stir together all ingredients *except* whipping cream, flour and ½ tsp. *(2 mL)* thyme leaves. Form into loaf; place in 13 × 9" *(33 × 23 cm)* baking pan. Bake for 55 to 65 min. or until browned. *Reserve pan juices.* In 1-qt. *(1-L)* saucepan stir together whipping cream, flour, ½ tsp. *(2 mL)* thyme leaves and reserved ¾ c. *(200 mL)* pan juices. Cook over med. heat, stirring occasionally, until slightly thickened (3 to 4 min.). Serve with meat loaf.

*Do not substitute lean ground beef for regular ground beef.

Herb-Spiced Meat Loaf

Bunkhouse Stroganoff Squares

A meat pie that is easily prepared and satisfies the heartiest appetite.

Stroganoff

2 c.	*(500 mL) (8 oz.) (225 g)* sliced ¼" *(0,5 cm)* fresh mushrooms
1 c.	*(250 mL) (2 med.)* chopped onions
2 lb.	*(900 g)* ground beef
1 c.	*(250 mL)* chopped fresh parsley
½ c.	*(125 mL)* fresh bread crumbs
8 oz.	*(250 g)* cream cheese, softened
1 tsp.	*(5 mL)* salt
½ tsp.	*(2 mL)* pepper
½ tsp.	*(2 mL)* thyme leaves

Crust

3 c.	*(750 mL)* all-purpose flour
2 tbsp.	*(30 mL)* instant minced onion
1 tsp.	*(5 mL)* salt
1 tsp.	*(5 mL)* sugar
¼ tsp.	*(1 mL)* pepper
½ c.	*(125 mL)* butter or margarine
½ c.	*(125 mL)* shortening
1	egg, slightly beaten
6 to 8 tbsp.	*(90 to 120 mL)* cold water
1	egg, slightly beaten
1 tbsp.	*(15 mL)* milk

Heat oven to 375°F *(190°C)*. In 10" *(25 cm)* skillet cook mushrooms, onions and ground beef over med. high heat, stirring occasionally, until browned (12 to 15 min.). Drain off fat. Stir in remaining stroganoff ingredients; cook over med. heat until cream cheese is melted (3 to 4 min.). In large bowl stir together flour, minced onion, 1 tsp. *(5 mL)* salt, sugar and ¼ tsp. *(1 mL)* pepper. Cut in butter and shortening until crumbly. With fork mix in 1 egg and water until flour is moistened. Divide dough in half; shape into 2 balls and flatten. Wrap 1 ball in plastic wrap; refrigerate. On lightly floured surface roll out other ball into 14" *(35 cm)* sq. Place in 9" *(23 cm)* sq. baking pan. Trim pastry to ½" *(1 cm)* from rim of pan. Fill with stroganoff mixture. Roll remaining pastry ball into 14" *(35 cm)* sq.; place over stroganoff mixture. Trim pastry to ½" *(1 cm)* from rim of pan. Roll edges of dough under to form rim inside of pan; crimp or flute crust. With sharp knife, cut X in each 3" *(7,5 cm)* sq. of pastry to decorate 9 squares. In small bowl stir together 1 egg and milk; brush over pastry. Bake for 35 to 45 min. or until crust is golden brown. Let stand 5 min.; cut into squares.

Bunkhouse Stroganoff Squares

Blue Cheese Stuffed Hamburgers

4 hamburgers
45 minutes

Blue cheese, mushrooms and onions are the fixings for this juicy hamburger.

1½ lb.	*(675 g)* ground beef
¼ tsp.	*(1 mL)* salt
¼ tsp.	*(1 mL)* pepper
⅓ c.	*(75 mL)* crumbled blue cheese
3 oz.	*(90 g)* cream cheese, softened
1 tbsp.	*(15 mL)* country-style Dijon mustard
4	onion buns

1½ c.	*(375 mL)* sliced ¼" *(0,5 cm)* fresh mushrooms
2	med. onions, sliced ⅛" *(0,2 cm)*
¼ tsp.	*(1 mL)* salt
¼ tsp.	*(1 mL)* pepper
1 tbsp.	*(15 mL)* Worcestershire sauce
4	slices ripe tomato

In medium bowl stir together ground beef, ¼ tsp. *(1 mL)* salt and ¼ tsp. *(1 mL)* pepper. Form into 8 large ¼" *(0,5 cm)* thick patties. In small bowl stir together blue cheese, cream cheese and mustard. Place about 2 tbsp. *(30 mL)* cheese mixture on top of each of 4 patties. Top each with remaining meat patty. Press around edges to seal. Place hamburgers in 10" *(25 cm)* skillet. Cook over med. heat, turning once, until desired doneness (12 to 15 min. for medium). Place hamburgers on buns. In same skillet with drippings place mushrooms and onions; add ¼ tsp. *(1 mL)* salt, ¼ tsp. *(1 mL)* pepper and Worcestershire sauce. Cook over med. high heat, stirring occasionally, until tender (4 to 5 min.). Meanwhile, place

tomato slice on each hamburger; top with grilled mushrooms and onions.

Microwave Directions: Assemble as directed left. Place hamburgers on microwave-safe bacon/roasting rack or 12 × 8" *(30 × 20 cm)* baking dish. Cover; microwave on HIGH, turning hamburgers over and rearranging after half the time, until desired doneness (5 to 8 min. for medium). In medium bowl combine remaining ingredients *except* buns and tomatoes. Cover; microwave on HIGH until crisply tender (2 to 3 min.). Assemble sandwiches as directed left.

To Stuff Burgers:

1. Form into 8 large ¼" *(0,5 cm)* thick patties.

2. Place about 2 tbsp. *(30 mL)* cheese mixture on top of each of 4 patties. Top each with remaining meat patty. Press around edges to seal.

Blue Cheese Stuffed Hamburgers

Cider-Glazed Baked Ham

10 to 12 servings
3 hours

Fruit-Stuffed Pork Loin

Slice into this succulent herb-roasted pork to reveal an exquisite display of fruit stuffing.

1 c.	*(250 mL)* water
1 c.	*(250 mL)* (1 med.) chopped tart cooking apple
1 c.	*(250 mL)* dried apricots
1 c.	*(250 mL)* dried pitted prunes
4 to 5 lb.	*(1,8 to 2,3 kg)* boneless center cut pork loin roast (2 loins tied)
1 tsp.	*(5 mL)* thyme leaves
½ tsp.	*(2 mL)* rosemary leaves, crushed
½ tsp.	*(2 mL)* sage leaves, crushed
½ tsp.	*(2 mL)* salt
½ tsp.	*(2 mL)* coarsely ground pepper
2 tbsp.	*(30 mL)* butter or margarine, melted
1 tbsp.	*(15 mL)* all-purpose flour
¼ tsp.	*(1 mL)* salt
2 c.	*(500 mL)* water

Heat oven to 325°F *(160°C)*. In 2-qt. *(2-L)* saucepan bring 1 c. *(250 mL)* water to a full boil; remove from heat. Add apple, apricots and prunes; let stand 5 min. Drain off water; set fruit aside. Untie roast; lay roast open. With sharp knife, cut ½" *(1 cm)* slit down center through thick muscle of pork loin lengthwise from one end to the other on both loins. With wooden spoon pack fruit into both slits. Place both loins back together; tie with string to secure. In small bowl stir together remaining ingredients *except* butter, flour, ¼ tsp. *(1 mL)* salt and water. Brush roast with melted butter; sprinkle herbs over entire roast. Place roast, fat side up, in roasting pan. Bake, basting with pan juices occasionally, for 2

to 2½ hr. or until meat thermometer reaches 165°F *(74°C)*. Remove from oven; let stand about 10 min. or until meat thermometer reaches 170°F *(76°C)*. Place roast on serving platter; *reserve pan juices.* In same roasting pan place ¼ c. *(50 mL)* reserved pan juices; stir in flour and ¼ tsp. *(1 mL)* salt. Cook over med. heat until smooth and bubbly (1 min.). Stir in 2 c. *(500 mL)* water; continue cooking, stirring occasionally, until mixture comes to a full boil (4 to 5 min.). Serve over carved roast.

Tip: Insert meat thermometer into center of loin. (Do not touch fruit stuffing.)

8 to 10 servings
1 hour 30 minutes

Cider-Glazed Baked Ham

As the ham bakes, basted with apple cider, its own wonderful honey-mustard sauce is made.

4 to 5 lb.	*(1,8 to 2,3 kg)* fully cooked boneless cured ham
1 c.	*(250 mL)* apple cider
¼ c.	*(50 mL)* firmly packed brown sugar
¼ c.	*(50 mL)* country-style Dijon mustard
¼ c.	*(50 mL)* honey
½ tsp.	*(2 mL)* liquid smoke
	Red, green and yellow apple slices

Heat oven to 350°F *(180°C)*. Place ham in 13 × 9" *(33 × 23 cm)* baking pan. Pour apple cider over ham. In medium bowl stir together remaining ingredients *except* apple slices. Spoon sauce over entire ham. Bake, basting every 15 min. with pan juices, for 60 to 70 min. or until heated through. Serve carved ham with pan juices; garnish with apple slices.

Microwave Directions: Place ham in 13 × 9" *(33 × 23 cm)* baking dish. Pour apple cider over ham. In medium bowl stir together remaining ingredients *except* apple slices. Spoon sauce over entire ham. Cover with plastic wrap. Microwave on HIGH 5 min. Reduce power to MEDIUM (50% power); microwave, basting every 15 min. with pan juices and turning ham over after half the time, until heated through (60 to 90 min.). If cut edge begins to dry, shield with aluminum foil. Serve carved ham with pan juices; garnish with apple slices.

Savory Pork Roast

8 to 10 servings
3 hours 20 minutes

A simply prepared roast, covered with sage and roasted to perfection.

4 to 5 lb. *(1,8 to 2,3 kg)* pork shoulder roast
2 to 3 tbsp. *(30 to 45 mL)* vegetable oil
3 tbsp. *(45 mL)* sage leaves, crushed

½ tsp. *(2 mL)* salt
¼ tsp. *(1 mL)* pepper

Heat oven to 350°F *(180°C)*. Coat roast with oil; rub sage over entire roast. Place roast, fat side up, on rack in roasting pan. Sprinkle with salt and pepper. Bake for 2 to 3 hr. or until meat thermometer reaches 170°F *(76°C)*.

Basil Tomato Pork Chops

6 servings
1 hour 30 minutes

Moist, tender pork chops cooked in a fresh vegetable sauce.

2 tbsp. *(30 mL)* butter or margarine
1 tsp. *(5 mL)* minced fresh garlic
8   pork chops, ½" *(1 cm)* thick
28-oz. *(796-mL)* can whole tomatoes
1 tsp. *(5 mL)* basil leaves
1 tsp. *(5 mL)* salt

½ tsp. *(2 mL)* pepper
½ c. *(125 mL)* water
3 tbsp. *(45 mL)* cornstarch
1   med. onion, sliced into rings
1   med. green pepper, sliced into rings

In Dutch oven melt butter until sizzling; stir in garlic. Add 4 pork chops; brown on both sides. Remove from pan; repeat with remaining pork chops. Return all pork chops to pan. Stir in remaining ingredients *except* water, cornstarch, onion and green pepper. Cover; cook over med. heat, stirring occasionally, until pork chops are fork tender (50 to 60 min.). Remove pork chops; keep warm. In small bowl stir together water and cornstarch. Stir cornstarch mixture into hot cooking liquid in Dutch oven; add onion and green pepper. Cook over med. high heat, stirring occasionally, until thickened and vegetables are crisply tender (5 to 6 min.). Serve sauce over pork chops.

Microwave Directions: In 13 × 9" *(33 × 23 cm)* baking dish melt butter on HIGH (40 to 50 sec.). Stir in garlic; add pork chops. In medium bowl stir together remaining ingredients *except* water, cornstarch, onion and green pepper. Pour over pork chops. Cover; microwave on HIGH, rearranging pork chops after half the time, until pork chops are fork tender (25 to 35 min.). Remove pork chops; keep warm. In small bowl stir together water and cornstarch. Stir cornstarch mixture into hot cooking liquid in baking dish; add onion and green pepper. Microwave on HIGH, stirring twice during the time, until thickened and vegetables are crisply tender (4 to 5 min.). Serve sauce over pork chops.

Basil Tomato Pork Chops

Apple-Nut Stuffed Pork Chops

6 servings
1 hour 30 minutes

Fresh apples add extra taste and color to hearty stuffed pork chops.

½ c.	*(125 mL)* butter or margarine	6	*(2 to 2¼" thick) (5 to 5,5 cm)* double rib pork chops, with 1½ to 2" *(3,5 to 5 cm)* pocket cut in rib side
⅓ c.	*(75 mL)* chopped onion		
⅓ c.	*(75 mL)* chopped walnuts		
⅓ c.	*(75 mL)* chopped apple	2 tbsp.	*(30 mL)* butter or margarine
1 c.	*(250 mL)* water		
8-oz.	*(225-g)* pkg. dried crumbly style herb seasoned stuffing		

Heat oven to 350°F *(180°C)*. In 10" *(25 cm)* skillet melt ½ c. *(125 mL)* butter until sizzling; add onion. Cook over med. heat until tender (4 to 5 min.). Remove from heat. Stir in walnuts, apple, water and stuffing. Fill pockets in pork chops with stuffing. In same skillet melt 2 tbsp. *(30 mL)* butter. Brown pork chops on both sides; place in 13 × 9" *(33 × 23 cm)* baking pan. Cover; bake for 60 to 70 min. or until no longer pink and thermometer reaches 170°F *(76°C)*.

Microwave Directions: *Eliminate 2 tbsp.* (30 mL) *butter.* In 13 × 9" *(33 × 23 cm)* baking dish melt ½ c. *(125 mL)* butter on HIGH (50 to 60 sec.); add onion. Cover; microwave on HIGH, stirring after half the time, until tender (2 to 3 min.). Stir in remaining ingredients *except* pork chops. Fill pockets in pork chops with stuffing. In same dish arrange pork chops with thickest edge to outside; *sprinkle with paprika.* Cover; microwave on HIGH, turning dish ½ turn after half the time, until no longer pink and thermometer reaches 170°F *(76°C)* (20 to 30 min.). Let stand 5 min.

Oven-Baked Pork Chops

6 servings
1 hour 30 minutes

Dinner is easy when pork chops and rice bake together in one pan.

6	*(1 to 1¼" thick) (2,5 to 3 cm)* pork loin or rib chops	3 c.	*(750 mL)* water
		4 tsp.	*(20 mL)* instant chicken bouillon
1 c.	*(250 mL) (2 stalks)* sliced ½" *(1 cm)* celery	1 tsp.	*(5 mL)* Italian herb seasoning*
1½ c.	*(375 mL)* uncooked long grain rice	½ tsp.	*(2 mL)* salt
1	med. sliced onion	1	med. green pepper, cut into 6 rings

Heat oven to 350°F *(180°C)*. In 10" *(25 cm)* skillet brown pork chops over med. heat. In 13 × 9" *(33 × 23 cm)* baking pan stir together celery and uncooked rice. Place onion slices over rice; top with pork chops. In 2-qt. *(2-L)* saucepan bring water to a full boil. Add remaining ingredients *except* green pepper. Stir to dissolve; pour over pork chops. Cover with aluminum foil; bake for 60 to 70 min. or until rice is cooked and pork chops are fork

tender. Remove foil; top pork chops with green pepper rings. Continue baking for 10 to 15 min. or until green pepper is crisply tender.

*¼ tsp. *(1 mL) each* oregano leaves, marjoram leaves and basil leaves and a pinch of rubbed sage can be substituted for 1 tsp. *(5 mL)* Italian herb seasoning.

Apple-Nut Stuffed Pork Chops

Pork Chops With Mushroom Pan Gravy

Serve tender pork chops over rice, then top with lots of traditional pan gravy.

6	slices bacon, cut into ½" *(1 cm)* pieces
2 c.	*(500 mL)* (2 med.) sliced ⅛" *(0,2 cm)* onions
4	(¾" thick) *(2 cm)* center cut pork chops
3 tbsp.	*(45 mL)* all-purpose flour
½ tsp.	*(2 mL)* salt
½ tsp.	*(2 mL)* thyme leaves

¼ tsp.	*(1 mL)* pepper
2 c.	*(500 mL)* half-and-half
2 c.	*(500 mL)* (8 oz.) *(225 g)* sliced ¼" *(0,5 cm)* fresh mushrooms

Cooked rice

In 10" *(25 cm)* skillet cook bacon and onions over med. high heat, stirring occasionally, until browned (8 to 10 min.). Add pork chops, arranging bacon and onions on top of pork chops. Cover; continue cooking for 10 min. or until browned. Turn pork chops. Reduce heat to med. Cover; cook until pork chops are tender (10 to 15 min.). Place pork chops on platter; keep warm while preparing gravy. In same skillet with drippings, brown particles, bacon and onions add remaining ingredients *except* half-and-half, mushrooms and rice. Cook over med. heat, stirring occasionally, until smooth and bubbly (1 min.). Stir in half-and-half and mushrooms. Continue cooking, stirring occasionally, until mixture is thickened (8 to 10 min.). Serve gravy over rice and pork chops.

Microwave Directions: In 12 × 8" *(30 × 20 cm)* baking dish microwave bacon and onion on HIGH, stirring after half the time, until tender (4 to 8 min.). Place pork chops in same dish, arranging bacon and onions on top of pork chops. Cover; microwave on HIGH, turning pork chops over and rearranging after half the time, until pork chops are tender (10 to 18 min.). Place pork chops on platter; keep warm while preparing gravy. Pour off fat. In same baking dish add remaining ingredients *except* half-and-half, mushrooms and rice. Microwave on HIGH, stirring after half the time, until bubbly (3 to 5 min.). Stir in half-and-half and mushrooms. Microwave on HIGH, stirring after half the time, until mixture is thickened (5½ to 7½ min.). Serve gravy over rice and pork chops.

Pork Chops With Mushroom Pan Gravy

Pan-Fried Pork Cutlets

Tender pork, lightly coated and pan-fried.

2 lb.	*(900 g)* pork tenderloin, cut into 12 slices		¾ c.	*(200 mL)* dry unseasoned bread crumbs
⅓ c.	*(75 mL)* all-purpose flour		1 tsp.	*(5 mL)* paprika
1 tsp.	*(5 mL)* salt		½ c.	*(125 mL)* butter or margarine
¼ tsp.	*(1 mL)* pepper			
1	egg, beaten			Lemon slices
2 tbsp.	*(30 mL)* milk			Parsley

Flatten each slice of pork to about ⅓" *(0,8 cm)* thickness by pounding between sheets of waxed paper; set aside. In pie pan combine flour, salt and pepper. In small bowl stir together egg and milk. In pie pan combine bread crumbs and paprika. Coat each slice of pork with flour mixture. Dip floured slices into egg mixture, then coat with bread crumb mixture. In 10" *(25 cm)* skillet melt ¼ c. *(50 mL)* butter over med. heat. Cook 6 slices at a time, turning once, until golden brown and done throughout (3 to 4 min. per side). Remove from pan to platter; keep warm in oven. Repeat with remaining slices. Garnish with lemon and parsley.

Honey-Smoked Pork Tenderloin

Country smokehouse flavor and hearty goodness.

3 tbsp.	*(45 mL)* butter or margarine		¼ tsp.	*(1 mL)* salt
1 lb.	*(450 g)* (2" *[5 cm]* diameter) pork tenderloin, sliced 2" *(5 cm)*		¼ tsp.	*(1 mL)* pepper
4	med. carrots, sliced 1" *(2,5 cm)*		¼ tsp.	*(1 mL)* sage
3	stalks celery, sliced 1" *(2,5 cm)*		3 tbsp.	*(45 mL)* honey
1	small onion, sliced ⅛" *(0,2 cm)*		2 tbsp.	*(30 mL)* lemon juice
½ tsp.	*(2 mL)* ginger		1 tsp.	*(5 mL)* liquid smoke
			½ tsp.	*(2 mL)* minced fresh garlic

In 10" *(25 cm)* skillet melt butter until sizzling; add pork and carrots. Cook over med. high heat, stirring occasionally, until meat is browned (5 to 6 min.). Reduce heat to med. Stir in remaining ingredients. Cover; cook, stirring occasionally, until vegetables are crisply tender (10 to 12 min.).

Microwave Directions: In 3-qt. *(2-L)* casserole melt butter on HIGH (30 to 45 sec.); add pork and carrots. Cover; microwave on HIGH, stirring after half the time, until pork is no longer pink (8 to 10 min.). Stir in remaining ingredients. Cover; microwave on HIGH, stirring after half the time, until vegetables are crisply tender (5 to 9 min.). Place pork and vegetables on platter; keep warm. *Combine 2 tsp.* (10 mL) *cornstarch with 2 tsp.* (10 mL) *water.* Stir into hot pan juices. Microwave on HIGH, stirring after half the time, until thickened (2 to 4 min.). Pour sauce over meat.

Honey-Smoked Pork Tenderloin

Autumn Squash With Savory Pork

4 servings
60 minutes

Autumn Squash With Savory Pork

Tantalizing pork served in acorn squash.

2	med. acorn squash, cut in half		½ tsp.	*(2 mL)* salt
½ c.	*(125 mL)* water		½ tsp.	*(2 mL)* marjoram leaves
½ c.	*(125 mL)* butter or margarine		½ tsp.	*(2 mL)* pepper
1 c.	*(250 mL)* (2 med.) chopped onions		½ tsp.	*(2 mL)* thyme leaves
1 c.	*(250 mL)* (2 stalks) sliced ¼" *(0,5 cm)* celery		2 c.	*(500 mL)* cubed 1" *(2,5 cm)* rye bread
¾ lb.	*(350 g)* pork tenderloin, cut into 2 × ½" *(5 × 1 cm)* strips		1 tbsp.	*(15 mL)* grated orange peel

Heat oven to 375°F *(190°C)*. Place squash in 13 × 9" *(33 × 23 cm)* baking pan; pour water in bottom of pan. Cover; bake for 45 to 50 min. or until fork tender. Meanwhile, in 10" *(25 cm)* skillet melt butter until sizzling. Add remaining ingredients *except* rye bread and orange peel. Cook over med. high heat, stirring occasionally, until meat is fork tender (15 to 20 min.). Stir in rye bread and orange peel. Continue cooking, stirring occasionally, until heated through (3 to 4 min.). To serve, divide mixture evenly among baked squash.

Microwave Directions: Place squash in 13 × 9" *(33 × 23 cm)* baking dish. Omit ½ c. *(125 mL)* water. Cover; microwave on HIGH, rearranging after half the time, until squash is tender. Let stand 5 min. Meanwhile, in medium bowl combine remaining ingredients *except* rye bread and orange peel. Cover; microwave on HIGH, stirring after half the time, until meat is no longer pink (8 to 10 min.). Stir in rye bread and orange peel. Cover; microwave until heated through (2 to 3 min.).

6 servings
40 minutes

Herb Roasted Pork Casserole

Pork roast dinner in a hearty casserole.

½ c.	*(125 mL)* butter or margarine		2 c.	*(500 mL)* crumbly style herb seasoned stuffing
3 c.	*(750 mL)* (4 med.) new red potatoes, cut into 1" *(2,5 cm)* pieces		1 c.	*(250 mL)* (2 stalks) sliced ½" *(1 cm)* celery
1 lb.	*(450 g)* pork roast, cut into 1" *(2,5 cm)* pieces		1 c.	*(250 mL)* chopped red onion
½ tsp.	*(2 mL)* salt		½ c.	*(125 mL)* apple juice
½ tsp.	*(2 mL)* crushed rosemary leaves		¼ c.	*(50 mL)* chopped fresh parsley
½ tsp.	*(2 mL)* pepper		2	med. ripe tomatoes, cut into 1" *(2,5 cm)* pieces
½ tsp.	*(2 mL)* sage			
1 tsp.	*(5 mL)* minced fresh garlic			

In deep 10" *(25 cm)* skillet melt ¼ c. *(50 mL)* butter until sizzling; add potatoes. Cook over med. high heat, stirring occasionally, until potatoes are lightly browned (10 to 15 min.). Add pork, salt, rosemary, pepper, sage and garlic. Continue cooking, stirring occasionally, until meat is browned (10 to 12 min.). Reduce heat to med. Add remaining ¼ c. *(50 mL)* butter and remaining ingredients *except* parsley and tomatoes. Cover; cook until heated through (7 to 9 min.). Stir in parsley and tomatoes. Cover; let stand 2 min. or until heated through.

Microwave Directions: In 3-qt. *(3-L)* casserole melt ¼ c. *(50 mL)* butter on HIGH (50 to 60 sec.). Stir in potatoes, pork, salt, rosemary, pepper, sage and garlic. Cover; microwave on HIGH, stirring after half the time, until pork is no longer pink (10 to 13 min.). Stir in remaining ¼ c. *(50 mL)* butter and remaining ingredients *except* parsley and tomatoes. Cover; microwave on HIGH, stirring after half the time, until heated through (3 to 5 min.). Stir in parsley and tomatoes. Cover; let stand 2 min. or until heated through.

Country Ham Steak With Glazed Apples

4 servings
20 minutes

Country Ham Steak With Glazed Apples

Brown sugar-glazed apples add heartwarming goodness to ham steak.

3 tbsp.   *(45 mL)* butter or margarine
¼ c.   *(50 mL)* firmly packed brown sugar
2 tbsp.   *(30 mL)* country-style Dijon mustard

2 c.   *(500 mL)* (2 med.) cored, sliced
    ⅛" *(0,2 cm)* tart apples
1 lb.   *(450 g) (½" [1 cm]* thick) ham steak

In 10" *(25 cm)* skillet melt butter until sizzling; stir in brown sugar and mustard. Add apples. Cook over med. heat, stirring occasionally, until apples are crisply tender (5 to 7 min.). Place ham steak in same skillet, arranging apples on ham steak. Cover; continue cooking until ham steak is heated through (5 to 7 min.).

Microwave Directions: In 13 × 9" *(33 × 23 cm)* baking dish melt butter on HIGH (30 to 45 sec.). Stir in brown sugar and mustard. Add apples. Place ham steak in baking dish, arranging apples on ham steak. Cover; microwave on HIGH, stirring apples after half the time, until apples are crisply tender and ham steak is heated through (5 to 8 min.).

6 servings
1 hour 30 minutes

Ham n' Cheese Scalloped Potatoes

This heartland favorite, scalloped potatoes, bakes in a rich Cheddar cheese sauce.

6 c.   *(1,5 L)* (4 large) thinly sliced potatoes
4 c.   *(1 L)* cubed 1" *(2,5 cm)* cooked ham
1 c.   *(250 mL)* (1 med.) thinly sliced onion,
    separated into rings
¼ c.   *(50 mL)* butter or margarine
⅓ c.   *(75 mL)* all-purpose flour

1 tsp.   *(5 mL)* dry mustard
½ tsp.   *(2 mL)* pepper
2 c.   *(500 mL)* milk
3 c.   *(750 mL)* (12 oz.) *(340 g)* shredded
    Cheddar cheese
2 tbsp.   *(30 mL)* chopped fresh chives

Heat oven to 350°F *(180°C)*. In 13 × 9" *(33 × 23 cm)* baking pan layer potatoes, ham and onion. In 2-qt. *(2-L)* saucepan melt butter until sizzling. Stir in flour, mustard and pepper. Cook over med. heat, stirring constantly, until smooth and bubbly (1 min.). Add milk. Continue cooking, stirring occasionally, until sauce is thickened (2 to 3 min.). Stir in cheese until melted (3 to 4 min.). Pour sauce over potatoes; sprinkle with chives. Bake for 60 to 75 min. or until bubbly and potatoes are fork tender.

Microwave Directions: In 13 × 9" *(33 × 23 cm)* baking dish layer potatoes, ham and onion. In 2-qt. *(2-L)* casserole melt butter on HIGH (60 to 70 sec.). Stir in flour, mustard and pepper. Microwave on HIGH until bubbly (30 to 45 sec.). Add milk. Microwave on HIGH, stirring after half the time, until sauce is thickened (4½ to 6 min.). Stir in cheese until melted. Pour sauce over potatoes. Cover with plastic wrap. Microwave on HIGH, stirring every 10 min., until bubbly and potatoes are fork tender (20 to 26 min.). Let stand 5 min. Sprinkle with chives.

6 servings
35 minutes

Spicy Sausage & Potatoes in a Skillet

*Spicy sausage and new red potatoes are pan-fried until crispy,
then cooked with green pepper and onion.*

1½ lb.   *(675 g)* (6 links) mild Italian sausage,
        cut into 1" *(2,5 cm)* pieces
10   small new red potatoes, quartered
½ tsp.   *(2 mL)* pepper
½ tsp.   *(2 mL)* thyme leaves

1 c.   *(250 mL)* sliced ⅛" *(0,2 cm)* red onion
¼ c.   *(50 mL)* chopped fresh parsley
1   green pepper, cut into
      1" *(2,5 cm)* pieces

In 10" *(25 cm)* skillet combine sausage, potatoes, pepper and thyme. Cook over med. high heat, stirring occasionally, until potatoes are browned (10 to 12 min.). Reduce heat to med. low. Cover; cook until potatoes are tender (8 to 10 min.). Stir in remaining ingredients. Continue cooking, uncovered, until vegetables are crisply tender (4 to 5 min.).

Microwave Directions: In 3-qt. *(3-L)* casserole combine sausage, potatoes, pepper and thyme. Cover; microwave on HIGH, stirring after half the time, until potatoes are tender (9 to 11 min.). Stir in remaining ingredients. Cover; microwave on HIGH until vegetables are crisply tender (4 to 6 min.).

---

4 servings
30 minutes

Bratwursts & Sauerkraut Skillet Supper

*Taste the unique flavor that apple juice gives
to bratwursts and sauerkraut in this skillet supper.*

6   bratwurst sausages
1 c.   *(250 mL)* apple juice
2 c.   *(500 mL)* sauerkraut, drained

2   med. green peppers, sliced into
      ¼" *(0,5 cm)* rings
2 tsp.   *(10 mL)* caraway seed

In 10" *(25 cm)* skillet place bratwursts. Cook over med. high heat, turning occasionally, until browned (5 min.). Reduce heat to med.; add apple juice. Cover; cook until fork tender (10 to 12 min.). Stir in remaining ingredients. Continue cooking, uncovered, until heated through (4 to 5 min.).

Microwave Directions: In 13 × 9" *(33 × 23 cm)* baking dish place bratwursts and apple juice. Cover; microwave on HIGH, turning bratwursts after half the time, until almost done (5 to 8 min.). Add remaining ingredients. Cover; microwave on HIGH until heated through and bratwursts are no longer pink (5 to 8 min.).

Spicy Sausage & Potatoes in a Skillet

Orange Glazed Stuffed Crown Roast

6 servings
2 hours 50 minutes

Serve this elegant spinach-stuffed roast when company's coming.

	Crown roast of lamb (3 to 4 lb.)
	(1,4 to 1,8 kg)
	Salt and pepper
¼ c.	*(50 mL)* butter or margarine
6-oz.	*(180-mL)* can frozen orange juice concentrate, thawed
2 tbsp.	*(30 mL)* Madeira wine, optional

Stuffing

2 c.	*(500 mL)* dried crumbly style herb seasoned stuffing
½ c.	*(125 mL)* butter or margarine, melted
2	*(10-oz.)* *(300-g)* pkg. frozen chopped spinach, thawed, drained
2	slices bacon, cut into ½" *(1 cm)* pieces
2	eggs, slightly beaten
½ tsp.	*(2 mL)* dry mustard
¼ tsp.	*(1 mL)* salt
¼ tsp.	*(1 mL)* pepper

Heat oven to 325°F *(160°C)*. Line shallow roasting pan with aluminum foil. Place roast, bone end up, on rack in roasting pan. Protect ends of bones with aluminum foil. Season with salt and pepper. Bake roast for 30 to 35 min. per lb. *(450 g)* or until meat thermometer reaches 160°F *(71°C)* (Medium). Meanwhile, in 1-qt. *(1-L)* saucepan combine ¼ c. *(50 mL)* butter, orange juice concentrate and wine. Cook over med. heat until butter is melted (4 to 5 min.). One hour before roast is done begin brushing orange juice mixture over roast every 15 min. and

prepare stuffing. In large bowl combine all stuffing ingredients; place in 1½-qt. *(1,5-L)* casserole. Bake in same oven for 35 to 40 min. or until heated through. Let roast stand 15 min. before carving. Stuff center of roast with stuffing and serve with warm orange juice mixture.

Tip: For crisp bacon, precook before adding to stuffing.

To Prepare Crown Roast:

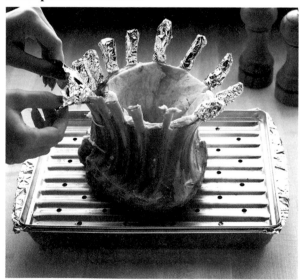

1. Line shallow roasting pan with aluminum foil. Place roast, bone end up, on rack in roasting pan. Protect ends of bones with aluminum foil.

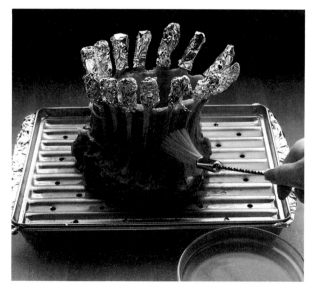

2. One hour before roast is done begin brushing orange juice mixture over roast every 15 min.

Orange Glazed Stuffed Crown Roast

Sausage-Stuffed Lamb Chops

4 to 6 servings
1 hour 20 minutes

Sausage-Stuffed Lamb Chops

The pairing of lamb and Italian sausage provides the perfect balance of savory flavors.

½ lb.	*(225 g)* mild Italian sausage
½ c.	*(125 mL)* (1 med.) finely chopped onion
1 c.	*(250 mL)* fresh bread crumbs
¼ c.	*(50 mL)* chopped fresh parsley
1 tsp.	*(5 mL)* thyme leaves
½ tsp.	*(2 mL)* marjoram leaves
½ tsp.	*(2 mL)* coarsely ground pepper

½ tsp.	*(2 mL)* grated orange peel
½ tsp.	*(2 mL)* minced fresh garlic
¼ c.	*(50 mL)* butter or margarine
½ tsp.	*(2 mL)* thyme leaves
½ tsp.	*(2 mL)* marjoram leaves
6	(2") *(5 cm)* double rib lamb chops, with 1½" *(3,5 cm)* pocket cut in loin side

Heat oven to 350°F *(180°C)*. In 10" *(25 cm)* skillet cook sausage and onion over med. high heat, stirring occasionally, until sausage is browned (7 to 9 min.). Drain off fat. Stir in remaining ingredients *except* butter, ½ tsp. *(2 mL)* thyme, ½ tsp. *(2 mL)* marjoram and lamb chops. Set aside. In same skillet melt butter until sizzling; stir in remaining ingredients *except* lamb chops. Add lamb chops. Cook over med. high heat until browned (2 to 3 min. on each side). Stuff each lamb chop with about ¼ c. *(50 mL)* filling. Place in 13 × 9" *(33 × 23 cm)* baking pan. Bake for 30 to 40 min. or until meat thermometer reaches 160°F *(71°C)* (Medium).

Microwave Directions: In 2-qt. *(2-L)* casserole combine sausage and onion. Cover; microwave on HIGH, stirring after half the time, until sausage is cooked (4 to 5½ min.). Drain off fat. Stir in remaining ingredients *except* butter, ½ tsp. *(2 mL)* thyme, ½ tsp. *(2 mL)* marjoram and lamb chops. Set aside. In 13 × 9" *(33 × 23 cm)* baking dish melt butter on HIGH (50 to 60 sec.). Stir in remaining ingredients *except* lamb chops. Stuff each lamb chop with about ¼ c. *(50 mL)* filling. Place in 13 × 9" *(33 × 23 cm)* dish; turn lamb chops over to coat each side with butter. Cover; microwave on HIGH, turning pan ¼ turn after half the time, 5 min. Reduce power to MEDIUM (50% power); microwave, turning lamb chops over and rearranging after half the time, until meat thermometer reaches 160°F *(71°C)* (10 to 15 min.).

Lamb	Internal Cooking Temperature
Rare	140°F *(60°C)*
Medium	160°F *(71°C)*
Well	170°F *(76°C)*

Country Vegetable & Lamb Kabobs

6 servings
1 hour 30 minutes

Leg of Lamb Roasted With Rosemary

Serve lamb with mint jelly, fresh peas and new potatoes for a traditional meal.

3 to 4 lb. *(1,4 to 1,8 kg)* leg of lamb
2 tbsp. *(30 mL)* minced fresh garlic
2 tsp. *(10 mL)* rosemary leaves, crushed

1 tsp. *(5 mL)* salt
½ tsp. *(2 mL)* pepper

Heat oven to 350°F *(180°C)*. Place lamb, fat side up, on rack in roasting pan. In small bowl stir together remaining ingredients. Spread over lamb. Bake for 60 to 90 min. or until meat thermometer reaches 160°F *(71°C)* (Medium).

Lamb	Internal Cooking Temperature
Rare	140°F *(60°C)*
Medium	160°F *(71°C)*
Well	170°F *(76°C)*

4 servings
60 minutes

Country Vegetable & Lamb Kabobs

A zesty marinade makes these colorful lamb kabobs irresistible.

Marinade
¼ c. *(50 mL)* butter or margarine
⅓ c. *(75 mL)* lemon juice
1 tbsp. *(15 mL)* sugar
1 tsp. *(5 mL)* thyme leaves
¾ tsp. *(3 mL)* salt
¼ tsp. *(1 mL)* oregano leaves
¼ tsp. *(1 mL)* pepper
2 tbsp. *(30 mL)* finely chopped onion
1 tsp. *(5 mL)* hot pepper sauce
½ tsp. *(2 mL)* minced fresh garlic

Kabobs
1 lb. *(450 g)* lamb, cut into about 32 (1") *(2,5 cm)* pieces
8 small mushrooms
8 cherry tomatoes
1 small green pepper, cut into 8 (1") *(2,5 cm)* pieces
1 small summer squash, cut into 8 (1") *(2,5 cm)* pieces
4 (12") *(30 cm)* metal skewers

Prepare grill placing coals to one side; heat until coals are ash white. Make aluminum foil drip pan; place opposite coals. In small saucepan combine all marinade ingredients. Cook over med. heat, stirring occasionally, until butter melts and mixture comes to a full boil (8 to 10 min.); remove from heat. Let cool 5 min. Stir in lamb pieces; set aside. Let marinate 15 min. To assemble kabobs on metal skewers, alternate lamb pieces with mushrooms, cherry tomatoes, green pepper and summer squash. Place kabobs on grill over drip pan. Grill, turning occasionally, until lamb is fork tender or desired doneness (10 to 15 min.). Heat remaining marinade; brush over kabobs before serving.

Broiling Directions: Prepare kabobs as directed left. Heat broiler. Place kabobs on greased broiler pan 4 to 5" *(10 to 12,5 cm)* from heat. Broil until brown (5 to 7 min.). Turn, brush with marinade; continue broiling until lamb is fork tender or desired doneness (5 to 7 min.). Heat remaining marinade; brush over kabobs before serving.

Microwave Directions: *Use 4 (12")* (30 cm) *wooden skewers.* Prepare kabobs as directed left. Place kabobs in *12 × 8" (30 × 20 cm)* baking dish. Microwave on HIGH 5 min. Turn kabobs over; brush with marinade. Microwave on HIGH until lamb is fork tender or desired doneness (4 to 5 min.). Heat remaining marinade; brush over kabobs before serving.

6 to 8 servings
1 day

Marinated Herb Veal Roast

A marinade with a blend of herbs imparts marvelous flavor to roasted veal.

Marinade

¼ c.	*(50 mL)*	olive or vegetable oil
1 tbsp.	*(15 mL)*	white wine vinegar
1 tbsp.	*(15 mL)*	sugar
1 tsp.	*(5 mL)*	basil leaves
1 tsp.	*(5 mL)*	thyme leaves
¾ tsp.	*(3 mL)*	salt
¼ tsp.	*(1 mL)*	pepper
2 tbsp.	*(30 mL)*	chopped fresh parsley
2 tsp.	*(10 mL)*	minced fresh garlic

2 to 3 lb.	*(1 to 1,4 kg))*	boneless shoulder veal roast

Sauce

½ c.	*(125 mL)*	chopped fresh mushrooms
½ c.	*(125 mL)*	chopped red pepper
1 tsp.	*(5 mL)*	grated lemon peel
2 tbsp.	*(30 mL)*	chopped fresh chives

In Dutch oven stir together oil and vinegar. Stir in remaining marinade ingredients *except* roast. Place roast in marinade; turn to coat all sides with herbs and oil. Cover; refrigerate 12 hr. or overnight. Heat oven to 350°F *(180°C)*. Cover; bake roast in marinade for 45 min. Uncover; continue baking, basting with pan juices occasionally, for 1 to 1½ hr. or until meat thermometer reaches 160°F *(71°C)* (Medium). *Reserve pan juices;* skim off fat. In 1-qt. *(1-L)* saucepan combine ⅓ c. *(75 mL)* reserved pan juices and all sauce ingredients *except*

chives. Cook over med. high heat until sauce comes to a full boil; boil 2 min. Stir in chives. Serve over carved roast.

Veal	Internal Cooking Temperature
Rare	140°F *(60°C)*
Medium	160°F *(71°C)*
Well	170°F *(76°C)*

6 servings
20 minutes

Veal With Artichokes & Mushrooms

A twist of fresh lemon flavors this quick, elegant entrée.

¼ c.	*(50 mL)*	all-purpose flour
¼ c.	*(50 mL)*	freshly grated Parmesan cheese
¼ tsp.	*(1 mL)*	salt
¼ tsp.	*(1 mL)*	pepper
6	*(¼" [0,5 cm])*	boneless veal cutlets
2		eggs, slightly beaten
¼ c.	*(50 mL)*	butter or margarine
2 tbsp.	*(30 mL)*	lemon juice
½ c.	*(125 mL)*	whipping cream

1 c.	*(250 mL)*	sliced ¼" *(0,5 cm)* fresh mushrooms
9-oz.	*(270-g)*	pkg. frozen artichoke hearts, thawed, drained
2 tbsp.	*(30 mL)*	freshly grated Parmesan cheese
¼ tsp.	*(1 mL)*	salt
		Dash cayenne pepper
2 tbsp.	*(30 mL)*	lemon juice
2 tbsp.	*(30 mL)*	chopped fresh parsley

In 9" *(23 cm)* pie pan stir together flour, ¼ c. *(50 mL)* Parmesan cheese, ¼ tsp. *(1 mL)* salt and pepper. Dip cutlets in eggs; lightly coat both sides of cutlets with flour mixture. In 10" *(25 cm)* skillet melt butter over med. heat until sizzling; stir in 2 tbsp. *(30 mL)* lemon juice. Place 3 cutlets in melted butter and lemon juice; fry until browned (3 min. on each side). Remove cutlets

to serving platter; keep warm. Repeat with remaining cutlets. In same skillet with drippings and brown particles stir in whipping cream. Add remaining ingredients *except* parsley. Cook over med. heat, stirring occasionally, until sauce is slightly thickened and artichokes are heated through (4 to 6 min.). Stir in parsley. Serve over cutlets.

Veal With Artichokes & Mushrooms

How To: Barbecue or Grill

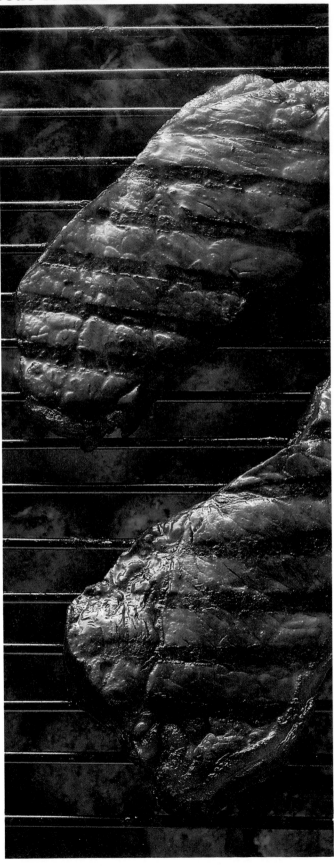

Many types of grills are available; the most common include:

- round covered kettle
- rectangular or square cooker with a hinged lid
- open brazier
- gas or electric grill

All work well and apply even heat to the food being cooked when properly used.

To Produce Best Results with a Grill:

Charcoal briquettes are most commonly used for barbecuing. All recipes in this cookbook were tested using charcoal briquettes and a gas grill. Other fuels available include mesquite, wood, hardwood charcoal and smoking or flavor chips. Each imparts a unique flavor to the cooked food.

To determine the number of charcoal briquettes needed, spread a single layer of charcoal briquettes 1" *(2,5 cm)* beyond the edge of the food for small cuts of meat. For longer cooking foods, use additional charcoal briquettes. Stack the charcoal briquettes in a pyramid shape to provide proper ventilation.

Ignite briquettes 30 to 40 minutes before you intend to cook. Be sure to open any vents on the grill. Preheat gas grill according to manufacturer's directions. For indirect grilling on a dual control gas grill, use single control, opposite meat placement.

To Ignite Briquettes:

Use a fluid starter according to package directions. Ignite briquettes with matches or with an electric starter.

The coals are ready when they have burned to an ash white color.

To Extinguish Coals:

Immediately after cooking, cover the grill and close all vents to extinguish the coals. Charcoal briquettes are reusable if thoroughly dried out. When relighting used charcoal briquettes, combine them with fresh charcoal briquettes and follow directions above.

There are two basic cooking methods used with the recipes in this cookbook: indirect and direct. The **indirect** method is a slower cooking method that minimizes flare-ups if dripping occurs. It is, therefore, the recommended method when sauces or marinades are applied. Indirect cooking is also used for large pieces of poultry, meat, fish or fatty foods to achieve more even cooking. Often the grill is covered to help distribute heat during cooking. The **direct** cooking method is faster since more intense heat is provided. Faster cooking meats or thin pieces of meat, poultry or fish are usually grilled over direct heat.

To Arrange Coals for Indirect Cooking:

1. Prepare grill placing coals to one side; heat until coals are ash white. Make aluminum foil drip pan; place opposite coals.

To Arrange Coals for Direct Cooking:

2. Prepare grill; heat until coals are ash white.

To Make Aluminum Foil Drip Pan: (Aluminum foil drip pans can be purchased ready-made.)

1. Tear off two sheets of heavy-duty aluminum foil that are 3" *(7,5 cm)* longer than the food to be grilled. With the two sheets together, fold all sides inward about 2" *(5 cm)*.

2. Turn aluminum foil over. Score aluminum foil about 1" *(2,5 cm)* from edge. At corners, score diagonally to edge.

3. Fold edges up and pinch corners.

4. Fold corners flat against sides. Bring all sides up to form pan.

FISH & SEAFOOD

Imagine a lazy summer day in the country. The sun is high and the fish are biting. So, you gather the fishing gear and head for the creek. But whether caught at the creek or selected at the market, nothing beats the lure of fresh fish and seafood cooked to perfection.

From virtually every part of this vast continent — the clear, inland lakes and streams, the icy-cold depths of the North Pacific, the rugged, rock-lined waters of the Atlantic — comes a bounty of fish and seafood. It's a rich and varied harvest, from sweet and tender scallops and shrimp to the distinctively robust taste of salmon.

Fish is delicious baked with seasoned stuffing or charcoal-grilled and dressed with a tangy herb sauce. To capture the delicate, mild flavor of fish, sauté it and serve with a simple lemon-butter mixture. Or perhaps you're hungry for the heartiness of old-fashioned country cooking. Invite a few friends in for a casual fish supper featuring light, flaky fillets coated in a special batter and fried to a crispy golden brown. No matter how it's prepared, fish is a delightfully versatile main course for family and company meals.

Seaside Harbor Dinner

4 servings
35 minutes

A hearty and flavorful fish and vegetable dinner in a skillet.

¼ c.	(50 mL) butter or margarine
6	small new red potatoes, quartered
3	stalks celery, sliced 1" (2,5 cm)
3	carrots, sliced 1" (2,5 cm)
½ tsp.	(2 mL) salt
½ tsp.	(2 mL) dry mustard

¼ tsp.	(1 mL) pepper
1 lb.	(450 g) fresh or frozen perch fillets, thawed, drained
1	med. ripe tomato, cut into 1" (2,5 cm) pieces

In 10" *(25 cm)* skillet melt butter until sizzling; add remaining ingredients *except* fish and tomato. Cover; cook over med. high heat, stirring occasionally, until vegetables are browned and crisply tender (12 to 15 min.). Reduce heat to med. Place fish in same skillet, arranging vegetables on top of fish. Sprinkle with tomato. Cover; cook until fish flakes with a fork (5 to 7 min.).

Microwave Directions: In 13 × 9" *(33 × 23 cm)* baking dish melt butter on HIGH (50 to 60 sec.). Stir in remaining ingredients *except* fish and tomato. Cover; microwave on HIGH, stirring after half the time, until vegetables are crisply tender (9 to 11 min.). Place fish in same baking dish, arranging vegetables on top of fish. Sprinkle with tomato. Cover; microwave on HIGH, turning after half the time, until fish flakes with a fork (5 to 7 min.).

Fishermen's Supper

4 servings
30 minutes

*Garlic butter complements the simple combination
of sole, zucchini and red onion.*

1 lb.	(450 g) fresh or frozen sole fillets, thawed, drained
1 c.	(250 mL) (1 med.) sliced ⅛" (0,2 cm) zucchini
1 c.	(250 mL) sliced ⅛" (0,2 cm) red onion, separated into rings

¼ c.	(50 mL) butter or margarine, melted
¼ tsp.	(1 mL) salt
¼ tsp.	(1 mL) pepper
1 tsp.	(5 mL) minced fresh garlic
2 tbsp.	(30 mL) chopped fresh parsley

Heat oven to 375°F *(190°C)*. Place fish in 9" *(23 cm)* sq. baking pan. Layer zucchini and red onion evenly over fish. In small bowl stir together remaining ingredients *except* parsley; pour over vegetables. Cover; bake for 20 to 25 min. or until vegetables are crisply tender and fish flakes with a fork. Sprinkle with parsley.

Microwave Directions: Place fish in 9" *(23 cm)* sq. baking dish. Place zucchini and red onion evenly over fish. In small bowl stir together remaining ingredients *except* parsley; pour over vegetables. Cover; microwave on HIGH, turning dish ¼ turn after half the time, until fish flakes with a fork (8 to 10 min.). Sprinkle with parsley.

Seaside Harbor Dinner

Crunchy Fish & Potatoes

6 servings
20 minutes

Pan-Fried Cornmeal Batter Fish

The catch of the day is dipped in a crispy cornmeal batter and pan-fried.

½ c.	*(125 mL)* all-purpose flour	
½ c.	*(125 mL)* milk	
1	egg	
1 tbsp.	*(15 mL)* sugar	
½ tsp.	*(2 mL)* salt	
½ tsp.	*(2 mL)* paprika	

¼ tsp.	*(1 mL)* cayenne pepper
¼ tsp.	*(1 mL)* oregano leaves
½ c.	*(125 mL)* yellow cornmeal
2 lb.	*(900 g)* fish fillets, steaks or pan-dressed fish, thawed, drained
½ c.	*(125 mL)* vegetable oil

In 9" *(23 cm)* pie pan stir together all ingredients *except* cornmeal, fish and oil. On waxed paper place cornmeal. Coat both sides of fish with cornmeal, then dip into batter. In 10" *(25 cm)* skillet heat oil until hot.

Place 3 to 4 fish in hot oil. Cook over med. heat until golden brown (3 to 4 min.). Turn; continue cooking until golden brown and fish flakes with a fork (2 to 3 min.). Repeat with remaining fish.

4 servings
60 minutes

Crunchy Fish & Potatoes

Perch fillets and potatoes team up in the same pan for a tasty dinner.

⅓ c.	*(75 mL)* butter or margarine
2 c.	*(500 mL)* (2 med.) sliced ¼" *(0,5 cm)* potatoes
¾ c.	*(200 mL)* crushed buttery crackers
1 tsp.	*(5 mL)* paprika

½ tsp.	*(2 mL)* garlic powder
¼ tsp.	*(1 mL)* salt
2 tbsp.	*(30 mL)* chopped fresh parsley
1 lb.	*(450 g)* fresh or frozen perch fillets, thawed, drained

Heat oven to 350°F *(180°C)*. In 13 × 9" *(33 × 23 cm)* baking pan melt butter in oven (5 to 7 min.). Add potato slices; stir to coat. Cover with aluminum foil; bake for 20 to 25 min. or until potato slices are fork tender. Meanwhile, in 9" *(23 cm)* pie pan stir together remaining ingredients *except* perch fillets. Spoon potatoes to one side of baking pan. Dip perch fillets into melted butter that potatoes were baked in, then coat with crumb mixture. Place fillets, to one side, in same baking pan with potatoes. Sprinkle fish and potatoes with remaining crumb mixture. Bake for 20 to 30 min. or until fish flakes with a fork.

Microwave Directions: In 13 × 9" *(33 × 23 cm)* baking dish melt butter on HIGH (60 to 70 sec.). Add potato slices; stir to coat. Cover; microwave on HIGH, stirring after half the time, until potato slices are fork tender (5 to 6 min.). Meanwhile, in 9" *(23 cm)* pie pan stir together remaining ingredients *except* perch fillets. Spoon potatoes to one side of baking dish. Dip perch fillets into melted butter that potatoes were baked in, then coat with crumb mixture. Place fillets, to one side, in same baking dish with potatoes. Sprinkle fish and potatoes with remaining crumb mixture. Microwave on HIGH until fish flakes with a fork (7 to 9 min.).

Codfish Cakes With Green Onions & Dill

6 cod cakes
20 minutes

Codfish cakes are fried until crispy and golden brown to provide a taste of the New England coast.

1 lb.	*(450 g)* fresh or frozen cod fillets, thawed, drained	½ tsp.	*(2 mL)* salt
2 c.	*(500 mL)* coarse fresh bread crumbs	¼ tsp.	*(1 mL)* dill weed
¼ c.	*(50 mL)* chopped green onions	¼ tsp.	*(1 mL)* pepper
2	eggs, slightly beaten	1 tbsp.	*(15 mL)* lemon juice
		¼ c.	*(50 mL)* butter or margarine

Flake cod fillets apart with fork or mallet. In medium bowl stir together flaked cod and remaining ingredients *except* butter. Form into 6 (3") *(7,5 cm)* patties. In 10" *(25 cm)* skillet melt butter until sizzling. Place 3 patties in same skillet. Cook over med. high heat until golden brown (4 to 5 min.). Turn; continue cooking until browned and fish flakes with a fork (3 to 4 min.). Repeat with remaining patties.

Microwave Directions: In medium bowl melt butter on HIGH (50 to 60 sec.). Flake cod fillets with fork or mallet. In same bowl stir together remaining ingredients and flaked cod. Form into 6 (3") *(7,5 cm)* patties; *sprinkle with paprika.* Place in 13 × 9" *(33 × 23 cm)* baking dish. Cover; microwave on HIGH, turning dish ½ turn after half the time, until fish flakes with a fork (5 to 7 min.).

Vegetable Garden Fish Kabobs

6 kabobs
45 minutes

*Serve with a fresh spinach salad, sourdough bread
and tall glasses of iced tea for a quick, relaxing summer meal.*

1 lb.	*(450 g)* fish fillets (cod or haddock), cut into 1" *(2,5 cm)* cubes	6	(12") *(30 cm)* metal skewers
1	med. zucchini, cut into ½" *(1 cm)* pieces	**Sauce**	
12	cherry tomatoes	½ c.	*(125 mL)* butter or margarine, melted
12	med. fresh mushrooms	¼ c.	*(50 mL)* teriyaki sauce or soy sauce
1	med. green pepper, cored, cut into 1" *(2,5 cm)* pieces	2 tbsp.	*(30 mL)* lemon juice

Prepare grill, placing coals to one side; heat until coals are ash white. Make aluminum foil drip pan; place opposite coals. Alternate cubes of fish and vegetables on skewers. In small bowl stir together all sauce ingredients; brush over kabobs. Place kabobs on grill over drip pan. Grill, turning occasionally and basting with sauce, 10 to 20 min. or until fish flakes with a fork. Serve with remaining sauce.

Microwave Directions: *Use 6 (12")* (30 cm) *wooden skewers.* Assemble kabobs and prepare sauce as directed left. Place kabobs in 13 × 9" *(33 × 23 cm)* baking dish or large microwave-safe cookie sheet. Cover; microwave on HIGH, turning and basting with sauce after half the time, until fish flakes with a fork (8 to 10 min.). Serve with remaining sauce.

Vegetable Garden Fish Kabobs

Lemon Sole & Carrot Bundles

4 servings
40 minutes

Fish fillets are rolled and stuffed with sweet, tender carrots and topped with the country goodness of herb stuffing.

4	med. carrots, cut into 5 × ¼" *(12,5 × 0,5 cm)* strips	½ tsp.	*(2 mL)* salt
1½ c.	*(375 mL)* crumbly style herb seasoned stuffing	¼ tsp.	*(1 mL)* pepper
⅓ c.	*(75 mL)* butter or margarine, melted	2 tbsp.	*(30 mL)* lemon juice
		1 lb.	*(450 g)* fresh or frozen sole fillets, thawed, drained

Heat oven to 375°F *(190°C)*. In 2-qt. *(2-L)* saucepan place carrots; add enough water to cover. Bring to a full boil. Cook over med. heat until carrots are crisply tender (6 to 8 min.). Meanwhile, in small bowl stir together remaining ingredients *except* fish; set aside. Separate fillets and divide carrots equally among fillets. Wrap each fillet around each portion of carrots. Place fillets, seam side down, in 9" *(23 cm)* sq. baking pan. Sprinkle with stuffing mixture. Cover; bake for 10 min. Uncover; continue baking for 8 to 10 min. or until fish flakes with a fork.

Microwave Directions: In 2-qt. *(2-L)* bowl combine ¼ c. *(50 mL)* water and carrots. Cover; microwave on HIGH, stirring after half the time, until crisply tender (5 to 6 min.). Meanwhile, in small bowl stir together remaining ingredients *except* fish; set aside. Separate fillets and divide carrots equally among fillets. Wrap each fillet around each portion of carrots. Place fillets, seam side down, in 1½-qt. *(1,5-L)* casserole. Sprinkle with stuffing mixture. Microwave on HIGH until fish flakes with a fork (7 to 9 min.).

To Wrap Fillets:

1. Separate fillets and divide carrots equally among fillets.

2. Wrap each fillet around each portion of carrots. Place fillets, seam side down, in 9" *(23 cm)* sq. baking pan.

Lemon Sole & Carrot Bundles

6 servings
1 hour 5 minutes

Sole Fillets Stuffed With Cheese

Fresh sole fillets are stuffed with cheese and tomato, and baked until the cheese is creamy and melted.

⅓ c.	*(75 mL)* butter or margarine	1	large ripe tomato, cut into 6 slices
1½ tsp.	*(7 mL)* garlic powder	12	*(3 × 1½ × ¼”) (7,5 × 3,5 × 0,5 cm)* slices
1½ tsp.	*(7 mL)* basil leaves		Monterey Jack cheese
2 tbsp.	*(30 mL)* chopped green onions	2 tbsp.	*(30 mL)* grated Parmesan cheese
6	*(5 oz.) (140 g)* fresh sole fillets, each cut in half		

Heat oven to 350°F *(180°C)*. In 13 × 9” *(33 × 23 cm)* baking pan melt butter. Stir in garlic powder, basil and green onions. Dip both sides of sole fillet halves into melted seasoned butter. Set 6 sole fillet halves aside. Place remaining 6 sole fillet halves in same baking pan; layer *each* with 1 tomato slice and 2 cheese slices. Top each with a remaining sole fillet half. Sprinkle with Parmesan cheese. Bake for 25 to 35 min. or until fish flakes with a fork. To serve, spoon remaining butter in bottom of pan over sole fillets.

6 servings
30 minutes

Rainbow Trout With Crunchy Gazpacho

This chunky cold tomato and vegetable sauce, ladled over rainbow trout, presents glorious color and flavor.

Gazpacho

2 c.	*(500 mL)* (2 med.) ripe tomatoes, cut into ½” *(1 cm)* pieces
1 c.	*(250 mL)* (1 med.) peeled cucumber, cut into ½” *(1 cm)* pieces
1 c.	*(250 mL)* (1 med.) red or green pepper, cut into ½” *(1 cm)* pieces
1 c.	*(250 mL)* red onion, cut into ¼” *(0,5 cm)* pieces
¼ c.	*(50 mL)* chopped fresh parsley
¼ c.	*(50 mL)* olive or vegetable oil
½ tsp.	*(2 mL)* salt
½ tsp.	*(2 mL)* pepper
3 tbsp.	*(45 mL)* red wine vinegar
1 tbsp.	*(15 mL)* Worcestershire sauce
¼ tsp.	*(1 mL)* hot pepper sauce

Trout

¼ c.	*(50 mL)* butter or margarine
½ tsp.	*(2 mL)* minced fresh garlic
½ c.	*(125 mL)* chopped red onion
¼ c.	*(50 mL)* chopped fresh parsley
½ tsp.	*(2 mL)* salt
¼ tsp.	*(1 mL)* pepper
6	*(½ to ¾ lb.) (225 to 340 g)* pan-dressed rainbow trout

In medium bowl stir together all gazpacho ingredients. In 5-c. *(1,3-L)* blender container place about 2 c. *(500 mL)* mixture. Blend on high speed until saucy (30 to 45 sec.). Stir back into remaining gazpacho mixture; set aside. In 10” *(25 cm)* skillet melt butter and garlic until sizzling. Meanwhile, in small bowl stir together remaining trout ingredients *except* trout. Place about 2 tbsp. *(30 mL)* mixture in cavity of each trout. Place 3 trout in same skillet; cook over med. high heat, turning once, until fish flakes with a fork (4 to 5 min. on each side). Remove to serving platter; keep warm. Repeat with remaining trout. Spoon 1 c. *(250 mL)* sauce over trout; serve remaining sauce with trout.

Grill Directions: *Omit butter and garlic.* Prepare gazpacho as directed left. Prepare grill; heat until coals are ash white. Prepare trout as directed left. Brush trout with vegetable oil. Grill trout over medium hot coals until fish flakes with a fork (7 to 10 min. on each side). Remove to serving platter. Spoon 1 c. *(250 mL)* sauce over trout; serve remaining sauce with trout.

Rainbow Trout With Crunchy Gazpacho

Hearty Salmon Pie

A chunky, fresh tomato sauce is served over a rich seafood pie.

Crust

¼ c.	*(50 mL)* butter or margarine
¾ c.	*(200 mL) finely* crushed dried crumbly style herb seasoned stuffing

Filling

2 c.	*(500 mL)* crushed dried crumbly style herb seasoned stuffing
1 c.	*(250 mL) (4 oz.) (110 g)* shredded Cheddar cheese
1 c.	*(250 mL)* water
½ c.	*(125 mL)* milk
16-oz.	*(439-g)* can red salmon, drained, bones removed, flaked*
2	eggs
1 tsp.	*(5 mL)* instant chicken bouillon
½ tsp.	*(2 mL)* dry mustard
2 tbsp.	*(30 mL)* chopped fresh parsley
1 tbsp.	*(15 mL)* finely chopped onion

Sauce

⅓ c.	*(75 mL)* butter or margarine
2 tbsp.	*(30 mL)* cornstarch
1⅓ c.	*(325 mL)* water
1 tsp.	*(5 mL)* dill weed
½ tsp.	*(2 mL)* salt
2 c.	*(500 mL)* (2 med.) cubed ½" *(1 cm)* ripe tomatoes

Heat oven to 350°F *(180°C)*. In 3-qt. *(3-L)* saucepan melt ¼ c. *(50 mL)* butter. Stir in ¾ c. *(200 mL)* finely crushed stuffing. Press stuffing mixture on bottom and up sides of greased 9" *(23 cm)* pie pan; set aside. In same saucepan stir together all filling ingredients; spoon into crust. Bake for 50 to 55 min. or until heated through; let stand 10 min. Meanwhile, in 2-qt. *(2-L)* saucepan melt ⅓ c. *(75 mL)* butter. Stir in cornstarch. Stir in remaining sauce ingredients *except* tomatoes. Cook over med. heat, stirring occasionally, until mixture comes to a full boil (5 to 7 min.). Add tomatoes; boil 1 min. To serve, cut pie into 6 wedges; serve sauce over wedges.

*3 (6½-oz.) *(184-g)* cans tuna, drained, flaked, can be substituted for 16-oz. *(439-g)* can salmon.

Hearty Salmon Pie

Garden Zucchini & Shrimp (top)
Skillet Jambalaya (bottom)

8 servings
40 minutes

Skillet Jambalaya

Spicy rice simmers in a skillet with shrimp and garden vegetables.

1 c.	*(250 mL)* water
10¾-oz.	*(284-mL)* can chicken broth
1 tbsp.	*(15 mL)* chili powder
¾ tsp.	*(3 mL)* salt
½ tsp.	*(2 mL)* paprika
½ tsp.	*(2 mL)* pepper
2 tbsp.	*(30 mL)* vegetable oil
1 tsp.	*(5 mL)* minced fresh garlic
1 c.	*(250 mL)* uncooked long grain rice
10-oz.	*(280-g)* pkg. frozen deveined large shrimp, thawed, drained

½ lb.	*(225-g)* fresh or frozen fish fillets, thawed, drained
2	med. ripe tomatoes, cut into 1" *(2,5 cm)* pieces
1	med. green pepper, cut into 1" *(2,5 cm)* pieces
1 c.	*(250 mL)* sliced ½" *(1 cm)* green onions
¼ c.	*(50 mL)* chopped fresh parsley
10-oz.	*(350-g)* pkg. frozen peas, thawed, drained

In 10" *(25 cm)* skillet stir together water, chicken broth, chili powder, salt, paprika, pepper, oil and garlic. Bring to a full boil. Stir in rice. Cover; cook over med. low heat for 15 min. Stir in remaining ingredients *except* onions, parsley and peas. Continue cooking, uncovered, until liquid is absorbed and rice is tender (10 to 15 min.). Stir in remaining ingredients. Continue cooking until heated through (4 to 5 min.).

Microwave Directions: In 3-qt. *(3-L)* casserole stir together water, chicken broth, chili powder, salt, paprika, pepper, oil, garlic and rice. Cover; microwave on HIGH, stirring after half the time, until rice is just tender (15 to 20 min.). Stir in remaining ingredients *except* onions, parsley and peas. Cover; microwave on HIGH, stirring after half the time, until fish flakes with fork (7 to 9 min.). Add remaining ingredients. Cover; microwave on HIGH until heated through (2 to 3 min.). Let stand 5 min.

4 servings
30 minutes

Garden Zucchini & Shrimp

Dill and garlic add a light flavor to this shrimp skillet meal.

⅓ c.	*(75 mL)* butter or margarine
2 c.	*(500 mL)* (2 med.) sliced ¼" *(0,5 cm)* zucchini
¼ c.	*(50 mL)* chopped fresh parsley
20	med. fresh or frozen raw shrimp, shelled, deveined, rinsed
½ tsp.	*(2 mL)* dill weed

¼ tsp.	*(1 mL)* salt
2 tbsp.	*(30 mL)* chopped onion
1 tbsp.	*(15 mL)* lemon juice
½ tsp.	*(2 mL)* minced fresh garlic
	Hot cooked rice

In 10" *(25 cm)* skillet melt butter over med. heat (3 to 6 min.). Stir in remaining ingredients *except* rice. Cook over med. heat, stirring occasionally, until shrimp turn pink and zucchini is crisply tender (5 to 8 min.). To serve, spoon shrimp with zucchini and butter sauce over hot cooked rice.

Microwave Directions: In 12 × 8" *(30 × 20 cm)* baking dish melt butter on HIGH (60 to 70 sec.). Stir in remaining ingredients *except* rice. Cover; microwave on HIGH, stirring after half the time, until shrimp turn pink and zucchini is crisply tender (3½ to 5 min.). To serve, spoon shrimp with zucchini and butter sauce over hot cooked rice.

4 servings
30 minutes

Marmalade-Glazed Shrimp

Orange marmalade and toasted coconut beautifully complement the flavor of sautéed shrimp.

1 lb.	*(450 g)* (about 24 med.) fresh or frozen raw shrimp
¼ c.	*(50 mL)* butter or margarine
½ tsp.	*(2 mL)* ground ginger
¼ tsp.	*(1 mL)* salt
¼ tsp.	*(1 mL)* pepper

1 tsp.	*(5 mL)* minced fresh garlic
½ c.	*(125 mL)* orange marmalade
2 tsp.	*(10 mL)* prepared horseradish
¼ c.	*(50 mL)* flaked coconut, toasted

Peel and devein shrimp, leaving tail intact. (If shrimp is frozen, do not thaw; peel under running cold water.) In 10" *(25 cm)* skillet melt butter until sizzling. Stir in ginger, salt, pepper and garlic; add shrimp. Cook over med. heat, stirring occasionally, until shrimp turn pink (5 to 7 min.). In small bowl stir together marmalade and horseradish; stir into shrimp. Continue cooking, stirring occasionally, until heated through (3 to 4 min.). If desired, sprinkle with toasted coconut.

Microwave Directions: Peel and devein shrimp, leaving tail intact. (If shrimp is frozen, do not thaw; peel under running cold water.) In 2-qt. *(2-L)* casserole melt butter on HIGH (50 to 60 sec.). Stir in ginger, salt, pepper and garlic; add shrimp. Cover; microwave on HIGH, stirring every 2 min., until shrimp turn pink (4 to 6 min.)*. In small bowl stir together marmalade and horseradish; stir into shrimp. Microwave on HIGH, stirring after half the time, until heated through (1 to 1½ min.). If desired, sprinkle with toasted coconut.

*If using frozen shrimp, microwave on HIGH, stirring every 2 min., until shrimp turn pink (6½ to 8½ min.).

---

8 servings
1 hour 30 minutes

Roasted Crab & Clam Bake

An informal and fun way to serve seafood, dazzling with flavor and color.

3 lb.	*(1,4 kg)* crab claws*
16	clams
8	new red potatoes, quartered
8	fresh ears of corn on the cob, husked, *each* cut into thirds
2	med. onions, cut into 2" *(5 cm)* pieces
1 c.	*(250 mL)* chopped fresh parsley
¼ c.	*(50 mL)* torn fresh basil leaves

1 c.	*(250 mL)* dry white wine or chicken broth
½ c.	*(125 mL)* olive or vegetable oil
1 tsp.	*(5 mL)* coarsely ground pepper
½ tsp.	*(2 mL)* salt
2 tsp.	*(10 mL)* minced fresh garlic
1 tsp.	*(5 mL)* hot pepper sauce
3	bay leaves
¼ c.	*(50 mL)* butter or margarine

Heat oven to 400°F *(200°C)*. In large roasting pan layer crab, clams, potatoes, corn and onions. In medium bowl stir together remaining ingredients *except* bay leaves and butter; pour over ingredients in roasting pan. Add bay leaves. Cover; bake for 30 min. Then, stir ingredients to baste with pan juices. Continue baking covered, stirring after 15 min., for 30 to 35 min. or until seafood is steamed and vegetables are fork tender. Remove bay leaves. Dot butter over top of seafood and vegetables; serve with pan juices.

*3 lb. *(1,4 kg)* crab legs and crab clusters (the knuckle of the crab leg) can be substituted for 3 lb. *(1,4 kg)* crab claws.

Roasted Crab & Clam Bake

Scallops & Tomatoes Over Crusty Bread

6 servings
60 minutes

Creamed Oysters with Spinach

*Ladle this rich creamed oyster and spinach medley over fresh-baked cornbread
or biscuits for delicious country-style fare.*

2 tbsp.	*(30 mL)* butter or margarine
½ c.	*(125 mL)* (1 med.) chopped onion
½ tsp.	*(2 mL)* minced fresh garlic
2 tbsp.	*(30 mL)* all-purpose flour
½ tsp.	*(2 mL)* salt
½ tsp.	*(2 mL)* coarsely ground pepper
½ tsp.	*(2 mL)* thyme leaves
½ c.	*(125 mL)* reserved oyster liquor or clam juice

½ c.	*(125 mL)* whipping cream
4 c.	*(1 L)* torn spinach leaves*
2 doz.	fresh shucked oysters, drained, *reserve liquor*
	Cornbread, biscuits or toast**

In 10" *(25 cm)* skillet melt butter until sizzling. Stir in onion and garlic. Cook over med. heat, stirring occasionally, until onion is tender (3 to 4 min.). Stir in flour, salt, pepper and thyme. Continue cooking, stirring constantly, until smooth and bubbly (30 sec.). Stir in reserved oyster liquor and whipping cream. Continue cooking, stirring occasionally, until mixture is thickened (3 to 5 min.). Stir in spinach and oysters; continue cooking until oysters are tender (5 to 6 min.). Serve over cornbread, biscuits or toast.

*2 (10-oz.) *(300-g)* pkg. frozen chopped spinach, thawed, well-drained, can be substituted for 4 c. *(1 L)* torn spinach leaves.

Microwave Directions: In 3-qt. *(3-L)* casserole melt butter on HIGH (30 to 60 sec.). Add onion and garlic. Microwave on HIGH until onion is tender (2 to 3 min.). Stir in flour, salt, pepper and thyme. Microwave on HIGH until bubbly (30 to 60 sec.). Add reserved oyster liquor and whipping cream. Microwave on HIGH until mixture is thickened (1½ to 2 min.). Stir in spinach and oysters. Cover; microwave on HIGH, stirring after half the time, until oysters are tender (4 to 5½ min.). Serve over cornbread, biscuits or toast.

**See Breads page 44 for Honey-Moist Cornbread or Flaky Buttermilk Biscuits.

6 servings
30 minutes

Scallops & Tomatoes Over Crusty Bread

Scallops simmer in a rich burgundy sauce and are served over crusty slices of toasted bread.

8	slices bacon, cut into ½" *(1 cm)* pieces
1 tbsp.	*(15 mL)* all-purpose flour
½ tsp.	*(2 mL)* thyme leaves
½ tsp.	*(2 mL)* coarsely ground pepper
1 tsp.	*(5 mL)* minced fresh garlic
3 tbsp.	*(45 mL)* tomato paste
1 lb.	*(450 g)* bay scallops, rinsed, drained

3 c.	*(750 mL)* (3 med.) ripe tomatoes, cut into 1" *(2,5 cm)* pieces
½ c.	*(125 mL)* pitted ripe olives, halved
2 tbsp.	*(30 mL)* dry red wine
¼ c.	*(50 mL)* chopped fresh parsley
6	diagonally cut slices crusty French bread

In 10" *(25 cm)* skillet cook bacon over med. high heat, stirring occasionally, until bacon is browned (6 to 8 min.). Stir in flour, thyme, pepper and garlic. Reduce heat to med. Cook, stirring constantly, until smooth and bubbly (30 sec.). Stir in tomato paste and remaining ingredients *except* wine, parsley and bread. Continue cooking, stirring occasionally, until scallops are white (4 to 5 min.). If desired, stir in wine. Stir in parsley. Toast bread in broiler or oven. Serve scallop mixture over toasted bread.

To Fillet Fish: # How To: Fillet Fish & Identify Forms of Fish

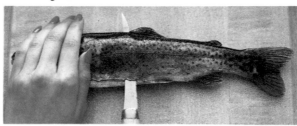

1. Lift pectoral fin. Using a thin, flexible sharp knife, angle the knife toward the back of the head and cut to the backbone.

2. Turn the blade parallel to the backbone. Cut toward tail with a sawing motion. Cut fillet off.

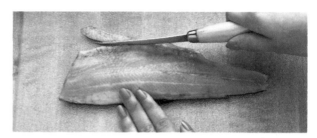

3. Remove rib bones by sliding the blade along the ribs. Turn fish over and remove second fillet.

4. Cut off the strip of fatty belly flesh. Discard guts, belly, bones and head.

5. If desired, skin the fillet by cutting into the tail flesh to the skin. Turn the blade parallel to the skin.

6. Pull the skin firmly while moving the knife in a sawing action between the skin and the flesh.

To Identify Forms of Fish:

Form	Definition
A. Whole	The entire fish.
B. Drawn or Pan-Dressed	The whole fish that has been eviscerated and scaled.
C. Fillets	Boneless pieces cut from the side of the fish.
D. Steaks	Pieces cut crosswise through the backbone.

EGGS & CHEESE

Farm-fresh eggs, gathered when the sun is just coming up in the east. Big rounds of richly robust sharp Cheddar. Creamy white bricks of mellow Monterey Jack. And wheels of sweet, nutty Swiss. These are the makings of country-style dishes that add a warm, comforting touch to any meal.

Eggs scrambled with bacon, new potatoes, onions and green pepper, then topped with shredded cheese. What a bright and cheerful way to wake up the family on a busy Saturday morning. If it's a cozy lunch or supper for two, enjoy your private time and good conversation over a puffy cheese omelet, dressed with a homemade herb sauce. Or if you're having a weekend brunch, an egg and cheese pie makes entertaining easy. As you greet your guests and welcome them into your home, the pie can be baking to its rich golden, delectable finish.

Whatever the time of day, whatever the occasion, dishes that start with eggs and cheese provide the kind of hearty nourishment and good eating that only country fare can.

Garden Grill Omelet

*A homemade herb sauce made with garden-ripened tomatoes
makes this zucchini, mushroom omelet absolutely delightful.*

Omelet

2 tbsp.	*(30 mL)* butter or margarine
1 c.	*(250 mL)* sliced ¼" *(0,5 cm)* fresh mushrooms
1 c.	*(250 mL)* (1 med.) sliced ¼" *(0,5 cm)* zucchini
4	eggs, slightly beaten
¼ tsp.	*(1 mL)* salt
¼ tsp.	*(1 mL)* pepper
3 tbsp.	*(45 mL)* water
1 tbsp.	*(15 mL)* butter or margarine
½ c.	*(125 mL)* (2 oz.) *(60 g)* shredded Mozzarella cheese

Tomato Sauce

1 tbsp.	*(15 mL)* butter or margarine
1	med. ripe tomato, cut into ½" *(1 cm)* pieces
2 tbsp.	*(30 mL)* chopped fresh parsley
½ tsp.	*(2 mL)* basil leaves
	Pinch of salt
½ tsp.	*(2 mL)* minced fresh garlic

In 8" *(20 cm)* omelet pan or 10" *(25 cm)* skillet melt 2 tbsp. *(30 mL)* butter until sizzling. Add mushrooms and zucchini. Cook over med. heat, stirring occasionally, until vegetables are crisply tender (4 to 5 min.). Remove from skillet; set aside. In small bowl stir together remaining omelet ingredients *except* butter and cheese. In same skillet melt 1 tbsp. *(15 mL)* butter until sizzling. Pour egg mixture into skillet. Cook over med. heat, lifting slightly with a spatula to allow uncooked portion to flow underneath, until omelet is set (3 to 4 min.). Place sautéed vegetables and cheese on half of omelet. Gently fold other half of omelet over filling. Meanwhile, in 1-qt. *(1-L)* saucepan melt 1 tbsp. *(15 mL)* butter; add remaining sauce ingredients. Cook over med. heat, stirring occasionally, until heated through (4 to 5 min.). Serve sauce over omelet.

Microwave Directions: In 10" *(25 cm)* quiche dish place 2 tbsp. *(30 mL)* butter, mushrooms and zucchini. Cover; microwave on HIGH, stirring after half the time, until vegetables are crisply tender (3 to 4 min.). Remove from quiche dish; set aside. Meanwhile, in small bowl combine remaining omelet ingredients *except* butter and cheese. In same quiche dish melt 1 tbsp. *(15 mL)* butter on HIGH (20 to 35 sec.). Pour egg mixture into dish. Cover; microwave on HIGH, stirring after half the time, until just set (2 to 4 min.). Place sautéed vegetables and cheese on half of omelet. Gently fold other half of omelet over filling. In small bowl combine sauce ingredients. Cover; microwave on HIGH, stirring after half the time, until heated through (2 to 3 min.). Serve sauce over omelet.

Garden Grill Omelet

4 servings
50 minutes

Country-Style Potato & Onion Pie

*This egg and Swiss cheese quiche-like pie is a satisfying food
that brings warmth to family gatherings at meal time.*

2 tbsp.	*(30 mL)* butter or margarine
1 c.	*(250 mL)* (3 small) sliced ⅛" *(0,2 cm)* new red potatoes
1	med. onion, sliced ⅛" *(0,2 cm)*, separated into rings
1 c.	*(250 mL)* (4 oz.) *(110 g)* shredded Swiss cheese

⅓ c.	*(75 mL)* chopped fresh parsley
⅓ c.	*(75 mL)* milk
8	eggs, slightly beaten
½ tsp.	*(2 mL)* salt
¼ tsp.	*(1 mL)* pepper
1	med. ripe tomato, sliced ¼" *(0,5 cm)*

Heat oven to 400°F *(200°C)*. In 10" *(25 cm)* ovenproof skillet melt butter in oven (3 to 4 min.). Add potatoes and onion. Bake, stirring once, for 15 to 20 min. or until vegetables are crisply tender. Meanwhile, in small bowl stir together remaining ingredients *except* tomato slices. Pour over baked potatoes and onion; arrange tomato slices over eggs. Return to oven; continue baking for 17 to 22 min. or until eggs are set and lightly browned.

Microwave Directions: In 10" *(25 cm)* quiche dish melt butter on HIGH (30 to 45 sec.). Add potatoes and onion. Cover; microwave on HIGH, stirring after half the time, until vegetables are crisply tender (3 to 5 min.). Let stand 5 min. Meanwhile, in medium bowl stir together remaining ingredients *except* tomato slices. Cover; microwave on HIGH, stirring every 2 min., until mixture is warm and starts to thicken (5 to 7 min.). Pour warmed egg mixture over potatoes and onion. Cover; microwave on HIGH, turning ½ turn after half the time, until eggs are set in center (5 to 7 min.). Top with tomatoes during last 2 min. of time.

6 servings
1 hour 30 minutes

Springtime Quiche

*Fresh chives in the crust and fresh asparagus in the quiche
create a savory springtime delight.*

Crust

1 c.	*(250 mL)* all-purpose flour
¼ tsp.	*(1 mL)* salt
⅓ c.	*(75 mL)* butter or margarine
2 tbsp.	*(30 mL)* chopped fresh chives
2 tbsp.	*(30 mL)* cold water

Filling

2 c.	*(500 mL)* (8 oz.) *(225 g)* shredded Cheddar cheese

1 c.	*(250 mL)* cooked, shredded chicken
6	slices crisply cooked bacon, cut into 1" *(2,5 cm)* pieces
¼ lb.	*(125 g)* fresh asparagus
1½ c.	*(375 mL)* half-and-half or milk
4	eggs, slightly beaten
¼ tsp.	*(1 mL)* salt
	Pinch of pepper

Heat oven to 400°F *(200°C)*. In medium bowl combine flour and salt; cut in butter until crumbly. Stir in chives and water (mixture will be crumbly). Shape into ball. On lightly floured surface, roll dough into 12" *(30 cm)* circle ⅛" *(0,2 cm)* thick. Fold into quarters; unfold and ease into 10" *(25 cm)* quiche pan, pressing firmly against bottom and sides. Flute edges. Spread cheese over bottom of crust; top with chicken. Sprinkle bacon over chicken. Place asparagus spears in spoke pattern on top of bacon. In small bowl stir together remaining filling ingredients. Pour over chicken mixture. Bake for 40 to 45 min. or until golden and set in center. Let stand 10 min.

Country-Style Potato & Onion Pie

Country Scrambled Eggs

Farm fresh eggs are scrambled with lots of healthy, hearty ingredients.

8	slices bacon, cut in ½" *(1 cm)* pieces
2 c.	*(500 mL)* cubed 1" *(2,5 cm)* new red potatoes
1 c.	*(250 mL)* (2 med.) chopped onions
½ c.	*(125 mL)* chopped green pepper
¼ c.	*(50 mL)* milk
8	eggs, slightly beaten
½ tsp.	*(2 mL)* salt
¼ tsp.	*(1 mL)* pepper
1 c.	*(250 mL)* (4 oz.) *(110 g)* shredded Cheddar cheese

In 10" *(25 cm)* skillet cook bacon over med. heat for 5 min. Add potatoes; continue cooking, stirring occasionally, until potatoes are browned and crisply tender (12 to 15 min.). Add onions and green pepper. Continue cooking until crisply tender (3 to 4 min.). Pour off fat. Meanwhile, in small bowl stir together remaining ingredients *except* cheese. Pour egg mixture over vegetables; stir to blend. Cook over med. heat, gently lifting portions with spatula so uncooked portion flows to bottom of pan, until eggs are set (4 to 5 min.). Sprinkle cheese over eggs; let stand until cheese is melted (2 to 4 min.).

Microwave Directions: In 3-qt. *(3-L)* casserole microwave bacon on HIGH until softened (2½ to 3 min.). Add potatoes. Cover; microwave on HIGH, stirring after half the time, until potatoes are crisply tender (5 to 8 min.). Stir in onions and green pepper. Cover; microwave on HIGH, stirring after half the time, until crisply tender (2 to 2½ min.). Pour off fat. Meanwhile, in small bowl stir together remaining ingredients *except* cheese. Pour egg mixture over vegetables; stir to blend. Cover; microwave on HIGH, stirring after half the time, until eggs are just dry and set (4 to 5 min.). Sprinkle cheese over eggs; let stand until cheese is melted (2 to 4 min.).

Country Scrambled Eggs

Cheddar Spinach Strata (top)
Sundown Oven Pancake (bottom)

4 servings
45 minutes

Sundown Oven Pancake

*An oven pancake that puffs up in the pan to form a shell
for crispy vegetables and Cheddar cheese.*

1 tbsp.	*(15 mL)* butter or margarine
½ c.	*(125 mL)* all-purpose flour
½ c.	*(125 mL)* milk
2	eggs, slightly beaten
¼ tsp.	*(1 mL)* salt
2 tbsp.	*(30 mL)* butter or margarine
2 c.	*(500 mL)* broccoli flowerets
1 c.	*(250 mL)* red onion, cut into 1" *(2,5 cm)* pieces
1 c.	*(250 mL)* (1 med.) green pepper, cut into 1" *(2,5 cm)* pieces
1 c.	*(250 mL)* (1 med.) ripe tomato, cut into 1" *(2,5 cm)* pieces
¼ tsp.	*(1 mL)* salt
¼ tsp.	*(1 mL)* pepper
1½ c.	*(375 mL)* (6 oz.) *(170 g)* shredded Cheddar cheese

Heat oven to 425°F *(220°C)*. In 9" *(23 cm)* pie pan melt 1 tbsp. *(15 mL)* butter in oven (2 to 3 min.). Meanwhile, in small bowl stir together flour, milk, eggs and ¼ tsp. *(1 mL)* salt. Pour into pie pan with melted butter. Bake for 12 to 15 min. or until golden brown. Meanwhile, in 10" *(25 cm)* skillet melt 2 tbsp. *(30 mL)* butter. Add remaining ingredients *except* cheese. Cook over med. heat, stirring occasionally, until vegetables are crisply tender (12 to 15 min.). Sprinkle ½ c. *(125 mL)* cheese in bottom of pancake; top with vegetable mixture. Sprinkle with remaining 1 c. *(250 mL)* cheese. Return to oven; continue baking for 5 to 7 min. or until cheese is melted.

8 servings
2 hours 30 minutes

Cheddar Spinach Strata

Make this strata the night before and bake it the next day for an easy brunch.

6 c.	*(1,5 L)* (8 slices) cubed ½" *(1 cm)* whole wheat bread
3 c.	*(750 mL)* (12 oz.) *(340 g)* shredded Cheddar cheese
2	(10-oz.) *(300-g)* pkg. frozen chopped spinach, thawed, drained
2-oz.	*(60-g)* jar diced pimiento, drained
6	eggs, beaten
3 c.	*(750 mL)* milk
1½ tsp.	*(7 mL)* onion salt
½ tsp.	*(2 mL)* pepper

In 13 × 9" *(33 × 23 cm)* baking pan layer: 3 c. *(750 mL)* bread cubes, cheese, spinach, pimiento and remaining 3 c. *(750 mL)* bread cubes. In medium bowl stir together remaining ingredients; pour over layered ingredients. Cover; refrigerate at least 1 hr. or overnight. Heat oven to 325°F *(160°C)*. Bake for 60 to 75 min. or until knife inserted near center comes out clean. Let stand 5 min. before serving.

Microwave Directions: In 13 × 9" *(33 × 23 cm)* baking dish assemble strata as directed left. Cover; refrigerate at least 1 hr. or overnight. Cover; microwave on HIGH, turning dish ½ turn twice during time, until knife inserted near center comes out clean (27 to 32 min.). Let stand 5 min. before serving.

1 dozen
2 hours

Shrimp Dilled Deviled Eggs

*Place these shrimp and dill-seasoned deviled eggs in an egg carton
for easy carrying to a picnic or barbecue.*

6		eggs
¼ c.	*(50 mL)*	mayonnaise
4¼-oz.	*(113-g)*	can deveined medium shrimp, rinsed, drained
2 tbsp.	*(30 mL)*	chopped green onions
1 tbsp.	*(15 mL)*	chopped fresh dill weed*

		Pinch of pepper
1 tbsp.	*(15 mL)*	lime juice
2 tsp.	*(10 mL)*	country-style Dijon mustard
¼ tsp.	*(1 mL)*	hot pepper sauce
		Fresh dill weed

In 2-qt. *(2-L)* saucepan place eggs; add enough cold water to come 1" *(2,5 cm)* above eggs. Cook over high heat until water comes to a full boil. Remove from heat. Cover; let stand 20 to 25 min. Immediately cool eggs in cold water to prevent further cooking; peel. Cut eggs crosswise in half. Remove yolks from egg whites; set egg whites aside. Place cooked egg yolks in medium bowl; mash with fork. Add mayonnaise, shrimp, onions, 1 tbsp. *(15 mL)* dill, pepper, lime juice, mustard and hot pepper sauce to egg yolks; stir to blend. Spoon about 1 tbsp. *(15 mL)* egg yolk mixture into each egg white; garnish with sprig of dill weed. Place in egg carton to transport; refrigerate until served.

*1 tsp. *(5 mL)* dried dill weed can be substituted for 1 tbsp. *(15 mL)* fresh dill weed.

6 servings
60 minutes

Fresh Herb-Baked Eggs

Eggs, soft-cooked in pastry shells, give an entirely new style to shirred eggs.

10-oz	*(283-g)*	pkg. (6) frozen ready-to-bake puff pastry shells
2 tbsp.	*(30 mL)*	butter or margarine, melted
1 tbsp.	*(15 mL)*	sherry, sherry cooking wine or vinegar
1 tsp.	*(5 mL)*	Worcestershire sauce

6		eggs
¼ tsp.	*(1 mL)*	salt
¼ tsp.	*(1 mL)*	pepper
¼ tsp.	*(1 mL)*	dill weed
1 tbsp.	*(15 mL)*	thinly sliced green onion

Prepare pastry shells according to pkg. directions *except* bake only 20 min. Heat oven to 350°F *(180°C)*. Place 6 baked pastry shells in greased 13 × 9" *(33 × 23 cm)* baking pan. In each pastry shell place 1 tsp. *(5 mL)* melted butter; sprinkle each pastry shell with ½ tsp. *(2 mL)* sherry and a few drops of Worcestershire sauce. Crack 1 egg into each pastry shell; season with dash of salt, pepper and dill weed. Sprinkle with ½ tsp. *(2 mL)* green onion. Bake for 20 to 25 min. or until egg white is set.

Shrimp Dilled Deviled Eggs

4 servings
45 minutes

Crispy Southwestern Supper

*A crispy fried tortilla is layered with pork sausage,
zucchini slices and lots of shredded cheese.*

½ c.	*(125 mL)* vegetable oil	1 c.	*(250 mL)* (4 oz.) *(110 g)* shredded Cheddar cheese
4	(7") *(17,5 cm)* flour tortillas	1 c.	*(250 mL)* (1 med.) chopped ripe tomato
6 oz.	*(170 g)* pork sausage		
3 c.	*(750 mL)* (3 med.) sliced ⅛" *(0,2 cm)* zucchini		Salsa
	Pinch of salt		Dairy sour cream
	Pinch of cayenne pepper		
1 c.	*(250 mL)* (4 oz.) *(110 g)* shredded Monterey Jack cheese		

Heat oven to 400°F *(200°C)*. In 10" *(25 cm)* skillet heat oil over med. high heat. Fry each tortilla in hot oil for 1 min.; turn. Continue frying until crispy and lightly browned (1 min.). Set aside. In 2-qt. *(2-L)* saucepan cook sausage over med. heat, stirring occasionally, until browned (4 to 5 min.). Stir in zucchini, salt and cayenne pepper. Continue cooking, stirring occasionally, until zucchini is crisply tender (4 to 5 min.). Pour off fat. Place tortillas on cookie sheet. Top each tortilla with about ¾ c. *(175 mL)* zucchini and sausage mixture, ¼ c. *(50 mL)* Monterey Jack cheese and ¼ c. *(50 mL)* Cheddar cheese. Sprinkle with ¼ c. *(50 mL)* chopped tomato. Bake for 8 to 12 min. or until heated through and cheese is melted. Serve with salsa and sour cream.

Microwave Directions: Fry tortillas as directed left. In 2-qt. *(2-L)* casserole crumble sausage. Cover; microwave on HIGH, stirring after half the time, until sausage is no longer pink (3 to 5 min.). Pour off fat. Stir in zucchini, salt and cayenne pepper. Cover; microwave on HIGH, stirring after half the time, until zucchini is crisply tender (3 to 4 min.). Assemble as directed left. Microwave one tortilla on HIGH until cheese is melted (1 to 1½ min.). Repeat with remaining tortillas.

To Fry Tortillas:

1. In 10" *(25 cm)* skillet heat oil over med. high heat. Fry each tortilla in hot oil for 1 min.; turn.

2. Continue frying until crispy and lightly browned (1 min.).

Crispy Southwestern Supper

Skillet Pan Pizza

*A homemade deep-dish pizza with a
buttery, tender crust that's baked in a skillet.*

Crust

2 tbsp.	*(30 mL)*	butter or margarine
1⅔ c.	*(425 mL)*	all-purpose flour
2 tsp.	*(10 mL)*	sugar
2 tsp.	*(10 mL)*	baking powder
½ tsp.	*(2 mL)*	salt
⅔ c.	*(175 mL)*	milk

Sauce

8-oz.	*(213-mL)*	can tomato sauce
6-oz.	*(156-mL)*	can tomato paste
1 tsp.	*(5 mL)*	basil leaves
½ tsp.	*(2 mL)*	oregano leaves
¼ tsp.	*(1 mL)*	pepper
½ tsp.	*(2 mL)*	minced fresh garlic

Topping

1½ c.	*(375 mL) (6 oz.) (170 g)*	shredded Mozzarella cheese
1 c.	*(250 mL)*	sliced ¼" *(0,5 cm)* fresh mushrooms
2 oz.	*(60 g)*	sliced pepperoni
1		med. green pepper, sliced ⅛" *(0,2 cm)*
1		med. ripe tomato, sliced ⅛" *(0,2 cm)*
½ c.	*(125 mL)*	pitted ripe olives, sliced ¼" *(0,5 cm)*

Heat oven to 425°F *(220°C)*. In 10" *(25 cm)* ovenproof skillet melt butter in oven (3 to 4 min.). Meanwhile, in medium bowl stir together all crust ingredients *except* milk. Stir in milk just until moistened. On lightly floured surface knead dough until smooth (1 min.). Press dough on bottom and halfway up sides of skillet with melted butter. Bake for 10 min. Meanwhile, in small bowl stir together all sauce ingredients. Spread tomato sauce over partially baked crust. Sprinkle with 1 c. *(250 mL)* cheese and mushrooms. Arrange pepperoni, green pepper and tomato on pizza; sprinkle with olives and remaining ½ c. *(125 mL)* cheese. Return to oven; continue baking for 15 to 20 min. or until heated through and cheese is melted.

Skillet Pan Pizza

Brunch Omelet Torte

248

Brunch Omelet Torte

This do-ahead recipe requires some time to prepare, but is sensational for a special breakfast or brunch.

17¼-oz. *(500-g)* pkg. (2 sheets) frozen
prerolled sheets of puff pastry, thawed

Potatoes

¼ c.	*(50 mL)* butter or margarine
3 c.	*(750 mL)* (6 med.) sliced
	⅛" *(0,2 cm)* new red potatoes
1 c.	*(250 mL)* (1 med.) sliced
	⅛" *(0,2 cm)* onion, separated into rings
¼ tsp.	*(1 mL)* salt
¼ tsp.	*(1 mL)* pepper

Omelet

2 tbsp.	*(30 mL)* butter or margarine
6	eggs
¼ c.	*(50 mL)* chopped fresh parsley
	Pinch of salt
	Pinch of pepper
2 tbsp.	*(30 mL)* water

Filling

½ lb.	*(225 g)* thinly sliced cooked ham
2 c.	*(500 mL)* (8 oz.) *(225 g)* shredded Cheddar cheese
1	egg, slightly beaten
1 tbsp.	*(15 mL)* water

On lightly floured surface roll each sheet of puff pastry into a 12" *(30 cm)* sq. Lay 1 sheet puff pastry into 10" *(25 cm)* pie pan; set aside. In 10" *(25 cm)* skillet melt ¼ c. *(50 mL)* butter until sizzling. Add potatoes, onion, ¼ tsp. *(1 mL)* salt and ¼ tsp. *(1 mL)* pepper. Cover; cook over med. high heat, turning occasionally, until potatoes are lightly browned and crisply tender (12 to 15 min.). Set aside. In cleaned skillet melt 1 tbsp. *(15 mL)* butter until sizzling. Meanwhile, in small bowl stir together all omelet ingredients *except* remaining 1 tbsp. *(15 mL)* butter. Pour half of omelet mixture (¾ c.) *(200 mL)* into skillet with sizzling 1 tbsp. *(15 mL)* butter. Cook over med. heat. As omelet mixture sets, lift slightly with spatula to allow uncooked portion to flow underneath. Continue cooking until set (2 to 3 min.). Slide omelet onto cookie sheet. Repeat with remaining butter and omelet mixture.

Layer ingredients into pie pan with puff pastry in the following order: 1 omelet, ¼ lb. *(110 g)* ham, half of fried potatoes, 1 c. *(250 mL)* shredded cheese, remaining potatoes, ham, cheese and omelet. Top with remaining sheet of puff pastry. Press together edges of both sheets of puff pastry to form a rim; trim off excess puff pastry. Crimp or flute edges of puff pastry. Cover; refrigerate overnight or heat oven to 375°F *(190°C)*. In small bowl stir together 1 egg and 1 tbsp. *(15 mL)* water; brush over puff pastry. Bake for 30 to 35 min. or until golden brown. Let stand 5 min.; cut into wedges. If torte is refrigerated overnight, let stand at room temperature 30 min. before baking. Bake as directed above.

Tip: Your favorite deli meats can be substituted for ham.

4 servings
45 minutes

Cheddar-Vegetable Stuffed Shells

Cheddar cheese and dill enhance vegetables nestled in pasta shells.

12	jumbo macaroni shells
2 c.	*(500 mL)* frozen vegetable medley
1½ c.	*(375 mL) (6 oz.) (170 g)* cubed ½" *(1 cm)* Cheddar or Colby cheese
2 tbsp.	*(30 mL)* butter or margarine, melted
½ tsp.	*(2 mL)* dill weed

Heat oven to 350°F *(180°C)*. Cook shells according to pkg. directions. Drain; rinse in cold water. Dry on paper towel. Place shells in 9" *(23 cm)* sq. baking pan. In small bowl stir together vegetables and cheese. Stuff each shell with about ¼ c. *(50 mL)* mixture. In small bowl stir together melted butter and dill weed; brush over shells. Cover; bake for 20 to 25 min. or until heated through.

Microwave Directions: Prepare and stuff pasta shells as directed left. Place shells in 9" *(23 cm)* sq. baking dish. In small bowl stir together melted butter and dill weed; brush over shells. Cover; microwave on HIGH until heated through (4½ to 5½ min.).

4 cups *(1 L)*
30 minutes

Country Vegetable Fondue

Vegetables create crunch and color in this quick-to-fix fondue.

½ c.	*(125 mL)* white wine or milk
16-oz.	*(450-g)* pkg. pasteurized process cheese spread, cut into cubes
8-oz.	*(250-g)* pkg. cream cheese, cut into cubes
¼ c.	*(50 mL)* chopped green onions
⅓ c.	*(75 mL)* chopped celery
10-oz.	*(300-g)* pkg. frozen chopped spinach, thawed, drained
2	(2-oz.) *(60-g)* jars chopped pimiento, drained
	Pinch of dry mustard
	Pinch of cayenne pepper
	Bread cubes
	Tortilla chips
	Vegetable sticks

In 2-qt. *(2-L)* saucepan or fondue pot stir together wine, cheese spread and cream cheese. Cook over med. heat, stirring occasionally, until cheeses are melted (8 to 10 min.). Stir in remaining ingredients *except* bread cubes, tortilla chips and vegetable sticks. Continue cooking, stirring occasionally, until heated through (8 to 10 min.). Serve with bread cubes, tortilla chips or vegetable sticks.

Microwave Directions: In 2-qt. *(2-L)* casserole stir together wine, cheese spread and cream cheese. Microwave on HIGH, stirring after half the time, until cheeses are melted (5 to 6 min.). Stir in remaining ingredients *except* bread cubes, tortilla chips and vegetable sticks. Microwave on HIGH, stirring after half the time, until heated through (3 to 4 min.). Serve with bread cubes, tortilla chips or vegetable sticks.

Country Vegetable Fondue

Lasagna Roll-Ups With Cream Sauce

8 servings
1 hour 15 minutes

Lasagna Roll-Ups With Cream Sauce

These lasagna roll-ups are filled with the fresh tastes of garden vegetables and herbs.

Lasagna

8	uncooked lasagna noodles
2 tbsp.	*(30 mL)* butter or margarine
1 tsp.	*(5 mL)* minced fresh garlic
1 c.	*(250 mL)* (1 med.) sliced ⅛" *(0,2 cm)* zucchini
1 c.	*(250 mL)* (1 med.) yellow, red or green pepper, cut into 1" *(2,5 cm)* pieces
½ c.	*(125 mL)* coarsely chopped red onion
½ tsp.	*(2 mL)* salt
¼ tsp.	*(1 mL)* pepper
2 tbsp.	*(30 mL)* torn fresh basil*
1 tsp.	*(5 mL)* chopped fresh oregano*
1	egg, slightly beaten
1 c.	*(250 mL)* (4 oz.) *(110 g)* shredded Mozzarella cheese
½ c.	*(125 mL)* freshly grated Parmesan cheese
15-oz.	*(475-g)* carton ricotta cheese**
2 c.	*(500 mL)* (2 med.) ripe tomatoes, cut into ½" *(1 cm)* pieces

Herb Sauce

2 tbsp.	*(30 mL)* butter or margarine
2 tbsp.	*(30 mL)* all-purpose flour
¼ tsp.	*(1 mL)* salt
¼ tsp.	*(1 mL)* pepper
1 c.	*(250 mL)* milk
1 c.	*(250 mL)* (4 oz.) *(110 g)* shredded Mozzarella cheese
¼ c.	*(50 mL)* chopped fresh parsley
1 tbsp.	*(15 mL)* torn fresh basil*
2 tbsp.	*(30 mL)* freshly grated Parmesan cheese

Heat oven to 350°F *(180°C)*. Cook lasagna noodles according to pkg. directions; rinse. In 10" *(25 cm)* skillet melt 2 tbsp. *(30 mL)* butter until sizzling; stir in garlic. Add remaining lasagna ingredients *except* egg, 1 c. *(250 mL)* Mozzarella cheese, ½ c. *(125 mL)* Parmesan cheese, ricotta cheese, tomatoes and lasagna noodles. Cook over med. heat, stirring occasionally, until vegetables are crisply tender (5 to 6 min.). Meanwhile, in large bowl stir together egg and cheeses. Stir in tomatoes and cooked vegetables. Place about ½ c. *(125 mL)* filling on one end of each lasagna noodle. Roll up lasagna noodle, jelly roll fashion. (Some filling will spill out each end.) Place, seam side down, in 12 × 8" *(30 × 20 cm)* baking pan. Fill in around roll-ups with excess filling. Set aside. In 2-qt. *(2-L)* saucepan melt 2 tbsp. *(30 mL)* butter over med. heat; stir in flour, ¼ tsp. *(1 mL)* salt and ¼ tsp. *(1 mL)* pepper. Cook, stirring occasionally, until smooth and bubbly (30 sec.). Add milk; continue cooking until sauce begins to thicken (1 to 2 min.). Stir in 1 c. *(250 mL)* Mozzarella cheese, 1 tbsp. *(15 mL)* parsley and 1 tbsp. *(15 mL)* basil. Continue cooking, stirring occasionally, until cheese is melted (2 to 4 min.). Pour over lasagna roll-ups; sprinkle with 2 tbsp. *(30 mL)* Parmesan cheese. Bake for 25 to 30 min. or until heated through.

*2 tsp. *(10 mL)* dried basil leaves can be substituted for 2 tbsp. *(30 mL)* torn fresh basil.

*¼ tsp. *(1 mL)* dried oregano leaves can be substituted for 1 tsp. *(5 mL)* chopped fresh oregano.

*1 tsp. *(5 mL)* dried basil leaves can be substituted for 1 tbsp. *(15 mL)* torn fresh basil.

**12-oz. *(340-g)* carton cottage cheese can be substituted for 15-oz. *(475-g)* carton ricotta cheese.

SALADS & SANDWICHES

What a great day to be outdoors. Fresh breezes are blowing, and puffy white clouds float lazily by as you bask in the warm sunshine of a perfect spring day. The first wild flowers of the season are in bloom, and the quiet is punctuated only by the sweet sound of birds singing in the trees.

It's not time for lunch yet, but somehow being outdoors seems to awaken your appetite. Perhaps it's knowing that the wicker basket is so close by. A peek inside reveals a banquet of picnic goodies. French loaves generously filled with slices of smoked meat and three kinds of cheese. Crunchy chicken salad on golden-brown rolls. Fresh vegetables and pasta tossed with a tangy mustard dressing. For dessert, there are sweet, fresh fruits and homemade cookies.

The fare is simple and delicious. Foods that are equally at home at a family supper or a backyard party. Sandwiches and salads re-create the pleasures of picnicking anytime, anywhere.

Lemon Dill Chicken Loaves

*Delicious, delightful and delectable describes sautéed chicken
served in French rolls and seasoned with cream cheese and dill.*

2 tbsp.	*(30 mL)* butter or margarine		4 oz.	*(110 g)* cream cheese, softened
¼ tsp.	*(1 mL)* salt		½ tsp.	*(2 mL)* dill weed
¼ tsp.	*(1 mL)* dill weed		¼ tsp.	*(1 mL)* salt
	Pinch of pepper		1 tbsp.	*(15 mL)* lemon juice
¼ tsp.	*(1 mL)* minced fresh garlic		4	French rolls or hoagie buns, split
2	whole, boneless chicken breasts, skinned, halved		4	lettuce leaves
⅔ c.	*(150 mL)* dairy sour cream		8	slices ripe tomato

In 10" *(25 cm)* skillet melt butter until sizzling; stir in salt, dill weed, pepper and garlic. Add chicken breasts. Cook over med. high heat, turning occasionally, until chicken is browned and fork tender (10 to 15 min.). Meanwhile, in small bowl stir together remaining ingredients *except* rolls, lettuce and tomato slices. To assemble each sandwich spread about 1 tbsp. *(15 mL)* cream cheese mixture over bottom half of roll. Top with 1 lettuce leaf, 2 slices tomato and sautéed chicken breast. Spoon about 1 tbsp. *(15 mL)* cream cheese mixture over chicken; top with remaining bun.

Microwave Directions: In 12 × 8" *(30 × 20 cm)* baking dish melt butter on HIGH (20 to 35 sec.). Stir in salt, dill weed, pepper and garlic. Place chicken in baking dish, turning to coat. Cover; microwave on HIGH, turning chicken over and rearranging after half the time, until chicken is no longer pink (5 to 7 min.). Assemble sandwiches as directed left.

Crunchy Chicken Salad Sandwich

*Fresh radish, celery and cucumber
add a crunchy new taste to a chicken sandwich.*

2 c.	*(500 mL)* cooked, cubed 1" *(2,5 cm)* chicken		½ c.	*(125 mL)* mayonnaise
½ c.	*(125 mL)* sliced ¼" *(0,5 cm)* celery		1 tsp.	*(5 mL)* dill weed
½ c.	*(125 mL)* sliced ¼" *(0,5 cm)* cucumber, cut in half		¼ tsp.	*(1 mL)* salt
⅓ c.	*(75 mL)* sliced ¼" *(0,5 cm)* radish, cut in half		12	small sandwich rolls Lettuce

In large bowl stir together all ingredients *except* rolls and lettuce. Cover; refrigerate at least 1 hr. to blend flavors. Spread on rolls; garnish with lettuce.

Crunchy Chicken Salad Sandwich (top)
Lemon Dill Chicken Loaves (bottom)

4 sandwiches
20 minutes

Avocado Chicken Clubhouse

Country-style mustard adds hearty flavor to this sandwich.

12	slices whole wheat bread
¼ c.	*(50 mL)* chopped green onions
⅔ c.	*(150 mL)* mayonnaise
3 tbsp.	*(45 mL)* country-style Dijon mustard
8	(1 oz.) *(30 g)* slices cooked chicken or turkey
1	med. avocado, peeled, sliced
8	slices ripe tomato
8	slices crisply cooked bacon, cut in half
	Lettuce

Toast bread. In small bowl stir together onions, mayonnaise and mustard. Spread mayonnaise mixture on 1 side of each slice of toast. To assemble each sandwich place 2 slices turkey on 1 slice toast, top with avocado slices. Top with 1 slice toast, mayonnaise side down; spread mayonnaise on toast. Place 2 tomato slices on toast; top with 4 pieces bacon and lettuce. Place toast on top. Repeat for remaining sandwiches. Secure with long wooden picks.

To Prepare Avocados:

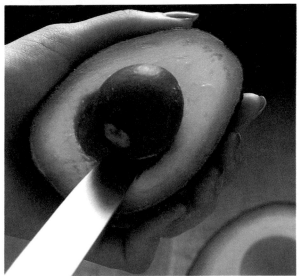

1. Cut avocado in half lengthwise, remove seed.

2. Peel off skin and slice.

Avocado Chicken Clubhouse

6 servings
20 minutes

Ranch-Hand Sandwich

After a hard day's work, enjoy this wholesome and hearty sandwich with a blue cheese spread.

¼ c.	*(50 mL)* butter or margarine, softened	1	med. ripe tomato, cut into 6 slices
¼ c.	*(50 mL)* crumbled blue cheese	12	*(½ oz.) (15 g)* thin slices cooked turkey
1 lb.	*(450 g)* loaf Italian bread or French bread, sliced in half lengthwise	12	*(¼ oz.) (7 g)* thin slices hard salami
8	lettuce leaves	4	*(1 oz.) (30 g)* slices Mozzarella cheese, cut in half

In small bowl stir together butter and blue cheese. Spread butter mixture on each half of bread. Place both halves of bread on cookie sheet. Broil 5 to 6" *(12 to 15 cm)* from heat for 2 to 4 min. or until butter is melted and bread is toasted. To assemble sandwich arrange lettuce leaves on bottom half of bun. Layer tomato, turkey, hard salami and cheese. Top with remaining bun. With serrated knife cut into individual servings.

4 sandwiches
20 minutes

Turkey n' Chive Sandwich

For that perfect picnic meal-on-a-bun.

8-oz.	*(250-g)* pkg. cream cheese, softened	1	med. ripe tomato, sliced ¼" *(0,5 cm)*
2 tbsp.	*(30 mL)* chopped fresh chives	1	med. green pepper, sliced into ¼" *(0,5 cm)* rings
4	individual French bread rolls, split		
4	lettuce leaves	4	*(1 oz.) (30 g)* slices Swiss cheese
8	*(1 oz.) (30 g)* slices cooked turkey		

In small bowl stir together cream cheese and chives. Spread on roll halves. To assemble each sandwich layer bottom half of roll with lettuce leaf, 2 slices turkey, tomato, green pepper and 1 slice cheese. Top with remaining roll. Repeat for remaining sandwiches.

Turkey n' Chive Sandwich

4 sandwiches
20 minutes

Horseradish Roast Beef Special

*The special of the day is this bountiful sandwich with sourdough bread,
a horseradish spread and roast beef.*

Horseradish Spread

½ c.	*(125 mL)* dairy sour cream
¼ tsp.	*(1 mL)* salt
	Pinch of pepper
1 tbsp.	*(15 mL)* country-style Dijon mustard
1 tsp.	*(5 mL)* prepared horseradish

Sandwich

¼ c.	*(50 mL)* butter or margarine, softened
½ tsp.	*(2 mL)* minced fresh garlic
8	slices sourdough bread
12	slices roast beef
8	slices ripe tomato
12	slices cucumber

In small bowl stir together all spread ingredients. In small bowl stir together butter and garlic. Spread 1 side of each slice bread with garlic butter. Place on cookie sheet. Broil 5 to 6" *(12 to 15 cm)* from heat for 3 to 4 min. or until bread is toasted. To assemble each sandwich layer 1 slice bread with 3 slices roast beef, 2 slices tomato and 3 slices cucumber. Spoon about 2 tbsp. *(30 mL)* spread over cucumbers. Top with 1 slice bread.

4 sandwiches
20 minutes

Best Ever Hoagie Sandwich

*Butter crisp fried buns enhance the tasty,
satisfying layers of meat and cheese in this hearty sandwich.*

¼ c.	*(50 mL)* butter or margarine, softened
4	individual hoagie buns or individual French rolls
¼ c.	*(50 mL)* chopped green onions
½ c.	*(125 mL)* dairy sour cream
¼ c.	*(50 mL)* country-style Dijon mustard
8 oz.	*(225 g)* sliced ham, roast beef or smoked turkey

4 oz.	*(110 g)* sliced Monterey Jack cheese
4 oz.	*(110 g)* sliced Cheddar cheese
4 oz.	*(110 g)* sliced Swiss cheese
1	med. ripe tomato, cut into 8 slices
	Leaf lettuce
4	(6") *(15 cm)* wooden picks

Spread butter inside top and bottom of buns. Heat 10" *(25 cm)* skillet or griddle. Fry bread, buttered side down, until golden brown (4 to 5 min.). Meanwhile, in small bowl stir together green onions, sour cream and mustard. Spread on fried buns. Divide meat and cheese evenly on bottom of buns. Top each with 2 tomato slices, leaf lettuce and top of bun. Secure with wooden picks.

Best Ever Hoagie Sandwich (top)
Horseradish Roast Beef Special (bottom)

Open-Faced Egg Salad Sandwich

4 sandwiches
40 minutes

Open-Faced Egg Salad Sandwich

Toasted whole wheat bread is topped with crispy cucumbers, juicy tomatoes, creamy egg salad and crisscrossed with bacon.

Egg Salad

6	eggs
1 c.	*(250 mL)* (2 stalks) sliced ¼" *(0,5 cm)* celery
¾ c.	*(175 mL)* mayonnaise
2 tbsp.	*(30 mL)* chopped green onion
¼ tsp.	*(1 mL)* salt
¼ tsp.	*(1 mL)* pepper
1 tsp.	*(5 mL)* prepared horseradish

Sandwich

8	slices bacon
4	slices whole wheat bread
4	lettuce leaves
8	slices ripe tomato
12	slices cucumber

In 2-qt. *(2-L)* saucepan place eggs; add enough cold water to come 1" *(2,5 cm)* above eggs. Cook over high heat until water comes to a full boil. Remove from heat. Cover; let stand 20 to 25 min. Immediately cool eggs in cold water to prevent further cooking; peel. Chop hard cooked eggs; place in medium bowl. Stir in remaining egg salad ingredients. Fry or microwave bacon until crispy (4 to 5 min.). Meanwhile, toast bread. Top each slice toast with 1 lettuce leaf, 2 slices tomato, 3 slices cucumber and ½ c. *(125 mL)* egg salad. Crisscross cooked bacon strips over sandwich.

8 sandwiches
20 minutes

Garden Tuna Melt

A family favorite — tuna — livened up with fresh vegetables.

¼ c.	*(50 mL)* chopped celery
¼ c.	*(50 mL)* mayonnaise
6½-oz.	*(184-g)* can tuna, drained
4	English muffins, split, toasted
8	green pepper rings

8	slices ripe tomato
8	(3¼ × 3¼") *(8 × 8 cm)* slices Cheddar cheese
2 tbsp.	*(30 mL)* sliced green onion

Heat oven to 350°F *(180°C)*. In medium bowl stir together celery, mayonnaise and tuna. Place English muffins on cookie sheet. Spread tuna mixture on muffins. Layer each with 1 green pepper ring and 1 tomato slice. Bake for 10 to 12 min. or until heated through. Remove from oven; top each with 1 slice cheese. Garnish with green onion. Continue baking for 1 to 2 min. or until cheese melts.

Microwave Directions: Prepare muffins as directed left. Top each with 1 slice cheese. Garnish with green onion. For each serving: place 2 muffins on a plate lined with paper towel. Microwave on HIGH until heated through (1½ to 2 min.).

8 sandwiches
30 minutes

Open-Face Turkey & Broccoli Sandwich

Broccoli, red onion and cheese top this broiled open-face turkey sandwich
flavored with a touch of tarragon.

½ c.	*(125 mL)* butter or margarine, softened
½ tsp.	*(2 mL)* tarragon leaves
1 lb.	*(450 g)* loaf French bread, cut into fourths, sliced horizontally
1 lb.	*(450 g)* cooked, sliced turkey
¾ c.	*(175 mL)* mayonnaise

¾ tsp.	*(3 mL)* tarragon leaves
3 c.	*(750 mL)* broccoli flowerets
1	med. sliced ¼" *(0,5 cm)* red onion, separated into rings
8	*(1 oz.) (30 g)* slices Monterey Jack cheese

Heat broiler. In small bowl stir together butter and ½ tsp. *(2 mL)* tarragon; spread on cut bread. Divide turkey among bread. In small bowl stir together mayonnaise and ¾ tsp. *(3 mL)* tarragon; spread over turkey, top with broccoli and onion rings. Place sandwiches on cookie sheet. Broil 3 to 4" *(7 to 10 cm)* from heat for 3 to 5 min. or until sandwiches are heated through. Top with cheese; broil 2 to 3 min. or until cheese is melted.

6 sandwiches
20 minutes

Horseradish Turkey n' Ham Melt

A hearty hot sandwich with the tang of horseradish and the crunch of green pepper.

6	slices rye bread
⅓ c.	*(75 mL)* butter or margarine, softened
2 tbsp.	*(30 mL)* prepared horseradish
6	*(1 oz.) (30 g)* slices cooked turkey

6	*(1 oz.) (30 g)* slices cooked ham
6	slices ripe tomato
1	med. green pepper, sliced into 6 rings
6	*(1 oz.) (30 g)* slices Cheddar cheese

Heat broiler. Toast bread. In small bowl stir together butter and horseradish; spread butter mixture on toast. Layer each slice toast with 1 slice turkey, 1 slice ham, 1 slice tomato and 1 slice green pepper. Place sandwiches on cookie sheet. Broil 3 to 4" *(7 to 10 cm)* from heat for 3 to 4 min. or until sandwiches are heated through. Top with cheese; broil 2 to 3 min. or until cheese is melted.

Microwave Directions: Prepare as directed left. Place 3 sandwiches on large plate. Microwave on MEDIUM (50% power), turning plate ¼ turn after half the time, until cheese is melted (3 to 3½ min.). Repeated with remaining sandwiches.

Open-Face Turkey & Broccoli Sandwich

<table>
<tr><td>4 servings
30 minutes</td></tr>
</table>

Ham & Maple Apple Stack

*Create this waffle stack with smoked ham and tart, crisp apples
that have been simmered in maple syrup.*

2 tbsp.	*(30 mL)* butter or margarine
2 c.	*(500 mL)* (2 med.) cored, sliced ¼" *(0,5 cm)* tart apples
¼ c.	*(50 mL)* maple syrup
¼ tsp.	*(1 mL)* nutmeg

8	(1 oz.) *(30 g)* slices cooked ham
8	frozen waffles
	Maple syrup

In 10" *(25 cm)* skillet melt butter until sizzling; add apples, syrup and nutmeg. Cook over med. heat, stirring occasionally, until apples are crisply tender (3 to 4 min.). Place ham in same skillet, placing apples on ham slices. Continue cooking until heated through (5 to 6 min.). Meanwhile, toast or bake waffles according to pkg. directions. Divide ham and apple mixture between 4 toasted waffles. Top with remaining toasted waffles. Serve with maple syrup.

Microwave Directions: In 13 × 9" *(33 × 23 cm)* baking dish melt butter on HIGH (20 to 30 sec.). Stir in apples, syrup and nutmeg. Place ham in baking dish; arrange apples over ham. Cover; microwave on HIGH until apples are crisply tender and ham is heated through (3 to 5 min.). Assemble sandwiches as directed left.

<table>
<tr><td>6 servings
45 minutes</td></tr>
</table>

Smokehouse Barbecued Pork

This rich, zesty barbecue sauce tastes like it has been simmering all day.

Sauce

¼ c.	*(50 mL)* firmly packed brown sugar
⅓ c.	*(75 mL)* country-style Dijon mustard
14-oz.	*(375-mL)* bottle catsup
¼ tsp.	*(1 mL)* oregano leaves
¼ tsp.	*(1 mL)* chili powder
2 tbsp.	*(30 mL)* cider vinegar
2 tbsp.	*(30 mL)* Worcestershire sauce
½ tsp.	*(2 mL)* liquid smoke
3	slices lemon

Pork

2 tbsp.	*(30 mL)* butter or margarine
½ c.	*(125 mL)* sliced ½" *(1 cm)* celery
1 lb.	*(450 g)* pork tenderloin, cut into 1" *(2,5 cm)* pieces*
2	med. onions, sliced ⅛" *(0,2 cm)*
¼ tsp.	*(1 mL)* salt
¼ tsp.	*(1 mL)* pepper
8	whole wheat buns

In 3-qt. *(3-L)* saucepan stir together all sauce ingredients. Cook over low heat, stirring occasionally, until heated through (5 to 10 min.). Meanwhile, in 10" *(25 cm)* skillet melt butter until sizzling. Add remaining pork ingredients *except* buns. Cook over med. high heat until meat is browned (13 to 18 min.). Add pork mixture to barbecue sauce. Serve barbecued pork in buns.

*3 c. *(750 mL)* shredded baked pork roast can be substituted for pork tenderloin.

Microwave Directions: In 3-qt. *(3-L)* casserole combine all sauce ingredients. Cover; microwave on HIGH, stirring after half the time, until heated through (3 to 5 min.). Stir in remaining pork ingredients *except* buns. Cover; microwave on HIGH, stirring after half the time, until meat is fork tender (10 to 13 min.). Assemble sandwiches as directed left.

Ham & Maple Apple Stack

Crusty Bread Stuffed With Sausage (top)
Grilled Sausage Patties on Rye (bottom)

Grilled Sausage Patties on Rye

4 servings
30 minutes

*Lots of Mozzarella cheese melts between sausage patties,
onions and grilled caraway rye bread.*

1 lb.	*(450 g)* pork sausage
1	med. onion, sliced ⅛" *(0,2 cm)*
8	green pepper rings

8	*(1 oz.) (30 g)* slices Mozzarella cheese
8	slices caraway rye bread
6 tbsp.	*(90 mL)* butter or margarine

Form sausage into 8 patties. Place in 10" *(25 cm)* skillet. Cook over med. heat, turning once, until browned and cooked through (6 to 8 min.). Add onion and green pepper. Continue cooking, stirring occasionally, until vegetables are crisply tender (4 to 5 min.). Remove sausage patties and vegetables from skillet; pour off fat. To assemble each sandwich place 1 slice cheese on slice of bread. Top with 2 sausage patties, ¼ of onion slices, 2 green pepper rings, 1 slice cheese and slice of bread. In same skillet melt 3 tbsp. *(45 mL)* butter until sizzling. Place 2 sandwiches in skillet. Cover; cook over med. heat until browned (3 min.). Turn. Cover; continue cooking until cheese is melted (2 to 3 min.). Remove

sandwiches to platter; keep warm while grilling remaining sandwiches in remaining 3 tbsp. *(45 mL)* butter.

Microwave Directions: Form sausage into 8 patties. Place in 13 × 9" *(33 × 23 cm)* baking dish. Cover; microwave on HIGH until partially cooked (3 to 4 min.). Turn patties over; add onion and green pepper. Cover; microwave on HIGH until vegetables are crisply tender and sausage is cooked through (3 to 4 min.). Pour off fat. Assemble sandwiches as directed left. Place in same baking dish. Cover; microwave on HIGH until cheese is melted (1½ to 2 min.).

Crusty Bread Stuffed With Sausage

6 servings
45 minutes

*Sourdough bread is filled with the savory and robust flavors of
sausage, onions, mushrooms, tomatoes and green pepper.*

1½ lb.	*(675 g)* (6 links) mild Italian sausage, cut into 1" *(2,5 cm)* pieces
2	med. onions, sliced ⅛" *(0,2 cm)*
2 c.	*(500 mL)* (½ lb.) *(225 g)* fresh mushrooms, halved
2 c.	*(500 mL)* (2 med.) ripe tomatoes, cut into 1" *(2,5 cm)* pieces
1	med. green pepper, cut into ½" *(1 cm)* strips

¼ c.	*(50 mL)* chopped fresh parsley
6-oz.	*(156-mL)* can tomato paste
1 tsp.	*(5 mL)* basil leaves
¼ tsp.	*(1 mL)* salt
¼ tsp.	*(1 mL)* pepper
1 lb.	*(450 g)* round loaf sourdough bread

Heat oven to 375°F *(190°C)*. In 10" *(25 cm)* skillet cook sausage and onions over med. high heat, stirring occasionally, until browned (8 to 10 min.). Pour off fat. Reduce heat to med. Add mushrooms, tomatoes and green pepper. Cook, stirring occasionally, until vegetables are crisply tender (5 to 7 min.). Stir in remaining ingredients *except* bread. Continue cooking, stirring

occasionally, until heated through (5 to 7 min.). Meanwhile, cut thin lengthwise slice off top of bread; reserve. Hollow out center of bread leaving 1" *(2,5 cm)* shell. (Save inside bread and use for fresh bread crumbs.) Place bread on cookie sheet; bake bread shell for 12 to 15 min. or until crusty. Fill hot bread with sausage mixture. With serrated knife cut into wedges.

Farmers' Market Sandwich (top)
Bacon Tomato Sandwich With Cheddar (bottom)

Bacon Tomato Sandwich With Cheddar

4 servings
20 minutes

*The familiar bacon tomato sandwich is made special
with zesty mayonnaise and melted Cheddar cheese.*

8	slices bacon
4	onion buns, split
⅓ c.	*(75 mL)* mayonnaise
1 tbsp.	*(15 mL)* country-style Dijon mustard
4	slices ripe tomato

12	red onion rings
12	slices cucumber
8	*(2¼ × 1 × ⅛")* *(11 × 2,5 × 0,2 cm)* strips Cheddar cheese

Heat oven to 375°F *(190°C)*. Fry or microwave bacon until crispy (4 to 5 min.). Place split onion buns on cookie sheet. In small bowl stir together mayonnaise and mustard. To assemble each sandwich spread about 1 tbsp. *(15 mL)* mayonnaise mixture on each bun half. Top bottom half of bun with 1 tomato slice, 3 onion rings and 3 cucumber slices. Crisscross 2 bacon strips over cucumber slices. Crisscross 2 slices cheese over bacon. Bake for 3 to 5 min. or until cheese is melted. Top with remaining bun.

Microwave Directions: Place bacon on microwave-safe bacon/roasting rack. Cover; microwave on HIGH until crisp (5 to 8 min.). Assemble sandwiches as directed left; place on large platter. Microwave on HIGH until cheese is melted (2 to 3 min.). Top with remaining bun.

Farmers' Market Sandwich

4 servings
30 minutes

*Gather the produce at the market to make these bagels
topped with sauteed fresh vegetables and Monterey Jack cheese.*

3 tbsp.	*(45 mL)* butter or margarine
2 c.	*(500 mL)* (2 med.) sliced ⅛" *(0,2 cm)* zucchini
1½ c.	*(375 mL)* sliced ¼" *(0,5 cm)* fresh mushrooms
½ c.	*(125 mL)* sliced ⅛" *(0,2 cm)* red onion, separated into rings
1 tsp.	*(5 mL)* basil leaves

¼ tsp.	*(1 mL)* salt
¼ tsp.	*(1 mL)* pepper
½ tsp.	*(2 mL)* minced fresh garlic
4	plain bagels, split
2 c.	*(500 mL)* (8 oz.) *(225 g)* shredded Monterey Jack cheese
8	slices ripe tomato

Heat oven to 375°F *(190°C)*. In 10" *(25 cm)* skillet melt butter until sizzling. Stir in remaining ingredients *except* bagels, cheese and tomato. Cook over med. heat, stirring occasionally, until vegetables are crisply tender (4 to 5 min.). Meanwhile, place bagels on cookie sheet; place 2 tbsp. *(30 mL)* cheese on each bagel half. Bake for 5 min. or until cheese is melted. Remove from oven; top each with 1 slice tomato. Divide zucchini mixture between bagels. Top with remaining cheese. Return to oven; continue baking 4 to 5 min. or until cheese is melted.

Microwave Directions: In 2-qt. *(2-L)* casserole melt butter on HIGH (30 to 45 sec.). Stir in remaining ingredients *except* bagels, cheese and tomato. Cover; microwave on HIGH, stirring after half the time, until vegetables are crisply tender (3 to 4 min.). Place bagels on large platter; place 2 tbsp. *(30 mL)* cheese on each bagel half. Microwave on HIGH until cheese is melted (1 to 1½ min.). Remove from microwave; top each with 1 slice tomato. Divide zucchini mixture between bagels. Top with remaining cheese. Microwave on HIGH until cheese is melted (2½ to 3½ min.).

Skillet Chicken Salad

Unique preparation and combinations in a creamy chicken salad.

3 tbsp.	*(45 mL)* butter or margarine
3	whole boneless chicken breasts, skinned, halved, cut into 3 × ½" *(7,5 × 1 cm)* strips
¼ tsp.	*(1 mL)* salt
¼ tsp.	*(1 mL)* pepper
¼ c.	*(50 mL)* sliced ¼" *(0,5 cm)* celery
¼ c.	*(50 mL)* chopped green onions
¼ c.	*(50 mL)* chopped fresh parsley
⅓ c.	*(75 mL)* dairy sour cream
⅓ c.	*(75 mL)* mayonnaise
½ tsp.	*(2 mL)* mustard seed
1 tbsp.	*(15 mL)* country-style Dijon mustard
1 tbsp.	*(15 mL)* lemon juice
8	lettuce leaves
1 c.	*(250 mL)* cherry tomato halves

In 10" *(25 cm)* skillet melt butter until sizzling. Stir in chicken, salt and pepper. Cook over med. high heat, stirring occasionally, until chicken is browned and fork tender (10 to 15 min.). Stir in remaining ingredients *except* lettuce leaves and cherry tomatoes. On platter or individual salad plates place lettuce leaves. Place chicken salad on lettuce; arrange cherry tomatoes around salad.

Southwestern Chicken Salad

Hot salsa will add extra spice to this chicken taco salad.

Dressing

1 c.	*(250 mL)* dairy sour cream
½ tsp.	*(2 mL)* chili powder
½ tsp.	*(2 mL)* cumin
½ tsp.	*(2 mL)* salt

Salad

2½ c.	*(625 mL)* cooked, cubed 1" *(2,5 cm)* chicken
⅓ c.	*(75 mL)* chopped onion
2	med. ripe tomatoes, cut into ½" *(1 cm)* pieces; *reserve 2 tbsp.* (30 mL)
½ c.	*(125 mL)* sliced ripe olives
4 c.	*(1 L)* shredded lettuce
1 c.	*(250 mL)* salsa
1 c.	*(250 mL)* shredded Cheddar cheese Tortilla chips

In large bowl stir together all dressing ingredients. Stir in chicken, onion, tomatoes *except* reserved 2 tbsp. *(30 mL)* and ripe olives. Cover; refrigerate at least 1 hr. To serve, line large serving platter with shredded lettuce. Top with chicken mixture. Spoon salsa over chicken mixture; sprinkle with cheese and reserved 2 tbsp. *(30 mL)* tomatoes. Garnish with tortilla chips.

Skillet Chicken Salad

Summer Light Chicken Salad

Hot Chicken & Lettuce Salad

4 servings
30 minutes

A tangy, warm salad dressing complements mandarin oranges and bacon in this delicious salad.

3 c.	*(750 mL)* torn leaf lettuce		2½ c.	*(625 mL)* cooked, shredded chicken
1 c.	*(250 mL)* torn spinach leaves		⅓ c.	*(75 mL)* cider vinegar
11-oz.	*(284-mL)* can mandarin orange segments, drained		¼ c.	*(50 mL)* vegetable oil
½ c.	*(125 mL)* sliced ¼" *(0,5 cm)* celery		½ tsp.	*(2 mL)* cracked pepper
¼ c.	*(50 mL)* chopped onion		1 tbsp.	*(15 mL)* Worcestershire sauce
8	slices bacon, cut into 1" *(2,5 cm)* pieces			

In large bowl combine lettuce, spinach and mandarin oranges; set aside. In 10" *(25 cm)* skillet cook celery, onion and bacon over med. heat, stirring occasionally, until bacon is browned and vegetables are crisply tender (8 to 10 min.). Stir in remaining ingredients. Cook over med. high heat, stirring occasionally, just until chicken is heated through (5 to 7 min.). Toss with lettuce. Serve immediately.

Microwave Directions: In large bowl combine lettuce, spinach and mandarin oranges; set aside. In 2-qt. *(2-L)* casserole microwave bacon on HIGH for 4 min. Stir in celery and onion. Microwave until bacon is cooked and vegetables are crisply tender (6 to 8 min.). With slotted spoon remove bacon-vegetable mixture. Drain fat *except* for 3 tbsp. *(45 mL)*. Stir remaining ingredients and bacon-vegetable mixture into reserved 3 tbsp. *(45 mL)* fat. Microwave on HIGH just until chicken is heated through (4 to 5 min.). Toss with lettuce. Serve immediately.

Summer Light Chicken Salad

4 to 6 servings
1 hour 30 minutes

A light dressing of lemon juice, oil and nutmeg makes this refreshing salad perfect for a hot summer day.

Dressing

⅓ c.	*(75 mL)* vegetable oil
⅓ c.	*(75 mL)* lemon juice
½ tsp.	*(2 mL)* salt
¼ tsp.	*(1 mL)* nutmeg
½ tsp.	*(2 mL)* minced fresh garlic

Salad

2½ c.	*(625 mL)* cooked, cubed 1" *(2,5 cm)* chicken
1 c.	*(250 mL)* halved, seedless red grapes
1 c.	*(250 mL)* (2 stalks) sliced ¼" *(0,5 cm)* celery
¼ c.	*(50 mL)* sliced green onions
4 c.	*(1 L)* shredded leaf lettuce

In jar with lid combine all dressing ingredients. Shake to mix. In large bowl combine all salad ingredients *except* lettuce. Toss salad with half of dressing.

Cover; refrigerate at least 1 hr. Place lettuce on serving platter; top with salad. Drizzle remaining dressing over salad and lettuce.

Apple Harvest Salad

6 servings
1 hour 15 minutes

*Sour cream and cinnamon are combined to make a smooth,
sparkling dressing for this harvest time salad.*

2½ c.	(625 mL) cooked, cubed 1" (2,5 cm) chicken		2 tbsp.	(30 mL) finely chopped onion
1 c.	(250 mL) walnut halves		½ tsp.	(2 mL) salt
½ c.	(125 mL) sliced ¼"(0,5 cm) celery		1 c.	(250 mL) dairy sour cream
2	med. tart apples, cubed ½" (1 cm)		½ tsp.	(2 mL) cinnamon
			6	lettuce cups

In large bowl stir together all ingredients *except* sour cream, cinnamon and lettuce. In small bowl stir together sour cream and cinnamon; fold into chicken mixture. Cover; refrigerate at least 1 hr. To serve, line six bowls with lettuce cups; fill each with salad.

Turkey in a Melon

6 servings
2 hours 30 minutes

*Cream cheese and nutmeg make a refreshing dressing
to serve with this turkey and melon salad.*

2   cantaloupes, cut into quarters, seeded, *reserve 2 quarters*

Salad

2 c.	(500 mL) cooked, cubed 1" (2,5 cm) turkey
½ c.	(125 mL) sliced ¼" (0,5 cm) celery
½ c.	(125 mL) chopped pecans
2 tbsp.	(30 mL) chopped green onion
	Leaf lettuce

Dressing

3 oz.	(90 g) cream cheese, softened
1 tbsp.	(15 mL) milk
¼ tsp.	(1 mL) nutmeg

Skin and cube reserved cantaloupe quarters. In large bowl stir together cubed cantaloupe and all salad ingredients *except* lettuce; set aside. In 5-c. (1,3-L) blender container combine dressing ingredients. Blend on high speed until smooth (1 to 2 min.). Fold dressing into turkey mixture. Cover; refrigerate at least 2 hr. To serve, place cantaloupe quarters on lettuce-lined plates; spoon salad into cantaloupe.

Turkey in a Melon

6 servings
15 minutes

Country Turkey & Grape Salad

The best made Parmesan-basil mayonnaise complements this and other salads.

Salad

4 c.	*(1 L)* cooked turkey, cut into 1½" *(3,5 cm)* pieces
1 c.	*(250 mL)* seedless green grapes
1 c.	*(250 mL)* seedless red grapes

Dressing

2	egg yolks
1 tsp.	*(5 mL)* basil leaves
¼ tsp.	*(1 mL)* salt
¼ tsp.	*(1 mL)* pepper

1 tbsp.	*(15 mL)* country-style Dijon mustard
1 c.	*(250 mL)* vegetable oil
¼ c.	*(50 mL)* lemon juice
⅓ c.	*(75 mL)* grated Parmesan cheese
8	lettuce leaves Clusters of seedless green and red grapes

In large bowl stir together all salad ingredients. In blender or food processor combine all dressing ingredients *except* oil, lemon juice and Parmesan cheese. Cover; blend on high until thoroughly combined. With blender still running, take off cover and slowly add ½ c. *(125 mL)* oil, lemon juice and remaining ½ c. *(125 mL)* oil. Blend until thickened (1 to 2 min.). By hand, stir in Parmesan cheese. Stir ½ c. *(125 mL)* dressing into salad. On platter or individual salad plates place lettuce leaves. Spoon turkey salad on lettuce; arrange clusters of grapes around salad. Serve with remaining dressing.

To Prepare Homemade Mayonnaise:

1. With blender still running, take off cover and slowly add ½ c. *(125 mL)* oil, lemon juice and remaining ½ c. *(125 mL)* oil.

2. Blend until thickened. By hand, stir in Parmesan cheese. Stir ½ c. *(125 mL)* dressing into salad.

Country Turkey & Grape Salad

6 servings
40 minutes

Springtime Ham & Asparagus Salad

Enjoy spring's bounty with a lemon cream dressing.

Salad

16	asparagus spears
4 c.	*(1 L)* torn lettuce
2 c.	*(500 mL)* cubed ½" *(1 cm)* cooked ham
2	hard cooked eggs, quartered

Dressing

½ c.	*(125 mL)* dairy sour cream
2 tbsp.	*(30 mL)* chopped fresh parsley
1 tbsp.	*(15 mL)* chopped fresh chives
	Pinch of salt
	Pinch of pepper
2 tbsp.	*(30 mL)* lemon juice
1 tbsp.	*(15 mL)* mayonnaise

In 10" *(25 cm)* skillet place asparagus; add enough water to cover. Cook over med. high heat until water comes to a full boil. Boil 1 to 2 min.; drain. Rinse with cold water. On platter or individual salad plates place lettuce. Arrange ham, eggs and asparagus spears on lettuce. In small bowl stir together all dressing ingredients. Pour dressing over salad.

6 servings
15 minutes

Orange Citrus Tuna Salad

Tuna salad with the freshness of orange and the spark of ginger.

Dressing

⅔ c.	*(150 mL)* mayonnaise
½ tsp.	*(2 mL)* ginger
¼ tsp.	*(1 mL)* pepper
2 tbsp.	*(30 mL)* orange juice
2 tbsp.	*(30 mL)* country-style Dijon mustard
½ tsp.	*(2 mL)* minced fresh garlic

Salad

1 c.	*(250 mL)* (2 stalks) coarsely chopped celery
2	*(6½-oz.)* *(184-g)* cans tuna, drained
2 tbsp.	*(30 mL)* chopped fresh parsley
4 c.	*(1 L)* torn lettuce
2	oranges, pared, sliced ¼" *(0,5 cm)*

In large bowl stir together all dressing ingredients. Stir in all salad ingredients *except* lettuce and oranges. On platter or individual salad plates place lettuce. Spoon tuna salad on lettuce; arrange orange slices around tuna salad.

Orange Citrus Tuna Salad (top)
Springtime Ham & Asparagus Salad (bottom)

283

Tarragon Beef & Pasta Salad

4 servings
30 minutes

Layered Pepperoni Pizza Salad

Deliver the savory taste of pizza in this fresh salad.

1 lb.	*(450 g)* ground beef
1½ c.	*(375 mL)* pizza sauce
2 oz.	*(60 g)* thinly sliced pepperoni, cut in half
4 c.	*(1 L)* chopped lettuce
1 c.	*(250 mL)* (1 med.) chopped ripe tomato

2 c.	*(500 mL)* (8 oz.) *(225 g)* shredded Mozzarella cheese
½ c.	*(125 mL)* sliced ripe olives
½ c.	*(125 mL)* cheese-flavored croutons

In 10" *(25 cm)* skillet brown ground beef (5 to 8 min.); drain. In same skillet stir in pizza sauce and pepperoni; continue cooking over med. heat, stirring occasionally, until meat mixture is heated through (2 to 3 min.). In large bowl layer 2 c. *(500 mL)* lettuce, tomato, 1 c. *(250 mL)* cheese, meat mixture, 2 c. *(500 mL)* lettuce, 1 c. *(250 mL)* cheese, olives and croutons. Serve immediately.

6 servings
1 hour 30 minutes

Tarragon Beef & Pasta Salad

Yogurt and fresh herbs dress this unique pasta salad.

Salad

1 c.	*(250 mL)* uncooked med. shell macaroni
8 oz.	*(225 g)* sliced, cooked roast beef, cut into 2 × ½" *(5 × 1 cm)* strips
1 c.	*(250 mL)* (2 stalks) sliced ½" *(1 cm)* celery
1 c.	*(250 mL)* halved cherry tomatoes
½ c.	*(125 mL)* sliced ¼" *(0,5 cm)* red onion, separated into rings

Dressing

1 c.	*(250 mL)* plain yogurt
½ c.	*(125 mL)* mayonnaise
¼ c.	*(50 mL)* chopped fresh parsley
¼ c.	*(50 mL)* chopped fresh chives
¾ tsp.	*(3 mL)* chopped fresh tarragon*
¼ tsp.	*(1 mL)* salt
¼ tsp.	*(1 mL)* pepper

Cook macaroni according to pkg. directions. Rinse with cold water. Drain; set aside. In large bowl stir together all remaining salad ingredients; stir in macaroni. Cover; refrigerate at least 1 hr. In small bowl stir together all dressing ingredients. Cover; refrigerate at least 1 hr. Pour dressing over salad; toss gently to coat.

*¼ tsp. *(1 mL)* dried tarragon leaves can be substituted for ¾ tsp. *(3 mL)* fresh tarragon.

6 servings
40 minutes

Market Pasta Salad

*Popular with the summer crowd, especially when made with fresh vegetables
right from the farmers' market.*

Salad

8 oz.	*(225 g)* uncooked, medium shell macaroni
2 c.	*(500 mL)* broccoli flowerets
½ c.	*(125 mL)* (1 med.) chopped onion
2	med. (2 c.) *(500 mL)* sliced ¼" *(0,5 cm)* yellow squash or zucchini
1	med. red pepper, cut into strips
1 c.	*(250 mL)* (4 oz.) *(110 g)* cubed ½" *(1 cm)* Cheddar cheese

Dressing

½ c.	*(125 mL)* vegetable oil
½ tsp.	*(2 mL)* salt
¼ tsp.	*(1 mL)* pepper
3 tbsp.	*(45 mL)* lemon juice
2 tbsp.	*(30 mL)* country-style Dijon mustard
1 tsp.	*(5 mL)* Worcestershire sauce
½ tsp.	*(2 mL)* minced fresh garlic
2 tbsp.	*(30 mL)* grated Parmesan cheese

Cook macaroni according to pkg. directions; drain. In large bowl stir together all salad ingredients *except* cheese; stir in hot macaroni. Refrigerate 10 min. Stir in cheese. Meanwhile, in medium bowl stir together all dressing ingredients *except* Parmesan cheese. Pour dressing over salad; toss to coat. Sprinkle with Parmesan cheese.

6 servings
45 minutes

Fettucine Chicken Salad

*A colorful mix of fresh vegetables, chicken and fettucine
make this a hearty main dish salad.*

Dressing

⅔ c.	*(150 mL)* vegetable oil
½ c.	*(125 mL)* white wine vinegar
1 tsp.	*(5 mL)* basil leaves
1 tsp.	*(5 mL)* oregano leaves
1 tsp.	*(5 mL)* minced fresh garlic
1 tsp.	*(5 mL)* salt
½ tsp.	*(2 mL)* pepper

Salad

6 oz.	*(180 g)* uncooked fettucine, broken into thirds
2½ c.	*(625 mL)* cooked, cubed 1" *(2,5 cm)* chicken or turkey
2 c.	*(500 mL)* broccoli flowerets
1 c.	*(250 mL)* (2 med.) sliced ¼" *(0,5 cm)* carrots
½	med. red onion, sliced into ⅛" *(0,2 cm)* rings
1 c.	*(250 mL)* halved cherry tomatoes

In jar with tight-fitting lid combine all dressing ingredients. Shake to mix; set aside. Cook fettucine according to pkg. directions; drain. Rinse with cold water. In large bowl combine remaining salad ingredients and drained fettucine. Gently stir in dressing.

Market Pasta Salad (top)
Fettucine Chicken Salad (bottom)

Sunshine Pasta Salad

4 servings
30 minutes

Sunshine Pasta Salad

Prepare this lemon pasta salad when tomatoes are garden-ripe and bursting with flavor.

4 oz.   *(110 g)* your favorite uncooked pasta
1 c.   *(250 mL)* (1 med.) sliced ⅛" *(0,2 cm)* cucumber
½ c.   *(125 mL)* chopped fresh parsley
6-oz.   *(170-mL)* jar marinated artichoke hearts, quartered, *reserve marinade*

½ tsp.   *(2 mL)* salt
½ tsp.   *(2 mL)* dill weed
¼ tsp.   *(1 mL)* pepper
1 tbsp. *(15 mL)* grated lemon peel
2 tbsp. *(30 mL)* lemon juice
4   med. ripe tomatoes

Cook pasta according to pkg. directions; drain. Rinse with cold water. In large bowl combine pasta and remaining ingredients *except* tomatoes. Toss to coat with reserved artichoke marinade. Remove stems from tomatoes; cut *each* tomato into 4 wedges, leaving ½" *(1 cm)* base to keep tomato intact. Serve 1 c. *(250 mL)* pasta over each tomato.

6 servings
1 hour 30 minutes

Dill n' Salmon Pasta Salad

A light refreshing summertime supper: serve with multi-grain bread and fresh fruit.

7-oz.   *(200-g)* pkg. uncooked corkscrew or twist pasta
8 oz.   *(225 g)* salmon fillet, cooked, chunked
2 c.   *(500 mL)* (8 oz.) *(225 g)* cubed ½" *(1 cm)* Cheddar cheese
⅓ c.   *(75 mL)* cubed ½" *(1 cm)* red pepper

2 tbsp. *(30 mL)* sliced green onion
⅓ c.   *(75 mL)* vegetable oil
¼ c.   *(50 mL)* lemon juice
1 tsp.   *(5 mL)* dill weed
½ tsp.   *(2 mL)* garlic salt
         Salt and pepper

Cook pasta according to pkg. directions; drain. Rinse with cold water. In large bowl stir together all ingredients; season with salt and pepper to taste. Cover; refrigerate at least 1 hr.

Tip: To cook salmon, place in 10" *(25 cm)* skillet; cover with water. Cook over med. heat until salmon flakes with a fork (12 to 15 min.).

Herb Garden Salad

8 servings
1 hour

Layered Rainbow Pasta Salad

Sun-kissed tomato and artichoke hearts combine with an array
of colorful ingredients in this main dish salad.

4 oz.	*(110 g)* uncooked corkscrew or twist pasta
4 c.	*(1 L)* torn leaf lettuce
3 c.	*(750 mL)* (12 oz.) *(340 g)* shredded Cheddar cheese
1	large ripe tomato, sliced ¼" *(0,5 cm)*, slices halved

14-oz.	*(398-g)* can artichoke hearts, drained, cut into 1" *(2,5 cm)* pieces
12	slices crisply cooked, crumbled bacon
2	slices crisply cooked bacon Italian dressing*

Cook pasta according to pkg. directions. Rinse with cold water; drain. To assemble salad, in large clear salad bowl layer 2 c. *(500 mL)* torn lettuce, 1½ c. *(375 mL)* cheese, tomato, pasta, 2 c. *(500 mL)* torn lettuce, artichoke hearts, crumbled bacon and remaining cheese.

Garnish top with bacon slices; serve with Italian dressing.

*Or serve with Basil Vinaigrette; see Sandwiches & Salads page 320.

---

6 servings
30 minutes

Herb Garden Salad

Cool and crisp, this garden-fresh salad is enhanced with herbs fresh from the garden.

Salad

4 c.	*(1 L)* torn lettuce
1 c.	*(250 mL)* sliced ¼" *(0,5 cm)* fresh mushrooms
1 c.	*(250 mL)* sliced ⅛" *(0,2 cm)* red onion, separated into rings
½ c.	*(125 mL)* torn fresh basil, parsley, mint or lemon balm
2	med. ripe tomatoes, each cut into 12 wedges
¾ lb.	*(340 g)* fresh green beans, blanched

Dressing

⅓ c.	*(75 mL)* olive or vegetable oil
½ tsp.	*(2 mL)* coarsely ground pepper
¼ tsp.	*(1 mL)* salt
2 tbsp.	*(30 mL)* red wine vinegar
1 tsp.	*(5 mL)* minced fresh garlic
1 tsp.	*(5 mL)* country-style Dijon mustard

In large bowl toss together all salad ingredients. In small bowl stir together all dressing ingredients. Pour dressing over salad; toss to coat.

Tip: To blanch green beans, place in boiling water for 7 to 9 min. Rinse in cold water.

Blue Cheese BLT Salad

6 servings
60 minutes

Backwoods Spinach Salad

A slightly sweet, warm bacon dressing tossed with spinach, wild rice and crispy radishes.

½ c.	*(125 mL)* uncooked wild rice	2 tbsp.	*(30 mL)* honey
8	slices bacon, cut into ½" *(1 cm)* pieces	4 c.	*(1 L)* torn spinach leaves
¼ c.	*(50 mL)* cider vinegar	1 c.	*(250 mL)* sliced ¼" *(0,5 cm)* fresh
¼ tsp.	*(1 mL)* salt		mushrooms
¼ tsp.	*(1 mL)* pepper	1 c.	*(250 mL)* sliced ¼" *(0,5 cm)* radishes

Cook wild rice according to pkg. directions. Meanwhile, in 10" *(25 cm)* skillet cook bacon over med. high heat, stirring occasionally, until browned (6 to 8 min.). Drain bacon fat, *reserving 2 tbsp.* (30 mL). In same skillet stir together vinegar, salt, pepper, honey and reserved bacon fat. Cook over med. heat, stirring occasionally, until heated through (3 to 4 min.). In large bowl combine remaining ingredients. Pour warm dressing over salad; toss to coat.

6 servings
20 minutes

Blue Cheese BLT Salad

Flavorful, colorful and delicious.

Dressing

¼ c.	*(50 mL)* cider vinegar
1 tbsp.	*(15 mL)* sugar
½ tsp.	*(2 mL)* pepper
¼ tsp.	*(1 mL)* salt
2 tbsp.	*(30 mL)* vegetable oil
1 tbsp.	*(15 mL)* lemon juice
½ tsp.	*(2 mL)* minced fresh garlic

Salad

4 c.	*(1 L)* torn lettuce
1	med. ripe avocado, peeled, cut into wedges
1	med. ripe tomato, cut into wedges
½ c.	*(125 mL)* sliced ⅛" *(0,2 cm)* onion, separated into rings
11-oz.	*(284-mL)* can mandarin orange segments, drained
½ c.	*(125 mL)* crumbled blue cheese
8	slices crisply cooked, crumbled bacon

In small bowl stir together all dressing ingredients. On platter or individual salad plates place lettuce. Arrange avocado, tomato, onion and mandarin orange segments on lettuce; sprinkle with blue cheese and bacon. Pour dressing over salad.

8 servings
2 hours 30 minutes

Spinach Salad With Yogurt Dressing

A homemade yogurt-based salad dressing is served with this fresh spinach salad.

Dressing
1 c.   *(250 mL)* plain yogurt
½ c.   *(125 mL)* mayonnaise
2 tbsp. *(30 mL)* sliced green onions
¼ tsp.   *(1 mL)* garlic salt
          Milk

Salad
6 c.   *(1,5 L)* fresh spinach, torn in
          bite-size pieces
2 c.   *(500 mL) (8 oz.) (225 g)* shredded
          Monterey Jack cheese
3   hard cooked eggs, quartered
⅓ c.   *(75 mL)* salted peanuts

In small bowl stir together all dressing ingredients *except* milk. Stir in milk until desired consistency is reached. Cover; refrigerate at least 2 hr. In large bowl toss together all salad ingredients; serve with dressing.

---

6 servings
30 minutes

Garden Tomato & Green Bean Salad

Summer salads — so flavorful with fresh tomatoes and green beans right from the garden.

1 lb.   *(450 g)* fresh green beans, trimmed
½ c.   *(125 mL)* mayonnaise
½ c.   *(125 mL)* dairy sour cream
1 tsp.   *(5 mL)* basil leaves
½ tsp.   *(2 mL)* pepper
¼ tsp.   *(1 mL)* salt

2 tbsp. *(30 mL)* chopped fresh parsley
2 tbsp. *(30 mL)* milk
1 tbsp. *(15 mL)* country-style Dijon mustard
2   med. ripe tomatoes, sliced ¼" *(0,5 cm)*
½ c.   *(125 mL)* sliced ⅛" *(0,2 cm)* red onion,
          separated into rings

Place beans in 3-qt. *(3-L)* saucepan; add enough water to cover. Bring to a full boil. Cook over med. heat until beans are crisply tender (12 to 15 min.). Meanwhile, in small bowl stir together remaining ingredients *except* tomatoes and onion. Rinse cooked green beans with cold water. On platter or individual salad plates arrange green beans, tomatoes and onion rings. Pour dressing over salad.

Spinach Salad With Yogurt Dressing (top)
Garden Tomato & Green Bean Salad (bottom)

Midsummer Artichoke Salad (top)
Picnic Potato Salad (bottom)

296

4 servings
40 minutes

Picnic Potato Salad

A comforting and familiar salad made even better with a hint of dill.

4 c.   *(1 L)* water
1 tsp.   *(5 mL)* salt
4 c.   *(1 L)* quartered small new red potatoes
⅓ c.   *(75 mL)* dairy sour cream
⅓ c.   *(75 mL)* mayonnaise
½ tsp.   *(2 mL)* dill weed
¼ tsp.   *(1 mL)* salt

¼ tsp.   *(1 mL)* pepper
2 tbsp.   *(30 mL)* chopped fresh parsley
1 tbsp.   *(15 mL)* country-style Dijon mustard
½ tsp.   *(2 mL)* minced fresh garlic
4   slices crisply cooked, crumbled bacon
2 tbsp.   *(30 mL)* sliced ⅛" *(0,2 cm)* green onion

In 3-qt. *(3-L)* saucepan bring water and salt to a full boil; add potatoes. Cook over high heat until potatoes are tender (12 to 15 min.). Rinse under cold water. In large bowl stir together remaining ingredients *except* bacon and green onion. Add potatoes; toss to coat. Sprinkle with bacon and green onion.

6 servings
15 minutes

Midsummer Artichoke Salad

Taste the sun in lush, ripe tomatoes tossed with artichokes, mushrooms and Mozzarella cheese.

3 c.   *(750 mL)* torn lettuce
2 c.   *(500 mL)* (½ lb.) *(225 g)* fresh mushrooms, halved
1 c.   *(250 mL)* (4 oz.) *(110 g)* cubed ½" *(1 cm)* Mozzarella cheese

2   (6-oz.) *(170-mL)* jars marinated artichoke hearts, *reserve marinade*
2   med. ripe tomatoes, cut into wedges
2 tbsp.   *(30 mL)* grated Parmesan cheese
¼ tsp.   *(1 mL)* coarsely ground pepper

In large bowl stir together all ingredients; toss to coat with reserved artichoke marinade.

6 servings
20 minutes

Summer Squash Salad

*A hearty fresh zucchini, yellow squash and ripe tomato salad
with a splash of Parmesan dressing.*

2 c.	*(500 mL)* (2 med.) sliced ⅛" *(0,2 cm)* zucchini
2 c.	*(500 mL)* (2 med.) halved lengthwise, sliced ⅛" *(0,2 cm)* yellow squash
¼ c.	*(50 mL)* grated Parmesan cheese
¼ c.	*(50 mL)* cider vinegar
¼ tsp.	*(1 mL)* salt
¼ tsp.	*(1 mL)* pepper
¼ tsp.	*(1 mL)* basil leaves
2 tbsp.	*(30 mL)* vegetable oil
½ tsp.	*(2 mL)* minced fresh garlic
½ c.	*(125 mL)* sliced ⅛" *(0,2 cm)* red onion, separated into rings
2	med. ripe tomatoes, cut into wedges

In 2-qt. *(2-L)* saucepan place zucchini and yellow squash; add enough water to cover. Cook over med. high heat until water comes to a full boil. Boil 1 to 2 min.; drain. Rinse with cold water. In large bowl stir together remaining ingredients *except* onion and tomatoes. Add zucchini, yellow squash, onion and tomatoes; toss to coat.

6 servings
15 minutes

Crispy Cucumbers in Dill Dressing

Cucumbers, tomatoes and onion add spark to simple summer fare.

¼ c.	*(50 mL)* cider vinegar
1 tsp.	*(5 mL)* sugar
½ tsp.	*(2 mL)* salt
½ tsp.	*(2 mL)* dill weed
¼ tsp.	*(1 mL)* pepper
2 tbsp.	*(30 mL)* vegetable oil
2 c.	*(500 mL)* (2 med.) sliced ⅛" *(0,2 cm)* cucumbers
1 c.	*(250 mL)* sliced ⅛" *(0,2 cm)* red onion, separated into rings
2	med. ripe tomatoes, cut into wedges

In large bowl stir together all ingredients *except* cucumbers, onion and tomatoes. Add remaining ingredients; toss to coat. Let stand 15 min. before serving.

298

Crispy Cucumbers in Dill Dressing

Crisp Vegetable Salad

6 servings
15 minutes

Crisp Vegetable Salad

Crisp and crunchy salad with an enticing cucumber dressing.

Dressing

⅓ c.   *(75 mL)* dairy sour cream
⅓ c.   *(75 mL)* mayonnaise
½ tsp.   *(2 mL)* dill weed
¼ tsp.   *(1 mL)* salt
¼ tsp.   *(1 mL)* dry mustard
         Pinch of pepper
1 tbsp. *(15 mL)* lemon juice
½ c.   *(125 mL)* chopped cucumber

Salad

2 c.   *(500 mL)* broccoli flowerets
2 c.   *(500 mL)* cauliflower flowerets
1 c.   *(250 mL)* (2 med.) sliced
        ¼" *(0,5 cm)* carrots
1 c.   *(250 mL)* (1 med.) sliced
        ⅛" *(0,2 cm)* cucumber

In large bowl stir together all dressing ingredients *except* cucumber. Stir in cucumber. Add all salad ingredients; toss to coat.

6 servings
20 minutes

Backporch Cabbage Slaw

A colorful layered cabbage salad that's perfect for barbecues and picnics.

Dressing

½ c.   *(125 mL)* dairy sour cream
3 oz.   *(90 g)* cream cheese, softened
2 tbsp. *(30 mL)* chopped fresh parsley
1 tsp.   *(5 mL)* salt
¼ tsp.   *(1 mL)* pepper
3 tbsp. *(45 mL)* milk
1 tbsp. *(15 mL)* lemon juice

Salad

4 c.   *(1 L)* shredded red cabbage
10-oz.   *(350-g)* pkg. frozen peas, thawed, drained
1 c.   *(250 mL)* (2 med.) shredded carrots
1 c.   *(250 mL)* (1 med.) sliced
         ⅛" *(0,2 cm)* cucumber
2 tbsp. *(30 mL)* chopped fresh parsley

In small bowl stir together all dressing ingredients. In large bowl layer 2 c. *(500 mL)* cabbage, 1 c. *(250 mL)* peas, ½ c. *(125 mL)* carrots and ½ c. *(125 mL)* cucumber.

Pour ½ c. *(125 mL)* dressing over salad. Repeat with remaining ingredients. Pour remaining dressing over salad. Sprinkle with 2 tbsp. *(30 mL)* parsley.

Blue Cheese Coleslaw

Adding crumbled blue cheese to homemade coleslaw provides a burst of flavor.

Dressing
¼ c.	*(50 mL)* sugar
¼ c.	*(50 mL) (2 oz.) (60 g)* blue cheese, crumbled
1 c.	*(250 mL)* mayonnaise
¼ c.	*(50 mL)* vinegar
½ tsp.	*(2 mL)* celery seed
½ tsp.	*(2 mL)* garlic salt
1 tbsp.	*(15 mL)* prepared mustard

Salad
8 c.	*(2 L)* finely shredded cabbage
1 c.	*(250 mL) (2 med.)* shredded carrots
¼ c.	*(50 mL)* sliced green onions
¼ c.	*(50 mL) (2 oz.) (60 g)* blue cheese, crumbled
1 c.	*(250 mL)* cherry tomato halves

In medium bowl stir together all dressing ingredients. Cover; refrigerate at least 2 hr. In large bowl combine cabbage, carrots and green onions. Just before serving, stir together dressing and cabbage mixture. Sprinkle with ¼ c. *(50 mL)* blue cheese. Garnish with cherry tomatoes. Serve immediately.

Bountiful Garden Salad With Pepper Salsa

This festive salad is perfect summer fare; it's casual, but dramatic, with colorful garden vegetables and a southwestern flavor.

6	fresh ears of corn on the cob, blanched*
3 c.	*(750 mL) (3 med.)* sliced ¼" *(0,5 cm)* zucchini or yellow squash
1 c.	*(250 mL) (1 med.)* sliced ⅛" *(0,2 cm)* cucumber
2	med. ripe tomatoes, *each* cut into 12 wedges

Salsa
½ tsp.	*(2 mL)* salt
½ tsp.	*(2 mL)* cumin
¼ tsp.	*(1 mL)* pepper
2 tbsp.	*(30 mL)* chopped fresh cilantro or parsley
2 tbsp.	*(30 mL)* lime juice
1 tbsp.	*(15 mL)* vegetable oil
1½ tsp.	*(7 mL)* minced jalapeño chilies
¾ c.	*(175 mL)* chopped green pepper
½ c.	*(125 mL)* chopped green onions

With sharp knife cut corn off cobs. In large bowl place cut corn, squash, cucumber and tomatoes. In medium bowl stir together all salsa ingredients *except* green pepper and onions. Stir in green pepper and onions. Stir salsa into salad ingredients; toss to coat.

*2 (9-oz.) *(300-g)* pkg. frozen whole kernel corn, thawed, can be substituted for 6 fresh ears of corn.

Tip: To blanch corn, place in boiling water for 2 min. Remove from heat; let stand 10 min. Rinse in cold water.

Bountiful Garden Salad With Pepper Salsa

Frosted Cranberry Squares

12 servings
7 hour 30 minutes

Frosted Cranberry Squares

This white-capped cranberry salad is the perfect accompaniment to your holiday meal.

Gelatin

2	(3-oz.) *(90-g)* pkg. raspberry flavor gelatin
2 c.	*(500 mL)* boiling water
12-oz.	*(300-g)* pkg. fresh or frozen cranberries, thawed
2 c.	*(500 mL)* sugar
⅔ c.	*(150 mL)* orange juice
20-oz.	*(568-mL)* can crushed pineapple in pineapple juice
1 tsp.	*(5 mL)* grated orange peel

Topping

3 oz.	*(90 g)* cream cheese, softened
1 c.	*(250 mL)* whipping cream
1 c.	*(250 mL)* miniature marshmallows

Orange slices or zest of orange peel
Sugared cranberries

In large bowl dissolve gelatin in boiling water; set aside. In 5-c. *(1,3-L)* blender container blend cranberries, half at a time, on high speed, stopping blender frequently to scrape sides, until well chopped (1 to 2 min.). Stir cranberries and remaining gelatin ingredients into dissolved gelatin mixture. Pour into 13 × 9" *(33 × 23 cm)* pan. Cover; refrigerate until firm (6 hr. or overnight). In small mixer bowl beat cream cheese at med. speed, scraping bowl often, until light and fluffy (1 to 2 min.). Scrape cheese off beaters; add whipping cream. Beat at low speed until mixed. Increase speed to high. Continue beating, scraping bowl often, until stiff peaks form (1 to 2 min.). By hand, fold in marshmallows. Spread over firm cranberry gelatin. Refrigerate at least 1 hr. Cut into squares. If desired, garnish with orange slices or zest of orange peel and sugared cranberries.

8 to 10 servings
7 hours

Chilled Peaches n' Cream Salad

Scoops of ice cream blend with chunky peaches in a chilled, refreshing gelatin salad.

2	(3-oz.) *(90-g)* pkg. peach flavor gelatin
1 c.	*(250 mL)* boiling water
1 c.	*(250 mL)* cold water
2 c.	*(500 mL)* vanilla ice cream, softened
	Pinch of nutmeg

1 lb.	*(450 g)* (3 to 4 med.) sliced fresh or frozen peaches, cut into ½" *(1 cm)* pieces, *reserve ½ fresh peach or 6 peach slices*
	Lettuce leaves

In large bowl dissolve gelatin in boiling water; stir in cold water, ice cream and nutmeg. Whisk until ice cream is melted. Refrigerate until slightly thickened (about 30 min.). Whisk mixture until smooth (1 to 2 min.); fold in peaches. Pour into greased 6-c. *(1,5-L)* mold. Refrigerate until firm (6 hr. or overnight). Unmold onto lettuce leaves; garnish with reserved peach slices.

8 to 10 servings
7 hour

Sparkling Fruit Molded Salad

*Ginger ale adds sparkle to this cool, refreshing salad layered
with red grapes, cantaloupe and green grapes.*

2	(¼-oz.) *(7-g)* envelopes unflavored gelatin
½ c.	*(125 mL)* water
½ c.	*(125 mL)* sugar
2 c.	*(500 mL)* ginger ale
2 tsp.	*(10 mL)* grated lime peel
2 tbsp.	*(30 mL)* lime juice

½ c.	*(125 mL)* seedless red grapes
1 c.	*(250 mL)* cubed 1" *(2,5 cm)* cantaloupe
1 c.	*(250 mL)* seedless green grapes
	Lime slices

In 1-qt. *(1-L)* saucepan soften gelatin in water. Cook over low heat, stirring occasionally, until gelatin is dissolved (3 to 5 min.). In large bowl stir together sugar and dissolved gelatin. Stir in ginger ale, lime peel and lime juice. Refrigerate until slightly thickened (about 45 min.). Pour 1 c. *(250 mL)* gelatin mixture into greased 6-c. *(1,5-L)* mold; refrigerate remaining slightly thickened gelatin. Add red grapes to gelatin in mold; refrigerate 15 min. Arrange cantaloupe on top of red grape gelatin mixture; spoon over just enough thickened gelatin to cover cantaloupe. Arrange green grapes on top of cantaloupe gelatin mixture. Spoon remaining thickened gelatin over green grapes. Refrigerate 6 hr. or overnight until firm. Unmold onto serving plate; garnish with lime slices.

8 servings
7 hours

Iced Banana Berry Salad

A mosaic of summer berries and bananas makes this simple frozen salad beautiful.

¾ c.	*(175 mL)* sugar
1 c.	*(250 mL)* dairy sour cream
1 tbsp.	*(15 mL)* grated lemon peel
2 tbsp.	*(30 mL)* lemon juice
1 c.	*(250 mL)* whipping cream
1 tsp.	*(5 mL)* vanilla
1 c.	*(250 mL)* (2 med.) sliced ¼" *(0,5 cm)* bananas

1 c.	*(250 mL)* blueberries*
1 c.	*(250 mL)* raspberries**
	Mint leaves
	Raspberries
	Blueberries

In large bowl stir together sugar, sour cream, lemon peel and lemon juice. In chilled small mixer bowl, beat chilled whipping cream at high speed, scraping bowl often, until stiff peaks form (1 to 2 min.). By hand, fold whipped cream, vanilla, bananas and berries into sour cream mixture. Spoon into individual ½-c. *(125-mL)* molds. Freeze 6 hr. or overnight. Unmold on small salad plates. If desired, garnish with mint leaves, raspberries and blueberries.

*1 c. *(250 mL)* frozen blueberries can be substituted for 1 c. *(250 mL)* blueberries.

**1 c. *(250 mL)* frozen raspberries can be substituted for 1 c. *(250 mL)* raspberries.

Tip: 8 × 4" *(20 × 10 cm)* loaf pan, lined with aluminum foil, can be substituted for individual ½-c. *(125-mL)* molds. Freeze 6 hr. or overnight. Lift salad from pan, using aluminum foil as handles. Remove aluminum foil. To serve, cut into 8 (1") *(2,5 cm)* slices.

Iced Banana Berry Salad (top)
Sparkling Fruit Molded Salad (bottom)

1 basket (1 cup *[250 mL]* dressing)
45 minutes

Star-Studded Fruit Basket

Become the "star" at your next picnic with this fruit-filled, watermelon showpiece.

Dressing

¼ c.	*(50 mL)*	honey
¼ c.	*(50 mL)*	frozen orange juice concentrate, thawed
½ c.	*(125 mL)*	whipping cream
1 tsp.	*(5 mL)*	poppy seed
¼ tsp.	*(1 mL)*	ginger

In small bowl stir together honey and orange juice concentrate. Stir in remaining dressing ingredients. Cover; refrigerate at least 1 hr. To make watermelon basket, measure and mark a horizontal line around the center of melon. Measure and mark a 2" *(5 cm)* wide center strip crosswise over top of melon for handle. Place 1½" *(3,5 cm)* star-shaped cookie cutter or cardboard pattern on marked horizontal line; trace around with pencil. Repeat, with star tips touching, all around middle of melon. Next, place star shape in center of 2" *(5 cm)* handle strip; trace around with pencil. Repeat, with

Basket

Large watermelon
Assorted fresh fruit pieces

star tips touching, over handle. With small sharp knife cut out stars, leaving bottom points attached to watermelon. Remove rind and melon. Cut out stars on handle, leaving bottom and top tips attached to one another. Carefully cut pink melon from handle, leaving white rind on handle. Remove remaining watermelon from basket with melon baller or spoon. Fill basket with assorted fresh fruit pieces. Serve dressing with fresh fruit.

Tip: Melon can be prepared one day ahead. Wrap tightly in plastic wrap and refrigerate.

To Prepare Basket:

1. Place 1½" *(3,5 cm)* star-shaped cookie cutter or cardboard pattern on marked horizontal line; trace around with pencil. Repeat, with star tips touching, all around middle of melon.

2. Next, place star shape in center of 2" *(5 cm)* handle strip; trace around with pencil. Repeat, with star tips touching, over handle.

3. With small sharp knife cut out stars, leaving bottom points attached to watermelon.

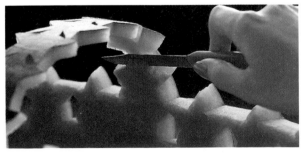

4. Carefully cut pink melon from handle, leaving white rind on handle.

Star-Studded Fruit Basket

6 servings
10 minutes

Summer Fruits With Lime Cooler

A squeeze of lime enhances fresh fruits and berries.

Dressing

½ c.	*(125 mL)* dairy sour cream
2 tbsp.	*(30 mL)* sugar
1 tsp.	*(5 mL)* grated lime peel
1 tbsp.	*(15 mL)* lime juice

Fruit

4	plums, sliced
2	peaches, sliced
1 pt.	*(500 mL)* strawberries, hulled, halved
½ pt.	*(250 mL)* raspberries

In small bowl stir together all dressing ingredients; set aside. In large bowl or individual fruit bowls toss together fruit. Serve dressing over fruit.

6 servings
20 minutes

Nutmeg Cream Melon Salad

So simple to make and refreshing to eat.

3 oz.	*(90 g)* cream cheese, softened
1 tbsp.	*(15 mL)* powdered sugar
¼ tsp.	*(1 mL)* nutmeg
	Pinch of salt
1 tbsp.	*(15 mL)* milk

2 c.	*(500 mL)* seedless red or green grapes
2 c.	*(500 mL)* cubed 1" *(2,5 cm)* cantaloupe
2 c.	*(500 mL)* cubed 1" *(2,5 cm)* honeydew

In large bowl stir together all ingredients *except* grapes, cantaloupe and honeydew. Add remaining ingredients; toss to coat.

Nutmeg Cream Melon Salad (top)
Summer Fruits With Lime Cooler (bottom)

4 to 6 servings
1 hour 30 minutes

Cinnamon Chicken Fruit Salad

For a special luncheon, serve this elegant chicken fruit salad in pineapple halves.

Salad

2½ c.	*(625 mL)*	cooked, cubed 1" *(2,5 cm)* chicken
2 c.	*(500 mL)*	seedless green grapes, cut in half
2 c.	*(500 mL)*	pitted sweet cherries
1 c.	*(250 mL)*	(2 stalks) sliced ¼" *(0,5 cm)* celery
2 tbsp.	*(30 mL)*	finely chopped onion
2 c.	*(500 mL)*	(1 large) fresh, cubed 1" *(2,5 cm)* pineapple; *reserve shell for serving*

Dressing

½ c.	*(125 mL)*	mayonnaise
½ c.	*(125 mL)*	vanilla yogurt
¼ tsp.	*(1 mL)*	ginger
¼ tsp.	*(1 mL)*	cinnamon
¼ c.	*(50 mL)*	toasted coconut

In large bowl combine all salad ingredients *except* pineapple; set aside. In small bowl stir together all dressing ingredients *except* coconut. Pour over salad; toss gently to coat. Cover; refrigerate at least 1 hr. Just before serving, place pineapple shells on large lettuce-lined platter. Stir cubed pineapple into salad. Spoon into pineapples; sprinkle with coconut.

Tip: Seedless red grapes can be substituted for the cherries.

To Prepare Pineapple Shells:

1. Leaving greens attached, cut pineapple into quarters or sixths lengthwise.

2. Holding pineapple securely, cut fruit from rind.

Cinnamon Chicken Fruit Salad

Orchard Salad With Almond Cream

6 servings
20 minutes

Orchard Salad With Almond Cream

Juicy ripe pears and crisp, tart apples blend with sweet apricots in a light almond whipped cream.

2	med. ripe pears, cut into 1" *(2,5 cm)* pieces
2	med. tart apples, cored, sliced ¼" *(0,5 cm)*
16-oz.	*(398-mL)* can apricot halves, drained, *reserve juice*

1 c.	*(250 mL)* whipping cream
2 tbsp.	*(30 mL)* sugar
¼ c.	*(50 mL)* reserved apricot juice
1 tbsp.	*(15 mL)* grated orange peel
½ tsp.	*(2 mL)* almond extract

In large bowl place pears, apples and apricots. In chilled small mixer bowl beat chilled whipping cream at high speed, scraping bowl often, until soft peaks form. Gradually add sugar; continue beating until stiff peaks form (1 to 2 min.). By hand, fold in remaining ingredients. Fold whipped cream into fruit mixture.

To Prepare Whipping Cream:

1. In chilled small mixer bowl beat chilled whipping cream at high speed, scraping bowl often, until soft peaks form. Gradually add sugar; continue beating until stiff peaks form (1 to 2 min.).

2. By hand, fold in remaining ingredients.

6 servings
30 minutes

Honey Glazed Citrus Salad

A refreshing combination of flavors.

2 tbsp.   *(30 mL)* vegetable oil
2 tbsp.   *(30 mL)* cider vinegar
2 tbsp.   *(30 mL)* honey
4 c.   *(1 L)* torn lettuce
½ c.   *(125 mL)* chopped red onion
¼ c.   *(50 mL)* chopped fresh parsley
2   oranges, pared, sectioned,
          drained
2   grapefruit, pared, sectioned,
          drained

In large bowl stir together oil, vinegar and honey. Add remaining ingredients; toss to coat.

To Section Grapefruit or Oranges:

1. Using sharp paring knife, remove the peel and white membrane by cutting in a spiral pattern.

2. For each section, cut toward the center of the fruit between the section and the membrane.

3. Turn knife, sliding knife down the other side of the section next to the membrane. Remove any seeds.

Honey Glazed Citrus Salad

Glazed Cranberry Citrus Compote

6 servings
40 minutes

Grandma's Winter Fruit Medley

A delicious fruit salad served with a thickened fruit juice dressing.

Fruit

2 c.	*(500 mL)* seedless green grapes
2 c.	*(500 mL)* seedless red grapes
20-oz.	*(568-mL)* can pineapple chunks, drained, *reserve juice*
11-oz.	*(284-mL)* can mandarin orange segments, drained, *reserve juice*
2	med. bananas, sliced ½" *(1 cm)*

Dressing

½ c.	*(125 mL)* sugar
¾ c.	*(175 mL) reserved* fruit juices
1	egg
1 tbsp.	*(15 mL)* all-purpose flour
1 tsp.	*(5 mL)* lemon juice

Place fruit in large bowl. In 1-qt. *(1-L)* saucepan stir together all dressing ingredients. Cook over med. heat, stirring occasionally, until dressing is thickened (3 to 5 min.). Let stand 5 min. Pour dressing over fruit; toss to coat. Chill 15 min.

6 servings
2 hours

Glazed Cranberry Citrus Compote

A refreshing, unique blend of chilled citrus fruits and sugar-glazed cranberries.

1 c.	*(250 mL)* fresh or frozen whole cranberries, thawed
¼ c.	*(50 mL)* sugar
1 tbsp.	*(15 mL)* grated fresh gingerroot

3	oranges, pared, sectioned, *reserve juice*
2	grapefruit, pared, sectioned, *reserve juice*
1 tbsp.	*(15 mL)* grated orange peel
1	kiwi, peeled, sliced ⅛" *(0,2 cm)*

In 2-qt. *(2-L)* saucepan place cranberries; sprinkle with sugar and gingerroot. Cover; cook over med. heat for 2 min. Stir cranberries. Continue cooking for 1 to 2 min. or until cranberries begin to soften but still hold their shape. Meanwhile, in large bowl stir together oranges, grapefruit and reserved juices; sprinkle with orange peel. Stir in glazed cranberries. Spoon into individual fruit dishes; top each with slice of kiwi. Refrigerate 1 hr. or until served.

Microwave Directions: In medium bowl combine cranberries, sugar and gingerroot. Cover with plastic wrap; microwave on HIGH until cranberries begin to soften but still hold their shape (1½ to 2 min.). Meanwhile, in large bowl stir together oranges, grapefruit and reserved juices; sprinkle with orange peel. Stir in glazed cranberries. Spoon into individual fruit dishes; top each with slice of kiwi. Refrigerate 1 hr. or until served.

1 cup *(250 mL)*
15 minutes

Basil Vinaigrette

This light basil dressing will make your garden-fresh lettuce and vegetables sparkle.

½ c.   *(125 mL)* vegetable or olive oil
⅓ c.   *(75 mL)* white vinegar
1 tbsp. *(15 mL)* torn fresh basil

1 tsp.   *(5 mL)* minced fresh garlic
¼ tsp.   *(1 mL)* salt
¼ tsp.   *(1 mL)* pepper

In jar with lid combine all ingredients. Shake well. Store refrigerated.

2 cups *(500 mL)*
1 hour 15 minutes

Creamy Herb Dressing

Herbs, fresh from the garden, are the secret to this flavorful dressing.

⅓ c.   *(75 mL)* chopped fresh parsley
¼ c.   *(50 mL)* chopped green onions
1 c.   *(250 mL)* dairy sour cream
¼ c.   *(50 mL)* mayonnaise

½ c.   *(125 mL)* buttermilk*
1 tsp.   *(5 mL)* chopped fresh thyme leaves**
¼ tsp.   *(1 mL)* salt
¼ tsp.   *(1 mL)* pepper

In small bowl stir together all ingredients. Cover; refrigerate at least 1 hr.

*1½ tsp. *(7 mL)* vinegar plus enough milk to equal ½ c. *(125 mL)* can be substituted for ½ c. *(125 mL)* buttermilk.

**½ tsp. *(2 mL)* dried thyme leaves, crushed, can be substituted for 1 tsp. *(5 mL)* fresh thyme leaves.

Basil Vinaigrette

PASTA, RICE & BEANS

Do you recall your favorite meal as a child? For many, it was macaroni and cheese. There was something so comforting about that dish, especially after a rough day at school or exhausting play with friends. As you came in the back door, you could smell that familiar aroma and just knew that Mom had made your favorite.

Think of the best baked beans you ever ate. They were lightly sweetened with brown sugar, and across the top were thick strips of bacon. Baked in a brown crock, the beans came from the oven bubbling hot and so tempting that you could hardly wait for the first delicious bite.

Then there was Mom's spaghetti. She made the sauce herself — a spicy-rich sauce that was chunky with stewed tomatoes and pepperoni. Lots of people asked for the recipe, but Mom's was always a little bit better.

Hearty, full-of-flavor dishes that start with pasta, rice or beans. Foods that satisfy so completely. The kind of old-fashioned food that memories are made of.

6 servings
45 minutes

Country Pasta With Mozzarella

A hearty home-style pasta filled with
bacon, broccoli and Mozzarella cheese.

8 oz.	*(225 g)* uncooked rigatoni
8	slices bacon, cut into 1" *(2,5 cm)* pieces
2 c.	*(500 mL)* broccoli flowerets
½ tsp.	*(2 mL)* minced fresh garlic
2 c.	*(500 mL) (8 oz.) (225 g)* shredded Mozzarella cheese

¼ c.	*(50 mL)* grated Parmesan cheese
	Pinch of cayenne pepper
¼ c.	*(50 mL)* chopped fresh parsley

Cook rigatoni according to pkg. directions; drain. Meanwhile, in 10" *(25 cm)* skillet cook bacon over med. high heat, stirring occasionally, until bacon is browned (6 to 8 min.). Reduce heat to med. Add broccoli and garlic. Cook, stirring occasionally, until broccoli is crisply tender (4 to 5 min.). Add rigatoni and remaining ingredients *except* parsley. Continue cooking, stirring occasionally, until cheese is melted (3 to 5 min.). Sprinkle with parsley.

Microwave Directions: Cook rigatoni according to pkg. directions; drain. In 3-qt. *(3-L)* casserole microwave bacon on HIGH until tender (4 to 5 min.). Add broccoli and garlic. Microwave on HIGH until broccoli is crisply tender (3 to 4 min.). Add rigatoni and remaining ingredients *except* parsley. Cover; microwave on HIGH, stirring after half the time, until heated through (2 to 3 min.). Let stand 2 min. Sprinkle with parsley.

6 servings
35 minutes

Spicy Spaghetti Sauce With Pepperoni

A chunky spaghetti sauce that's ready when you are
and abundant in taste and aroma.

8 oz.	*(225 g)* uncooked spaghetti
1 c.	*(250 mL)* sliced ½" *(1 cm)* fresh mushrooms
1 c.	*(250 mL)* (2 med.) chopped onions
1 c.	*(250 mL)* pitted ripe olives, sliced ½" *(1 cm)*
½ c.	*(125 mL)* chopped fresh parsley
1 c.	*(250 mL)* water

2	*(14½-oz.) (398-mL)* cans stewed tomatoes
6-oz.	*(156-mL)* can tomato paste
2 tsp.	*(10 mL)* basil leaves
½ tsp.	*(2 mL)* oregano leaves
¼ tsp.	*(1 mL)* pepper
1 tbsp.	*(15 mL)* country-style Dijon mustard
1 tsp.	*(5 mL)* minced fresh garlic
3 oz.	*(90 g)* sliced pepperoni

Cook spaghetti according to pkg. directions; drain. Meanwhile, in 3-qt. *(3-L)* saucepan combine all ingredients *except* pepperoni. Cook over over med. heat, stirring occasionally, until sauce is thickened (15 to 20 min.). Stir in pepperoni; continue cooking until heated through (4 to 5 min.). Serve over spaghetti.

Microwave Directions: Cook spaghetti according to pkg. directions; drain. In 3-qt. *(3-L)* casserole combine ¾ c. *(175 mL)* water and remaining ingredients *except* pepperoni. Cover; microwave on HIGH, stirring after half the time, until heated through (8 to 10 min.). Stir in pepperoni. Microwave on HIGH until pepperoni is heated through (2 to 3 min.). Serve over spaghetti.

Country Pasta With Mozzarella

Home-Style Macaroni & Cheese

6 servings
40 minutes

Home-Style Macaroni & Cheese

*Macaroni with chunks of Cheddar cheese is baked until bubbling
for a soothing and satisfying supper.*

7-oz.	*(200-g)* pkg. uncooked elbow macaroni
¼ c.	*(50 mL)* butter or margarine
3 tbsp.	*(45 mL)* all-purpose flour
2 c.	*(500 mL)* milk
8-oz.	*(250-g)* pkg. cream cheese, softened
½ tsp.	*(2 mL)* salt
½ tsp.	*(2 mL)* pepper

2 tsp.	*(10 mL)* country-style Dijon mustard
2 c.	*(500 mL)* (8 oz.) *(225 g)* cubed ½" *(1 cm)* Cheddar cheese
1 c.	*(250 mL)* fresh bread crumbs
2 tbsp.	*(30 mL)* butter or margarine, melted
2 tbsp.	*(30 mL)* chopped fresh parsley

Heat oven to 400°F *(200°C)*. Cook macaroni according to pkg. directions; drain. Meanwhile, in 3-qt. *(3-L)* saucepan melt ¼ c. *(50 mL)* butter; stir in flour. Cook over med. heat, stirring occasionally, until smooth and bubbly (1 min.). Stir in milk, cream cheese, salt, pepper and mustard. Continue cooking, stirring occasionally, until sauce is thickened (3 to 4 min.). Stir in macaroni and cheese. Pour into 2-qt. *(2-L)* casserole. In small bowl stir together remaining ingredients; sprinkle over macaroni and cheese. Bake for 15 to 20 min. or until golden brown and heated through.

Microwave Directions: Cook macaroni according to pkg. directions; drain. Meanwhile, in 3-qt. *(3-L)* casserole melt ¼ c. *(50 mL)* butter on HIGH (50 to 60 sec.). Stir in flour. Microwave on HIGH until bubbly (1 to 1½ min.). Stir in milk, cream cheese, salt, pepper and mustard. Microwave on HIGH, stirring after half the time, until thickened (4 to 5 min.). Stir in macaroni and cheese. In small bowl stir together remaining ingredients; sprinkle over macaroni and cheese. Microwave on HIGH until heated through (8 to 10 min.).

6 servings
30 minutes

Herb Garden & Lemon Pasta

Toss fresh garden ingredients together with pasta
for an enjoyable light supper.

8 oz.	*(225 g)* uncooked corkscrew or twist pasta	¼ c.	*(50 mL)* chopped fresh chives
⅓ c.	*(75 mL)* vegetable oil	¼ c.	*(50 mL)* chopped fresh parsley
3 c.	*(750 mL)* (3 med.) sliced	2	med. ripe tomatoes, cut into wedges
	¼" *(0,5 cm)* zucchini	½ tsp.	*(2 mL)* salt
1 c.	*(250 mL)* chopped red onion	½ tsp.	*(2 mL)* pepper
¼ c.	*(50 mL)* freshly grated Parmesan cheese	2 tbsp.	*(30 mL)* lemon juice
¼ c.	*(50 mL)* chopped fresh basil		

Cook pasta according to pkg. directions; drain. Meanwhile, in 10" *(25 cm)* skillet heat oil; add zucchini and onion. Cook over med. heat, stirring occasionally, until zucchini is crisply tender (5 to 7 min.). Add remaining ingredients and pasta. Cover; let stand 2 min. or until tomatoes are heated through.

Microwave Directions: Cook pasta according to pkg. directions; drain. In 3-qt. *(3-L)* casserole combine oil, zucchini and onion. Cover; microwave on HIGH, stirring after half the time, until zucchini is crisply tender (3 to 4 min.). Add remaining ingredients and pasta. Cover; microwave on HIGH, stirring after half the time, until tomatoes are heated through (1 to 2 min.).

4 servings
25 minutes

Fettucine With Spinach Cream Sauce

Butter and cream make this delicate spinach sauce rich in flavor.

8 oz.	*(225 g)* uncooked fettucine	10-oz.	*(300-g)* pkg. frozen chopped spinach, thawed, drained
3 tbsp.	*(45 mL)* butter or margarine	15	cherry tomatoes, halved
1 c.	*(250 mL)* sliced ¼" *(0,5 cm)* fresh mushrooms	1 tsp.	*(5 mL)* basil leaves
1 tbsp.	*(15 mL)* all-purpose flour	½ tsp.	*(2 mL)* salt
¼ c.	*(50 mL)* grated Parmesan cheese	¼ tsp.	*(1 mL)* pepper
1½ c.	*(375 mL)* half-and-half		

Cook fettucine according to pkg. directions; drain. Meanwhile, in 10" *(25 cm)* skillet melt butter; add mushrooms. Cook over med. heat, stirring occasionally, until mushrooms are tender (2 to 3 min.). Stir in flour until smooth and bubbly (1 min.). Stir in remaining ingredients. Continue cooking, stirring occasionally, until heated through (6 to 8 min.). Serve over fettucine.

Microwave Directions: Cook fettucine according to pkg. directions; drain. Meanwhile, in 2-qt. *(2-L)* casserole melt butter on HIGH (30 to 40 sec.). Stir in mushrooms. Microwave on HIGH until mushrooms are tender (1 to 2 min.). Stir in flour. Microwave on HIGH until smooth and bubbly (1 to 1½ min.). Add remaining ingredients *except* spinach and tomatoes. Microwave on HIGH until thickened (2 to 3 min.). Stir in spinach and tomatoes. Microwave on HIGH until heated through (1 to 2 min.). Serve over fettucine.

Herb Garden & Lemon Pasta

6 servings
45 minutes

Creamy Vegetables & Fettuccine

A colorful pasta side dish; serve with roast beef and a green salad for a hearty meal.

2 c.	*(500 mL)* (4 med.) diagonally sliced ½" *(1 cm)* carrots
6 oz.	*(170 g)* uncooked fettuccine
2 c.	*(500 mL)* broccoli flowerets
6 tbsp.	*(90 mL)* butter or margarine

2 tbsp.	*(30 mL)* all-purpose flour
½ tsp.	*(2 mL)* salt
½ tsp.	*(2 mL)* nutmeg
1 c.	*(250 mL)* milk
¼ c.	*(50 mL)* grated Parmesan cheese

In 3-qt. *(3-L)* saucepan bring 8 c. *(2 L)* water to a full boil. Add carrots and fettuccine. Cook over med. heat 6 min. Add broccoli; continue cooking until carrots and broccoli are crisply tender (4 to 5 min.); drain. Rinse with hot water; set aside. In same saucepan melt butter. Stir in flour, salt and nutmeg until smooth and bubbly (1 min.). Add milk; cook over med. heat, stirring occasionally, until mixture comes to a full boil (4 to 6 min.). Boil 1 min. Stir in fettuccine mixture. Reduce heat to low; continue cooking until heated through (3 to 4 min.). To serve, sprinkle with Parmesan cheese.

6 servings
30 minutes

Poppy Seed Noodles n' Cream

· Poppy seed and sour cream bring old world flavor to this quick side dish.

8 oz.	*(225 g)* uncooked extra wide egg noodles
1 c.	*(250 mL)* dairy sour cream
¼ c.	*(50 mL)* butter or margarine

2 tsp.	*(10 mL)* poppy seed
½ tsp.	*(1 mL)* salt

In 3-qt. *(3-L)* saucepan cook noodles according to pkg. directions; drain well. Return to pan; add remaining ingredients. Cook over med. heat, stirring constantly, until smooth and heated through (1 to 2 min.).

Creamy Vegetables & Fettuccine

Skillet Pasta & Vegetables (top)
Fresh Herb Linguine (bottom)

4 servings
15 minutes

Fresh Herb Linguine

A buttery, fresh herb sauce makes this pasta a perfect accompaniment to most any meat.

8 oz.	*(225 g)* uncooked linguine		1½ tsp.	*(7 mL)* chopped fresh oregano leaves*
⅓ c.	*(75 mL)* butter or margarine		1 tbsp.	*(15 mL)* lemon juice
½ tsp.	*(2 mL)* minced fresh garlic			
⅓ c.	*(75 mL)* chopped fresh parsley		1 c.	*(250 mL)* freshly grated Parmesan cheese

In 3-qt. *(3-L)* saucepan cook linguine according to pkg. directions; drain. In same saucepan place butter and garlic. Cook over med. heat until butter is melted (3 to 4 min.). Stir in linguine and remaining ingredients *except* Parmesan cheese. Cook over med. heat, stirring constantly, until heated through (2 to 3 min.). Sprinkle with Parmesan cheese.

*½ tsp. *(2 mL)* dried oregano leaves can be substituted for 1½ tsp. *(7 mL)* fresh oregano leaves.

Microwave Directions: Cook linguine according to pkg. directions; drain. In 2-qt. *(2-L)* casserole place butter and garlic. Microwave on HIGH until butter is melted (60 to 70 sec.). Stir in linguine and remaining ingredients *except* Parmesan cheese. Microwave on HIGH until heated through (1½ to 2 min.). Sprinkle with Parmesan cheese.

4 servings
30 minutes

Skillet Pasta & Vegetables

A new way to use the plentiful zucchini from your garden.

4 oz.	*(110 g)* uncooked bow tie pasta*		1 tsp.	*(5 mL)* basil leaves
¼ c.	*(50 mL)* butter or margarine		½ tsp.	*(2 mL)* salt
1 tsp.	*(5 mL)* minced fresh garlic		½ tsp.	*(2 mL)* pepper
1	med. zucchini, cut into ½" *(1 cm)* pieces		1½ c.	*(375 mL) (6 oz.) (170 g)* shredded
1	small eggplant, cut into ½" *(1 cm)* pieces			Mozzarella cheese
1	med. red onion, cut into eighths			

Cook pasta according to pkg. directions; drain. In 10" *(25 cm)* skillet melt butter until sizzling; stir in garlic. Stir in remaining ingredients *except* pasta and cheese. Cook over med. heat, stirring occasionally, until vegetables are crisply tender (4 to 6 min.). Stir in pasta. Continue cooking, stirring occasionally, until heated through (2 to 3 min.). Stir in cheese. Serve immediately.

*4 oz. *(110 g)* of your favorite uncooked pasta can be substituted for 4 oz. *(110 g)* uncooked bow tie pasta.

Microwave Directions: Cook pasta according to pkg. directions; drain. In 3-qt. *(3-L)* casserole melt butter on HIGH (40 to 50 sec.); stir in garlic. Microwave on HIGH 1 min. Stir in remaining ingredients *except* pasta and cheese. Cover; microwave on HIGH, stirring after half the time, until vegetables are crisply tender (5 to 6 min.). Stir in pasta. Microwave, stirring after half the time, until heated through (2 to 3 min.). Stir in cheese. Serve immediately.

Cheesy Confetti Rice (top)
Savory Rice & Vegetables (bottom)

8 servings
40 minutes

Savory Rice & Vegetables

There's no need for a dressing on this hearty salad.

Rice

1 c.	*(250 mL)* uncooked long grain rice
¼ c.	*(50 mL)* vegetable oil
¾ c.	*(175 mL)* water
10¾-oz.	*(284-mL)* can chicken broth
1 tsp.	*(5 mL)* paprika
¼ tsp.	*(1 mL)* salt
¼ tsp.	*(1 mL)* pepper
	Pinch of cayenne pepper

Vegetables

2 c.	*(500 mL)* broccoli flowerets
1 c.	*(250 mL)* pitted ripe olives
¼ c.	*(50 mL)* sliced ¼" *(0,5 cm)* green onions
¼ c.	*(50 mL)* chopped fresh parsley
1	med. ripe tomato, cut into wedges
1	med. green pepper, cut into strips
8 oz.	*(225 g)* sliced ⅛" *(0,2 cm)* summer sausage, halved

In 10" *(25 cm)* skillet combine rice and oil. Cook over med. low heat, stirring occasionally, until rice is browned (5 min.). Stir in remaining rice ingredients. Cover; continue cooking until liquid is absorbed (15 to 20 min.). Meanwhile, in large bowl stir together all vegetable ingredients. Pour hot rice over vegetables; toss to combine.

6 (⅔ cup) *(150 mL)* servings
50 minutes

Cheesy Confetti Rice

Cheese combines with rice and vegetables for a colorful and tasty side dish.

¼ c.	*(50 mL)* butter or margarine
1 c.	*(250 mL)* uncooked long grain rice
¼ c.	*(50 mL)* chopped onion
2½ c.	*(625 mL)* water
4-oz.	*(110-g)* can diced mild green chilies, drained
1 tbsp.	*(15 mL)* instant chicken bouillon
1 c.	*(250 mL)* (4 oz.) *(110 g)* shredded Monterey Jack cheese
¼ c.	*(50 mL)* sliced ripe olives
2-oz.	*(60-g)* jar diced pimiento, drained
2 tbsp.	*(30 mL)* chopped fresh parsley

In 2-qt. *(2-L)* saucepan melt butter. Add rice and onion. Cook over med. heat, stirring constantly, until rice is a golden color (8 to 10 min.). Slowly add water, green chilies and chicken bouillon. Continue cooking until mixture comes to a full boil (8 to 10 min.); reduce heat to low. Cover; simmer until rice is tender (25 to 30 min.). Stir in remaining ingredients. Serve immediately.

Microwave Directions: In 3-qt. *(3-L)* casserole melt butter on HIGH (50 to 60 sec.). Add rice and onion. Cover; microwave on HIGH until rice is a golden color (5 to 6 min.). Slowly add water, green chilies and chicken bouillon. Cover; microwave on HIGH until mixture comes to a full boil (5 to 6 min.). Reduce power to MEDIUM (50% power); microwave until rice is tender (10 to 12 min.). Stir in remaining ingredients. Serve immediately.

Springtime Garden Pilaf

8 (⅔ cup) *(150 mL)* servings
35 minutes

Crunchy almonds and colorful vegetables liven up rice.

2¾ c.	*(675 mL)* water	1¼ c.	*(300 mL)* uncooked long grain rice
¼ c.	*(50 mL)* butter or margarine	½ c.	*(125 mL)* finely chopped carrots
2 tbsp.	*(30 mL)* instant chicken bouillon	½ c.	*(125 mL)* slivered almonds, toasted
¼ tsp.	*(1 mL)* salt	¼ c.	*(50 mL)* chopped fresh parsley
	Pinch of pepper	2 tbsp.	*(30 mL)* sliced green onion
¼ tsp.	*(1 mL)* minced fresh garlic		

In 2-qt. *(2-L)* saucepan bring water, butter, chicken bouillon, salt, pepper and garlic to a full boil (5 to 7 min.). Add rice and carrots; return to a full boil. Reduce heat to low; simmer until rice is tender (25 to 30 min.). Stir in remaining ingredients.

Microwave Directions: In 3-qt. *(3-L)* casserole combine water, butter, chicken bouillon, salt, pepper and garlic. Cover; microwave on HIGH until mixture comes to a full boil (4 to 5 min.). Add rice and carrots. Cover; microwave on HIGH 5 min. Reduce power to MEDIUM (50% power); microwave until rice is tender (10 to 15 min.). Stir in remaining ingredients. Cover; let stand 5 min.

Crunchy Rice Medley

6 (½ cup) *(125 mL)* servings
25 minutes

Water chestnuts add crunch to this flavorful side dish.

6-oz.	*(170-g)* pkg. long grain & wild rice mix	4-oz.	*(110-g)* can sliced mushrooms, drained
¼ c.	*(50 mL)* butter or margarine	2-oz.	*(60-g)* jar chopped pimiento, drained
8-oz.	*(199-mL)* can sliced water chestnuts, drained		

Cook rice according to pkg. directions. Stir in remaining ingredients. Continue cooking until butter is melted and vegetables are heated through (3 to 4 min.).

Springtime Garden Pilaf

6 servings
60 minutes

Trappers' Wild Rice

A sweet, full-flavored wild rice that is a perfect accompaniment to game or roasted meat.

1 c.	*(250 mL)* uncooked wild rice		½ tsp.	*(2 mL)* pepper
4 c.	*(1 L)* water		2 tsp.	*(10 mL)* minced fresh garlic
2	med. carrots, sliced ⅛" *(0,2 cm)*		1 tsp.	*(5 mL)* grated fresh gingerroot
1	med. onion, sliced ⅛" *(0,2 cm)*		½ c.	*(125 mL)* apple juice
1 tsp.	*(5 mL)* salt		3 tbsp.	*(45 mL)* honey
1 tsp.	*(5 mL)* sage leaves, rubbed		2 tbsp.	*(30 mL)* chopped fresh parsley

Rinse wild rice. In 2-qt. *(2-L)* saucepan combine wild rice and remaining ingredients *except* apple juice, honey and parsley. Bring to a full boil (6 to 8 min.). Cover; cook over med. heat until wild rice is tender (45 to 50 min.). Drain off any excess liquid; stir in apple juice and honey. Continue cooking until heated through (4 to 5 min.). Stir in parsley.

Microwave Directions: Rinse wild rice. In 2-qt. *(2-L)* casserole combine wild rice and remaining ingredients *except* apple juice, honey and parsley. Cover; microwave on HIGH until mixture comes to full boil (9 to 12 min.). Reduce power to MEDIUM (50% power); microwave, stirring occasionally, until wild rice is tender (40 to 50 min.). Drain off any excess liquid; stir in apple juice and honey. Microwave on HIGH until heated through (2 to 3 min.). Stir in parsley.

8 servings
3 hours 30 minutes

Barn-Raising Beans

Serve these mildly spiced beans with accompaniments of rice, sour cream and green onions.

1 lb.	*(450 g)* dried red beans*		1½ tsp.	*(7 mL)* salt
6	slices bacon, cut into ½" *(1 cm)* pieces		½ tsp.	*(2 mL)* cumin
1 c.	*(250 mL)* (2 med.) chopped onions		½ tsp.	*(2 mL)* thyme leaves
¼ c.	*(50 mL)* chopped fresh cilantro or parsley		2	bay leaves
¼ c.	*(50 mL)* butter or margarine		2	whole cloves
2	med. carrots, coarsely chopped		2 tsp.	*(10 mL)* minced fresh garlic
1 tbsp.	*(15 mL)* chili powder		4 c.	*(1 L)* water

In large bowl place beans; cover with water. Soak for 1 hr. Meanwhile, in 3-qt. *(3-L)* saucepan cook bacon over med. high heat, stirring occasionally, until bacon is browned (6 to 8 min.). Reduce heat to med. Add remaining ingredients *except* 4 c. *(1 L)* water and beans. Cook, stirring occasionally, until onions are crisply tender (2 to 3 min.). Drain beans; add to vegetable mixture.

Add 4 c. *(1 L)* water. Cook over high heat until mixture comes to a full boil. Reduce heat to med. Cover; cook, stirring occasionally, until beans are fork tender (1½ to 2 hr.). Remove bay leaves and cloves.

*1 lb. *(450 g)* dried kidney beans can be substituted for 1 lb. *(450 g)* dried red beans. Cook for 60 to 70 min.

Trappers' Wild Rice (top)
Barn-Raising Beans (bottom)

8 cups *(2 L)*
1 day

Robust Country Baked Beans

Long, slow cooking brings out old-time flavor in these hearty baked beans.

2 c.	*(500 mL)* dried Great Northern beans		¼ c.	*(50 mL)* dark molasses
1 c.	*(250 mL)* dried kidney beans		½ lb.	*(225 g)* thick-sliced bacon, cut into
⅔ c.	*(150 mL)* firmly packed brown sugar			1" *(2,5 cm)* pieces
1½ c.	*(375 mL)* boiling water		½ lb.	*(225 g)* salt pork, cubed 1" *(2,5 cm)*
¼ c.	*(50 mL)* country-style Dijon mustard		2	med. onions, chopped

In Dutch oven stir together Great Northern beans, kidney beans and enough cold water to cover beans; soak overnight. If needed, add more water to cover beans. Cook over high heat until water comes to a full boil. Reduce heat to med.; continue cooking 30 to 45 min. or until beans are tender. Heat oven to 325°F *(160°C)*. Drain beans. In large bean pot or Dutch oven combine beans and remaining ingredients. Bake, stirring occasionally, for 6 to 9 hr. or until beans are a rich brown color and sauce has thickened. If beans become dry during baking, add 1 to 2 c. *(250 to 500 mL)* water.

Same Day: For same day preparation do not soak overnight. Instead, cook over high heat until water comes to a full boil. Reduce heat to med.; boil 2 min. Remove from heat. Cover; let stand 1 hr. Continue as directed left, beginning at "If needed, add more water to cover beans."

---

4 servings
30 minutes

Southern Style Black-Eyed Peas & Rice

A variation on a southern specialty called Hopping John.

2 c.	*(500 mL)* cooked black-eyed peas		2 tbsp.	*(30 mL)* grated Parmesan cheese
1 c.	*(250 mL)* cooked long grain rice		½ tsp.	*(2 mL)* salt
¼ c.	*(50 mL)* butter or margarine		¼ tsp.	*(1 mL)* hot pepper sauce
4 c.	*(1 L)* torn fresh spinach*		1 c.	*(250 mL) (4 oz.) (110 g)* shredded
4	slices bacon, cut into 1" *(2,5 cm)* pieces			Cheddar cheese

Have cooked black-eyed peas and rice ready. In 2-qt. *(2-L)* saucepan melt butter. Stir in spinach and bacon. Cook over med. heat, stirring occasionally, until spinach is tender (4 to 6 min.). Stir in black-eyed peas, rice and remaining ingredients *except* Cheddar cheese. Continue cooking, stirring occasionally, until heated through (7 to 10 min.). Just before serving, stir in Cheddar cheese.

*10-oz. *(300-g)* pkg. frozen chopped spinach, thawed and drained, can be substituted for 4 c. *(1 L)* torn fresh spinach.

Microwave Directions: Have cooked black-eyed peas and rice ready. In 2-qt. *(2-L)* casserole melt butter on HIGH (50 to 60 sec.). Stir in spinach and bacon. Microwave on HIGH, stirring after half the time, until spinach is tender (3 to 4 min.). Stir in black-eyed peas, rice and remaining ingredients *except* Cheddar cheese. Microwave on HIGH, stirring after half the time, until heated through (4 to 5 min.). Just before serving, stir in Cheddar cheese.

Robust Country Baked Beans (top)
Southern Style Black-Eyed Peas & Rice (bottom)

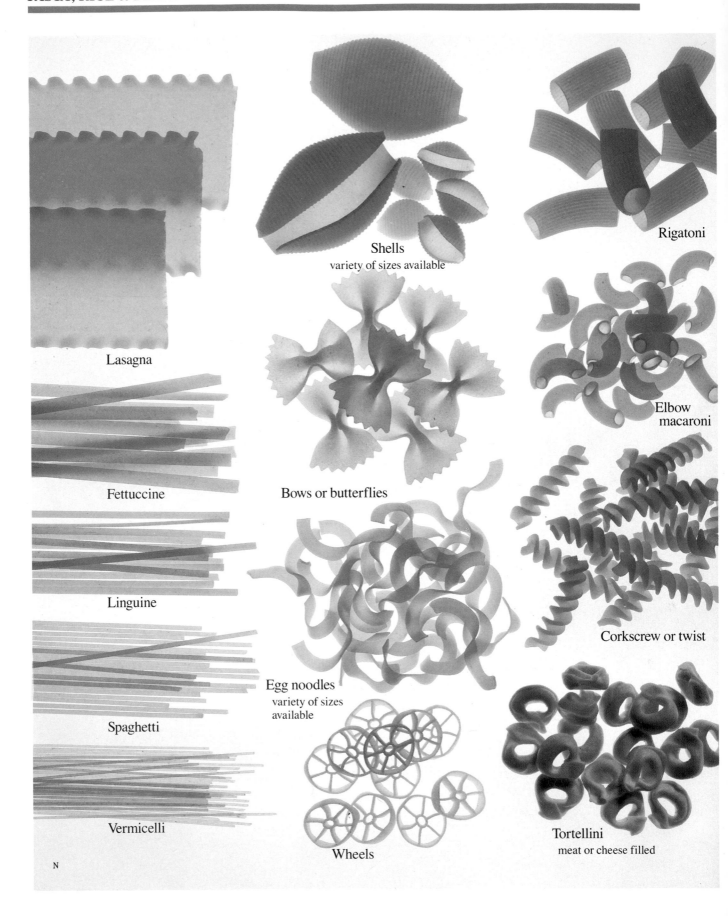

Lasagna

Fettuccine

Linguine

Spaghetti

Vermicelli

Shells
variety of sizes available

Bows or butterflies

Egg noodles
variety of sizes
available

Wheels

Rigatoni

Elbow
macaroni

Corkscrew or twist

Tortellini
meat or cheese filled

N

Wild:
Seed of grass grown in marshes and shallow lakes.

Split peas

Black-eyed peas

Brown:
Whole grain, unpolished, hull and part of bran removed.

Navy beans

Great Northern beans

Regular, short grain or long grain:
Milled to remove hull, germ and part of bran.

Converted, parboiled or processed:
Treated before milling to force nutrients into the starchy part of the grain.

Pinto beans

Red beans

Precooked or instant:
Long grain rice that has been cooked, rinsed and dried.

Kidney beans

Lima beans

VEGETABLES

Fresh from the farm or country roadside stand, vegetables present a kaleidoscope of shapes, sizes, colors and tastes. And no matter which way you turn, each variety looks more inviting than the last.

Fresh green beans, crisp enough to snap between your fingers. Imagine them cooked with bacon and rings of red onion. You can almost taste the flavor. And carrots with their lacy-leafed tops, so good whether creamed, glazed or as part of an old-fashioned pot roast dinner. Plump, vine-ripened tomatoes, bright red inside and out and sweeter than you ever imagined. Tender ears of corn, still in their fresh green husks with silky, golden topknots. The pleasures of sweet corn-on-the-cob, served piping hot with plenty of butter, are nothing less than legendary.

As beautiful as they are delicious, these are the fruits of the earth. And every vegetable dish you prepare brings a touch of the country into your home.

Tender Asparagus Spears With Garlic Mustard

From the garden or market an abundance of asparagus is always a joy.

1 lb.	*(450 g)* (24) asparagus spears, trimmed	2 tbsp.	*(30 mL)* country-style Dijon mustard
¼ c.	*(50 mL)* butter or margarine	¼ tsp.	*(1 mL)* pepper
2 c.	*(500 mL)* (½ lb.) *(225 g)* sliced		Pinch of salt
	¼" *(0,5 cm)* fresh mushrooms	½ tsp.	*(2 mL)* minced fresh garlic

In 10" *(25 cm)* skillet place asparagus spears; add enough water to cover. Bring to a full boil. Cook over med. heat until asparagus is crisply tender (5 to 7 min.). Drain; return to skillet. Add remaining ingredients, pushing asparagus to side just until butter is melted. Cook over med. heat, stirring occasionally, until heated through (5 to 7 min.).

Microwave Directions: In 12 × 8" *(30 × 20 cm)* baking dish melt butter on HIGH (50 to 60 sec.). Stir in all ingredients *except* asparagus and mushrooms; mix well. Place asparagus, heads toward center of dish, and mushrooms in dish; turn to coat with butter mixture. Cover; microwave on HIGH, stirring after half the time, until vegetables are crisply tender (6 to 9 min.). Let stand 2 min.

Garden Green Beans With Bacon

*Fresh, tender green beans cooked with flavorful bacon and onion
provide old-fashioned goodness.*

1 lb.	*(450 g)* fresh green beans, trimmed	3 tbsp.	*(45 mL)* butter or margarine
4	slices bacon, cut into ½" *(1 cm)* pieces	½ tsp.	*(2 mL)* pepper
1 c.	*(250 mL)* sliced ⅛" *(0,2 cm)* red onion, separated into rings	¼ tsp.	*(1 mL)* salt

In 3-qt. *(3-L)* saucepan place beans and bacon; add enough water to cover. Bring to a full boil. Cook over med. heat, stirring occasionally, until beans are crisply tender (20 to 25 min.); drain. Return to pan; add remaining ingredients. Cook over med. heat, stirring occasionally, until onion is crisply tender (5 to 7 min.).

Microwave Directions: In 3-qt. *(3-L)* casserole combine beans and ½ c. *(125 mL)* water. Cover; microwave on HIGH, stirring after half the time, until beans are crisply tender (8 to 10 min.). Drain; return to casserole. Add remaining ingredients. Cover; microwave on HIGH until heated through (3 to 5 min.).

Garden Green Beans With Bacon (top)
Tender Asparagus Spears With Garlic Mustard (bottom)

Country Vegetable Simmer

6 servings
45 minutes

Country Vegetable Simmer

*Simmer fresh green beans, sweet new potatoes and juicy tomatoes
with just a hint of basil for a hearty vegetable dish.*

½ lb.	*(225 g)* fresh green beans, trimmed
4	small new red potatoes, quartered
2	small onions, quartered
3 tbsp.	*(45 mL)* butter or margarine
8	fresh mushrooms, halved
1	med. ripe tomato, cut into ½" *(1 cm)* pieces

1 tsp.	*(5 mL)* basil leaves
¼ tsp.	*(1 mL)* salt
¼ tsp.	*(1 mL)* pepper
¼ tsp.	*(1 mL)* thyme leaves
2 tbsp.	*(30 mL)* tomato paste
½ tsp.	*(2 mL)* minced fresh garlic
¼ c.	*(50 mL)* chopped fresh parsley

In 3-qt. *(3-L)* saucepan combine beans, potatoes and onions. Add enough water to cover; bring to a full boil. Cook over med. heat, stirring occasionally, until vegetables are crisply tender (15 to 20 min.); drain. Return to pan; add remaining ingredients *except* parsley. Cook over med. heat, stirring occasionally, until heated through (10 to 12 min.). Stir in parsley.

Microwave Directions: In 3-qt. *(3-L)* casserole combine beans, potatoes, onions and ½ c. *(125 mL)* water. Cover; microwave on HIGH, stirring after half the time, until vegetables are crisply tender (10 to 13 min.). Drain; return to casserole. Add remaining ingredients *except* parsley. Cover; microwave on HIGH until heated through (2 to 3 min.). Stir in parsley.

4 servings
15 minutes

Family Favorite Green Beans

Green beans special enough for a party, but perfect for a family meal.

3 tbsp.	*(45 mL)* butter or margarine
1	med. onion, cut into eighths
10-oz.	*(300-g)* pkg. frozen French-style green beans
½ tsp.	*(2 mL)* rosemary
¼ tsp.	*(1 mL)* salt

	Pinch of pepper
8-oz.	*(227-g)* pkg. fresh mushrooms, cut into thirds
½ c.	*(125 mL)* (2 oz.) *(60 g)* shredded Monterey Jack cheese

In 2-qt. *(2-L)* saucepan melt butter. Stir in onion; cook over med. heat until tender (2 to 3 min.). Add remaining ingredients *except* mushrooms and cheese. Cover; continue cooking, stirring occasionally, until beans are thawed and separated (3 to 5 min.). Remove cover. Stir in mushrooms; continue cooking, stirring occasionally, until beans are crisply tender (5 to 7 min.). Sprinkle with cheese. Cover; let stand 1 min.

Microwave Directions: In 1½-qt. *(1,5-L)* casserole melt butter on HIGH (40 to 50 sec.). Stir in onion. Cover; microwave on HIGH 1 min. Stir in remaining ingredients *except* cheese. Cover; microwave on HIGH, stirring after half the time, until beans are crisply tender (4 to 5 min.). Sprinkle with cheese. Cover; let stand 1 min.

4 to 6 servings
30 minutes

Southern Lima Beans & Bacon

A hearty, stick-to-the-ribs country way to prepare lima beans.

2 tbsp.	*(30 mL)* butter or margarine		14-oz.	*(398-mL)* can stewed tomatoes
4	slices thick-sliced bacon, cut into		10-oz.	*(300-g)* pkg. frozen lima beans
	1" *(2,5 cm)* pieces		¼ tsp.	*(1 mL)* pepper
1	med. onion, cut into eighths		¼ tsp.	*(1 mL)* celery seed
1 c.	*(250 mL)* frozen whole kernel corn			

In 10" *(25 cm)* skillet melt butter until sizzling; stir in bacon and onion. Cook over med. high heat, stirring occasionally, 5 min.; drain. Reduce heat to med.; stir in remaining ingredients. Continue cooking, stirring occasionally, until lima beans are tender (8 to 10 min.).

Microwave Directions: In 3-qt. *(3-L)* casserole melt butter on HIGH (30 to 40 sec.). Stir in bacon and onion. Microwave on HIGH, stirring after half the time, 3 min.; drain. Stir in remaining ingredients. Cover; microwave on HIGH, stirring after half the time, until lima beans are tender (5 to 8 min.).

4 servings
60 minutes

Home-Style Beets With Sour Cream

This duo of fresh beets and carrots, accented with chives, is a fall favorite.

5	med. fresh beets		½ tsp.	*(2 mL)* salt
1 c.	*(250 mL)* (2 med.) sliced		½ tsp.	*(2 mL)* dill weed
	¼" *(0,5 cm)* carrots			Pinch of pepper
3 tbsp.	*(45 mL)* butter or margarine			
1 tbsp.	*(15 mL)* chopped fresh chives			Dairy sour cream

In 2-qt. *(2-L)* saucepan bring 3 c. *(750 mL)* water to a full boil. Add beets. Cover; cook over med. heat until beets are fork tender (35 to 45 min.). Drain. Run cold water over beets; slip off skins and remove root ends. Cut beets into ½" *(1 cm)* cubes; set aside. In 1-qt. *(1-L)* saucepan bring ¾ c. *(175 mL)* water to a full boil. Add carrots. Cover; cook over med. heat until carrots are crisply tender (8 to 10 min.). Drain; set aside. In same 2-qt. *(2-L)* saucepan melt butter. Add beets, carrots and remaining ingredients *except* sour cream. Cover; cook over med. heat, stirring occasionally, until heated through (5 to 7 min.). Serve with a dollop of sour cream.

Microwave Directions: In 2-qt. *(2-L)* casserole combine ¼ c. *(50 mL)* water and beets. Cover; microwave on HIGH, stirring after half the time, until beets are fork tender (15 to 17 min.). Let stand 2 min. Drain. Run cold water over beets; slip off skins and remove root ends. Cut beets into ½" *(1 cm)* cubes; set aside. In 1-qt. *(1-L)* casserole combine ½ c. *(125 mL)* water and carrots. Cover; microwave on HIGH, stirring after half the time, until carrots are crisply tender (4 to 5 min.). Let stand 1 min. Drain; set aside. In same 2-qt. *(2-L)* casserole melt butter on HIGH (40 to 50 sec.). Add beets, carrots and remaining ingredients *except* sour cream. Cover; microwave on HIGH, stirring after half the time, until heated through (3 to 4 min.). Let stand 1 min. Serve with a dollop of sour cream.

Home-Style Beets With Sour Cream

4 servings
20 minutes

Lemon Pepper Broccoli

Fresh broccoli spears are simply seasoned with cayenne pepper and zest of lemon.

1	med. (1½ lb.) *(625 g)* bunch of broccoli, cut into 12 spears
3 tbsp.	*(45 mL)* butter or margarine
2-oz.	*(60-g)* jar diced pimiento, drained

	Pinch of salt
	Pinch of cayenne pepper
2 tsp.	*(10 mL)* grated lemon peel

In 10" *(25 cm)* skillet place broccoli spears; add enough water to cover. Bring to a full boil. Cook over med. heat until broccoli is crisply tender (5 to 7 min.). Drain; return to skillet. Add remaining ingredients, pushing broccoli to side just until butter is melted. Cook over med. heat, stirring occasionally, until broccoli is heated through (5 to 7 min.).

Microwave Directions: In 12 × 8" *(30 × 20 cm)* baking dish place broccoli spears with heads toward center. Dot with butter; sprinkle with remaining ingredients. Cover; microwave on HIGH, turning dish ½ turn after half the time, until crisply tender (6 to 8 min.).

6 servings
60 minutes

Broccoli & Onion Au Gratin

Rosemary adds excitement to broccoli baked in a creamy Swiss cheese sauce.

Cheese Sauce

2 tbsp.	*(30 mL)* butter or margarine
2 tbsp.	*(30 mL)* all-purpose flour
½ tsp.	*(2 mL)* salt
¼ tsp.	*(1 mL)* rosemary leaves, crushed
¼ tsp.	*(1 mL)* pepper
1½ c.	*(375 mL)* milk
1 c.	*(250 mL)* shredded Swiss cheese

2 c.	*(500 mL)* broccoli flowerets
1	med. onion, cut into eighths

Topping

2 c.	*(500 mL)* fresh bread crumbs
⅓ c.	*(75 mL)* butter or margarine, melted
¼ c.	*(50 mL)* chopped fresh parsley

Heat oven to 350°F *(180°C)*. In 1-qt. *(1-L)* saucepan melt 2 tbsp. *(30 mL)* butter; stir in flour, salt, rosemary and pepper. Cook over med. heat, stirring constantly, until smooth and bubbly (30 sec.). Stir in milk. Continue cooking, stirring occasionally, until mixture thickens and comes to a full boil (4 to 5 min.). Boil 1 min. Remove from heat; stir in cheese until smooth. Set aside. In greased shallow 1-qt. *(1-L)* casserole or 9" *(23 cm)* sq. baking pan place broccoli and onion. Stir in cheese sauce. In small bowl stir together all topping ingredients. Sprinkle over broccoli mixture. Bake for 25 to 35 min. or until top is golden brown and broccoli is crisply tender.

Microwave Directions: In small bowl melt 2 tbsp. *(30 mL)* butter on HIGH (40 to 50 sec.). Stir in flour, salt, rosemary and pepper. Microwave on HIGH until smooth and bubbly (20 to 30 sec.). Stir in milk. Microwave on HIGH, stirring every min., until mixture thickens (5 to 6 min.). Stir in cheese until smooth; set aside. In greased shallow 1-qt. *(1-L)* baking dish or 10" *(25 cm)* quiche dish place broccoli and onion. Stir in cheese sauce. In small bowl stir together all topping ingredients. Sprinkle over broccoli mixture. Microwave on HIGH, turning ½ turn after half the time, until broccoli is crisply tender (6 to 7 min.).

Lemon Pepper Broccoli (top)
Broccoli & Onion Au Gratin (bottom)

Broccoli With Three Cheeses

Broccoli With Three Cheeses

*Cream cheese, Cheddar cheese and blue cheese blend together to make
a smooth, rich sauce for broccoli spears.*

1	med. (1½ lb.) *(675 g)* bunch of broccoli, cut into spears
1 c.	*(250 mL)* water
2 tbsp.	*(30 mL)* butter or margarine
2 tbsp.	*(30 mL)* all-purpose flour
¼ tsp.	*(1 mL)* pepper

1 c.	*(250 mL)* milk
3 oz.	*(90 g)* cream cheese, softened
1 c.	*(250 mL)* (4 oz.) *(125 g)* shredded Cheddar cheese
⅓ c.	*(75 mL)* crumbled blue cheese
¼ c.	*(50 mL)* chopped pecans

In Dutch oven place broccoli spears; add water. Cover; bring to a full boil. Cook over med. heat until broccoli is crisply tender (5 to 7 min.); drain. Meanwhile, in 1-qt. *(1-L)* saucepan melt butter; stir in flour and pepper. Cook over med. heat, stirring constantly, until smooth and bubbly (30 sec.). Stir in milk and cream cheese. Continue cooking, stirring occasionally, until mixture thickens and comes to a full boil (4 to 5 min.). Stir in Cheddar cheese and blue cheese. Continue cooking, stirring occasionally, until cheeses are melted (1 to 2 min.). Serve cheese sauce over broccoli; sprinkle with pecans.

Microwave Directions: *Decrease water to ½ c.* (125 mL). In 8" *(20 cm)* sq. baking dish place broccoli spears with heads toward center. Add ½ c. *(125 mL)* water. Cover with plastic wrap; microwave on HIGH, turning dish ½ turn after half the time, until crisply tender (6 to 8 min.). Let stand covered while preparing sauce; drain. In small bowl melt butter on HIGH (30 to 60 sec.). Stir in flour and pepper. Microwave on HIGH until bubbly (30 to 60 sec.). Stir in milk and cream cheese. Microwave on HIGH, stirring after half the time, until mixture thickens and comes to a full boil (2 to 3 min.). Stir until smooth. Stir in Cheddar cheese and blue cheese. Microwave on HIGH until cheeses are melted (1 to 1½ min.). Serve cheese sauce over broccoli; sprinkle with pecans.

Broccoli With Garlic Butter & Cashews

Tender broccoli spears served with melted butter, flavored with garlic and soy sauce.

1	med. (1½ lb.) *(675 g)* bunch of broccoli, cut into spears
1 c.	*(250 mL)* water
⅓ c.	*(75 mL)* butter or margarine
1 tbsp.	*(15 mL)* firmly packed brown sugar

¼ tsp.	*(1 mL)* pepper
3 tbsp.	*(45 mL)* soy sauce
2 tsp.	*(10 mL)* vinegar
¼ tsp.	*(1 mL)* minced fresh garlic
⅓ c.	*(75 mL)* salted whole cashews

In Dutch oven place broccoli spears; add water. Cover; bring to a full boil. Cook over med. heat until crisply tender (5 to 7 min.); drain. Remove to serving platter; keep warm. In same Dutch oven melt butter.

Add remaining ingredients *except* cashews. Cook over med. heat, stirring occasionally, until mixture comes to a full boil (3 to 4 min.). Stir in cashews. Serve broccoli with sauce.

6 servings
30 minutes

Lemon Chive Brussels Sprouts

Chives with their sweet oniony flavor and lemon add zest to Brussels sprouts.

1 lb.	*(450 g)* (40) Brussels sprouts, trimmed
¼ c.	*(50 mL)* butter or margarine
2 tbsp.	*(30 mL)* chopped fresh chives
2 tsp.	*(10 mL)* grated lemon peel
1½ tsp.	*(7 mL)* fresh dill weed*
¼ tsp.	*(1 mL)* salt
¼ tsp.	*(1 mL)* pepper

In 2-qt. *(2-L)* saucepan place Brussels sprouts; add enough water to cover. Bring to a full boil. Cook over med. heat until Brussels sprouts are crisply tender (12 to 15 min.); drain. Return to pan; add remaining ingredients. Cook over med. heat, stirring occasionally, until heated through (4 to 6 min.).

*½ tsp. *(2 mL)* dried dill weed can be substituted for 1½ tsp. *(7 mL)* fresh dill weed.

Microwave Directions: In 2-qt. *(2-L)* casserole place Brussels sprouts and ¼ c. *(50 mL)* water. Cover; microwave on HIGH until crisply tender (3 to 4 min.). Add remaining ingredients. Cover; microwave on HIGH, stirring after half the time, until heated through (2½ to 4 min.).

To Trim Brussels Sprouts:

1. To trim Brussels sprouts: remove any loose or discolored leaves.

2. Cut off stem ends, leaving enough stem to prevent outer leaves from falling off during cooking.

Lemon Chive Brussels Sprouts

Buttery Apples n' Cabbage

6 servings
20 minutes

Buttery Apples n' Cabbage

Crisp fall apples complement buttery cabbage; the perfect side dish to serve with pork.

1 c.	*(250 mL)* water
4 c.	*(1 L)* (½ small head) cubed
	1" *(2,5 cm)* cabbage
¼ c.	*(50 mL)* butter or margarine

½ tsp.	*(2 mL)* salt
¼ tsp.	*(1 mL)* nutmeg
2 c.	*(500 mL)* (2 med.) unpeeled, cubed
	½" *(1 cm)* tart red apples
2 tbsp.	*(30 mL)* chopped fresh parsley

In 2-qt. *(2-L)* saucepan bring water to a full boil; add cabbage. Cover; cook over med. heat, stirring occasionally, until cabbage is crisply tender (5 to 6 min.). Drain; stir in remaining ingredients *except* apples and parsley. Cover; cook over med. heat, stirring occasionally, until butter is melted (1 to 2 min.). Stir in apples. Cover; continue cooking, stirring occasionally, until apples are crisply tender (3 to 4 min.). Sprinkle with parsley.

Microwave Directions: *Decrease water to ¼ c.* (50 mL). In 2-qt. *(2-L)* casserole combine water and cabbage. Cover; microwave on HIGH, stirring after half the time, until cabbage is crisply tender (6 to 7 min.). Let stand 1 min.; drain. Cut butter into pieces. In same casserole combine cabbage, butter and remaining ingredients *except* parsley. Cover; microwave on HIGH, stirring after half the time, until butter is melted and apples are crisply tender (2 to 3 min.). Let stand 1 min. Sprinkle with parsley.

6 servings
30 minutes

Garden Carrot Medley

Serve this colorful medley when the vegetables are ready to be picked fresh from the garden.

¾ c.	*(175 mL)* water
2 c.	*(500 mL)* (4 med.) carrots, cut
	into 2 × ¼" *(5 × 0,5 cm)* strips
3 tbsp.	*(45 mL)* butter or margarine
2 c.	*(500 mL)* (1 med.) yellow summer squash
	or zucchini, trim off ends,
	cut in half lengthwise
	and cut crosswise into ¼" *(0,5 cm)* slices

¼ c.	*(50 mL)* chopped green pepper
½ tsp.	*(2 mL)* salt
½ tsp.	*(2 mL)* basil leaves

In 2-qt. *(2-L)* saucepan bring water to a full boil. Add carrots. Cover; cook over med. heat until carrots are crisply tender (8 to 10 min.). Drain; add butter, stirring until melted. Stir in remaining ingredients. Cover; cook over med. heat, stirring occasionally, until squash is crisply tender (6 to 8 min.).

Microwave Directions: *Decrease water to ½ c.* (125 mL). In 2-qt. *(2-L)* casserole combine water and carrots. Cover; microwave on HIGH, stirring after half the time, until carrots are crisply tender (5 to 6 min.). Let stand 1 min. Drain; add butter, stirring until melted. Stir in remaining ingredients. Cover; microwave on HIGH, stirring after half the time, until squash is crisply tender (4 to 5 min.). Let stand 1 min.

4 servings
30 minutes

Chuckwagon Carrots

Crisp bacon gives smoked flavor to hearty chunks of carrots.

3 c.   *(750 mL)* (6 med.) sliced
          ½" *(1 cm)* carrots
¼ c.   *(50 mL)* cooked, crumbled bacon
3 tbsp.   *(45 mL)* butter or margarine

1 tbsp.   *(15 mL)* firmly packed brown sugar
2 tbsp.   *(30 mL)* sliced ⅛" *(0,2 cm)* green onions
¼ tsp.   *(1 mL)* salt
          Pinch of pepper

In 2-qt. *(2-L)* saucepan place carrots; add enough water to cover. Bring to a full boil. Cook over med. heat until carrots are crisply tender (8 to 12 min.). Drain; return to pan. Add remaining ingredients. Cover; cook over med. heat, stirring occasionally, until heated through (5 to 7 min.).

Microwave Directions: In 2-qt. *(2-L)* casserole combine ½ c. *(125 mL)* water and carrots. Cover; microwave on HIGH, stirring after half the time, until carrots are crisply tender (6 to 8 min.). Let stand 1 min. Drain; set aside. In same casserole melt butter on HIGH (40 to 50 sec.). Stir in carrots and remaining ingredients. Cover; microwave on HIGH, stirring after half the time, until heated through (3 to 4 min.). Let stand 1 min.

6 servings
30 minutes

Glazed Orange Ginger Carrots

*The natural sweetness of carrots is intriguing
when combined with a unique blend of ginger and caraway.*

10   med. carrots, cut into 1" *(2,5 cm)* pieces
3 tbsp.   *(45 mL)* butter or margarine
1 tbsp.   *(15 mL)* firmly packed brown sugar
½ tsp.   *(2 mL)* ginger

½ tsp.   *(2 mL)* caraway seed
1 tbsp.   *(15 mL)* grated orange peel
2 tbsp.   *(30 mL)* orange juice

In 2-qt. *(2-L)* saucepan place carrots; add enough water to cover. Bring to a full boil. Cook over med. heat until carrots are crisply tender (10 to 12 min.); drain. Return to pan; add remaining ingredients. Cook over med. heat, stirring occasionally, until heated through (4 to 7 min.).

Microwave Directions: In 2-qt. *(2-L)* casserole combine carrots and 2 tbsp. *(30 mL)* water. Cover; microwave on HIGH, stirring after half the time, until carrots are crisply tender. Drain; return to casserole. Add remaining ingredients. Cover; microwave on HIGH (1 to 1½ min.). Let stand 2 min.

Chuckwagon Carrots

Pan-Roasted Vegetables

6 servings
30 minutes

Pick of the Season Minted Carrots

A sprinkling of mint brings out the sweetness of fresh-picked carrots.

10	med. carrots with tops, peeled*	1 tbsp.	*(15 mL)* grated orange peel
2 tbsp.	*(30 mL)* butter or margarine	2 tbsp.	*(30 mL)* orange juice
	Pinch of salt	2 tbsp.	*(30 mL)* chopped fresh mint
	Pinch of pepper		

Cut carrots into 2" *(5 cm)* pieces, leaving 2" *(5 cm)* greens on top of carrots. In 2-qt. *(2-L)* saucepan place carrots; add enough water to cover. Bring to a full boil. Cook over med. heat until carrots are crisply tender (10 to 15 min.); drain. Return to pan; add remaining ingredients *except* mint. Cook over med. heat, stirring occasionally, until butter is melted (3 to 4 min.). Sprinkle with mint.

*Carrots without tops can be substituted for carrots with tops.

Microwave Directions: Cut carrots into 2" *(5 cm)* pieces, leaving 2" *(5 cm)* greens on top of carrots. In 2-qt. *(2-L)* casserole combine carrots and ¼ c. *(50 mL)* water. Cover; microwave on HIGH, stirring after half the time, until carrots are crisply tender (8 to 11 min.). Drain; return to casserole. Add remaining ingredients *except* mint. Cover; microwave on HIGH until butter is melted (1½ to 2 min.). Let stand 2 min. Sprinkle with mint.

6 servings
40 minutes

Pan-Roasted Vegetables

Pan-roasting vegetables with herbs brings out their natural flavors.

⅓ c.	*(75 mL)* butter or margarine	2 c.	*(500 mL)* broccoli flowerets
½ tsp.	*(2 mL)* thyme leaves	2 c.	*(500 mL)* (4 med.) carrots, cut into
¼ tsp.	*(1 mL)* salt		julienne strips
¼ tsp.	*(1 mL)* pepper	2	small onions, quartered
3 c.	*(750 mL)* cauliflower flowerets		

Heat oven to 400°F *(200°C)*. In 13 × 9" *(33 × 23 cm)* baking pan melt butter in oven (5 to 6 min.). Stir in thyme, salt and pepper. Add remaining ingredients; toss to coat. Cover with aluminum foil; bake for 22 to 27 min. or until vegetables are crisply tender.

Microwave Directions: In 13 × 9" *(33 × 23 cm)* baking dish melt butter on HIGH (60 to 70 sec.). Stir in thyme, salt and pepper. Add remaining ingredients; toss to coat. Cover with plastic wrap; microwave on HIGH, stirring after half the time, until vegetables are crisply tender (7 to 9 min.).

6 servings
25 minutes

Smokehouse Cauliflower Medley

The smoky bacon flavor enhances fresh cauliflower and parsley.

¼ c.	*(50 mL)* butter or margarine		1 tsp.	*(5 mL)* dry mustard
1	med. head cauliflower, cut into flowerets		½ tsp.	*(2 mL)* salt
¼ lb.	*(125 g)* bacon, cooked, cut into 1" *(2,5 cm)* pieces		2 tbsp.	*(30 mL)* water
2-oz.	*(60-g)* jar sliced pimiento, drained		1 tbsp.	*(15 mL)* chopped fresh parsley

In 3-qt. *(3-L)* saucepan melt butter. Stir in remaining ingredients *except* parsley. Cover; cook over med. heat, stirring occasionally, until cauliflower is crisply tender (10 to 12 min.). Sprinkle with parsley.

Microwave Directions: In 2-qt. *(2-L)* casserole melt butter on HIGH (50 to 60 sec.). Stir in remaining ingredients *except* parsley. Cover; microwave on HIGH, stirring after half the time, until cauliflower is crisply tender (5 to 6 min.). Sprinkle with parsley; let stand 1 min.

4 servings
15 minutes

Garden Patch Corn

Basil and parsley spice up this vegetable trio.

⅓ c.	*(75 mL)* butter or margarine		½ tsp.	*(2 mL)* salt
10-oz.	*(300-g)* pkg. frozen sweet whole kernel corn		1 c.	*(250 mL)* (1 med.) cubed ½" *(1 cm)* ripe tomato
½ c.	*(125 mL)* chopped green pepper		1 tbsp.	*(15 mL)* fresh chopped parsley
1 tsp.	*(5 mL)* basil leaves			

In 2-qt. *(2-L)* saucepan melt butter. Stir in remaining ingredients *except* tomato and parsley. Cover; cook over med. heat, stirring occasionally, until vegetables are crisply tender (10 to 12 min.). Remove from heat. Stir in tomato and parsley. Cover; let stand 1 min. or until tomato is heated through.

Microwave Directions: In 1½-qt. *(1,5-L)* casserole melt butter on HIGH (60 to 70 sec.). Stir in remaining ingredients *except* tomato and parsley. Cover; microwave on HIGH, stirring after half the time, until vegetables are crisply tender (5 to 8 min.). Stir in tomato and parsley. Cover; let stand 1 min. or until tomato is heated through.

Garden Patch Corn (top)
Smokehouse Cauliflower Medley (bottom)

Zesty Horseradish Corn on the Cob

*Sweet yellow, tender ears of corn are enticing
with a horseradish mustard butter.*

½ c.	*(125 mL)* butter or margarine, softened
½ tsp.	*(2 mL)* salt
¼ tsp.	*(1 mL)* pepper
1 tbsp.	*(15 mL)* chopped fresh parsley

2 tbsp.	*(30 mL)* country-style Dijon mustard
2 tsp.	*(10 mL)* prepared horseradish
8	fresh ears of corn on the cob, husked

Prepare grill or heat oven to 375°F *(190°C)*. In small bowl stir together all ingredients *except* corn. Spread about 1 tbsp. *(15 mL)* butter mixture evenly over each ear of corn. Wrap tightly in heavy-duty double thickness aluminum foil, sealing well. Place on grill rack directly over coals or low flame, turning every 5 min., for 20 to 25 min. or until tender. If baking, place foil-wrapped corn on jelly roll pan. Bake for 40 to 45 min. or until heated through.

Tip: Horseradish butter can be used as a spread for sandwiches or vegetables.

Microwave Directions: In 13 × 9" *(33 × 23 cm)* baking dish stir together all ingredients *except* corn. Place corn in dish; turn to coat. Cover; microwave on **HIGH**, turning dish ½ turn after half the time, until corn is heated through (14 to 18 min.). Let stand 3 min.

Zesty Horseradish Corn on the Cob

Oven-Roasted Corn on the Cob

6 servings
60 minutes

Garlic, herbs and tomato add a special flavor to corn on the cob.

6	fresh ears of corn on the cob, husked
½ c.	*(125 mL)* olive or vegetable oil
1½ tsp.	*(7 mL)* salt
1 tsp.	*(5 mL)* basil leaves

½ tsp.	*(2 mL)* thyme leaves
½ tsp.	*(2 mL)* pepper
2 tsp.	*(10 mL)* minced fresh garlic
1	med. ripe tomato, cut into 12 wedges

Heat oven to 350°F *(180°C)*. Cut each ear of corn into thirds; set aside. In small bowl combine all ingredients *except* corn and tomato. Place corn in 13 × 9" *(33 × 23 cm)* baking pan; pour oil mixture over corn. Cover with aluminum foil. Bake, turning corn after 30 min., for 60 to 70 min. or until corn is tender. Add tomato wedges; return to oven for 5 min. or until tomato is heated through.

Microwave Directions: *Add 2 tbsp.* (30 mL) *water and omit salt.* Cut each ear of corn into thirds; set aside. In small bowl combine oil, basil, thyme, pepper and garlic. Dip corn into oil mixture; place in 13 × 9" *(33 × 23 cm)* baking dish. Add 2 tbsp. *(30 mL)* water. Cover with plastic wrap. Microwave on HIGH, rearranging corn after half the time, until corn is tender (12 to 15 min.). Add tomato wedges. Cover with plastic wrap; let stand 3 min. or until tomato is heated through. If desired, season with salt.

Southwestern-Style Corn in Tomato Shells

8 servings
45 minutes

Taste a southwestern sensation in this quick corn dish served in hollowed-out tomatoes.

4	med. ripe tomatoes
1 tbsp.	*(15 mL)* butter or margarine
1 c.	*(250 mL)* red onion, cut into ½" *(1 cm)* pieces
1 c.	*(250 mL)* chunky-style salsa
16-oz.	*(500-g)* pkg. frozen whole kernel corn, thawed, drained

1 tsp.	*(5 mL)* cumin
1 tbsp.	*(15 mL)* lime juice
½ c.	*(125 mL)* sliced ¼" *(0,5 cm)* ripe olives
½ c.	*(125 mL)* chopped fresh parsley
	Dairy sour cream

Heat oven to 350°F *(180°C)*. Cut tomatoes in half. Hollow out tomato pulp to form ½" *(1 cm)* shells; *reserve pulp.* Set aside. In 2-qt. *(2-L)* saucepan melt butter over med. heat. Stir in remaining ingredients *except* olives, parsley, sour cream and tomatoes. Stir in reserved tomato pulp. Continue cooking, stirring occasionally, until heated through (10 to 12 min.). Stir in olives and parsley. Place tomato halves on oven-proof serving platter or in 13 × 9" *(33 × 23 cm)* baking pan. Fill each tomato half with about ½ c. *(125 mL)* corn mixture; spoon remaining corn around tomatoes. Bake for 10 to 12 min. or until tomato halves are heated through. Serve with sour cream.

Tip: Tomato shells can be omitted; serve corn in serving dish.

Microwave Directions: Prepare tomatoes as directed left; *reserve pulp.* Set aside. In 3-qt. *(3-L)* bowl melt butter on high (15 to 30 sec.). Stir in remaining ingredients *except* olives, parsley, sour cream and tomatoes. Stir in reserved tomato pulp. Cover; microwave on HIGH, stirring after half the time, until heated through (6 to 8 min.). Stir in olives and parsley. Place tomato halves on microwave-safe serving platter. Fill each tomato half with about ½ c. *(125 mL)* corn mixture; spoon remaining corn around tomatoes. Cover; microwave on HIGH until tomato halves are heated through (5 to 7 min.). Serve with sour cream.

Southwestern-Style Corn in Tomato Shells

Bacon Crackle Corn Bake

8 servings
45 minutes

*This creamy corn casserole, topped with crispy bacon,
fresh snipped parsley and chives, is full of country goodness.*

6	slices bacon, cut into ½" *(1 cm)* pieces
½ c.	*(125 mL)* (1 med.) chopped onion
2 tbsp.	*(30 mL)* all-purpose flour
½ tsp.	*(2 mL)* salt
½ tsp.	*(2 mL)* pepper
½ tsp.	*(2 mL)* minced fresh garlic
1 c.	*(250 mL)* dairy sour cream
2	(16-oz.) *(500-g)* pkg. frozen whole kernel corn, thawed, drained
1 tbsp.	*(15 mL)* chopped fresh parsley
1 tbsp.	*(15 mL)* chopped fresh chives

Heat oven to 350°F *(180°C)*. In 10" *(25 cm)* skillet cook bacon over med. high heat, stirring occasionally, until partially cooked (4 min.). Add onion; continue cooking until bacon is browned (4 to 5 min.). Drain off fat *except* for 1 tbsp. *(15 mL)*; set bacon and onion aside. Stir flour, salt, pepper and garlic into reserved 1 tbsp. *(15 mL)* fat. Cook over med. heat, stirring constantly, until smooth and bubbly (30 sec.). Stir in sour cream, corn and ⅓ of bacon and onion mixture. Pour into 1½-qt. *(1,5-L)* casserole; sprinkle with remaining bacon and onion mixture. Bake for 25 to 30 min. or until heated through. Sprinkle with parsley and chives.

Microwave Directions: *Do not thaw corn.* Place bacon in 2-qt. *(2-L)* casserole. Cover with waxed paper. Microwave on HIGH, stirring after half the time, until partially cooked (4 to 5½ min.). Add onion; microwave on HIGH until bacon is cooked (2 to 3 min.). Drain off fat *except* for 1 tbsp. *(15 mL)*; set bacon and onion aside. Stir flour, salt, pepper and garlic into reserved 1 tbsp. *(15 mL)* fat. Microwave on HIGH until bubbly (30 to 60 sec.). Stir in sour cream, *frozen* corn and ⅓ of bacon and onion mixture; sprinkle with remaining bacon and onion mixture. Cover with plastic wrap; microwave on HIGH, stirring every 3 min., until heated through (10 to 13 min.). Sprinkle with parsley and chives.

Garlic Parmesan Eggplant Slices

4 servings
30 minutes

These crispy eggplant slices are pan-fried and topped with garden-fresh tomato.

1	med. (1 lb.) *(450 g)* sliced ¼" *(0,5 cm)* eggplant
1 tsp.	*(5 mL)* salt
½ c.	*(125 mL)* all-purpose flour
½ c.	*(125 mL)* seasoned bread crumbs
¼ c.	*(50 mL)* freshly grated Parmesan cheese
1 tbsp.	*(15 mL)* basil leaves
⅓ c.	*(75 mL)* olive or vegetable oil
½ tsp.	*(2 mL)* pepper
1 tsp.	*(5 mL)* minced fresh garlic
2	eggs, slightly beaten
1 c.	*(250 mL)* (1 med.) chopped ripe tomato

Place eggplant slices on 15 × 10 × 1" *(37,5 × 25 × 2,5 cm)* jelly roll pan; sprinkle with salt. In 9" *(23 cm)* pie pan stir together flour, bread crumbs, Parmesan cheese and basil. In 10" *(25 cm)* skillet cook olive oil, pepper and garlic over med. heat until sizzling. Meanwhile, dip eggplant slices into eggs; coat with flour mixture. Fry ½ of eggplant slices in olive oil until golden brown (2 to 3 min. on each side). Remove to serving platter; keep warm. Repeat with remaining eggplant slices. Remove to serving platter; sprinkle with tomato. Cover with aluminum foil; let stand 2 min. or until tomato is heated through.

Bacon Crackle Corn Bake (top)
Garlic Parmesan Eggplant Slices (bottom)

6 to 8 servings
30 minutes

Burgundy Mushrooms

A delicious side dish for roasted or grilled meats.

¼ c.   *(50 mL)* butter or margarine
1 tbsp.   *(15 mL)* all-purpose flour
½ tsp.   *(2 mL)* salt
½ tsp.   *(2 mL)* coarsely ground pepper
¼ tsp.   *(1 mL)* dry mustard
1 tsp.   *(5 mL)* minced fresh garlic
⅓ c.   *(75 mL)* dry red wine or beef broth

1 c.   *(250 mL)* (1 med.) green pepper, cut into ½" *(1 cm)* pieces
1 c.   *(250 mL)* thinly sliced red onion, separated into rings
2   (8-oz.) *(227-g)* pkg. fresh mushrooms, halved

In 10" *(25 cm)* skillet melt butter over med. heat. Stir in flour, salt, pepper, mustard and garlic; continue cooking until smooth and bubbly (30 sec.). Stir in wine; add remaining ingredients. Continue cooking, stirring occasionally, until mushrooms are tender (10 to 12 min.).

Microwave Directions: *Increase flour to 2 tbsp.* (30 mL). In 2-qt. *(2-L)* casserole melt butter on HIGH (50 to 60 sec.). Stir in 2 tbsp. *(30 mL)* flour, salt, pepper, mustard and garlic. Microwave on HIGH until smooth and bubbly (15 to 30 sec.). Stir in wine; add remaining ingredients. Microwave on HIGH, stirring after half the time, until mushrooms are tender (5 to 7 min.). Let stand 2 min.

4 servings
15 minutes

Savory Mushroom Sauté

Fresh mushrooms with savory herbs make a perfect accompaniment for grilled meat, chicken or fish.

⅓ c.   *(75 mL)* butter or margarine
3   (8-oz.) *(227-g)* pkg. fresh mushrooms, halved
2 tbsp.   *(30 mL)* chopped onion
½ tsp.   *(2 mL)* tarragon leaves

½ tsp.   *(2 mL)* nutmeg
¼ tsp.   *(1 mL)* salt
¼ tsp.   *(1 mL)* pepper
¼ c.   *(50 mL)* chopped fresh parsley

In 10" *(25 cm)* skillet melt butter. Stir in remaining ingredients *except* parsley. Cook over med. heat, stirring occasionally, until mushrooms are tender (3 to 4 min.). Stir in parsley.

Savory Mushroom Sauté

Sliced Onions n' Blue Cheese Bake

6 servings
40 minutes

Sliced Onions n' Blue Cheese Bake

Onions, blended with blue cheese and mushrooms,
add zest and richness when served with grilled meats.

4	med. onions, sliced ¼" *(0,5 cm)*
½ c.	*(125 mL)* crumbled blue cheese
2 c.	*(500 mL) (8 oz.) (227 g)* sliced ¼" *(0,5 cm)* fresh mushrooms
¼ c.	*(50 mL)* butter or margarine, softened
1 tsp.	*(5 mL)* dill weed
¼ tsp.	*(1 mL)* pepper
1 tbsp.	*(15 mL)* Worcestershire sauce
¼ c.	*(50 mL)* chopped fresh parsley

Heat oven to 400°F *(200°C)*. In 9" *(23 cm)* sq. baking pan layer half of onions. In small bowl combine ¼ c. *(50 mL)* blue cheese and remaining ingredients *except* parsley and remaining onions; stir to blend. Sprinkle cheese mixture over onions; top with remaining onions. Bake for 10 min.; stir. Crumble remaining ¼ c. *(50 mL)* blue cheese over onions; sprinkle with parsley. Continue baking for 10 to 15 min. or until onions are crisply tender.

Microwave Directions: *Add 2 tbsp.* (30 mL) *all-purpose flour.* In medium bowl mix onions with 2 tbsp. *(30 mL)* flour. In 2-qt. *(2-L)* casserole layer half of onions. In small bowl combine ¼ c. *(50 mL)* blue cheese and remaining ingredients *except* parsley and remaining onions; stir to blend. Sprinkle cheese mixture over onions; top with remaining onions. Cover; microwave on HIGH until onions are crisply tender (2½ to 3½ min.). Stir; top with remaining ¼ c. *(50 mL)* blue cheese and parsley. Cover; microwave on HIGH until cheese starts to melt (1 to 1½ min.). Let stand 2 min.

6 servings
30 minutes

Cream-Glazed Onion Halves With Peas

When Vidalia onions are in season, take advantage of their glorious, sweet taste.

3	med. (3") *(7,5 cm)* Vidalia or sweet onions
¼ c.	*(50 mL)* butter or margarine
¾ tsp.	*(3 mL)* seasoned salt
¼ tsp.	*(1 mL)* pepper
½ c.	*(125 mL)* whipping cream
10-oz.	*(350-g)* pkg. frozen tender tiny peas, thawed, drained
¼ c.	*(50 mL)* chopped fresh parsley

Peel onions; cut each in half. Hollow out inner 2 to 3 rings of onions to form shells; chop removed onion. In 10" *(25 cm)* skillet melt butter until sizzling; stir in chopped onion, seasoned salt and pepper. Place onions, cut side down, in skillet. Cook over med. heat for 10 min. Carefully turn onions over; stir in whipping cream. Continue cooking for 3 to 5 min. or until cream mixture is bubbly. Place some peas into each onion shell; sprinkle remaining peas and parsley into cream mixture. Continue cooking, stirring occasionally, until peas are crisply tender (8 to 10 min.).

Microwave Directions: *Do not thaw peas.* Peel onions; cut each in half. Hollow out inner 2 to 3 rings of onions to form shells; chop removed onion. In 8" *(20 cm)* sq. baking dish melt butter on HIGH (50 to 60 sec.). Stir in chopped onion, seasoned salt and pepper. Place onions, cut side down, in dish. Cover with plastic wrap. Microwave on HIGH until onions just begin to soften (3 to 4 min.). Carefully turn onions over; stir in whipping cream. Cover; microwave on HIGH, stirring after half the time, until cream mixture is bubbly (2 to 3 min.). Place some frozen peas into each onion shell; sprinkle remaining peas and parsley into cream mixture. Cover; microwave on HIGH until peas are crisply tender (5 to 7 min.).

4 to 6 servings
30 minutes

Butter-Fried Parsnips

Parsnips with a new twist — seasoned and pan-fried in butter.

5 to 6   med. parsnips, peeled, cut
          lengthwise into quarters
4 c.   *(1 L)* water

½ c.   *(125 mL)* butter or margarine, melted
¼ c.   *(50 mL)* all-purpose flour
½ tsp.   *(2 mL)* seasoned salt

In covered 3-qt. *(3-L)* saucepan boil parsnips in water until tender (8 to 10 min.); drain. Dip parsnips in ¼ c. *(50 mL)* melted butter. In plastic bag combine flour and seasoned salt. Add parsnips; shake to coat with flour mixture. In 10" *(25 cm)* skillet melt ¼ c. *(50 mL)* butter until sizzling. Add parsnips. Cook over med. high heat, turning occasionally, until all sides are golden brown (8 to 10 min.).

4 servings
15 minutes

Indian Summer Medley

Simply seasoned and prepared, a delightful pea, corn and tomato medley.

3 tbsp.   *(45 mL)* butter or margarine
¼ c.   *(50 mL)* chopped fresh parsley
10-oz.   *(350-g)* pkg. frozen peas, thawed, drained
8-oz.   *(199-mL)* can whole kernel corn, drained

½ tsp.   *(2 mL)* salt
          Pinch of pepper
1   med. ripe tomato, cut into wedges

In 2-qt. *(2-L)* saucepan melt butter over med. heat. Add remaining ingredients *except* tomato. Continue cooking until vegetables are crisply tender (5 to 7 min.). Add tomato wedges. Cover; let stand 2 min. or until tomatoes are heated through.

Microwave Directions: In 1-qt. *(1-L)* casserole combine all ingredients *except* tomatoes. Cover; microwave on HIGH, stirring after half the time, until vegetables are crisply tender (3½ to 5½ min.). Add tomato wedges. Cover; microwave on HIGH until tomatoes are heated through (1 min.). Let stand 3 min.

Butter-Fried Parsnips

Aunt Rebecca's Creamed Potatoes & Peas (top)
Honey-Glazed Pea Pods & Carrots (bottom)

6 servings
30 minutes

Aunt Rebecca's Creamed Potatoes & Peas

Tender potatoes and tiny peas are served in a rich, bacon-flavored cream sauce.

12	small new red potatoes, cut into 1½" *(3,5 cm)* pieces
8	slices bacon, cut into ½" *(1 cm)* pieces
1 c.	*(250 mL)* red onion, cut into ½" *(1 cm)* pieces
2 tbsp.	*(30 mL)* all-purpose flour

¾ tsp.	*(3 mL)* thyme leaves
½ tsp.	*(2 mL)* salt
½ tsp.	*(2 mL)* pepper
1 c.	*(250 mL)* whipping cream
10-oz.	*(350-g)* pkg. frozen tender tiny peas, thawed, drained

In 2-qt. *(2-L)* saucepan place potatoes. Add enough water to cover; bring to a full boil. Cook over med. heat, stirring occasionally, until potatoes are tender (10 to 15 min.). Meanwhile, in 10" *(25 cm)* skillet cook bacon over med. high heat, stirring occasionally, until partially cooked (4 min.). Add onion; continue cooking until browned (4 to 5 min.). Drain off fat *except* for 2 tbsp. *(30 mL)*; set bacon and onion aside. Stir flour, thyme leaves, salt and pepper into reserved 2 tbsp. *(30 mL)* fat. Cook over med. heat, stirring constantly, until smooth and bubbly (30 sec.). Stir in whipping cream, peas, bacon, onion and potatoes. Continue cooking, stirring occasionally, until mixture thickens and is heated through (3 to 4 min.).

Microwave Directions: In 2-qt. *(2-L)* casserole place potatoes. Add ¼ c. *(50 mL)* water. Cover; microwave on HIGH, stirring after half the time, until potatoes are tender (8 to 10 min.). Let stand covered 3 min.; drain. Set aside. In same 2-qt. *(2-L)* casserole place bacon. Cover with waxed paper. Microwave on HIGH until partially cooked (3 to 4 min.). Stir in onion. Cover; microwave on HIGH until onion is tender and bacon is cooked (2 to 3 min.). Drain off fat *except* for 2 tbsp. *(30 mL)*. Stir in flour, thyme leaves, salt and pepper. Microwave on HIGH until bubbly (30 to 60 sec.). Stir in whipping cream; microwave on HIGH until mixture just comes to a boil (1 to 2 min.). Add peas and potatoes. Cover; microwave on HIGH, stirring after half the time, until mixture thickens and is heated through (4 to 6 min.).

6 servings
30 minutes

Honey-Glazed Pea Pods & Carrots

A touch of golden honey flavors these tender pea pods mixed with sweet carrots.

¾ c.	*(175 mL)* water
2 c.	*(500 mL)* (4 med.) diagonally sliced ¼" *(0,5 cm)* carrots
8 oz.	*(225 g)* fresh pea pods, washed, remove tips and strings*

3 tbsp.	*(45 mL)* butter or margarine
½ tsp.	*(2 mL)* cornstarch
2 tbsp.	*(30 mL)* honey

In 2-qt. *(2-L)* saucepan bring water to a full boil. Add carrots. Cover; cook over med. heat until carrots are crisply tender (10 to 12 min.). Add pea pods. Continue cooking until pea pods are crisply tender (1 to 2 min.). Drain; set aside. In same pan melt butter; stir in cornstarch. Add carrots, pea pods and honey. Cook over med. heat, stirring occasionally, until heated through (2 to 3 min.).

*2 (6-oz.) *(170-g)* pkg. frozen pea pods can be substituted for 8 oz. *(225 g)* fresh pea pods.

Microwave Directions: *Decrease water to ½ c.* (125 mL). In 2-qt. *(2-L)* casserole combine water and carrots. Cover; microwave on HIGH, stirring after half the time, until carrots are crisply tender (8 to 10 min.). Add pea pods. Cover; microwave on HIGH until pea pods are crisply tender (1 to 2 min.). Drain; set aside. In same casserole melt butter on HIGH (50 to 60 sec.). Stir in cornstarch. Microwave on HIGH 1 min. Stir in carrots, pea pods and honey. Cover; microwave on HIGH until heated through (1 to 2 min.).

5 servings
15 minutes

Skillet Green Peppers

A unique and easy way to prepare garden-fresh green peppers.

¼ c.	*(50 mL)* butter or margarine
3 c.	*(750 mL)* (2 med.) green peppers, cut into ¼" *(0,5 cm)* strips
1 tsp.	*(5 mL)* Italian herb seasoning*

½ tsp.	*(2 mL)* minced fresh garlic
½ c.	*(125 mL)* halved cherry tomatoes
½ c.	*(125 mL)* croutons

In 10" *(25 cm)* skillet melt butter. Stir in remaining ingredients *except* tomatoes and croutons. Cook over med. heat, stirring occasionally, until peppers are crisply tender (6 to 8 min.). Add tomatoes. Continue cooking 1 min. Sprinkle with croutons; serve immediately.

*¼ tsp. *(1 mL)* each* oregano leaves, marjoram leaves and basil leaves and a pinch of rubbed sage can be substituted for 1 tsp. *(5 mL)* Italian herb seasoning.

Microwave Directions: In 1½-qt. *(1,5-L)* casserole melt butter on HIGH (50 to 60 sec.). Stir in remaining ingredients *except* tomatoes and croutons. Cover; microwave on HIGH, stirring after half the time, until peppers are crisply tender (4 to 5 min.). Add tomatoes. Cover; microwave on HIGH 1 min. Let stand 1 min. Sprinkle with croutons; serve immediately.

4 to 6 servings
30 minutes

Hot & Tangy German Potatoes

Serve these tangy potatoes with hearty sausage and applesauce.

4	med. red potatoes, cooked, peeled, sliced ¼" *(0,5 cm)*
8	slices thick-sliced bacon, cut into 1" *(2,5 cm)* pieces
1 c.	*(250 mL)* (2 stalks) sliced ½" *(1 cm)* celery
2	med. onions, cut into eighths

¼ c.	*(50 mL)* sugar
¾ c.	*(175 mL)* cider vinegar
¼ c.	*(50 mL)* water
½ tsp.	*(2 mL)* salt
¼ tsp.	*(1 mL)* pepper
¼ c.	*(50 mL)* chopped fresh parsley

Have potatoes ready. In 3-qt. *(3-L)* saucepan cook bacon, stirring constantly, over high heat 3 min. Stir in celery and onions. Reduce heat to med; continue cooking, stirring occasionally, until vegetables are crisply tender (5 to 8 min.). Stir in remaining ingredients *except* potatoes and parsley. Continue cooking, stirring occasionally, until mixture comes to a full boil (3 to 5 min.). Stir in potatoes; continue cooking until potatoes are heated through (5 to 10 min.). Sprinkle with parsley.

Microwave Directions: Have potatoes ready. In 3-qt. *(3-L)* casserole microwave bacon on HIGH 3 min. Stir in celery and onions. Cover; microwave on HIGH, stirring after half the time, until vegetables are crisply tender (3 to 4 min.). Stir in remaining ingredients *except* potatoes and parsley. Microwave on HIGH, stirring after half the time, until mixture comes to a full boil (3 to 4 min.). Stir in potatoes. Microwave on HIGH, stirring after half the time, until potatoes are heated through (6 to 7 min.). Sprinkle with parsley.

Hot & Tangy German Potatoes (top)
Skillet Green Peppers (bottom)

Garlic Roasted Potato Wedges (top)
New Potatoes With Lemon Horseradish (bottom)

6 servings
40 minutes

Garlic Roasted Potato Wedges

Garlic and potato lovers' delight.

4	large red potatoes	1 tsp.	*(5 mL)* minced fresh garlic
¼ c.	*(50 mL)* butter or margarine	½ tsp.	*(2 mL)* salt
¼ c.	*(50 mL)* grated Parmesan cheese	¼ tsp.	*(1 mL)* pepper

Heat oven to 425°F *(220°C)*. Cut potatoes in half lengthwise; cut each half into 4 wedges. In 3-qt. *(3-L)* saucepan place potato wedges; add enough water to cover. Bring to a full boil. Cook over med. heat until potatoes are tender (8 to 12 min.); drain. In 13 × 9" *(33 × 23 cm)* baking pan melt butter in oven (5 to 6 min.). Stir in remaining ingredients. Add potato wedges; coat both sides with butter mixture. Bake for 10 min.; turn potatoes. Continue baking for 10 to 15 min. or until lightly browned.

Microwave Directions: Prepare potatoes as directed left. In 10" *(25 cm)* pie plate melt butter on HIGH (50 to 60 sec.). Stir in remaining ingredients. Add potato wedges; coat both sides with butter mixture. Cover; microwave on HIGH, stirring after half the time, until potatoes are tender (11 to 15 min.).

4 to 6 servings
1 hour 20 minutes

New Potatoes With Lemon Horseradish

New potatoes served with a zesty twist.

¼ c.	*(50 mL)* butter or margarine	12	*(1½ lb.) (575 g)* tiny new potatoes, washed, unpeeled *except* for ½" *(1 cm)* strip around center of potato
½ tsp.	*(2 mL)* salt		
	Pinch of pepper		
1 tbsp.	*(15 mL)* prepared horseradish	6	slices ¼" *(0,5 cm)* lemon
2 tsp.	*(10 mL)* lemon juice	2 tbsp.	*(30 mL)* chopped fresh parsley

Heat oven to 350°F *(180°C)*. In 2-qt. *(2-L)* casserole melt butter in oven (6 to 8 min.). Stir in salt, pepper, horseradish and lemon juice. Stir in potatoes until well coated with butter. Cover; bake for 55 to 65 min. or until potatoes are fork tender. Garnish with lemon slices and sprinkle with parsley. To serve, spoon butter sauce over potatoes.

Microwave Directions: In 2-qt. *(2-L)* casserole melt butter on HIGH (50 to 60 sec.). Stir in salt, pepper, horseradish and lemon juice. Stir in potatoes until well coated with butter. Cover; microwave on HIGH, stirring after half the time, until potatoes are fork tender (10 to 12 min.). Let stand 5 min. Garnish with lemon slices and sprinkle with parsley. Serve as directed left.

6 servings
1 hour 30 minutes

Apple-Filled Sweet Potatoes

Twice-baked sweet potatoes, subtly flavored with orange peel and nutmeg.

6	med. sweet potatoes or yams
¼ c.	*(50 mL)* firmly packed brown sugar
½ c.	*(125 mL)* butter or margarine
	Pinch of nutmeg
½ tsp.	*(2 mL)* grated orange peel

1 c.	*(250 mL)* (1 med.) peeled, cored, coarsely chopped apple
¼ c.	*(50 mL)* chopped pecans, toasted
	Pecan halves

Heat oven to 375°F *(190°C)*. Prick sweet potatoes with fork to allow steam to escape. Bake for 35 to 45 min. or until fork tender. Cut thin lengthwise slice from top of each sweet potato; scoop out inside, leaving a thin shell. Set shells aside. In large mixer bowl place hot sweet potato and remaining ingredients *except* apple, chopped pecans and pecan halves. Beat at med. speed, scraping bowl often, until well mixed and no lumps remain (2 to 3 min.). By hand, stir in apple and chopped

pecans. Place shells on 15 × 10 × 1" *(40 × 25 × 2,5 cm)* baking pan; fill shells with sweet potato mixture. If desired, garnish each sweet potato with pecan halves. Bake for 15 to 20 min. or until heated through.

Tip: If desired, do not stuff shells. Spoon hot sweet potato mixture into serving bowl. If desired, toast pecan halves and use to garnish sweet potato mixture.

---

5 servings
45 minutes

Elegant Spinach Timbales

Cheese sauce crowns these delightful individual servings of spinach.

Timbales

2	(10-oz.) *(300-g)* pkg. frozen chopped spinach
4	eggs
¼ c.	*(50 mL)* butter or margarine, softened
½ tsp.	*(2 mL)* salt
1 tbsp.	*(15 mL)* lemon juice

Cheese Sauce

2 tbsp.	*(30 mL)* butter or margarine
2 tbsp.	*(30 mL)* all-purpose flour
½ tsp.	*(2 mL)* dry mustard
¼ tsp.	*(1 mL)* salt
¼ tsp.	*(1 mL)* pepper
1 c.	*(250 mL)* milk
1½ c.	*(375 mL)* (6 oz.) *(170 g)* shredded Cheddar cheese

Cook spinach according to pkg. directions; drain. In small mixer bowl beat eggs at med. speed until foamy (1 to 2 min.). By hand, stir in cooked spinach and remaining timbale ingredients. Divide mixture between 5 greased 6-oz. *(170-mL)* custard cups. Place custard cups on a rack in 10" *(25 cm)* skillet. Add hot (not boiling) water to just below rack. Cover; cook over med. heat for 18 to 22 min. or until knife inserted in center comes

out clean. If water begins to boil, reduce heat to low. Meanwhile, in 1-qt. *(1-L)* saucepan melt 2 tbsp. *(30 mL)* butter. Add flour, mustard, ¼ tsp. *(1 mL)* salt and pepper. Cook over med. heat until smooth and bubbly (30 sec.). Stir in milk. Continue cooking, stirring occasionally, until sauce comes to a full boil (4 to 5 min.); boil 1 min. Stir in cheese until melted. Loosen edges of timbales with knife; unmold. Serve cheese sauce over timbales.

Apple-Filled Sweet Potatoes

6 servings
30 minutes

Zucchini & Onions With Mozzarella

Midsummer vegetables are a delight sautéed with herbs and lots of Mozzarella cheese.

3 tbsp.	*(45 mL)* butter or margarine	¼ tsp.	*(1 mL)* oregano leaves
3 c.	*(750 mL)* (3 med.) sliced		Pinch of salt
	⅛" *(0,2 cm)* zucchini	½ tsp.	*(2 mL)* minced fresh garlic
1 c.	*(250 mL)* (1 med.) sliced	1	med. ripe tomato, cut into wedges
	⅛" *(0,2 cm)* onion	1 c.	*(250 mL)* (4 oz.) *(125 g)* shredded
½ tsp.	*(2 mL)* basil leaves		Mozzarella cheese

In 10" *(25 cm)* skillet melt butter over med. heat. Add remaining ingredients *except* tomato and cheese. Continue cooking, stirring occasionally, until zucchini is crisply tender (7 to 10 min.). Add tomato wedges; sprinkle with cheese. Cover; let stand 2 min. or until cheese is melted.

Microwave Directions: In 2-qt. *(2-L)* casserole melt butter on HIGH (30 to 45 sec.). Add remaining ingredients *except* tomato and cheese. Cover; microwave on HIGH, stirring after half the time, until zucchini is crisply tender (3 to 4½ min.). Add tomato wedges; sprinkle with cheese. Cover; let stand 2 min. or until cheese is melted.

6 servings
15 minutes

Quick Skillet Squash Medley

The entire family will enjoy this slightly sweet, colorful squash medley.

¼ c.	*(50 mL)* butter or margarine	1 tbsp.	*(15 mL)* firmly packed brown sugar
1½ c.	*(375 mL)* peeled, cubed 1" *(2,5 cm)*		Pinch of nutmeg
	butternut squash	1½ c.	*(375 mL)* unpeeled, sliced
1½ c.	*(375 mL)* unpeeled, quartered, sliced		⅛" *(0,2 cm)* zucchini
	½" *(1 cm)* yellow squash		

In 10" *(25 cm)* skillet melt butter; stir in remaining ingredients *except* zucchini. Cook over med. heat, stirring occasionally, 5 min. Stir in zucchini; continue cooking until squash are crisply tender (4 to 5 min.).

Microwave Directions: In 2-qt. *(2-L)* casserole melt butter on HIGH (50 to 60 sec.). Stir in butternut squash. Cover; microwave on HIGH 1½ min. Stir in remaining ingredients. Cover; microwave on HIGH, stirring after half the time, until squash are crisply tender (6 to 7 min.).

Zucchini & Onions With Mozzarella

Savory Herb Tomato Halves (top)
Harvest Acorn Squash (bottom)

4 servings
60 minutes

Harvest Acorn Squash

*The tartness of apples and sweetness of acorn squash blend with honey
to make a mouth-watering delight.*

2	med. acorn squash, halved, remove seeds
½ c.	*(125 mL)* apple juice or water
¼ c.	*(50 mL)* butter or margarine, melted
¼ tsp.	*(1 mL)* nutmeg

2 tbsp.	*(30 mL)* honey
1 tsp.	*(5 mL)* grated orange peel
2	med. tart apples, cored, sliced ⅛" *(0,2 cm)*

Heat oven to 375°F *(190°C)*. In 13 × 9" *(33 × 23 cm)* baking pan place squash cut side up. Pour apple juice in pan; set aside. In small bowl combine remaining ingredients *except* apples. Divide apple slices evenly among squash halves. Pour about 2 tbsp. *(30 mL)* butter mixture over apple slices. Cover with aluminum foil; bake for 45 to 50 min. or until squash is fork tender.

Microwave Directions: In 12 × 8" *(30 × 20 cm)* baking dish place squash cut side up. Pour apple juice in pan; set aside. In small bowl combine remaining ingredients *except* apples. Divide apple slices evenly among squash halves. Pour about 2 tbsp. *(30 mL)* butter mixture over apple slices. Cover with plastic wrap; microwave on HIGH, turning ¼ turn after half the time, until squash is fork tender (12 to 15 min.). Let stand 5 min.

8 servings
40 minutes

Savory Herb Tomato Halves

Fresh bread crumbs and herbs top tomato halves to make an easy and delicious side dish.

1¼ c.	*(300 mL)* fresh bread crumbs
⅓ c.	*(75 mL)* butter or margarine, melted
1 tbsp.	*(15 mL)* chopped fresh parsley
1 tsp.	*(5 mL)* basil leaves
¼ tsp.	*(1 mL)* garlic powder
¼ tsp.	*(1 mL)* salt

¼ tsp.	*(1 mL)* oregano leaves
¼ tsp.	*(1 mL)* cracked pepper
4	med. ripe tomatoes, stems removed, halved crosswise

Heat oven to 350°F *(180°C)*. In small bowl stir together all ingredients *except* tomatoes. Place tomatoes, cut side up, on 15 × 10 × 1" *(37,5 × 25 × 2,5 cm)* jelly roll pan. Spoon a heaping tablespoonful of crumb mixture on each tomato half. Bake for 15 to 18 min. or until tomatoes are heated through, yet firm.

Microwave Directions: In small bowl stir together all ingredients *except* tomatoes. Place four tomato halves, cut side up, in pie plate. Spoon a heaping tablespoonful of crumb mixture on each tomato half. Cover with plastic wrap. Microwave on HIGH, turning plate ½ turn after half the time, until tomatoes are heated through, yet firm (2½ to 3½ min.). Repeat with remaining tomato halves.

4 servings
15 minutes

Buttery Crunch-Topped Tomatoes

Skillet tomatoes with the oh-so-good taste of stuffed tomatoes.

2 tbsp. *(30 mL)* butter or margarine, melted
⅓ c. *(75 mL)* coarsely crushed buttery crackers
½ c. *(125 mL)* (2 oz.) *(60 g)* shredded
Cheddar cheese
1 tbsp. *(15 mL)* chopped fresh parsley
2 tbsp. *(30 mL)* butter or margarine

½ tsp. *(2 mL)* caraway seed
¼ tsp. *(1 mL)* salt
Pinch of pepper
1 tbsp. *(15 mL)* chopped onion
2 large ripe tomatoes, each cut
into 10 wedges

In small bowl stir together 2 tbsp. *(30 mL)* melted butter, crushed crackers, cheese and parsley; set aside. In 10" *(25 cm)* skillet melt 2 tbsp. *(30 mL)* butter. Stir in caraway seed, salt, pepper and onion. Add tomatoes. Cover; cook over med. heat, stirring occasionally, until tomatoes are heated through (2 to 3 min.). Sprinkle with cheese mixture. Cover; let stand 1 min. Serve immediately.

Microwave Directions: In small bowl stir together 2 tbsp. *(30 mL)* melted butter, crushed crackers, cheese and parsley; set aside. In 2-qt. *(2-L)* casserole melt 2 tbsp. *(30 mL)* butter on HIGH (25 to 35 sec.). Stir in caraway seed, salt, pepper and onion. Add tomatoes. Cover; microwave on HIGH, stirring every 2 min., until tomatoes are heated through (4½ to 5½ min.). Sprinkle with cheese mixture. Cover; let stand 1 min. Serve immediately.

6 servings
25 minutes

Tomato Zucchini Relish

Serve this flavorful homemade relish as a menu accompaniment at your next barbecue or picnic.

2 tbsp. *(30 mL)* sugar
3 tbsp. *(45 mL)* cider vinegar
1 tbsp. *(15 mL)* country-style Dijon mustard
¼ tsp. *(1 mL)* salt
Pinch of pepper
Pinch of celery seed
Pinch of mustard seed

1 c. *(250 mL)* sliced ⅛" *(0,2 cm)* red onion,
separated into rings
3 c. *(750 mL)* (3 med.) zucchini, cut
into ½" *(1 cm)* pieces
1 c. *(250 mL)* (1 med.) ripe tomato, cut
into ½" *(1 cm)* pieces

In 2-qt. *(2-L)* saucepan combine all ingredients *except* onion, zucchini and tomato. Cook over med. heat, stirring occasionally, until mixture comes to a full boil. Add vegetables; continue cooking, stirring occasionally, until vegetables are crisply tender (6 to 8 min.). Serve warm or at room temperature. Store refrigerated.

Microwave Directions: In 2-qt. *(2-L)* casserole combine all ingredients *except* onion, zucchini and tomato. Cover; microwave on HIGH, stirring after half the time, until mixture comes to a full boil (2 to 3 min.). Add vegetables. Cover; microwave on HIGH, stirring after half the time, until vegetables are crisply tender (2 to 4 min.). Serve warm or at room temperature. Store refrigerated.

Buttery Crunch-Topped Tomatoes

How To: Buy Fresh Vegetables

Vegetable:	Peak Season:	Look for:
Asparagus	Spring	Tender green spears with closed tips.
Beans, Green	Summer	Bright green color, firm crisp pods.
Beans, Lima	Summer and fall	Light green, crisp, full pods.
Beets	Summer and fall	Firm, smooth, round beets with deep red color and fresh tops.
Broccoli	All year	Firm, tight, dark green clusters.
Brussels Sprouts	Fall and winter	Unblemished, firm, bright green sprouts.
Cabbage	All year	Firm, heavy heads of light green color.
Carrots	All year	Firm, well-shaped carrots with good color.
Cauliflower	Fall and early winter	Clean, compact flowerets with green outer leaves.
Corn	Summer	Bright green husks, fresh looking silk, plump, but not too large, kernels.
Eggplant	All year	Firm, well-shaped, shiny purple skin.
Mushrooms	All year	Creamy white to light tan caps that are firm and plump.
Parsnips	Winter	Small to medium size, smooth, firm and well-shaped parsnips.
Peas	Spring and summer	Bright green, plump and tender pea pods.
Peppers, Green	Summer and fall	Well-shaped, shiny, medium to dark green peppers with firm sides.
Spinach	All year	Tender, fresh, unblemished leaves of bright green color.
Squash, Acorn	Fall and winter	Dark green color and hard, tough rinds.
Squash, Butternut	Fall and winter	Good yellow or orange color, hard, tough rinds.
Squash, Pattypan	Summer	Small, smooth-skinned, light green, flat, round, scalloped edge squash.
Squash, Summer, Yellow or Crookneck	Summer	Firm, bright yellow, blemish-free skin.
Zucchini	Summer	Firm squash with shiny smooth skin.

DESSERTS, CAKES & PIES

Whether held in the church basement, at a neighbor's house or in the local park by the river, the old-fashioned potluck dinner offered the best eating of the year. You could be sure that everyone would bring out their finest dishes. You had your favorites, of course. The desserts!

Apple pie with a crust so rich and flaky that you feared it would blow right off the top of the pie. Cherry pie with sugar-crusted strips of pastry criss-crossed atop the filling in a beautiful lattice pattern. Sometimes the pie pan would be so full that the filling would dribble over the edge, which made the pie even more tempting.

There was bread pudding, still warm from the oven. Cobblers and crisps with a pitcher of thick cream nearby. And for a light touch, fresh berries with custard sauce.

Next came the cakes. Dozens of them. Wedges of home-made carrot cake with a creamy smooth frosting. Chocolate cake, so rich that it glistened. Spicy gingerbread and old-fashioned blueberry buckle.

They were all so tempting. Who could fault you for slyly running your finger around the edge of the layer cake with its creamy frosting. Or trying every cake, pie and dessert on that table!

6 dumplings
1 hour 30 minutes

Apple Dumplings & Brandy Sauce

*A tender butter crust, baked to a golden brown,
surrounds these pecan-filled apple dumplings smothered in a rich sauce.*

Dumplings

2 c.	*(500 mL)* all-purpose flour
¼ tsp.	*(1 mL)* salt
½ c.	*(125 mL)* butter or margarine, cut into pieces
⅔ c.	*(150 mL)* dairy sour cream
6	med. tart cooking apples, cored, peeled
⅓ c.	*(75 mL)* sugar
⅓ c.	*(75 mL)* chopped pecans
2 tbsp.	*(30 mL)* butter or margarine, softened
	Milk

Sauce

½ c.	*(125 mL)* firmly packed brown sugar
2 tbsp.	*(30 mL)* butter or margarine
½ c.	*(125 mL)* whipping cream
1 tbsp.	*(15 mL)* brandy*

Heat oven to 400°F *(200°C)*. In medium bowl stir together flour and salt. Cut in ½ c. *(125 mL)* butter until mixture forms coarse crumbs. With fork, stir in sour cream until mixture leaves sides of bowl and forms a ball. On lightly floured surface roll dough into 19 × 12" *(47,5 × 30 cm)* rectangle. Cut 1" *(2,5 cm)* strip off 19" *(47,5 cm)* end; reserve. Cut remaining dough into six (6") *(15 cm)* squares. Place apple in center of each square. In small bowl stir together sugar, pecans and 2 tbsp. *(30 mL)* butter. Stuff 1½ tbsp. *(20 mL)* into cored center of each apple. Fold dough up around apple; seal seams well. Place seam side down on greased

15 × 10 × 1" *(37,5 × 25 × 2,5 cm)* jelly roll pan. Brush dough with milk; prick dough with fork. Cut leaf designs out of reserved 1" *(2,5 cm)* strip of dough. Brush with milk; place on wrapped apples. Bake for 35 to 50 min. or until apples are fork tender. If crust browns too quickly, cover with aluminum foil. In 1-qt. *(1-L)* saucepan combine all sauce ingredients. Cook over med. heat, stirring occasionally, until mixture comes to a full boil (3 to 4 min.). Serve sauce over warm dumplings.

*1 tsp. *(5 mL)* brandy extract can be substituted for 1 tbsp. *(15 mL)* brandy.

6 servings
30 minutes

Skillet Maple Apples

Old-fashioned baked apple goodness in a skillet.

¼ c.	*(50 mL)* butter or margarine
⅓ c.	*(75 mL)* sugar
2 tbsp.	*(30 mL)* cornstarch
2 c.	*(500 mL)* half-and-half

¼ c.	*(50 mL)* pure maple syrup
1 tsp.	*(5 mL)* vanilla
3	med. tart apples, cored, cut in half crosswise

In 10" *(25 cm)* skillet melt butter; stir in sugar and cornstarch. Stir in remaining ingredients *except* apples. Cook over med. low heat, stirring constantly, until thickened (6 to 8 min.). Place apples, cut side down, in cream mixture. Cover; continue cooking, spooning

sauce over apples occasionally, until apples are fork tender (12 to 15 min.). Remove apples to individual dessert dishes. With wire whisk, whisk sauce until smooth. Serve sauce over apple halves.

Apple Dumplings & Brandy Sauce

6 servings
60 minutes

Old-Fashioned Banana Bread Pudding

A cozy kind of dessert that's comforting and scrumptious.

Bread Pudding

¼ c.	*(50 mL)*	butter or margarine
4 c.	*(1 L)*	cubed 1" *(2,5 cm)* stale French or sourdough bread
3		eggs
½ c.	*(125 mL)*	sugar
2 c.	*(500 mL)*	milk
½ tsp.	*(2 mL)*	cinnamon
½ tsp.	*(2 mL)*	nutmeg
¼ tsp.	*(1 mL)*	salt
2 tsp.	*(10 mL)*	vanilla
1 c.	*(250 mL)* (2 med.)	sliced ¼" *(0,5 cm)* bananas

Sauce

3 tbsp.	*(45 mL)*	butter or margarine
2 tbsp.	*(30 mL)*	sugar
1 tbsp.	*(15 mL)*	cornstarch
¾ c.	*(175 mL)*	milk
¼ c.	*(50 mL)*	light corn syrup
1 tsp.	*(5 mL)*	vanilla

Heat oven to 375°F *(190°C)*. In 2-qt. *(2-L)* casserole melt ¼ c. *(50 mL)* butter in oven (4 to 6 min.). Stir in bread cubes. In medium bowl slightly beat eggs; stir in remaining pudding ingredients *except* bananas. Stir in bananas. Pour over bread cubes; stir to coat. Bake for 40 to 50 min. or until knife inserted near center comes out clean. Meanwhile, in 1-qt. *(1-L)* saucepan melt 3 tbsp. *(45 mL)* butter over med. heat. Stir in sugar and cornstarch; add remaining ingredients *except* vanilla. Continue cooking, stirring occasionally, until sauce comes to a full boil (3 to 4 min.). Boil 1 min. Stir in vanilla. Serve sauce over warm pudding.

9 servings
45 minutes

Streusel Blueberry Buckle

*A homespun dessert that's so good
you'll bake it for breakfast, brunch or picnics.*

Blueberry Buckle

2 c.	*(500 mL)*	all-purpose flour
¾ c.	*(175 mL)*	sugar
½ c.	*(125 mL)*	milk
¼ c.	*(50 mL)*	butter or margarine, softened
1		egg
2 tsp.	*(10 mL)*	baking powder
½ tsp.	*(2 mL)*	salt
½ tsp.	*(2 mL)*	nutmeg
1 c.	*(250 mL)*	fresh or frozen blueberries

Streusel Topping

½ c.	*(125 mL)*	sugar
⅓ c.	*(75 mL)*	all-purpose flour
½ tsp.	*(2 mL)*	cinnamon
½ tsp.	*(2 mL)*	nutmeg
¼ c.	*(50 mL)*	butter or margarine, softened

Heat oven to 375°F *(190°C)*. In large mixer bowl combine all blueberry buckle ingredients *except* blueberries. Beat at low speed, scraping bowl often, until well mixed (1 to 2 min.). By hand, fold blueberries into batter. Spread into greased and floured 9" *(23 cm)* sq. baking pan. In small bowl stir together all streusel ingredients *except* butter. Cut in butter until crumbly; sprinkle over batter. Bake for 30 to 35 min. or until wooden pick inserted in center comes out clean.

Streusel Blueberry Buckle

Stars & Stripes Tart

6 servings
45 minutes

Grandma Ruth's Cherry Crumble

This country favorite gets its name from fruit being baked with a crumbly mixture on top.

Crumble

½ c.	*(125 mL)*	all-purpose flour
½ c.	*(125 mL)*	old-fashioned rolled oats
⅓ c.	*(75 mL)*	firmly packed brown sugar
½ tsp.	*(2 mL)*	nutmeg
⅓ c.	*(75 mL)*	butter or margarine
½ c.	*(125 mL)*	sliced almonds

Heat oven to 350°F *(180°C)*. In large bowl stir together all crumble ingredients *except* butter and almonds. Cut in butter until crumbly; stir in almonds. Set aside. In medium bowl stir together all filling ingredients *except* ice cream. Place about ½ c. *(125 mL)* filling in each of 6 (6-oz.) *(170-mL)* custard cups or ramekins. Sprinkle each cup with about ¼ c. *(50 mL)* crumble mixture; place cups on 15 × 10 × 1" *(37,5 × 25 × 2,5 cm)* jelly roll pan. Bake for 25 to 30 min. or until bubbly and lightly browned. Serve warm with vanilla ice cream.

Filling

2		(16-oz.) *(398-mL)* cans pitted tart cherries, drained
½ c.	*(125 mL)*	sugar
1 tbsp.	*(15 mL)*	all-purpose flour
1 tsp.	*(5 mL)*	vanilla
		Vanilla ice cream

Microwave Directions: Prepare crumble and filling as directed left. Place about ½ c. *(125 mL)* filling in each of 6 (6-oz.) *(170-mL)* custard cups or ramekins. Sprinkle each cup with about ¼ c. *(50 mL)* crumble mixture. Arrange custard cups in circle in microwave. Microwave on HIGH, rearranging custard cups after half the time, until topping is set (10 to 13 min.). Serve warm with vanilla ice cream.

Tip: Grandma Ruth's Cherry Crumble can be baked in 1½-qt. *(1,5-L)* casserole. Bake for 30 to 35 min.

12 servings
2 hours

Stars & Stripes Tart

A rich fruit tart.

Crust

1 c.	*(250 mL)*	butter or margarine, softened
½ c.	*(125 mL)*	sugar
2½ c.	*(625 mL)*	all-purpose flour
⅓ c.	*(75 mL)*	milk

Filling

3		(3-oz.) *(250-g)* pkg. cream cheese, softened
¾ c.	*(175 mL)*	powdered sugar
1 tsp.	*(5 mL)*	grated orange peel
1 tbsp.	*(15 mL)*	orange juice

Topping

1 pt.	*(500 mL)*	strawberries, hulled, sliced, or raspberries*
½ pt.	*(250 mL)*	blueberries*
¼ c.	*(50 mL)*	apple jelly, melted

Heat oven to 400°F *(200°C)*. In large mixer bowl combine butter and sugar. Beat at med. speed, scraping bowl often, until light and fluffy (1 to 2 min.). Add flour and milk; beat at low speed until well mixed. Press dough on bottom and ½" *(1 cm)* up sides of 13 × 9" *(33 × 23 cm)* baking pan. Prick bottom with fork. Bake for 14 to 18 min. or until lightly browned. Cool. In small mixer bowl combine all filling ingredients; beat at med. speed, scraping bowl often, until light and fluffy (1 to 2 min.).

Spread over top of cooled crust. Refrigerate 1 hr. or until firm. Just before serving, arrange fruit on filling in design of American flag using strawberry slices for stripes and blueberries for stars. Brush fruit and filling with melted apple jelly.

*4 c. *(1 L)* of your favorite fruit (kiwi, mandarin orange segments, pineapple, etc.), arranged in any design, can be substituted for strawberries and blueberries.

Caramel Rum Fruit Dip

1½ cups
20 minutes

Rich and creamy, this dip is an indulgent way to dress up fruit.

½ c.   *(125 mL)* butter or margarine
14-oz.   *(400-g)* pkg. caramels, unwrapped
¼ c.   *(50 mL)* chopped pecans

1 tbsp.   *(15 mL)* milk
1 tbsp.   *(15 mL)* rum*

In 2-qt. *(2-L)* saucepan melt butter and caramels over low heat, stirring occasionally, until caramels are melted (12 to 15 min.). Stir in pecans, milk and rum. Stir vigorously to incorporate butter. Keep warm; use as a dip for slices of apples, pears and bananas or serve over ice cream.

*1 tsp. *(5 mL)* rum extract can be substituted for 1 tbsp. *(15 mL)* rum.

Microwave Directions: In medium bowl melt butter and caramels on HIGH, stirring twice during time, until caramels are melted (3 to 4 min.). Stir in pecans, milk and rum. Stir vigorously to incorporate butter. Serve as directed left.

Summertime Melon Melba

6 to 8 servings
15 minutes

A favorite warm weather dessert that's simply delicious!

1   honeydew or cantaloupe melon
            Vanilla ice cream
½ c.   *(125 mL)* raspberry preserves, melted

Cut melon in half crosswise and remove seeds. Slice melon into 1" *(2,5 cm)* rings. Remove rind. Fill each ring with scoops of ice cream. Top with melted preserves. Serve immediately.

Summertime Melon Melba

Granny's Peaches & Cream Cobbler

8 servings
60 minutes

This irresistible cobbler brings memories of visits to Grandma's house.

Filling

1 c.	*(250 mL)*	sugar
2		eggs, slightly beaten
2 tbsp.	*(30 mL)*	all-purpose flour
½ tsp.	*(2 mL)*	nutmeg
4 c.	*(1 L)*	(4 to 6 med.) peeled, sliced fresh peaches*

Cobbler

1½ c.	*(375 mL)*	all-purpose flour
2 tbsp.	*(30 mL)*	sugar
1 tsp.	*(5 mL)*	baking powder
½ tsp.	*(2 mL)*	salt
⅓ c.	*(75 mL)*	butter or margarine, softened
1		egg, slightly beaten
3 tbsp.	*(45 mL)*	milk
3 tbsp.	*(45 mL)*	sugar

Whipping cream

Heat oven to 400°F *(200°C)*. In large bowl stir together all filling ingredients *except* peaches. Stir in peaches. Pour into 13 × 9" *(33 × 23 cm)* baking pan. In medium bowl stir together all cobbler ingredients *except* butter, egg and milk. Cut in butter until crumbly. Stir in egg and milk just until moistened. Crumble mixture over peaches; sprinkle with 3 tbsp. *(45 mL)* sugar. Bake for 40 to 45 min. or until golden brown and bubbly around edges. Serve with whipping cream.

*2 (16-oz.) *(500-g)* pkg. sliced frozen peaches can be substituted for 4 c. *(1 L)* sliced fresh peaches.

Pear Pandowdy

9 servings
1 hour 15 minutes

Pandowdy — a traditional favorite — features fresh fruit baked with buttery cinnamon-sugar and topped with biscuits.

1 c.	*(250 mL)*	firmly packed brown sugar
½ c.	*(125 mL)*	butter or margarine, softened
2 tbsp.	*(30 mL)*	all-purpose flour
¼ tsp.	*(1 mL)*	cinnamon
2 tbsp.	*(30 mL)*	lemon juice
5 c.	*(1,3 L)*	(5 med.) peeled, cored, sliced ⅛" *(0,2 cm)* pears*

Biscuits

1½ c.	*(375 mL)*	buttermilk baking mix
½ c.	*(125 mL)*	milk
1 tbsp.	*(15 mL)*	sugar
¼ tsp.	*(1 mL)*	cinnamon

Vanilla ice cream or whipping cream

Heat oven to 400°F *(200°C)*. In large mixer bowl combine brown sugar, butter, flour, ¼ tsp. *(1 mL)* cinnamon and lemon juice. Beat at med. speed, scraping bowl often, until well mixed (1 to 2 min.). Add pears; toss to coat. Spoon into 2-qt. *(2-L)* casserole. Cover; bake for 25 to 35 min. or until pears are crisply tender. Meanwhile, in small bowl combine baking mix and milk; stir until just moistened. Drop dough by spoonfuls onto hot pear mixture to make 9 biscuits. In small bowl stir together sugar and cinnamon. Sprinkle sugar mixture over biscuits. Return to oven, uncovered; continue baking for 15 to 20 min. or until biscuits are lightly browned. Serve warm with ice cream or whipping cream.

*5 c. *(1,3 L)* (5 med.) peeled, cored, sliced ⅛" *(0,2 cm)* apples can be substituted for 5 c. *(1,3 L)* sliced pears.

Granny's Peaches & Cream Cobbler

Berry Time Shortcake

This strawberry shortcake is an easy summertime dessert.

Cake

1¼ c.	*(300 mL)* all-purpose flour
¾ c.	*(175 mL)* sugar
⅓ c.	*(75 mL)* butter or margarine, softened
⅔ c.	*(150 mL)* milk
2	eggs

2½ tsp.	*(10 mL)* baking powder
½ tsp.	*(2 mL)* salt
1 tsp.	*(5 mL)* vanilla
	Strawberries
	Sweetened whipped cream

Heat oven to 400°F *(200°C)*. In small mixer bowl combine all cake ingredients *except* strawberries and sweetened whipped cream. Beat at med. speed, scraping bowl often, until well mixed (1 to 2 min.). Spread into greased and floured 9" *(23 cm)* sq. baking pan.

Bake for 20 to 25 min. or until lightly browned. Cool completely. Cut into squares. If desired, split each square in half horizontally. Serve with strawberries and sweetened whipped cream.

Lemon Picnic Cake With Berries

An old-fashioned butter cake, served with fresh berries, is the perfect dessert for a picnic or potluck.

Cake

4	eggs, separated
2 c.	*(500 mL)* sugar
1 c.	*(250 mL)* butter or margarine, softened
3 c.	*(750 mL)* all-purpose flour
2 tsp.	*(10 mL)* baking powder
1 c.	*(250 mL)* milk
2 tsp.	*(10 mL)* grated lemon peel
1 tbsp.	*(15 mL)* lemon juice
1 tsp.	*(5 mL)* vanilla

Glaze

⅓ c.	*(75 mL)* sugar
⅓ c.	*(75 mL)* lemon juice
1 tbsp.	*(15 mL)* grated lemon peel
	Fresh berries

Heat oven to 350°F *(180°C)*. In small mixer bowl beat egg whites at high speed, scraping bowl often, just until stiff peaks form (2 to 3 min.). Set aside. In large mixer bowl combine 2 c. *(500 mL)* sugar and butter. Beat at low speed, scraping bowl often, until light and fluffy (1 to 2 min.). Add egg yolks; continue beating until creamy (1 to 2 min.). In small bowl stir together flour and baking powder. Gradually add flour mixture alternately with milk to butter mixture while beating at low speed. Add lemon peel, lemon juice and vanilla. By hand, fold egg whites into cake batter. Pour into greased and floured 10" *(25 cm)* tube or Bundt pan. Bake for 50 to 65 min. or until wooden pick inserted in center comes out clean. In 1-qt. *(1-L)* saucepan stir together all glaze ingredients *except* berries. Cook over med. heat, stirring occasionally, until sugar is dissolved (3 to 4 min.). With wooden pick poke holes in top of cake; pour glaze over cake. Cool 15 min.; remove from pan. If desired, leave cake in pan to transport. Serve with fresh berries.

Lemon Picnic Cake With Berries

Orange Pecan Delight

This tender, moist dessert bakes while you eat dinner.

¼ c.	*(50 mL)* butter or margarine
⅓ c.	*(75 mL)* crushed vanilla wafers
¼ c.	*(50 mL)* all-purpose flour
½ c.	*(125 mL)* milk
½ c.	*(125 mL)* orange juice
4	eggs, separated
2 tbsp.	*(30 mL)* sugar

⅓ c.	*(75 mL)* sugar
½ tsp.	*(2 mL)* vanilla
½ c.	*(125 mL)* finely chopped pecans
1 c.	*(250 mL)* whipping cream
2 tbsp.	*(30 mL)* sugar
2 tsp.	*(10 mL)* grated orange peel

Grease bottoms only of 8 individual soufflé dishes or custard cups. In 2-qt. *(2-L)* saucepan melt butter over low heat. Stir in crushed vanilla wafers and flour; gradually stir in milk and juice. Cook over med. heat, stirring constantly, until mixture thickens and comes to a full boil (6 to 8 min.). Remove from heat; cool 20 min. Heat oven to 325°F *(160°C)*. In small mixer bowl beat egg whites at high speed, scraping bowl often, until soft peaks form (1 to 2 min.). Continue beating, gradually adding 2 tbsp. *(30 mL)* sugar, until stiff peaks form (1 to 2 min.); set aside. In large mixer bowl combine egg yolks, ⅓ c. *(75 mL)* sugar and vanilla. Beat at med. speed, scraping bowl often, until thickened and lemon colored (2 to 3 min.). Stir pecans and wafer mixture into yolks. Fold in egg whites just until mixed. Spoon

into prepared dishes. Place dishes inside two 9" *(23 cm)* sq. baking pans; place in oven. Pour 1" *(2,5 cm)* hot water into pans. Bake for 40 to 50 min. or until knife inserted in center comes out clean. Meanwhile, in small chilled mixer bowl, beat chilled whipping cream at high speed, scraping bowl often, until soft peaks form. Gradually add 2 tbsp. *(30 mL)* sugar and orange peel; continue beating until stiff peaks form. Serve hot dessert immediately with orange whipped cream.

Tip: 1½-qt. *(1,5-L)* soufflé dish can be substituted for 8 individual soufflé dishes. Bake for 75 to 90 min. or until knife inserted halfway between edge and center comes out clean.

To Prepare Orange Pecan Delight:

1. Cook over med. heat, stirring constantly, until mixture thickens and comes to a full boil (6 to 8 min.). Remove from heat; cool 20 min.

2. In small mixer bowl beat egg whites at high speed, scraping bowl often, until soft peaks form (1 to 2 min.). Continue beating, gradually adding 2 tbsp. *(30 mL)* sugar, until stiff peaks form (1 to 2 min.); set aside.

Orange Pecan Delight

Sweetheart Cheesecake

10 servings

Sweetheart Cheesecake

Rich homemade cheesecake sweetened with a decorative ring of hearts.

Crust

1⅓ c.	*(325 mL)* crushed chocolate wafer cookies
¼ c.	*(50 mL)* butter or margarine, melted
2 tbsp.	*(30 mL)* sugar

Filling

4	eggs, separated
½ c.	*(125 mL)* butter or margarine, softened
2	(8-oz.) *(250-g)* pkg. cream cheese, softened
1 c.	*(250 mL)* sugar
1 tbsp.	*(15 mL)* cornstarch
1 tsp.	*(5 mL)* baking powder
1 tbsp.	*(15 mL)* lemon juice

Topping

1 c.	*(250 mL)* dairy sour cream
2 tbsp.	*(30 mL)* sugar
1 tsp.	*(5 mL)* vanilla
21-oz.	*(540-mL)* can cherry pie filling
3 tbsp.	*(45 mL)* cherry-flavored liqueur

Heat oven to 325°F *(160°C)*. In small bowl stir together all crust ingredients. Press crumb mixture evenly onto bottom of 9" *(23 cm)* springform pan. Bake 10 min.; cool. In small mixer bowl beat egg whites at high speed, scraping bowl often, until soft peaks form (1 to 2 min.); set aside. In large mixer bowl combine ½ c. *(125 mL)* butter, cream cheese and egg yolks. Beat at med. speed, scraping bowl often, until smooth and creamy (2 to 3 min.). Add remaining filling ingredients *except* egg whites. Continue beating, scraping bowl often, until well mixed (1 to 2 min.). By hand, fold in beaten egg whites. Spoon filling into prepared pan. Bake for 60 to 80 min. or until center is set and firm to the touch. (Cheesecake surface will be cracked.) Cool 15 min.; loosen sides of cheesecake from pan by running knife around inside of pan. Cool completely. (Cheesecake center will dip slightly upon cooling.) In small bowl stir together sour cream, 2 tbsp. *(30 mL)* sugar and vanilla. Spread evenly over top of cheesecake. Spoon out 2 to 3 tbsp. *(30 to 45 mL)* of cherry sauce from pie filling; drop by teaspoonfuls onto sour cream topping. Carefully pull knife or spatula through cherry sauce forming hearts. Cover; refrigerate 4 hr. or overnight. In medium bowl stir together remaining pie filling and, if desired, liqueur. Serve over slices of cheesecake.

To Prepare Cheesecake:

1. Spoon out 2 to 3 tbsp. *(30 to 45 mL)* of cherry sauce from pie filling; drop by teaspoonfuls onto sour cream topping.

2. Carefully pull knife or spatula through cherry sauce forming hearts.

Chocolate-Marbled Almond Cheesecake

12 servings
12 hours

Chocolate-Marbled Almond Cheesecake

*This rich, dark chocolate-marbled cheesecake, on an almond crust,
was meant for those with a passion for chocolate.*

2 c.	*(500 mL)* sugar
4	(8-oz.) *(250-g)* pkg. cream cheese, softened
4	eggs
1 c.	*(250 mL)* dairy sour cream
1 tbsp.	*(15 mL)* unsweetened cocoa

2 tsp.	*(10 mL)* vanilla
1 tsp.	*(5 mL)* almond extract
12-oz.	*(300-g)* pkg. semi-sweet chocolate chips, melted
2-oz.	*(60-g) (½ c.) (125 mL)* pkg. blanched almonds, finely chopped

Heat oven to 325°F *(160°C)*. In large mixer bowl combine sugar and cream cheese. Beat at med. speed, scraping bowl often, until light and fluffy (3 to 4 min.). Continue beating, adding eggs one at a time, until creamy (1 to 2 min.). Add remaining ingredients *except* chocolate chips and almonds. Continue beating, scraping bowl often, until well mixed (1 to 2 min.). By hand, fold in melted chocolate chips to swirl chocolate throughout batter for marbled effect. Lightly butter 9" *(23 cm)* springform pan; press almonds firmly on bottom of pan. Pour batter into prepared pan. Bake for 65 to 75 min. or until set. Turn off oven; leave cheesecake in oven for 2 hr. Loosen sides of cheesecake from pan by running knife around inside of pan. Cool completely. Cover; refrigerate 8 hr. or overnight. Store refrigerated.

8 servings
2 hours

Apricot-Laced Cream Puffs

An apricot cream cheese filling provides an interesting twist to cream puffs, a heartwarming classic.

Cream Puffs

1 c.	*(250 mL)* water
½ c.	*(125 mL)* butter or margarine
1 c.	*(250 mL)* all-purpose flour
4	eggs

Apricot Cream

½ c.	*(125 mL)* whipping cream
¼ c.	*(50 mL)* powdered sugar
8-oz.	*(250-g)* pkg. cream cheese, softened
½ tsp.	*(2 mL)* ginger
2 tbsp.	*(30 mL)* apricot preserves
½ c.	*(125 mL)* apricot preserves, melted Powdered sugar

Heat oven to 400°F *(200°C)*. In 2-qt. *(2-L)* saucepan bring water and butter to a full boil. Stir in flour. Cook over low heat, stirring vigorously, until mixture forms a ball. Add eggs, one at a time, beating until smooth. Drop about ⅓ c. *(75 mL)* dough 3" *(7,5 cm)* apart onto cookie sheet. Bake for 35 to 40 min. or until puffed and golden brown. Cool completely. In chilled small mixer bowl, beat chilled whipping cream at high speed, scraping bowl often, until soft peaks form. Gradually add ¼ c. *(50 mL)* powdered sugar; continue beating until stiff peaks form (1 to 2 min.). Add remaining apricot cream ingredients *except* ½ c. *(125 mL)* apricot preserves and powdered sugar. Continue beating, scraping bowl often, until smooth (2 to 3 min.). Cut off cream puff tops; pull out any filaments of soft dough. Fill puffs with apricot cream; replace tops. Drizzle with melted apricot preserves; sprinkle with powdered sugar.

Bananas Foster With Crepes

Buttery crepes served in a rich banana-rum sauce.

6 servings
45 minutes

Crepes

¾ c.	*(175 mL)*	all-purpose flour
1½ tsp.	*(7 mL)*	sugar
¼ tsp.	*(1 mL)*	baking powder
¼ tsp.	*(1 mL)*	salt
1 c.	*(250 mL)*	milk
1		egg
1 tbsp.	*(15 mL)*	butter or margarine, melted
¼ tsp.	*(1 mL)*	vanilla
1 tsp.	*(5 mL)*	butter or margarine

Sauce

½ c.	*(125 mL)*	butter or margarine
1¾ c.	*(425 mL)*	powdered sugar
¼ c.	*(50 mL)*	milk
½ tsp.	*(2 mL)*	cinnamon
2 tbsp.	*(30 mL)*	rum*
3		med. bananas, sliced ¼" *(0,5 cm)*
2 tbsp.	*(30 mL)*	lemon juice

In small mixer bowl combine flour, sugar, baking powder and salt. Add remaining crepe ingredients *except* 1 tsp. *(5 mL)* butter. Beat at med. speed, scraping bowl often, until smooth (1 to 2 min.). Melt 1 tsp. *(5 mL)* butter in 6 or 8" *(15 to 20 cm)* skillet until sizzling. For each of 6 crepes, pour about ¼ c. *(50 mL)* batter into skillet; immediately rotate skillet until thin film covers bottom. Cook over med. heat until lightly browned (2 to 3 min.). Run wide spatula around edge to loosen; turn. Continue cooking until lightly browned (2 to 3 min.). Place crepes on plate, placing waxed paper between each. Cover crepes; set aside. In 10" *(25 cm)* skillet melt ½ c. *(125 mL)*

butter over med. heat. Stir in powdered sugar, ¼ c. *(50 mL)* milk, cinnamon and rum. In small bowl combine bananas and lemon juice; toss to coat bananas. Gently stir bananas into sauce in skillet. Fold each crepe in half; fold in half again to form triangles. Arrange crepes in skillet; spoon sauce over crepes. Cook over med. heat, spooning sauce over crepes occasionally, until heated through (4 to 6 min.). Serve immediately.

*1 tsp. *(5 mL)* rum extract can be substituted for 2 tbsp. *(30 mL)* rum.

To Prepare Bananas Foster:

1. Immediately rotate skillet until thin film covers bottom.

2. Run wide spatula around edge to loosen; turn. Continue cooking until lightly browned (2 to 3 min.).

Bananas Foster With Crepes

2 cups *(500 mL)*
15 minutes

Luscious Berries With Custard Sauce

Delightful custard sauce poured over sun-ripened berries.

1½ c.	*(375 mL)* whipping cream
½ c.	*(125 mL)* sugar
1 tbsp.	*(15 mL)* cornstarch
4	egg yolks
2 tsp.	*(10 mL)* vanilla

Fresh raspberries, strawberries and blueberries

In 2-qt. *(2-L)* saucepan cook cream over med. heat until just comes to a boil (6 to 8 min.). Remove from heat. Meanwhile, in medium bowl gradually whisk sugar and cornstarch into egg yolks. Whisk until mixture is light and creamy (3 to 4 min.). Gradually whisk hot cream into beaten egg yolks. Return mixture to same saucepan; stir in vanilla. Cook over med. heat, stirring constantly, until custard is thick enough to coat back of metal spoon (3 to 4 min.). (Do not boil because egg yolks will curdle.) Serve warm or cool over fresh berries.

Microwave Directions: In 1-qt. *(1-L)* casserole microwave cream on HIGH until just comes to a boil (2 to 4 min.). Meanwhile, in medium bowl gradually whisk sugar and cornstarch into egg yolks. Whisk until mixture is light and creamy (3 to 4 min.). Gradually whisk hot cream into beaten egg yolks. Return mixture to same casserole; stir in vanilla. Microwave on HIGH, stirring after half the time, until custard is thick enough to coat back of metal spoon (1½ to 2½ min.). (Do not boil because egg yolks will curdle.) Serve warm or cool over fresh berries.

To Prepare Custard Sauce:

1. Gradually whisk hot cream into beaten egg yolks.

2. Cook over med. heat, stirring constantly, until custard is thick enough to coat back of metal spoon.

Luscious Berries With Custard Sauce

Best Ever Baked Custard

6 servings
1 hour 15 minutes

Best Ever Baked Custard

Each spoonful of custard is rich, creamy and so comforting.

½ c.	*(125 mL)* sugar		½ c.	*(125 mL)* whipping cream
6	egg yolks		2 tsp.	*(10 mL)* vanilla
1½ c.	*(375 mL)* milk			Pinch of nutmeg

Heat oven to 325°F *(160°C)*. In medium bowl gradually whisk sugar into egg yolks. Gradually whisk remaining ingredients *except* nutmeg into egg mixture. Pour into 6 (6-oz.) *(170-mL)* custard cups or ramekins. Place custard cups in 13 × 9" *(33 × 23 cm)* baking pan; fill around custard cups with 1" *(2,5 cm)* of warm water. Sprinkle top of custards with nutmeg. Bake for 50 to 60 min. or until knife inserted in center comes out clean. Serve warm.

To Prepare Custard:

1. Place custard cups in 13 × 9" *(33 × 23 cm)* baking pan; fill around custard cups with 1" *(2,5 cm)* of warm water.

2. Bake for 50 to 60 min. or until knife inserted in center comes out clean.

6 to 8 servings
3 hours

Chocolate Truffle Pudding

Indulge in this truffle-like pudding to satisfy chocolate cravings.

1 c.	*(250 mL)* milk	2	egg yolks, slightly beaten
1 c.	*(250 mL)* whipping cream	2 tbsp.	*(30 mL)* butter or margarine
½ c.	*(125 mL)* sugar	1 tsp.	*(5 mL)* vanilla
3 tbsp.	*(45 mL)* unsweetened cocoa		
2 tbsp.	*(30 mL)* cornstarch		Sweetened whipped cream
¾ c.	*(175 mL)* semi-sweet real chocolate chips		Zest of orange peel
1	egg, slightly beaten		Unsweetened cocoa

In 2-qt. *(2-L)* saucepan stir together milk and whipping cream. Cook over med. heat until warm (3 to 5 min.). In small bowl stir together sugar, 3 tbsp. *(45 mL)* cocoa and cornstarch. Gradually add to milk mixture. Add remaining ingredients *except* whipped cream, zest of orange peel and cocoa. Continue cooking, stirring constantly, until pudding just begins to thicken (5 to 10 min.). Pour pudding into 6 or 8 (½-c.) *(125-mL)* individual dessert dishes. Cool 30 min. Cover; refrigerate at least 2 hr. Pipe with sweetened whipped cream; top with zest of orange peel and sprinkle with cocoa.

6 servings
2 hours

Home-Style Rice Pudding

This creamy, old-fashioned pudding is topped with a delicious sweet meringue.

Pudding

½ c.	*(125 mL)* sugar
1 tbsp.	*(15 mL)* cornstarch
½ tsp.	*(2 mL)* salt
¼ tsp.	*(1 mL)* nutmeg
2½ c.	*(625 mL)* milk
2	egg yolks, *reserve egg whites*
½ tsp.	*(2 mL)* vanilla
1½ c.	*(375 mL)* cooked rice

Meringue

2	reserved egg whites
2 tbsp.	*(30 mL)* sugar

Heat oven to 350°F *(180°C)*. In large bowl stir together ½ c. *(125 mL)* sugar, cornstarch, salt and nutmeg. Add milk, egg yolks and vanilla; with wire whisk, beat until smooth. Stir in rice. Pour into 1½-qt. *(1,5-L)* casserole. Place casserole in 9" *(23 cm)* sq. baking pan. Place in oven; pour hot water 1" *(2,5 cm)* deep into sq. pan. Bake, stirring occasionally, until pudding is creamy and milk is absorbed (about 1½ hr.). Remove from oven; remove 1½-qt. *(1,5-L)* casserole from sq. pan. Increase oven to 400°F *(200°C)*. In small mixer bowl beat egg whites at high speed, scraping bowl often, until soft peaks form (1 to 2 min.). Continue beating, gradually adding sugar, until stiff peaks form (1 to 2 min.). Spread over pudding, sealing around edges. Bake for 5 to 8 min. or until meringue is lightly browned. Serve warm or cold.

Chocolate Truffle Pudding

12 servings
2 hours 20 minutes

Steamed Cranberry Pudding

Old-fashioned, warmly spiced steamed pudding is sure to become a family holiday tradition.

Pudding

2 c.	*(500 mL)* all-purpose flour
1 c.	*(250 mL)* sugar
1 c.	*(250 mL)* milk
1	egg
2 tbsp.	*(30 mL)* butter or margarine, softened
1 tsp.	*(5 mL)* baking soda
1 tsp.	*(5 mL)* cinnamon
1 tsp.	*(5 mL)* nutmeg
¼ c.	*(50 mL)* all-purpose flour
2 c.	*(500 mL)* fresh or frozen whole cranberries

Sauce

½ c.	*(125 mL)* sugar
½ c.	*(125 mL)* firmly packed brown sugar
½ c.	*(125 mL)* butter or margarine
½ c.	*(125 mL)* whipping cream
1 tsp.	*(5 mL)* vanilla

In large mixer bowl combine all pudding ingredients *except* ¼ c. *(50 mL)* flour and cranberries. Beat at med. speed, scraping bowl often, until well mixed (1 to 2 min.). In small bowl toss together ¼ c. *(50 mL)* flour and cranberries. By hand, stir cranberry mixture into batter. Pour into greased 1½-qt. *(1,5-L)* metal mold or casserole. Cover tightly with aluminum foil. Place rack in Dutch oven or roasting pan; add boiling water to just below rack. Place mold on rack. Cover; cook over med.

heat at a low boil for about 2 hr. or until wooden pick inserted in center comes out clean. Add boiling water occasionally to keep water level just below rack. Remove; let stand 2 to 3 min. Remove aluminum foil and unmold. Serve warm or cold with warm sauce. In 1-qt. *(1-L)* saucepan combine all sauce ingredients *except* vanilla. Cook over med. heat, stirring occasionally, until mixture thickens and comes to a full boil (4 to 5 min.). Boil 1 min. Stir in vanilla. Store sauce refrigerated.

To Prepare Steamed Cranberry Pudding:

1. Pour into greased 1½-qt. *(1,5-L)* metal mold or casserole. Cover tightly with aluminum foil.

2. Place rack in Dutch oven or roasting pan; add boiling water to just below rack.

Steamed Cranberry Pudding

6 servings
3 hours

Individual Fruit-Filled Meringues

*These heart-shaped meringues showcase a cloud of whipped cream
and a colorful arrangement of fresh fruit.*

Meringues
4	egg whites
2 tsp.	*(10 mL)* cornstarch
¼ tsp.	*(1 mL)* cream of tartar
1 tsp.	*(5 mL)* lemon juice
1 c.	*(250 mL)* sugar
⅓ c.	*(75 mL)* powdered sugar

Whipped Cream
1 c.	*(250 mL)* whipping cream
¼ c.	*(50 mL)* sugar
1 tsp.	*(5 mL)* vanilla
1 c.	*(250 mL)* sliced fresh strawberries
1 c.	*(250 mL)* 1" *(2,5 cm)* pieces fresh pineapple
1	kiwi, cut into 6 slices

Heat oven to 275°F *(140°C)*. In large mixer bowl beat egg whites, cornstarch, cream of tartar and lemon juice at high speed, scraping bowl often, until soft peaks form (1 to 2 min.). Continue beating, gradually adding 1 c. *(250 mL)* sugar and powdered sugar, until glossy and stiff peaks form (6 to 8 min.). On brown paper or parchment paper-lined cookie sheet, shape or pipe 6 (about 4") *(10 cm)* individual heart-shaped or round meringues, building up sides. Bake for 1 hr. Turn off oven; leave meringues in oven with door closed for 1 hr. Finish cooling meringues at room temperature. In chilled small mixer bowl, beat chilled whipping cream at high speed, scraping bowl often, until soft peaks form. Gradually add ¼ c. *(50 mL)* sugar; continue beating until stiff peaks form (1 to 2 min.). By hand, fold in vanilla. Fill meringue shells with whipped cream; top with strawberries, pineapple and kiwi.

To Prepare Meringues:

1. Continue beating, gradually adding 1 c. *(250 mL)* sugar and powdered sugar, until glossy and stiff peaks form (6 to 8 min.).

2. On brown paper or parchment paper-lined cookie sheet, shape or pipe 6 (about 4") *(10 cm)* individual heart-shaped or round meringues, building up sides.

Individual Fruit-Filled Meringues

15 servings
6 hours 30 minutes

Chocolate Mousse Squares

Mousse-like dessert that's easy enough to prepare for a large group.

2 c.	*(500 mL)* (about 25) finely crushed chocolate sandwich cookies
⅓ c.	*(75 mL)* butter or margarine, melted
2 c.	*(500 mL)* powdered sugar
1 c.	*(250 mL)* butter or margarine, softened
8-oz.	*(250-g)* pkg. cream cheese, softened
4	(1-oz.) *(30-g)* sq. unsweetened chocolate, melted, cooled

4	eggs
2 tsp.	*(10 mL)* vanilla
1 c.	*(250 mL)* flaked coconut
1 c.	*(250 mL)* chopped walnuts
1½ c.	*(375 mL)* whipping cream

In medium bowl stir together crushed cookies and ⅓ c. *(75 mL)* melted butter. *Reserve ¼ c. (50 mL) crumb mixture;* set aside. Press remaining crumb mixture on bottom of 13 × 9" *(33 × 23 cm)* pan. In large mixer bowl combine powdered sugar, 1 c. *(250 mL)* butter, cream cheese, chocolate, eggs and vanilla. Beat at med. speed, scraping bowl often, until smooth and fluffy (2 to 3 min.). By hand, stir in coconut and walnuts. In chilled bowl, beat chilled whipping cream at high speed, scraping bowl often, until soft peaks form. Fold into chocolate mixture; pour over crumb crust. Sprinkle with reserved ¼ c. *(50 mL)* crumb mixture. Cover; refrigerate at least 6 hr. Cut into squares. Store refrigerated.

8 servings
3 hours 30 minutes

Chocolate Mint Mallow Cups

A little extra time is needed for these individual mint delights, but everyone will praise the results.

1 c.	*(250 mL)* semi-sweet chocolate chips
½ c.	*(125 mL)* milk
24	large marshmallows
	Pinch of salt
1 tsp.	*(5 mL)* vanilla

	Pinch of peppermint extract
6	drops red food coloring
1 c.	*(250 mL)* (½ pt.) whipping cream
⅓ c.	*(75 mL)* crushed starlight peppermint candy, *reserve 1 tbsp.* (15 mL)

In 1-qt. *(1-L)* saucepan melt chocolate chips over *low* heat, stirring occasionally, until chips are melted (4 to 5 min.). Place 8 paper liners in a muffin pan. With pastry brush coat inside of each liner evenly with melted chocolate, about ⅛" *(0,2 cm)* thick, bringing coating almost to top of liner, but not over edge. Refrigerate until firm (30 min.). Meanwhile, in 2-qt. *(2-L)* saucepan combine milk and marshmallows; cook over *low* heat, stirring occasionally, until marshmallows are melted (9 to 12 min.). Remove from heat; stir in salt, vanilla, peppermint extract and red food coloring. Refrigerate until mixture mounds slightly when dropped from a spoon (about 1 hr.). Meanwhile, in chilled mixer bowl, beat chilled whipping cream at high speed, scraping bowl often, until stiff peaks form. Stir marshmallow mixture until smooth. Fold marshmallow mixture and crushed peppermint candy *except* reserved 1 tbsp. *(15 mL)* into whipped cream. Spoon about ⅓ c. *(75 mL)* filling into each chocolate cup. Refrigerate at least 2 hr. Carefully remove paper liners from chocolate cups. To serve, sprinkle with reserved 1 tbsp. *(15 mL)* crushed candy.

Microwave Directions: In small bowl microwave chocolate chips on HIGH, stirring every 30 sec., until chips are melted (1½ to 2½ min.). Prepare chocolate cups as directed left. In medium bowl microwave milk and marshmallows on HIGH, stirring every min., until marshmallows are melted (1½ to 2½ min.). Continue as directed left.

Chocolate Mint Mallow Cups

Fresh Strawberry Mousse Soufflé

12 servings
6 hours 30 minutes

Fresh Strawberry Mousse Soufflé

This cold soufflé has a mousse-like texture and the flavor of fresh strawberries.

1 c.	*(250 mL)* sugar		1 c.	*(250 mL)* dairy sour cream
2	(¼-oz.) *(7-g)* envelopes unflavored gelatin		1½ tsp.	*(7 mL)* almond extract
4 c.	*(1 L)* (2 pt.) whipping cream		1 tsp.	*(5 mL)* vanilla
4	egg whites			Strawberries
4 c.	*(1 L)* (1 qt.) sliced ¼" *(0,5 cm)* strawberries			

Make a 4" *(10 cm)* strip of double layer aluminum foil 2" *(5 cm)* longer than circumference of 2-qt. *(2-L)* soufflé dish. Collar soufflé dish with strip, securing strip around outside edge with string or tape. In 2-qt. *(2-L)* saucepan combine sugar and gelatin. Stir in 2 c. *(500 mL)* whipping cream; let stand 1 min. Cook over med. heat, stirring occasionally, until gelatin is dissolved (4 to 6 min.). Refrigerate, stirring occasionally, until mixture begins to thicken (about 1 hr.). In small mixer bowl beat egg whites at high speed until stiff peaks form (2 to 3 min.); set aside. In another chilled small mixer bowl, beat 2 c. *(500 mL)* chilled whipping cream at high speed, scraping bowl often, until stiff peaks form (3 to 4 min.). Set aside. In large mixer bowl combine 4 c. *(1 L)* strawberries, sour cream, almond extract, vanilla and thickened gelatin mixture. Beat at low speed, scraping bowl often, until strawberries are broken into pieces (2 to 3 min.). Fold in beaten egg whites and whipped cream. Pour into oiled and collared 2-qt. *(2-L)* soufflé dish. Cover; refrigerate until firm (5 to 6 hr.). To serve, remove collar and garnish with strawberries.

To Prepare Soufflé:

1. Make a 4" *(10 cm)* strip of double layer aluminum foil 2" *(5 cm)* longer than circumference of 2-qt. *(2-L)* soufflé dish. Collar soufflé dish with strip, securing strip around outside edge with string or tape.

2. Refrigerate, stirring occasionally, until mixture begins to thicken (about 1 hr.).

Strawberry Trifle

8 servings
2 hours 30 minutes

Strawberry Trifle

*Layers of fresh strawberries, pudding and whipping cream
make this dessert as pretty as it is good to eat.*

3½-oz. *(135-g)* pkg. vanilla flavored instant
pudding and pie filling mix
1 c. *(250 mL)* dairy sour cream
1 c. *(250 mL)* milk
1 tsp. *(5 mL)* grated orange peel

2 c. *(500 mL)* (1 pt.) whipping cream, whipped
½ *(10")* *(25 cm)* tube angel food cake, cut
into bite-size pieces
2 pt. *(1 L)* fresh strawberries, hulled, sliced

In large mixer bowl place instant pudding, sour cream, milk and orange peel. Beat at low speed, scraping bowl often, until thick and well mixed (1 to 2 min.). By hand, fold in whipped cream. In large serving bowl layer: ½ of cake pieces, ⅓ strawberries and ½ pudding mixture. Repeat layers. Arrange remaining strawberries on top. Cover; refrigerate at least 2 hr.

15 servings
8 hours

Banana Split Squares

Crowd-pleasing banana splits.

Crust
½ c. *(125 mL)* butter or margarine
2 c. *(500 mL)* graham cracker crumbs
¼ c. *(50 mL)* sugar

Filling
3 bananas, sliced ¼" *(0,5 cm)*
½ gal. *(2 L)* vanilla ice cream, slightly softened
1 c. *(250 mL)* chopped walnuts

Sauce
2 c. *(500 mL)* powdered sugar
½ c. *(125 mL)* butter or margarine
12-oz. *(385-mL)* can evaporated milk
6-oz. *(175-g)* pkg. semi-sweet real
chocolate chips
1 tsp. *(5 mL)* vanilla

Topping
1 c. *(250 mL)* whipping cream
Maraschino cherries

In 2-qt. *(2-L)* saucepan melt ½ c. *(125 mL)* butter. Stir in crumbs and sugar. Press crumb mixture on bottom of 13 × 9" *(33 × 23 cm)* pan. Layer banana slices over crumb mixture. Spread ice cream over bananas. Sprinkle with chopped nuts. Cover; freeze until firm (about 4 hr.). Meanwhile, in 2-qt. *(2-L)* saucepan combine all sauce ingredients. Cook over low heat, stirring occasionally, until mixture thickens and comes to a full boil (20 to 25 min.). Boil 1 min. Cool completely; pour evenly over ice cream. Cover; freeze until firm (about 3 hr.). In chilled bowl, beat chilled whipping cream at high speed, scraping bowl often, until soft peaks form. Spread over sauce. If desired, garnish with maraschino cherries. Serve immediately or freeze until served.

6 servings
5 hours 30 minutes

Maple-Nut Cream Cheese Cups

A creamy, rich dessert with the flavor of cheesecake.

¼ c.	*(50 mL)* milk		¼ c.	*(50 mL)* pure maple syrup or maple flavored syrup
⅓ c.	*(75 mL)* sugar		2 tbsp.	*(30 mL)* graham cracker crumbs
8-oz.	*(250-g)* pkg. cream cheese, softened		¼ c.	*(50 mL)* chopped pecans
1	egg			
½ tsp.	*(2 mL)* vanilla			

Line 6 muffin cups with paper liners; set aside. In large mixer bowl combine all ingredients *except* maple syrup, graham cracker crumbs and pecans. Beat at med. speed, scraping bowl often, until smooth (2 to 3 min.). Pour cream cheese mixture evenly into prepared muffin cups. Freeze until firm (4 to 5 hr.). In small bowl stir together maple syrup and graham cracker crumbs. Cover; refrigerate at least 2 hr. To serve, place each dessert upside down on dessert plate. Let stand at room temperature 10 to 15 min.; remove paper. Spoon 1 tbsp. *(15 mL)* maple syrup mixture over each dessert; sprinkle with nuts.

9 servings
4 hours 30 minutes

Lemon Raspberry Ice Squares

A light, refreshing dessert for a warm summer day.

1 c.	*(250 mL)* (about 18) crushed lemon flavored sugar cookies		1 c.	*(250 mL)* buttermilk*
¼ c.	*(50 mL)* sugar		⅓ c.	*(75 mL)* sugar
3 tbsp.	*(45 mL)* butter or margarine, melted		2 c.	*(500 mL)* frozen raspberries
1 c.	*(250 mL)* raspberry flavored yogurt			Sweetened whipped cream

In small bowl stir together crushed cookies, ¼ c. *(50 mL)* sugar and butter. Press on bottom of 9" *(23 cm)* sq. baking pan; set aside. In medium bowl stir together remaining ingredients *except* raspberries and whipped cream. Fold in raspberries. Pour yogurt mixture over cookie crust. Cover; freeze until firm (3 to 4 hr.). To serve, let stand at room temperature 10 to 15 min. Cut into squares; garnish with sweetened whipped cream.

*1 tbsp. *(15 mL)* vinegar plus enough milk to equal 1 c. *(250 mL)* can be substituted for 1 c. *(250 mL)* buttermilk.

Tip: Blueberry flavored yogurt and frozen blueberries or strawberry flavored yogurt and halved frozen strawberries can be substituted for raspberry flavored yogurt and frozen raspberries.

Maple-Nut Cream Cheese Cups (top)
Lemon Raspberry Ice Squares (bottom)

Banana n' Chocolate Chip Ice Cream Sandwiches

12 ice cream sandwiches
6 hours

Banana n' Chocolate Chip Ice Cream Sandwiches

Ice cream, bananas and coconut are sandwiched between chewy chocolate chip cookies for frozen ice cream treats.

24	(3") *(7 cm)* chewy chocolate chip cookies	½ c.	*(125 mL)* flaked coconut
4 c.	(1 qt.) *(1 L)* chocolate chip ice cream, slightly softened	1	med. banana, chopped

Prepare or purchase your favorite chewy chocolate chip cookies. In large bowl stir together ice cream, coconut and banana just until blended. Freeze mixture for 2 hr. Spread about ¼ c. *(50 mL)* ice cream on each of 12 cookies. Top each with additional cookie; press together to form a sandwich. With metal spatula go around edges of each ice cream sandwich to remove excess ice cream. Wrap each ice cream sandwich with plastic wrap; freeze at least 4 hr.

Tip: A variety of cookies can be used. If smaller cookies are used, adjust measurement of ice cream proportionately. Leftover ice cream can be served as a milk shake.

9 servings
9 hours

Honey Peanut Butter Ice Cream Squares

This peanut butter ice cream dessert will quickly become a family tradition.

Crust

½ c.	*(125 mL)* all-purpose flour
⅓ c.	*(75 mL)* quick-cooking oats
¼ c.	*(50 mL)* sugar
¼ c.	*(50 mL)* butter or margarine
¼ tsp.	*(1 mL)* baking soda

Ice Cream

½ c.	*(125 mL)* crunchy-style peanut butter
⅓ c.	*(75 mL)* light corn syrup
2 tbsp.	*(30 mL)* honey
½ gal.	*(2 L)* vanilla ice cream, slightly softened
1 c.	*(250 mL)* chopped salted peanuts

Heat oven to 350°F *(180°C)*. Line 9" *(23 cm)* sq. baking pan with aluminum foil, extending excess foil over edges. In large mixer bowl combine all crust ingredients. Beat at med. speed, scraping bowl often, until crumbly (1 to 2 min.). Press on bottom of prepared pan. Bake for 12 to 20 min. or until lightly browned. Cool completely. In small bowl stir together peanut butter, corn syrup and honey. Spread half of peanut butter mixture over crust. Spread half of ice cream over peanut butter mixture. Drop by spoonfuls and spread remaining peanut butter mixture over ice cream; sprinkle with ½ c. *(125 mL)* peanuts. Spread and swirl remaining ice cream over peanuts. Sprinkle with remaining peanuts. Freeze 8 hr. or overnight or until firm. To serve, lift ice cream square from pan, using aluminum foil as handles. Remove aluminum foil. Cut into squares; serve immediately.

Homemade Ice Cream

3 quarts *(3 L)*
1 hour 30 minutes

Everyone takes a turn cranking when making this creamy sensation.

4 c.	*(1 L)* milk		5	eggs
4 c.	*(1 L)*(2 pt.) whipping cream		1½ tsp.	*(7 mL)* vanilla
1½ c.	*(375 mL)* sugar			Pinch of salt

In 3-qt. *(3-L)* saucepan combine milk and whipping cream. Cook over low heat until warm (6 to 8 min.). In large mixer bowl combine remaining ingredients. Beat at med. speed, scraping bowl often, until smooth (2 to 3 min.). Gradually stir into milk mixture. Cool to room temperature. Pour into ice cream canister. Freeze in ice cream maker according to manufacturer's directions.

Lemon Ice

3 quarts *(3 L)*
8 hours 30 minutes

The flavor of old-fashioned lemonade, frozen in a refreshing ice.

2 c.	*(500 mL)* sugar		3	eggs
4 c.	*(1 L)* milk		½ tsp.	*(2 mL)* salt
2 c.	*(500 mL)* (1 pt.) whipping cream		1 tbsp.	*(15 mL)* lemon peel
⅔ c.	*(150 mL)* lemon juice			

In large mixer bowl combine all ingredients. Beat at low speed, scraping bowl often, until well mixed (1 to 2 min.). Pour into 13 × 9" *(33 × 23 cm)* pan. Cover; freeze until firm (about 4 hr.). Spoon into large mixer bowl. Beat at med. speed, scraping bowl often, until light and fluffy but not thawed (2 to 3 min.). Return to pan; freeze at least 4 hr. or until firm.

Homemade Ice Cream

3 cups *(750 mL)*
20 minutes

Spiced Pears in Cider Sauce

Serve this flavorful sauce over gingerbread, spice cake or ice cream.

2 c.   *(500 mL)* apple cider
2 tbsp. *(30 mL)* cornstarch
2 tbsp. *(30 mL)* firmly packed brown sugar
         Pinch of allspice
         Dash of ground clove

2 c.   *(500 mL)* (2 med.) ripe Red Bartlett,
         Bartlett, Anjou or Bosc pears, cut into
         ½" *(1 cm)* pieces
2 tbsp. *(30 mL)* lemon juice

In 2-qt. *(2-L)* saucepan stir together all ingredients *except* pears and lemon juice. Cook over med. heat, stirring occasionally, until mixture is slightly thickened (5 to 7 min.). Stir in pears and lemon juice. Continue cooking, stirring occasionally, until pears are tender (3 to 5 min.). Serve warm sauce over gingerbread, spice cake or ice cream.

Microwave Directions: In 2-qt. *(2-L)* casserole combine all ingredients *except* pears and lemon juice. Microwave on HIGH, stirring after half the time, until mixture is slightly thickened (5½ to 7 min.). Stir in pears and lemon juice. Microwave on HIGH until pears are tender (1 to 1½ min.). Serve warm sauce over gingerbread, spice cake or ice cream.

2 cups *(500 mL)*
15 minutes

Apricot Crème Sauce

This creamy apricot sauce brings a delightful touch to desserts.

14½-oz. *(398-mL)* can apricot halves in their own
         juice, drained, *reserve juice*
1 tbsp. *(15 mL)* cornstarch
½ c.   *(125 mL)* apricot preserves

½ c.   *(125 mL)* whipping cream
¼ tsp.   *(1 mL)* nutmeg
1 tbsp. *(15 mL)* lemon juice

Slice apricots into ¼" *(0,5 cm)* slices; set aside. In 1-qt. *(1-L)* saucepan combine ⅔ c. *(150 mL)* reserved apricot juice and cornstarch; whisk to blend. Cook over med. heat, stirring occasionally, until thickened (4 to 6 min.). Stir in remaining ingredients and apricots. Continue cooking, stirring occasionally, until apricots are warm (4 to 5 min.). Serve sauce over pound cake, meringues, cream puffs or ice cream.

Microwave Directions: Slice apricots into ¼" *(0,5 cm)* slices; set aside. In 1-qt. *(1-L)* casserole combine ⅔ c. *(150 mL)* reserved apricot juice and cornstarch; whisk to blend. Stir in remaining ingredients *except* apricots. Microwave on HIGH, stirring every min., until thickened (3 to 4 min.). Stir in apricots; microwave on HIGH until apricots are warm (1 to 2 min.). Serve sauce over pound cake, meringues, cream puffs or ice cream.

Spiced Pears in Cider Sauce

Dreamy Chocolate Mint Sauce

4 cups *(1 L)*
15 minutes

Dreamy Chocolate Mint Sauce

A rich-tasting dessert sauce that's reminiscent of after dinner mints.

1 c.	*(250 mL)* sugar
½ c.	*(125 mL)* butter or margarine, cut into pieces
¾ c.	*(175 mL)* water

¼ c.	*(50 mL)* light corn syrup
12-oz.	*(300-g)* pkg. semi-sweet real chocolate chips
¼ c.	*(50 mL)* creme de menthe*

In 2-qt. *(2-L)* saucepan combine sugar, butter, water and corn syrup. Cook over med. heat, stirring constantly, until mixture comes to a full boil (5 to 8 min.). Boil 3 min.; remove from heat. Immediately add chocolate chips; beat with a wire whisk or rotary beater until smooth. Stir in creme de menthe. Serve warm or cool over ice cream or cake.

*1 tsp. *(5 mL)* peppermint extract can be substituted for creme de menthe.

Microwave Directions: In 2-qt. *(2-L)* casserole combine sugar, butter, water and corn syrup. Microwave on HIGH, stirring after half the time, until mixture comes to a full boil (4 to 7 min.). Boil 3 min. Immediately add chocolate chips; beat with a wire whisk or rotary beater until smooth. Stir in creme de menthe. Serve warm or cool over ice cream or cake.

2¼ cups *(550 mL)*
15 minutes

Homemade Caramel Sauce

Serve this rich dessert sauce over ice cream, gingerbread or pound cake.

¾ c.	*(175 mL)* firmly packed brown sugar
¾ c.	*(175 mL)* sugar
⅓ c.	*(75 mL)* butter or margarine

½ c.	*(125 mL)* light corn syrup
⅔ c.	*(150 mL)* whipping cream

In 2-qt. *(2-L)* saucepan combine all ingredients *except* whipping cream. Cook over med. heat, stirring occasionally, until mixture comes to a full boil (5 to 8 min.). Cool 5 min. Stir in whipping cream. Serve warm or divide sauce into 3 (¾ c.) *(175 mL)* portions and prepare variations as directed below. Store refrigerated.

Microwave Directions: In 2-qt. *(2-L)* casserole combine all ingredients *except* whipping cream. Microwave on HIGH, stirring every min., until mixture comes to a full boil (4 to 5 min.). Cool 5 min. Stir in whipping cream. Serve warm or divide sauce into 3 (¾ c.) *(175 mL)* portions and prepare variations as directed below. Store refrigerated.

Variations:

Rum Raisin Sauce: While still warm, stir ¼ c. *(50 mL)* raisins and ¼ tsp. *(1 mL)* rum extract into ¾ c. *(175 mL)* sauce.

Banana Sauce: Cool ¾ c. *(175 mL)* sauce completely. Cut 1 banana into cubes; stir into cooled sauce.

Praline Sauce: While still warm, stir ½ c. *(125 mL)* toasted pecan halves into ¾ c. *(175 mL)* sauce.

Icebox Banana Cake With Chocolate Cream

Icebox Banana Cake With Chocolate Cream

12 servings
4 hours

This cake tastes great from the refrigerator or it freezes beautifully for a chilled treat.

Cake

1 c.	*(250 mL)* sugar
⅔ c.	*(150 mL)* butter or margarine, softened
2 tsp.	*(10 mL)* vanilla
2	eggs
1 c.	*(250 mL)* (2 med.) mashed ripe bananas
¼ c.	*(50 mL)* dairy sour cream
1½ c.	*(375 mL)* all-purpose flour
1 tsp.	*(5 mL)* baking soda

Chocolate Cream

1½ c.	*(375 mL)* whipping cream
3 tbsp.	*(45 mL)* powdered sugar
1 tsp.	*(5 mL)* vanilla
½ c.	*(125 mL)* semi-sweet chocolate chips, melted
2	bananas
2 tbsp.	*(30 mL)* chopped pecans

Heat oven to 350°F *(180°C)*. In large mixer bowl combine sugar, butter and 2 tsp. *(10 mL)* vanilla. Beat at low speed, scraping bowl often, until light and fluffy (1 to 2 min.). Continue beating, adding eggs one at a time, until creamy (1 to 2 min.). By hand, stir in 1 c. *(250 mL)* bananas and sour cream. Fold in flour and baking soda. Pour into 2 greased and floured 8" *(20 cm)* round cake pans. Bake for 25 to 30 min. or until wooden pick inserted in center comes out clean. Cool 5 min.; remove from pans. Cool completely. In chilled small mixer bowl, beat chilled whipping cream at high speed, scraping bowl often, until soft peaks form. Gradually add sugar and 1 tsp. *(5 mL)* vanilla; continue beating until stiff peaks form (1 to 2 min.). Add melted chocolate; continue beating until well mixed (1 min.). (Do not overbeat.) On serving plate, place 1 cake layer. Spread with half of chocolate cream. Slice 1 banana; lay banana slices on top of chocolate cream. Top with remaining cake layer. Frost top of cake with remaining chocolate cream. Refrigerate or freeze cake 2 hr. or overnight. To serve, slice remaining banana; arrange banana slices around outside edge of cake. Sprinkle pecans in center of cake. Serve immediately or freeze to prevent bananas from browning.

Tip: 2 (9") *(23 cm)* round cake pans can be substituted for 2 (8") *(20 cm)* round cake pans. Bake for 20 to 25 min.

10 servings
60 minutes

Glazed Carrot Cake Wedges

*No one can resist a wedge of this rich carrot cake
with an orange, cream cheese glaze.*

Cake

1½ c.	*(375 mL)*	all-purpose flour
1 c.	*(250 mL)*	sugar
1½ tsp.	*(7 mL)*	baking soda
1 tsp.	*(5 mL)*	cinnamon
½ tsp.	*(2 mL)*	salt
¾ c.	*(175 mL)*	vegetable oil
2		eggs, slightly beaten
1 tsp.	*(5 mL)*	vanilla

1½ c.	*(375 mL)*	(3 med.) finely shredded carrots
1 c.	*(250 mL)*	flaked coconut

Glaze

1 c.	*(250 mL)*	powdered sugar
3-oz.	*(90-g)*	pkg. cream cheese, softened
1 tbsp.	*(15 mL)*	grated orange peel
1 tbsp.	*(15 mL)*	orange juice

Heat oven to 350°F *(180°C)*. In large bowl combine flour, sugar, baking soda, cinnamon and salt. Stir in oil, eggs and vanilla until well mixed. Stir in carrots and coconut. (Batter is thick.) Spread into greased and floured 9" *(23 cm)* round cake pan. Bake for 40 to 45 min. or until wooden pick inserted in center comes out clean. Meanwhile, in small mixer bowl combine all glaze ingredients. Beat at low speed, scraping bowl often, until smooth (1 min.). Pour over warm cake. Cut into wedges.

9 servings
45 minutes

Spiced Orange Gingerbread

Gingerbread sweetly glazed with orange that is sure to warm your heart.

1⅔ c.	*(400 mL)*	all-purpose flour
⅓ c.	*(75 mL)*	sugar
½ c.	*(125 mL)*	butter or margarine, melted
½ c.	*(125 mL)*	light molasses
¼ c.	*(50 mL)*	water
¼ c.	*(50 mL)*	orange juice
1		egg
1 tsp.	*(5 mL)*	baking soda

1 tsp.	*(5 mL)*	ginger
1 tsp.	*(5 mL)*	cinnamon
½ tsp.	*(2 mL)*	salt
½ tsp.	*(2 mL)*	cloves
½ c.	*(125 mL)*	orange marmalade

Sweetened whipped cream

Heat oven to 350°F *(180°C)*. In large mixer bowl combine all ingredients *except* orange marmalade and whipped cream. Beat at low speed, scraping bowl often, until well mixed (1 to 2 min.). Pour into greased and floured 9" *(23 cm)* sq. baking pan. Bake for 30 to 35 min. or until top springs back when touched lightly in center. In 1-qt. *(1-L)* saucepan place orange marmalade. Cook over low heat, stirring occasionally, until heated through (5 min.). Spread over warm gingerbread. Serve with whipped cream.

Spiced Orange Gingerbread (top)
Glazed Carrot Cake Wedges (bottom)

9 servings
40 minutes

Chocolate Chip Pound Cake Squares

A dessert that is reminiscent of old-fashioned pound cake with a sauce that is a chocolate dream.

Cake

1 c.	*(250 mL)* sugar
⅔ c.	*(150 mL)* butter or margarine, softened
3	eggs
1¼ c.	*(300 mL)* all-purpose flour
½ c.	*(125 mL)* mini semi-sweet chocolate chips
1 tbsp.	*(15 mL)* vanilla

Sauce

1 c.	*(250 mL)* mini semi-sweet chocolate chips
½ c.	*(125 mL)* whipping cream

Heat oven to 350°F *(180°C)*. In large mixer bowl combine sugar and butter. Beat at low speed, scraping bowl often, until light and fluffy (1 to 2 min.). Continue beating, adding eggs one at a time, until creamy (1 to 2 min.). By hand, fold in remaining cake ingredients. Pour into greased 9" *(23 cm)* sq. baking pan. Bake for 30 to 35 min. or until wooden pick inserted in center comes out clean. In 1-qt. *(1-L)* saucepan place 1 c. *(250 mL)* chocolate chips and whipping cream. Cook over low heat, stirring constantly, until chocolate is melted (4 to 6 min.). Serve sauce over squares.

15 servings
1 hour 30 minutes

Chocolate Rocky Road Cake

Chocolate, marshmallows and peanuts top this moist chocolate cake.

Cake

2 c.	*(500 mL)* all-purpose flour
1½ c.	*(375 mL)* sugar
½ c.	*(125 mL)* unsweetened cocoa
½ c.	*(125 mL)* butter or margarine, softened
1 c.	*(250 mL)* water
3	eggs
1¼ tsp.	*(7 mL)* baking powder
1 tsp.	*(5 mL)* baking soda
1 tsp.	*(5 mL)* vanilla

Frosting

2 c.	*(500 mL)* miniature marshmallows
¼ c.	*(50 mL)* butter or margarine
3-oz.	*(90-g)* pkg. cream cheese
1-oz.	*(30-g)* sq. unsweetened chocolate
2 tbsp.	*(30 mL)* milk
3 c.	*(750 mL)* powdered sugar
1 tsp.	*(5 mL)* vanilla
½ c.	*(125 mL)* coarsely chopped salted peanuts

Heat oven to 350°F *(180°C)*. In large mixer bowl combine all cake ingredients. Beat at low speed, scraping bowl often, until ingredients are moistened. Beat at high speed, scraping bowl often, until smooth (1 to 2 min.). Pour into greased and floured 13 × 9" *(33 × 23 cm)* baking pan. Bake for 30 to 40 min. or until wooden pick inserted in center comes out clean. Sprinkle with marshmallows. Continue baking 2 min. or until marshmallows are softened. Meanwhile, in 2-qt. *(2-L)* saucepan combine ¼ c. *(50 mL)* butter, cream cheese, chocolate and milk. Cook over med. heat, stirring occasionally, until melted (8 to 10 min.). Remove from heat; stir in powdered sugar and vanilla until smooth. Pour over marshmallows and swirl together. Sprinkle with peanuts.

Chocolate Chip Pound Cake Squares (top)
Chocolate Rocky Road Cake (bottom)

16 servings
45 minutes

Pumpkin Pecan Layer Cake

Three layers of festive fall flavors create this memorable cake.

Cake

2 c.	*(500 mL)* crushed vanilla wafers
1 c.	*(250 mL)* chopped pecans
¾ c.	*(175 mL)* butter or margarine, softened
18-oz.	*(500-g)* pkg. spice cake mix
16-oz.	*(398-mL)* can pumpkin
¼ c.	*(50 mL)* butter or margarine, softened
4	eggs

Filling

3 c.	*(750 mL)* powdered sugar
⅔ c.	*(150 mL)* butter or margarine, softened
4 oz.	*(125 g)* cream cheese, softened
2 tsp.	*(10 mL)* vanilla
¼ c.	*(50 mL)* caramel topping
1 c.	*(250 mL)* pecan halves

Heat oven to 350°F *(180°C)*. In large mixer bowl combine wafer crumbs, chopped pecans and ¾ c. *(175 mL)* butter. Beat at med. speed, scraping bowl often, until crumbly (1 to 2 min.). Press mixture evenly on bottom of 3 greased and floured 9" *(23 cm)* round cake pans. In same bowl combine cake mix, pumpkin, ¼ c. *(50 mL)* butter and eggs. Beat at med. speed, scraping bowl often, until well mixed (2 to 3 min.). Spread 1¾ c. *(425 mL)* batter over crumbs in each pan. Bake for 20 to 25 min. or until wooden pick inserted in center comes out clean. Cool 5 min.; remove from pans. Cool completely. In small mixer bowl combine cream cheese, ⅔ c. *(150 mL)*

butter, powdered sugar and vanilla. Beat at med. speed, scraping bowl often, until light and fluffy (2 to 3 min.). On serving plate layer 3 cakes (nut side down) with ½ c. *(125 mL)* filling spread between each layer. With remaining filling, frost sides only of cake. Spread caramel topping over top of cake, drizzling some over the frosted sides. Arrange pecan halves in rings on top of cake. Store refrigerated.

Tip: To remove cake easily from pan, place wire rack on top of cake and invert; repeat with remaining layers.

To Prepare Cake:

1. Press mixture evenly on bottom of 3 greased and floured 9" *(23 cm)* round cake pans

2. On serving plate layer 3 cakes, nut side down, with ½ c. *(125 mL)* filling spread between each layer. With remaining filling, frost sides only of cake.

Pumpkin Pecan Layer Cake

Chocolate Cherry Surprise Cake.

16 servings
1 hour 30 minutes

Chocolate Cherry Surprise Cake

Two favorite taste treats combine to create a luscious cake.

Cake

2	(10-oz.) *(284-mL)* jars maraschino cherries, drained, *reserve juice*
2	eggs, separated
2 c.	*(500 mL)* sugar
⅔ c.	*(150 mL)* butter or margarine, softened
2	(1-oz.) *(30-g)* sq. unsweetened chocolate, melted
3 c.	*(750 mL)* all-purpose flour
2 tsp.	*(10 mL)* baking soda
½ tsp.	*(2 mL)* salt
	Reserved cherry juice plus enough *buttermilk* to equal 2 c. *(500 mL)*

Frosting

¾ c.	*(175 mL)* sugar
⅓ c.	*(75 mL)* light corn syrup
3 tbsp.	*(45 mL)* water
3	egg whites
1½ tsp.	*(7 mL)* vanilla
1 c.	*(250 mL)* flaked coconut

Heat oven to 350°F *(180°C)*. Cut maraschino cherries in half; set aside. In small mixer bowl beat 2 egg whites at high speed, scraping bowl often, until soft peaks form (1 to 2 min.); set aside. In large mixer bowl combine 2 egg yolks, 2 c. *(500 mL)* sugar, butter and chocolate. Beat at med. speed, scraping bowl often, until well mixed (1 to 2 min.). Add flour, baking soda and salt alternately with cherry juice and buttermilk mixture. Continue beating until smooth (1 to 2 min.). By hand, fold in cherries, then egg whites. Pour into 3 greased and floured 9" *(23 cm)* round cake pans. Bake for 30 to 35 min. or until wooden pick inserted in center comes out clean. Cool 5 min.; remove from pans. Cool completely. In 1-qt. *(1-L)* saucepan stir together ¾ c. *(175 mL)* sugar, corn syrup and water. Cover; cook over med. heat until mixture comes to a full boil (3 to 5 min.). Remove cover; continue boiling until small amount of mixture dropped into ice water forms a firm ball or candy thermometer reaches 242°F *(117°C)* (8 to 12 min.). Meanwhile, in large mixer bowl beat 3 egg whites at high speed just until stiff peaks form (1 to 2 min.). Continue beating, pouring hot syrup mixture slowly into egg whites, until stiff peaks form (6 to 8 min.). Add vanilla; continue beating until well mixed. On serving plate layer 3 cakes with ½ c. *(125 mL)* frosting spread between each layer. Frost entire cake. Sprinkle top and sides of cake with coconut. Store loosely covered.

Tip: Three (8") *(20 cm)* round cake pans can be substituted for 3 (9") *(23 cm)* round cake pans. Bake for 35 to 40 min. or until wooden pick inserted in center comes out clean.

Tip: To cut cake easily, dip knife into water before cutting each slice of cake; clean knife if cake and frosting stick.

Chocolate Chip Macaroon Angel Food

Homemade angel food cake, light as a cloud and worth the extra effort.

Cake

1½ c.	*(375 mL)* powdered sugar
1 c.	*(250 mL)* cake flour*
1½ c.	*(375 mL)* (about 12) egg whites
1½ tsp.	*(7 mL)* cream of tartar
1 c.	*(250 mL)* sugar
¼ tsp.	*(1 mL)* salt

1 tsp.	*(5 mL)* almond extract
1 tsp.	*(5 mL)* vanilla
1 c.	*(250 mL)* mini semi-sweet chocolate chips
½ c.	*(125 mL)* flaked coconut
2 c.	*(500 mL)* sweetened whipped cream
1 c.	*(250 mL)* toasted flaked coconut

Heat oven to 375°F *(190°C)*. In small bowl stir together powdered sugar and flour; set aside. In large mixer bowl beat egg whites and cream of tartar at med. speed until foamy (1 to 2 min.). Beating at high speed, gradually add 1 c. *(250 mL)* sugar, 2 tbsp. *(30 mL)* at a time. Continue beating, scraping bowl often, adding salt, almond extract and vanilla until stiff and glossy (6 to 8 min.). By hand, gradually fold in flour mixture, ¼ c. *(50 mL)* at a time. Fold in just until flour mixture disappears. Fold in chocolate chips and ½ c. *(125 mL)* coconut. Spread batter into 10" *(25 cm)* tube pan. Cut gently through batter with metal spatula. Bake for 30 to 35 min. or

until cracks feel dry and top springs back when touched lightly. Invert pan on heat-proof funnel or bottle; let cool 1½ hr. Remove from pan. Decrumb cake with fingertips. Place cake on serving plate. Pipe top and around bottom of cake with sweetened whipped cream; sprinkle with toasted coconut.

*1 c. *(250 mL)* minus 2 tbsp. *(30 mL)* all-purpose flour can be substituted for 1 c. *(250 mL)* cake flour.

Tip: 16-oz. *(410-g)* pkg. angel food cake mix can be substituted for homemade cake.

To Prepare Cake:

1. By hand, gradually fold in flour mixture, ¼ c. *(50 mL)* at a time.

2. Cut gently through batter with metal spatula.

3. Invert pan on heat-proof funnel or bottle; let cool 1½ hr.

4. Decrumb cake with fingertips.

Chocolate Chip Macaroon Angel Food

Blue Ribbon Apple Pie

8 servings
2 hours

Blue Ribbon Apple Pie

*Pour whipping cream into this delectable apple pie;
the cream thickens and settles around juicy apples.*

Crust

2 c.	*(500 mL)*	all-purpose flour
1 tsp.	*(5 mL)*	sugar
¼ tsp.	*(1 mL)*	salt
¼ tsp.	*(1 mL)*	cinnamon
¼ tsp.	*(1 mL)*	nutmeg
⅓ c.	*(75 mL)*	butter or margarine
⅓ c.	*(75 mL)*	shortening
4 to 5 tbsp.	*(60 to 75 mL)*	cold water

Filling

½ c.	*(125 mL)*	sugar
¼ c.	*(50 mL)*	firmly packed brown sugar
¼ c.	*(50 mL)*	all-purpose flour
½ tsp.	*(2 mL)*	cinnamon
½ tsp.	*(2 mL)*	nutmeg
6 c.	*(1,5 L)*	peeled, cored, sliced ¼" *(0,5 cm)* tart cooking apples
1 tbsp.	*(15 mL)*	butter or margarine
1 tsp.	*(5 mL)*	sugar
½ c.	*(125 mL)*	whipping cream

Heat oven to 400°F *(200°C)*. In large bowl stir together 2 c. *(500 mL)* flour, 1 tsp. *(5 mL)* sugar, salt, ¼ tsp. *(1 mL)* cinnamon and ¼ tsp. *(1 mL)* nutmeg. Cut in ⅓ c. *(75 mL)* butter and shortening until crumbly. With fork mix in water until flour is moistened. Divide dough in half; shape into 2 balls and flatten. Wrap 1 ball in plastic wrap; refrigerate. On lightly floured surface roll out other ball into 12" *(30 cm)* circle. Place in 9" *(23 cm)* pie pan. Trim pastry to ½" *(1 cm)* from rim of pan; set aside. In large bowl combine all filling ingredients *except* apples, 1 tbsp. *(15 mL)* butter, 1 tsp. *(5 mL)* sugar and whipping cream. Add apples; toss lightly to coat. Spoon into prepared crust. Roll remaining pastry ball into 12" *(30 cm)* circle; cut 8 large slits in top crust. Place over pie; crimp or flute crust. Brush with melted 1 tbsp. *(15 mL)* butter; sprinkle with 1 tsp. *(5 mL)* sugar. Cover edge of crust with 2" *(5 cm)* strip of aluminum foil. Bake for 35 min.; remove aluminum foil. Continue baking for 10 to 20 min. or until crust is lightly browned and juice begins to bubble through slits in crust. Remove from oven; run knife through slits to open. Pour whipping cream evenly through all slits. Return to oven for 5 min. to warm whipping cream. Cool pie 30 min.; serve warm.

Tip: If desired, omit whipping cream for a traditional apple pie.

Cherry Orchard Pie

Grated orange peel spices this eye-catching lattice top cherry pie.

Crust

2 c.	*(500 mL)* all-purpose flour
¼ tsp.	*(1 mL)* salt
⅔ c.	*(150 mL)* butter or margarine
4 to 5 tbsp.	*(60 to 75 mL)* cold water

Filling

1 c.	*(250 mL)* sugar
⅓ c.	*(75 mL)* all-purpose flour
	Pinch of salt
2	(16-oz.) *(398-mL)* cans red tart pitted cherries, drained
1 tsp.	*(5 mL)* grated orange peel
	Milk
	Sugar

Heat oven to 400°F *(200°C)*. In large bowl stir together 2 c. *(500 mL)* flour and ¼ tsp. *(1 mL)* salt. Cut in butter until crumbly. With fork mix in water until flour is moistened. Divide dough in half; shape into 2 balls and flatten. Wrap 1 ball in plastic wrap; refrigerate. On lightly floured surface roll out other ball into 12" *(30 cm)* circle. Place in 9" *(23 cm)* pie pan. Trim pastry to ½" *(1 cm)* from rim of pan; set aside. In large bowl combine sugar, ⅓ c. *(75 mL)* flour and a pinch of salt. Add cherries and orange peel; toss lightly to coat. Spoon into prepared crust. With remaining pastry ball prepare lattice top. (See Desserts, Cakes & Pies page 471.) Brush strips with milk; sprinkle with sugar. Cover edge of crust with 2" *(5 cm)* strip of aluminum foil. Bake for 50 to 60 min. or until crust is golden brown and filling bubbles in the center. If desired, remove aluminum foil during last 5 min. If browning too quickly, shield lattice strips with aluminum foil.

Crumb Top Rhubarb Pie

Pecans and a crumb topping crown this delicious country favorite.

Crust

1 c.	*(250 mL)* all-purpose flour
	Pinch of salt
⅓ c.	*(75 mL)* shortening
3 to 4 tbsp.	*(45 to 60 mL)* cold water

Filling

1¼ c.	*(300 mL)* sugar
3 tbsp.	*(45 mL)* cornstarch
½ tsp.	*(2 mL)* cinnamon
¼ tsp.	*(1 mL)* nutmeg
4 c.	*(1 L)* sliced ¼" *(0,5 cm)* rhubarb
⅔ c.	*(170 mL)* chopped pecans

Topping

1 c.	*(250 mL)* all-purpose flour
⅔ c.	*(150 mL)* sugar
½ c.	*(125 mL)* butter or margarine

Heat oven to 400°F *(200°C)*. In large bowl stir together 1 c. *(250 mL)* flour and salt. Cut in shortening until crumbly. With fork mix in water until flour is moistened. Shape into a ball. On lightly floured surface roll into 12" *(30 cm)* circle. Place in 9" *(23 cm)* deep-dish pie pan. Crimp or flute crust; set aside. In large bowl stir together all filling ingredients *except* rhubarb and pecans. Stir in rhubarb until well coated with sugar mixture. Spoon into pie shell. Sprinkle with pecans; set aside. In medium bowl stir together 1 c. *(250 mL)* flour and ⅔ c. *(150 mL)* sugar. Cut in butter until crumbly. Sprinkle mixture over rhubarb. Cover edge of crust with 2" *(5 cm)* strip of aluminum foil. Bake for 50 to 60 min. or until topping is golden brown and filling bubbles around edges. If desired, remove aluminum foil during last 10 min.

Cherry Orchard Pie (right)
Crumb Top Rhubarb Pie (left)

Fresh Strawberry Almond Pie

8 servings
4 hours

Shortbread cookies and almonds create a delightful crust for this refreshing summer pie.

Crust

1½ c.	*(375 mL)* crushed shortbread cookies
¼ c.	*(50 mL)* finely chopped blanched whole or slivered almonds
⅓ c.	*(75 mL)* butter or margarine, melted

Filling

6 c.	*(1,5 L)* (3 pt.) strawberries, hulled
1 c.	*(250 mL)* sugar
3 tbsp.	*(45 mL)* cornstarch
⅓ c.	*(75 mL)* water
¼ tsp.	*(1 mL)* salt
½ tsp.	*(2 mL)* almond extract

Sweetened whipped cream

Heat oven to 350°F *(180°C)*. In small bowl stir together all crust ingredients. Press on bottom and up sides of 9" *(23 cm)* pie pan. Bake for 8 min. Cool completely. Mash enough strawberries to equal 1 c. *(250 mL)*. In 2-qt. *(2-L)* saucepan combine sugar and cornstarch. Stir in mashed strawberry mixture and water. Cook over med. heat, stirring constantly, until mixture thickens and comes to a full boil (8 to 15 min.). Boil 1 min.; remove from heat. Stir in salt and almond extract; cool 10 min. Fill baked crust with remaining strawberries; pour cooked strawberry mixture over strawberries. Refrigerate at least 3 hr.; garnish with sweetened whipped cream. Serve immediately.

Creamy Banana Pie With Lemon Zest

8 servings
8 hours

This banana cream pie is heavenly light and luscious.

9"	*(23 cm)* baked pie shell
¾ c.	*(175 mL)* sugar
¼ c.	*(50 mL)* cornstarch
1	*(¼-oz.)* *(7-mL)* envelope unflavored gelatin
2½ c.	*(625 mL)* milk
4	egg yolks, slightly beaten
2 tbsp.	*(30 mL)* butter or margarine
1 tbsp.	*(15 mL)* vanilla
2 tsp.	*(10 mL)* grated lemon peel
2 tbsp.	*(30 mL)* lemon juice
3	med. bananas, sliced ¼" *(0,5 cm)*
¾ c.	*(175 mL)* whipping cream
¼ c.	*(50 mL)* apple jelly
1 tbsp.	*(15 mL)* lemon juice
1	med. banana, sliced ¼" *(0,5 cm)*

In 2-qt. *(2-L)* saucepan combine sugar, cornstarch and gelatin. Gradually stir in milk and egg yolks. Cook over med. heat, stirring constantly, until mixture comes to a full boil (10 to 12 min.). Stir in butter, vanilla and lemon peel until butter is melted; pour filling into large bowl. Cover; refrigerate until thickened (about 2 hr.). Place 2 tbsp. *(30 mL)* lemon juice in small bowl; dip 3 sliced bananas into lemon juice. In chilled small mixer bowl, beat chilled whipping cream, scraping bowl often, until stiff peaks form (1 to 2 min.). By hand, fold whipped cream and bananas into pudding mixture. Pour into baked pie shell. Refrigerate at least 5 hr. or until firm. Just before serving, in 1-qt. *(1-L)* saucepan stir together apple jelly and 1 tbsp. *(15 mL)* lemon juice. Cook over low heat, stirring occasionally, until apple jelly is melted (3 to 4 min.). Arrange remaining sliced banana 1" *(2,5 cm)* from outside edge of pie to form a circle. Spoon or drizzle apple jelly mixture over bananas.

Creamy Banana Pie With Lemon Zest (top)
Fresh Strawberry Almond Pie (bottom)

8 servings
3 hours

Country Lemon Cream Pie

This refreshing lemon pie is creamy and rich.

9"   *(23 cm)* baked pie shell

Filling
1 c.   *(250 mL)* sugar
¼ c.   *(50 mL)* cornstarch
1½ c.   *(375 mL)* milk
         Pinch of salt

3   egg yolks, slightly beaten
¼ c.   *(50 mL)* butter or margarine
¼ c.   *(50 mL)* lemon juice
2 tsp.   *(10 mL)* grated lemon peel
½ c.   *(125 mL)* dairy sour cream

         Sweetened whipped cream

In 2-qt. *(2-L)* saucepan combine sugar, cornstarch, milk and salt. Cook over med. heat, stirring constantly, until mixture comes to a full boil (10 to 12 min.). Reduce heat to low. Continue cooking, stirring constantly, 2 min. Remove from heat. In small bowl gradually stir 1 c. *(250 mL)* hot mixture into egg yolks. Return mixture to saucepan. Cook over med. heat, stirring constantly, 2 min. Remove from heat; stir in butter, lemon juice and lemon peel until butter is melted. Stir in sour cream; pour into baked pie shell. Refrigerate at least 2 hr. or until firm. Just before serving, garnish with sweetened whipped cream.

8 servings
3 hours

Chocolate Mint Silk Pie

Mint adds a refreshing touch to this delectable pie.

Crust
1½ c.   *(375 mL)* crushed chocolate sandwich cookies
¼ c.   *(50 mL)* butter or margarine, melted

Filling
1 c.   *(250 mL)* sugar
¾ c.   *(175 mL)* butter or margarine, softened
3   *(1-oz.) (30-g)* sq. semi-sweet chocolate, melted, cooled
½ tsp.   *(2 mL)* peppermint extract
3   eggs

         Sweetened whipped cream

In medium bowl stir together crust ingredients. Press on bottom and sides of 9" *(23 cm)* pie pan. Refrigerate 10 min. In small mixer bowl combine sugar and ¾ c. *(175 mL)* butter. Beat at med. speed, scraping bowl often, until well mixed (2 to 3 min.). Add chocolate and peppermint extract; continue beating until well mixed (1 to 2 min.). Add eggs; continue beating, scraping bowl often, until light and fluffy (5 min.). Spoon into prepared crust. Refrigerate at least 3 hr. or until set. If desired, garnish with sweetened whipped cream.

Chocolate Mint Silk Pie

Chocolate-Laced Pecan Pie

8 servings
5 hours

Chocolate-Laced Pecan Pie

Two all-time favorites — pecan pie and chocolate — come together in this extra rich pie.

Single crust pie pastry*

⅔ c.	*(150 mL)* sugar
⅓ c.	*(75 mL)* butter or margarine, melted
1 c.	*(250 mL)* light corn syrup
3	eggs
½ tsp.	*(2 mL)* salt

1 c.	*(250 mL)* pecan halves
½ c.	*(125 mL)* semi-sweet chocolate chips

Pecan halves
Semi-sweet chocolate chips, melted
Sweetened whipped cream

Heat oven to 375°F *(190°C)*. Line 9" *(23 cm)* pie pan with pastry; crimp or flute crust. Set aside. In small mixer bowl combine sugar, butter, corn syrup, eggs and salt. Beat at med. speed, scraping bowl often, until well mixed (1 to 2 min.). By hand, stir in 1 c. *(250 mL)* pecans and ½ c. *(125 mL)* chocolate chips. Pour into prepared pie shell; if desired, turn pecan halves right side up. Cover pie loosely with aluminum foil. Bake for 30 min. Remove aluminum foil; continue baking 10 to 15 min. or until filling is set. If browning too quickly, re-cover with aluminum foil. Cool; refrigerate at least 4 hr. or until ready to serve. If desired, dip additional pecan halves halfway in melted chocolate chips; refrigerate until set. Serve pie with sweetened whipped cream; garnish with dipped pecan halves.

Tip: If desired, omit semi-sweet chocolate chips for a traditional pecan pie.

*See Desserts, Cakes & Pies page 456 for single crust pie pastry recipe.

---

8 servings
2 hours

Maple Pecan Pumpkin Pie

A hint of maple in the filling, a drizzling over the pecans and a touch in the whipped cream makes traditional pumpkin pie extra ordinary.

Single crust pie pastry*

16-oz.	*(450-mL)* can pumpkin
¼ c.	*(50 mL)* sugar
2	eggs, slightly beaten
1 c.	*(250 mL)* whipping cream
½ c.	*(125 mL)* pure maple syrup or maple flavored syrup
1 tsp.	*(5 mL)* cinnamon
½ tsp.	*(2 mL)* nutmeg

¼ tsp.	*(1 mL)* ground ginger
¼ tsp.	*(1 mL)* ground cloves
½ c.	*(125 mL)* pecan halves
2 tbsp.	*(30 mL)* pure maple syrup or maple flavored syrup
½ c.	*(125 mL)* whipping cream
1 tbsp.	*(15 mL)* pure maple syrup or maple flavored syrup

Heat oven to 375°F *(190°C)*. Line 9" *(23 cm)* pie pan with pastry; crimp or flute crust. Set aside. In large bowl stir together pumpkin, sugar and eggs. Add remaining ingredients *except* pecans, 2 tbsp. *(30 mL)* maple syrup, ½ c. *(125 mL)* whipping cream and 1 tbsp. *(15 mL)* maple syrup. Pour into prepared pie shell. Cover edge of crust with 2" *(5 cm)* strip of aluminum foil. Bake for 40 min. Remove aluminum foil. Bake for 15 to 25 min. or until knife inserted in center comes out clean. Arrange pecan halves on top of pie; drizzle or brush 2 tbsp. *(30 mL)* maple syrup over pecans. In chilled small mixer bowl, beat chilled whipping cream at high speed, scraping bowl often, until soft peaks form. Gradually add 1 tbsp. maple syrup; continue beating until stiff peaks form (1 to 2 min.). Serve pie with whipped cream.

*See Desserts, Cakes & Pies page 456 for single crust pie pastry recipe.

8 servings
2 hours

Chewy Caramel Brownie Pie

*This brownie pie is exceedingly rich, chewy, gooey and irresistible
when topped with a scoop of ice cream.*

Brownie

½ c.	*(125 mL)* butter or margarine
2	*(1-oz.) (30-g)* sq. unsweetened chocolate
1 c.	*(250 mL)* sugar
¾ c.	*(175 mL)* all-purpose flour
2	eggs, slightly beaten
½ tsp.	*(2 mL)* salt
½ tsp.	*(2 mL)* baking powder
1 tsp.	*(5 mL)* vanilla

Caramel

8 oz.	*(250 g)* (30) caramels, unwrapped
3 tbsp.	*(45 mL)* whipping cream
½ c.	*(125 mL)* chopped pecans
¼ c.	*(50 mL)* semi-sweet chocolate chips
	Vanilla ice cream

Heat oven to 350°F *(180°C)*. In 2-qt. *(2-L)* saucepan combine butter and unsweetened chocolate. Cook over med. heat, stirring occasionally, until melted (4 to 6 min.). Stir in remaining brownie ingredients. Spread batter into greased 9" *(23 cm)* pie pan. Bake for 20 to 25 min. or until brownie is firm to the touch. Meanwhile, in 1-qt. *(1-L)* saucepan cook caramels and whipping cream over med. low heat, stirring occasionally, until caramels are melted (5 to 6 min.). Remove brownie from oven; spread melted caramel mixture over entire baked brownie. Sprinkle with pecans and chocolate chips. Return to oven; bake for 3 to 5 min. or until caramel mixture is bubbly. Let stand 30 to 45 min.; cut into wedges. Serve warm with ice cream.

8 servings
9 hours

Celebration Ice Cream Pie

*This mile-high pie is snow-capped with a marshmallow cream meringue;
choose your favorite ice cream combinations for a celebration.*

9"	*(23 cm)* baked pie shell
4 c.	*(1 L)* (1 qt.) praline pecan ice cream, slightly softened*
4 c.	*(1 L)* (1 qt.) chocolate almond fudge ice cream, slightly softened*
6	egg whites

2 c.	*(500 mL)* marshmallow cream
	Chocolate sauce
	Caramel sauce
	Raspberry purée

In bottom of baked pie shell spread praline pecan ice cream. Freeze for 1 hr. Spread chocolate almond fudge ice cream on top of praline pecan ice cream. Freeze for 1 hr. Heat oven to 425°F *(220°C)*. Meanwhile, in large mixer bowl beat egg whites on high speed, scraping bowl often, until stiff peaks form (2 to 3 min.). Reduce speed to low. Gradually beat in marshmallow cream until smooth. Spread carefully onto frozen pie, sealing to edges of crust. Bake for 3 to 5 min. or until lightly browned. Freeze 6 hr. or overnight or until firm. Serve with chocolate sauce, caramel sauce or raspberry purée.

*Other Ice Cream Flavor Combinations:

Chocolate Chip and Rocky Road
Strawberry and Chocolate
Peppermint Bon Bon and Chocolate Chip
Strawberry Revel and Chocolate Revel
Vanilla and Chocolate

Tip: To prepare raspberry purée, place 2 c. *(500 mL)* fresh raspberries or 10-oz. *(300-g)* pkg. frozen raspberries, thawed, in 5-c. *(1,3-L)* blender container. Blend on high speed until puréed. If desired, strain sauce to remove seeds. Sweeten with sugar to taste.

Celebration Ice Cream Pie

Chocolate Lover's Ice Cream Pie

Straight from the ice house, this is a chocolate lover's ultimate dessert.

2 c.   *(500 mL)* crushed chocolate chip cookies
⅓ c.   *(75 mL)* butter or margarine, melted
4 c.   *(1 L)* (1 qt.) chocolate ice cream, slightly softened

Chocolate-flavored syrup
Sweetened whipped cream
Chocolate chip cookies, broken into pieces

In medium bowl stir together crushed cookies and butter. Press on bottom and sides of 9" *(23 cm)* pie pan. Freeze until firm (10 min.). Spread ice cream over crust. Cover; freeze until firm (6 hr. or overnight).

Just before serving, drizzle pie with chocolate syrup. If desired, garnish with sweetened whipped cream and pieces of chocolate chip cookies.

Blueberry-Peach Ice Cream Torte

Fresh peaches swirled in ice cream and topped with a blueberry sauce make an elegant presentation.

2 c.   *(500 mL)* (3 med.) fresh peaches, peeled, sliced*
2 tbsp.   *(30 mL)* sugar
1 pkg.   (12) ladyfingers, split
½ gal.   *(2 L)* vanilla ice cream, slightly softened

Sauce
⅓ c.   *(75 mL)* sugar
2 tbsp.   *(30 mL)* cornstarch
1 c.   *(250 mL)* water
2 tbsp.   *(30 mL)* butter or margarine
2 tbsp.   *(30 mL)* lemon juice
1 tsp.   *(5 mL)* grated lemon peel
2 c.   *(500 mL)* fresh or frozen blueberries (do not thaw)

In 5-c. *(1,3-L)* blender container combine peach slices and 2 tbsp. *(30 mL)* sugar. Cover; blend at high speed until well blended (30 to 40 sec.). Set aside. Place split ladyfingers upright (rounded side out) around edge of 10" *(25 cm)* springform pan, fitting closely together. Place ice cream in large bowl. Swirl in peach mixture. Place, by spoonfuls, evenly into prepared pan, pressing gently to level ice cream. Cover with aluminum foil; freeze at least 12 hr. or overnight. In 2-qt. *(2-L)* saucepan combine ⅓ c. *(75 mL)* sugar and cornstarch; stir in water. Cook over med. heat, stirring occasionally, until mixture thickens and comes to a full boil (3 to 5 min.). Boil 1 min. Stir in butter, lemon juice and lemon peel.

Cool 10 min. Stir in blueberries. Just before serving, pour sauce over top of torte.

*2 c. *(500 mL)* frozen sliced peaches, thawed, can be substituted for 2 c. *(500 mL)* fresh peaches.

Tip: 9" *(23 cm)* round cake pan can be substituted for 10" *(25 cm)* springform pan. Line with aluminum foil, extending excess aluminum foil over edges. After torte is frozen, lift torte from pan, using aluminum foil as handles. Remove aluminum foil.

Tip: Fresh blueberries make a clear sauce; frozen blueberries make a blueberry-colored sauce.

Blueberry-Peach Ice Cream Torte (top)
Chocolate Lover's Ice Cream Pie (bottom)

How To: Buy Fresh Fruits

Fruit:	Peak Season:	Look for:
Apples	All year	Firm, bruise-free apples. Choose specific varieties according to use.
Avocados	All year	Avocados which yield to gentle pressure, are bruise-free and do not have dark, soft, sunken spots.
Bananas	All year	Yellow or yellow tipped with green, bruise-free peel.
Blueberries	Summer	Round, firm, uniform dark blueberries with a silvery cast.
Cherries	Summer	Dark red colored skins, green stems and plump cherries.
Cranberries	Fall	Shiny, firm, red, plump berries.
Grapes	All year	Plump, slightly soft grapes that are well attached to stems. Green grapes should be yellow-green; red grapes should be predominantly red.
Kiwi Fruit	Spring, summer and fall	Plump, blemish-free fruits.
Lemons, Limes and Oranges	All year	Smooth, blemish-free, thin-skinned, full-color fruits.
Melons	Spring, summer and fall	Firm, heavy melons with good color, aroma and smooth stem ends. Cantaloupes should have pronounced netting, green honeydew should have a waxy, white rind barely tinged with green. Watermelon should have symmetrical shape, a dull surface and an underside that's yellowish or cream colored.
Peaches	Summer	Firm for slightly soft peaches with a creamy yellow background color.
Pears	All year	Slightly firm pears. A minor scar or surface blemish does not affect the fruit's flesh.
Pineapples	All year	Plump, slightly firm fruit with green leaves and fragrant aroma.
Raspberries	Summer	Plump berries of medium red color with no stems attached.
Rhubarb	Spring	Firm, crisp stalks with fresh looking leaves.
Strawberries	Spring, summer and fall	Plump, bright red berries with fresh green caps.

M

To Roll Out Pastry:

1. Using a stockinet-covered or floured rolling pin, roll out pastry on lightly floured pastry cloth. For a uniform circle, roll pastry from center to outside edge in four directions. For even thickness, lift rolling pin as you approach the edge.

2. To keep circular, occasionally push edges in gently with sides of hands. Prevent sticking by gently lifting pastry occasionally and sprinkling cloth with flour, if necessary.

3. To transfer pastry to pie pan, fold pastry into quarters. Place in pie pan with point in center. Gently unfold and ease into pie pan, pressing pastry gently with fingertips to fit snugly into pie pan. This prevents stretching and shrinking of pastry.

To Prepare Decorative Pie Pastries:

Forked: Flatten pastry evenly on rim of pie pan. With kitchen shears trim pastry even with edge of pie pan. Dip tines of fork into flour. Press firmly into edge of pastry. Continue around entire edge.

Crimped: Fold and roll edge of pastry under — even with pie pan. Pinch pastry in V-shape between thumb and index finger on outside edge of pastry with other index finger on inside edge of pastry. Continue around entire edge.

Diagonally Fluted or Rope: Fold and roll edge of pastry under — even with pie pan. Press thumb at an angle into edge of crust. Pinch pastry between thumb and knuckle of index finger. Place thumb in groove left by knuckle and repeat. Continue around entire edge.

Decorative Leaf: With paring knife, cut leaf shapes from pastry scraps. With tip of knife, draw line down center of each leaf, creating a vein. Flatten pastry evenly on rim of pie pan. With kitchen shears, trim pastry even with edge of pie pan. Dampen edge of pastry and arrange leaves in overlapping pattern around entire edge.

Ruffle: Fold and roll pastry under — even with pie pan. With hand inside of pastry edge, place thumb and index finger 1" *(2,5 cm)* apart on outside of pastry edge. With other hand on outside of pastry edge, place index finger on inside of pastry between thumb and index finger. Pull pastry toward outside. Continue around entire edge.

Simple Lattice Top: With kitchen shears, trim bottom pastry to ½" *(1 cm)* from rim of pie pan. Fill. Roll top pastry into 11" *(28 cm)* circle. With sharp knife or pastry wheel, cut circle into 10 (½") *(1 cm)* strips. Place 5 strips, 1" *(2,5 cm)* apart, across filling in pie pan. Place remaining 5 strips, 1" *(2,5 cm)* apart, at right angles to the strips already in place. With kitchen shears, trim strips. Fold trimmed edge of bottom pastry over strips; build up an edge. Seal; flute edge as desired.

COOKIES & CANDY

When Saturday was baking day, the big kitchen was abuzz with activity. Never mind that the heat of the stove made the room almost too warm to bear. If you stayed around long enough, and especially if you offered to help, you could win the first samples.

During the holiday season, baking became a marathon event that went on day after delicious day. There were gifts of sweets for everyone. A tin of cookies for the mailman. Sugar cookies that you helped decorate. Spicy drop cookies, plump with raisins. And chewy caramel nut bars.

But the best treats of baking day were the ones you got to eat. There were always special surprises in your lunchbox, like a gingerbread man with creamy white frosting, a crunchy piece of peanut brittle or brownies, unbelievably fudgy and rich with a cream cheese filling to add even more goodness.

And after every baking day, an assortment of sweets was packed away in boxes and tins so that friends and neighbors who dropped by could share in the sweet treasury of the kitchen.

Double Fudge Cream Cheese Brownies

*Two kinds of chocolate and cream cheese
make these homemade brownies absolutely yummy.*

Brownies

1 c.	*(250 mL)* butter or margarine
4	(1 oz.) *(30 g)* sq. unsweetened chocolate
2 c.	*(500 mL)* sugar
1½ c.	*(375 mL)* all-purpose flour
4	eggs, slightly beaten
1 tsp.	*(5 mL)* salt
1 tsp.	*(5 mL)* baking powder
2 tsp.	*(10 mL)* vanilla
1 c.	*(250 mL)* semi-sweet chocolate chips

Filling

¼ c.	*(50 mL)* sugar
2 tbsp.	*(30 mL)* butter or margarine, softened
3-oz.	*(90-g)* pkg. cream cheese, softened
1	egg
1 tbsp.	*(15 mL)* all-purpose flour
½ tsp.	*(2 mL)* vanilla

Heat oven to 350°F *(180°C)*. In 2-qt. *(2-L)* saucepan combine 1 c. *(250 mL)* butter and unsweetened chocolate. Cook over med. heat, stirring occasionally, until melted (4 to 6 min.). Stir in remaining brownie ingredients *except* chocolate chips. Fold in chocolate chips. Spread half of batter into greased 13 × 9" *(33 × 23 cm)* baking pan. In small bowl stir together all filling ingredients. Spread over brownie mixture. Spoon remaining batter over cream cheese. (Batter will not entirely cover cream cheese mixture.) Bake for 30 to 35 min. or until brownies begin to pull away from sides of pan.

Caramel N' Chocolate Pecan Bars

Popular candy flavors combined in an easy bar.

Crust

2 c.	*(500 mL)* all-purpose flour
1 c.	*(250 mL)* firmly packed brown sugar
½ c.	*(125 mL)* butter or margarine, softened
1 c.	*(250 mL)* pecan halves

Caramel Layer

⅔ c.	*(150 mL)* butter or margarine
½ c.	*(125 mL)* firmly packed brown sugar
1 c.	*(250 mL)* semi-sweet chocolate chips

Heat oven to 350°F *(180°C)*. In large mixer bowl combine all crust ingredients *except* pecans. Beat at med. speed, scraping bowl often, until well mixed and particles are fine (2 to 3 min.). Press on bottom of 13 × 9" *(33 × 23 cm)* baking pan. Sprinkle pecans evenly over unbaked crust. In 1-qt. *(1-L)* saucepan combine ⅔ c. *(150 mL)* butter and ½ c. *(125 mL)* brown sugar. Cook over med. heat, stirring constantly, until mixture comes to a full boil. Boil, stirring constantly, until small amount of mixture dropped into ice water forms a firm ball or candy thermometer reaches 242°F *(117°C)* (about 1 min.). Pour evenly over pecans and crust. Bake for 18 to 22 min. or until entire caramel layer is bubbly. Remove from oven. Immediately sprinkle with chips; allow to melt slightly (2 to 3 min.). Swirl chips leaving some whole for a marbled effect. Cool completely; cut into bars.

Double Fudge Cream Cheese Brownies (right)
Caramel N' Chocolate Pecan Bars (left)

Cheesecake Squares (top)
Lemon-Butter Bars (bottom)

16 bars
50 minutes

Cheesecake Squares

The flavor of cheesecake in an easy-to-make bar.

Crust

1 c.	*(250 mL)* all-purpose flour
½ c.	*(125 mL)* firmly packed brown sugar
⅓ c.	*(75 mL)* butter or margarine, softened
½ c.	*(125 mL)* chopped walnuts or pecans

Filling

8-oz.	*(250-g)* pkg. cream cheese, softened
¼ c.	*(50 mL)* sugar
1	egg
2 tbsp.	*(30 mL)* milk
2 tbsp.	*(30 mL)* lemon juice
½ tsp.	*(2 mL)* vanilla

Heat oven to 350°F *(180°C)*. In large mixer bowl combine flour, brown sugar and butter. Beat at low speed, scraping bowl often, until mixture is crumbly (2 to 3 min.). By hand, stir in nuts. *Reserve 1 c.* (250 mL) *of mixture for topping*; press remaining mixture on bottom of 8" *(20 cm)* sq. baking pan. Bake for 8 to 10 min. or until lightly browned. Meanwhile, in small mixer bowl combine all filling ingredients. Beat at med. speed, scraping bowl often, until smooth (4 to 5 min.). Spread over hot crust. Sprinkle with reserved crumb mixture. Continue baking for 23 to 30 min. or until golden brown. Cool; cut into bars. Store refrigerated.

Holiday Squares: Stir ¼ c. *(50 ml)* red and ¼ c. *(50 mL)* green chopped candied cherries into filling mixture.

16 bars
50 minutes

Lemon-Butter Bars

Tangy lemon and creamy butter combine to make these classic bars.

Crust

1⅓ c.	*(325 mL)* all-purpose flour
¼ c.	*(50 mL)* sugar
½ c.	*(125 mL)* butter or margarine, softened

Filling

¾ c.	*(175 mL)* sugar
2	eggs
2 tbsp.	*(30 mL)* all-purpose flour
¼ tsp.	*(1 mL)* baking powder
3 tbsp.	*(45 mL)* lemon juice
	Powdered sugar

Heat oven to 350°F *(180°C)*. In small mixer bowl combine all crust ingredients. Beat at low speed, scraping bowl often, until mixture is crumbly (2 to 3 min.). Press on bottom of 8" *(20 cm)* sq. baking pan. Bake for 15 to 20 min. or until edges are lightly browned. Meanwhile, in small mixer bowl combine all filling ingredients. Beat at low speed, scraping bowl often, until well mixed. Pour filling over hot crust. Continue baking for 18 to 20 min. or until filling is set. Sprinkle with powdered sugar; cool.

Microwave Directions: Prepare crust as directed left. Press on bottom of 8" *(20 cm)* sq. baking dish. Microwave on HIGH until top looks dry (4 to 5 min.). Meanwhile, in small microwave-safe mixer bowl combine all filling ingredients. Beat at low speed, scraping bowl often, until well mixed. Microwave filling on HIGH, stirring every min., until warm and slightly thickened (2 to 4 min.). Pour over hot crust. Microwave on HIGH, turning dish ¼ turn after half the time, until filling is just set in center (2 to 5 min.). Sprinkle with powdered sugar; cool.

Glazed Apple Pie Bars

Glazed Apple Pie Bars

3 dozen
2 hours

Apple pie — an all-time favorite crowd-pleasing treat.

Crust

2½ c.	*(625 mL)*	all-purpose flour
1 tsp.	*(5 mL)*	salt
1 c.	*(250 mL)*	butter or margarine, softened
1		egg, separated, yolk beaten with enough milk to equal ⅔ c. *(150 mL)*, *reserve white*

Filling

1 c.	*(250 mL)*	crushed cornflake cereal
8 c.	*(2 L)* (8 to 10 med.)	cooking apples, cored, peeled, sliced
1 c.	*(250 mL)*	sugar
1½ tsp.	*(7 mL)*	cinnamon
½ tsp.	*(2 mL)*	nutmeg
1		*reserved* egg white
2 tbsp.	*(30 mL)*	sugar
½ tsp.	*(2 mL)*	cinnamon

Glaze

1 c.	*(250 mL)*	powdered sugar
1 to 2 tbsp.	*(15 to 30 mL)*	milk
½ tsp.	*(2 mL)*	vanilla

Heat oven to 350°F *(180°C)*. In medium bowl combine flour and salt; cut in butter until crumbly. With fork stir in egg yolk and milk until dough forms a ball; divide in half. On lightly floured surface roll half of dough into 15 × 10" *(38 × 25 cm)* rectangle; place on bottom of ungreased 15 × 10 × 1" *(38 × 25 × 2,5 cm)* jelly roll pan. Sprinkle with cereal; layer apples over cereal. In small bowl combine 1 c. *(250 mL)* sugar, 1½ tsp. *(7 mL)* cinnamon and nutmeg. Sprinkle over apples. Roll remaining half of dough into 15½ × 10½" *(39 × 26 cm)* rectangle; place over apples. In small bowl beat egg white with fork until foamy; brush over top crust. In small bowl stir together 2 tbsp. *(30 mL)* sugar and ½ tsp. *(2 mL)* cinnamon; sprinkle over crust. Bake for 45 to 60 min. or until lightly browned. In small bowl stir together all glaze ingredients; drizzle over warm crust. Cut into bars.

Graham Cracker Caramel Crisps

4 dozen
45 minutes

Graham crackers are topped with marshmallows, buttery syrup and lots of almonds and coconut.

12		double graham crackers
2 c.	*(500 mL)*	miniature marshmallows
¾ c.	*(175 mL)*	butter or margarine
¾ c.	*(175 mL)*	firmly packed brown sugar
1 tsp.	*(5 mL)*	cinnamon
1 tsp.	*(5 mL)*	vanilla
1 c.	*(250 mL)*	sliced almonds
1 c.	*(250 mL)*	flaked coconut

Heat oven to 350°F *(180°C)*. Line 15 × 10 × 1" *(38 × 25 × 2,5 cm)* jelly roll pan with graham crackers. Sprinkle marshmallows evenly over crackers. In 2-qt. *(2-L)* saucepan combine butter, brown sugar, cinnamon and vanilla. Cook over med. heat, stirring constantly, until brown sugar is dissolved and butter is melted (4 to 5 min.). Pour evenly over crackers and marshmallows; sprinkle with almonds and coconut. Bake for 8 to 12 min. or until lightly browned. Cool completely; cut into bars.

Frosted Orange Date Bars

4 dozen
60 minutes

*Luxuriously moist, old-fashioned date bars are accented with orange peel
and a buttery orange frosting.*

Bars

¾ c.	*(175 mL)* sugar
½ c.	*(125 mL)* butter or margarine
½ c.	*(125 mL)* water
8-oz.	*(250-g)* pkg. chopped dates
1¼ c.	*(300 mL)* all-purpose flour
1 c.	*(250 mL)* chopped pecans
¾ c.	*(175 mL)* milk
¼ c.	*(50 mL)* orange juice
2	eggs
¾ tsp.	*(3 mL)* baking soda
½ tsp.	*(2 mL)* salt
1 tbsp.	*(15 mL)* grated orange peel

Frosting

3 c.	*(750 mL)* powdered sugar
⅓ c.	*(75 mL)* butter or margarine, softened
3-oz.	*(90-g)* pkg. cream cheese, softened
1 tbsp.	*(15 mL)* grated orange peel
2 to 3 tbsp.	*(30 to 45 mL)* orange juice

Heat oven to 350°F *(180°C)*. In 3-qt. *(3-L)* saucepan combine sugar, ½ c. *(125 mL)* butter, water and dates. Cook over low heat, stirring constantly, until dates are softened (5 to 8 min.). Remove from heat. By hand, stir in remaining bar ingredients until well mixed. Spread into greased 15 × 10 × 1" *(38 × 25 × 2,5 cm)* jelly roll pan. Bake for 15 to 20 min. or until wooden pick inserted in center comes out clean. Cool completely. In small mixer bowl combine all frosting ingredients. Beat at med. speed, scraping bowl often, until light and fluffy (2 to 3 min.). Spread over cooled bars; cut into bars.

Old-World Raspberry Bars

2 dozen
60 minutes

Rich, moist bars filled with flavorful raspberry preserves.

2¼ c.	*(550 mL)* all-purpose flour
1 c.	*(250 mL)* sugar
1 c.	*(250 mL)* chopped pecans
1 c.	*(250 mL)* butter or margarine, softened
1	egg
10-oz.	*(300-mL)* (¾ c.) *(175 mL)* jar raspberry preserves*

Heat oven to 350°F *(180°C)*. In large mixer bowl combine all ingredients *except* raspberry preserves. Beat at low speed, scraping bowl often, until well mixed (2 to 3 min.). *Reserve 1½ c. (375 mL) mixture;* set aside. Press remaining mixture into greased 8" *(20 cm)* sq. baking pan; spread preserves to within ½" *(1 cm)* from edge. Crumble reserved 1½ c. *(375 mL)* mixture over preserves. Bake for 40 to 50 min. or until lightly browned. Cool completely; cut into bars.

*10-oz. *(300-mL)* jar of your favorite flavor preserves can be substituted for 10-oz. *(300-mL)* jar raspberry preserves.

Old-World Raspberry Bars

3 dozen
45 minutes

Nutty Chocolate Chunk Cookies

Everyone loves these buttery cookies chock full of chocolate and nuts.

¾ c.	*(175 mL)* firmly packed brown sugar
½ c.	*(125 mL)* sugar
1 c.	*(250 mL)* butter or margarine, softened
1	egg
1½ tsp.	*(7 mL)* vanilla
2¼ c.	*(550 mL)* all-purpose flour

1 tsp.	*(5 mL)* baking soda
½ tsp.	*(2 mL)* salt
1 c.	*(250 mL)* coarsely chopped walnuts
8-oz.	*(250-g)* milk chocolate candy bar, cut into ¼" *(1 cm)* pieces

Heat oven to 375°F *(190°C)*. In large mixer bowl combine brown sugar, sugar, butter, egg and vanilla. Beat at med. speed, scraping bowl often, until well mixed (1 to 2 min.). Add flour, baking soda and salt. Continue beating until well mixed (1 to 2 min.). By hand, stir in walnuts and chocolate. Drop dough by rounded tablespoonfuls 2" *(5 cm)* apart onto cookie sheets. Bake for 9 to 11 min. or until lightly browned. Cool 1 min. before removing from cookie sheets.

2 dozen
30 minutes

Jumbo Candy & Nut Cookies

These oversized cookies are a family favorite.

1 c.	*(250 mL)* sugar
1 c.	*(250 mL)* firmly packed brown sugar
1 c.	*(250 mL)* butter or margarine, softened
2	eggs
1 tbsp.	*(15 mL)* vanilla
2 c.	*(500 mL)* all-purpose flour

1½ c.	*(375 mL)* quick-cooking oats
1 tsp.	*(5 mL)* baking soda
½ tsp.	*(2 mL)* salt
2 c.	*(500 mL)* (1 lb.) *(450 g)* candy coated milk chocolate pieces
1 c.	*(250 mL)* coarsely chopped peanuts

Heat oven to 350°F *(180°C)*. In large mixer bowl combine sugar, brown sugar, butter, eggs and vanilla. Beat at med. speed, scraping bowl often, until light and fluffy (2 to 3 min.). Add remaining ingredients *except* candy and peanuts. Beat at low speed, scraping bowl often, until well mixed (2 to 3 min.). By hand, stir in candy and peanuts. Drop dough by scant ¼ cupfuls *(50 mL)* 2" *(5 cm)* apart onto greased cookie sheets. Bake for 13 to 16 min. or until light golden brown.

Nutty Chocolate Chunk Cookies (left)
Jumbo Candy & Nut Cookies (right)

Old-Fashioned Oatmeal Cookies (right)
Chunky Peanut Cookies (left)

4 dozen
60 minutes

Old-Fashioned Oatmeal Cookies

These tasty, chewy cookies will remind you of Grandma's always-full cookie jar.

3 c.	*(750 mL)* quick-cooking oats		1 tsp.	*(5 mL)* cinnamon
2 c.	*(500 mL)* firmly packed brown sugar		½ tsp.	*(2 mL)* salt
1 c.	*(250 mL)* butter or margarine, softened		2 tsp.	*(10 mL)* vanilla
2	eggs		1¾ c.	*(425 mL)* all-purpose flour
1 tsp.	*(5 mL)* baking soda		1½ c.	*(375 mL)* raisins

Heat oven to 375°F *(190°C)*. In large mixer bowl combine all ingredients *except* flour and raisins. Beat at low speed, scraping bowl often, until well mixed (1 to 2 min.). Add flour; continue beating until well mixed (1 to 2 min.). By hand, stir in raisins. Drop dough by rounded teaspoonfuls 2" *(5 cm)* apart onto greased cookie sheets. Bake for 8 to 10 min. or until edges are lightly browned.

4 dozen
60 minutes

Chunky Peanut Cookies

A peanutty tasting lunchbox cookie.

1¾ c.	*(425 mL)* all-purpose flour		1 tsp.	*(5 mL)* salt
½ c.	*(125 mL)* sugar		½ tsp.	*(2 mL)* baking soda
½ c.	*(125 mL)* firmly packed brown sugar		½ tsp.	*(2 mL)* vanilla
½ c.	*(125 mL)* butter or margarine, softened		2 c.	*(500 mL)* salted peanuts
2	eggs			

Heat oven to 350°F *(180°C)*. In large mixer bowl combine all ingredients *except* peanuts. Beat at low speed, scraping bowl often, until well mixed (2 to 3 min.). By hand, stir in peanuts. Drop dough by rounded teaspoonfuls 2" *(5 cm)* apart onto greased cookie sheets. Bake for 8 to 12 min. or until lightly browned.

4 dozen
60 minutes

Sugar-Topped Butter Cookies

Old-fashioned crisp butter cookies—delicious served at "tea time" or dipped in milk.

2¼ c.	*(550 mL)* all-purpose flour
1 c.	*(250 mL)* sugar
1 c.	*(250 mL)* butter or margarine, softened

1	egg
1 tsp.	*(5 mL)* baking soda
1 tsp.	*(5 mL)* vanilla

Heat oven to 350°F *(180°C)*. In large mixer bowl combine all ingredients. Beat at med. speed, scraping bowl often, until well mixed (2 to 3 min.). Shape rounded teaspoonfuls of dough into 1" *(2,5 cm)* balls; place 2" *(5 cm)* apart on greased cookie sheets. Flatten cookies to ¼" *(0,5 cm)* thickness with bottom of glass dipped in sugar. Bake for 8 to 11 min. or until edges are very lightly browned.

Chocolate Chip Butter Cookies: By hand, stir 1 c. *(250 mL)* mini semi-sweet chocolate chips into dough.

Brickle Bit Butter Cookies: By hand, stir 6-oz. *(180-mL)* pkg. almond brickle bits into dough.

3 dozen
60 minutes

Holiday Thumbprint Cookies

Make a beautiful cookie tray using one cookie dough with many variations.

Cookies

2 c.	*(500 mL)* all-purpose flour
½ c.	*(125 mL)* firmly packed brown sugar
1 c.	*(250 mL)* butter or margarine, softened
2	eggs, separated
	Pinch of salt
1 tsp.	*(5 mL)* vanilla or almond extract

Suggested Coatings

1½ c.   *(375 mL)* finely chopped peanuts, almonds, pecans or walnuts
Colored sugars
Cinnamon and sugar

Suggested Toppings

Chocolate stars
Candied cherries
Caramels, cut in half
Maraschino cherries
Fruit preserves

Heat oven to 350°F *(180°C)*. In large mixer bowl combine all cookie ingredients *except* egg whites. Beat at low speed, scraping bowl often, until well mixed (2 to 3 min.). Shape rounded teaspoonfuls of dough into 1" *(2,5 cm)* balls. In small bowl beat egg whites with fork until foamy. Dip each ball of dough into egg white; roll in choice of nuts. (If using colored sugars or cinnamon and sugar, do not dip balls of dough in egg white. Roll balls of dough in colored sugars or cinnamon and sugar.) Place 1" *(2,5 cm)* apart on greased cookie sheets. Make a depression in center of each cookie with back of teaspoon. Bake for 8 min.; remove from oven. Fill centers with choice of suggested toppings; continue baking for 6 to 10 min. or until lightly browned.

Holiday Thumbprint Cookies

Melt-In-Your-Mouth Spritz

5 dozen
60 minutes

Melt-In-Your-Mouth Spritz

Perfect spritz cookies every time, plus five variations to create variety.

⅔ c. *(150 mL)* sugar
1 c. *(250 mL)* butter or margarine, softened
1 egg

½ tsp. *(2 mL)* salt
2 tsp. *(10 mL)* vanilla
2¼ c. *(550 mL)* all-purpose flour

Heat oven to 400°F *(200°C)*. In large mixer bowl combine all ingredients *except* flour. Beat at med. speed, scraping bowl often, until mixture is light and fluffy (2 to 3 min.). Add flour. Reduce speed to low. Continue beating, scraping bowl often, until well mixed (2 to 3 min.). If desired, add the ingredients from one of the following variations. If dough is too soft, cover; refrigerate until firm enough to form cookies (30 to 45 min.). Place dough into cookie press; form desired shapes 1" *(2,5 cm)* apart on cookie sheets. Bake for 6 to 8 min. or until edges are lightly browned.

Variations:

Spiced Spritz: To dough add: 1 tsp. *(5 mL)* each cinnamon and nutmeg, ½ tsp. *(2 mL)* allspice, ¼ tsp. *(1 mL)* cloves. Glaze: In small bowl stir together 1 c. *(250 mL)* powdered sugar, 2 tbsp. *(30 mL)* milk and ½ tsp. *(2 mL)* vanilla until smooth. Drizzle over warm cookies.

Eggnog Spritz: To dough add: 1 tsp. *(5 mL)* nutmeg. Glaze: In small bowl stir together 1 c. *(250 mL)* powdered sugar, ¼ c. *(50 mL)* softened butter, 2 tbsp. *(30 mL)* water and ¼ tsp. *(1 mL)* rum extract until smooth. Drizzle over warm cookies.

Chocolate Flecked Spritz: To dough add: ¼ c. *(50 mL)* coarsely grated semi-sweet chocolate.

Pina Colada Spritz: Omit vanilla in dough recipe above and add: 1 tbsp. *(15 mL)* pineapple juice and ¼ tsp. *(1 mL)* rum extract; stir in ½ c. *(125 mL)* finely chopped coconut. Frosting: In small mixer bowl combine 1 c. *(250 mL)* powdered sugar, 2 tbsp. *(30 mL)* softened butter, 2 tbsp. *(30 mL)* pineapple preserves and 1 tbsp. *(15 mL)* pineapple juice. Beat at med. speed, scraping bowl often, until light and fluffy (2 to 3 min.). Spread on cooled cookies. If desired, sprinkle with toasted coconut.

Chocolate Mint Spritz: To dough add: ¼ tsp. *(1 mL)* mint extract. Immediately after removing cookies from oven place 1 chocolate candy kiss on each cookie.

3 dozen
60 minutes

Butter Pecan Tartlets

These mini tarts taste like pecan pie.

Tart Shells

½ c.	*(125 mL)* butter or margarine, softened
½ c.	*(125 mL)* sugar
1	egg
1 tsp.	*(5 mL)* almond extract
1¾ c.	*(425 mL)* all-purpose flour

Filling

1 c.	*(250 mL)* powdered sugar
½ c.	*(125 mL)* butter or margarine
⅓ c.	*(75 mL)* dark corn syrup
1 c.	*(250 mL)* chopped pecans
36	pecan halves

Heat oven to 400°F *(200°C)*. In large mixer bowl combine all tart shell ingredients. Beat at med. speed, scraping bowl often, until mixture is crumbly (2 to 3 min.). Press 1 tbsp. *(15 mL)* mixture into cups of mini muffin pans to form 36 (1¾" to 2") *(4,5 to 5 cm)* shells. Bake for 7 to 10 min. or until very lightly browned. Remove from oven. Reduce oven to 350°F *(180°C)*. Meanwhile, in 2-qt. *(2-L)* saucepan combine all filling ingredients *except* chopped pecans and pecan halves. Cook over med. heat, stirring occasionally, until mixture comes to a full boil (4 to 5 min.). Remove from heat; stir in chopped pecans. Spoon into baked shells. Top each with a pecan half. Bake for 5 min. Cool; remove from pans.

Butter Pecan Tartlets

Orange Spiced Gingerbread Cookies

*Traditional cut-out gingerbread cookies are spiced with grated orange peel
for a subtle new taste sensation.*

Cookies

⅓ c.	*(75 mL)* firmly packed brown sugar
⅓ c.	*(75 mL)* butter or margarine, softened
⅔ c.	*(150 mL)* light molasses
1	egg
2 tsp.	*(10 mL)* grated orange peel
2¾ c.	*(675 mL)* all-purpose flour
1 tsp.	*(5 mL)* ginger
½ tsp.	*(2 mL)* baking soda
½ tsp.	*(2 mL)* salt

Frosting

4 c.	*(1 L)* powdered sugar
½ c.	*(125 mL)* butter or margarine, softened
3 to 4 tbsp.	*(45 to 60 mL)* milk
2 tsp.	*(10 mL)* vanilla

In large mixer bowl combine brown sugar, ⅓ c. *(75 mL)* butter, molasses, egg and orange peel. Beat at med. speed, scraping bowl often, until smooth and creamy (1 to 2 min.). Add remaining cookie ingredients. Reduce to low speed. Continue beating, scraping bowl often, until well mixed (1 to 2 min.). Cover; refrigerate at least 2 hr. Heat oven to 375°F *(190°C)*. Roll out dough, ½ at a time (keeping remaining dough refrigerated), on well floured surface to ¼" *(0,5 cm)* thickness. Cut with 3 to 4" *(7,5 to 10 cm)* cookie cutters. Place 1" *(2,5 cm)* apart on greased cookie sheets. Bake for 6 to 8 min. or until no indentation remains when touched. Cool completely. In small mixer bowl combine all frosting ingredients. Beat at low speed, scraping bowl often, until fluffy (1 to 2 min.). If desired, color frosting with food coloring. Decorate cookies with frosting.

Homemade Caramel Corn n' Nuts

This best-ever caramel corn is made extra special with the addition of mixed nuts.

20 c.	*(5 L)* popped popcorn
2 c.	*(500 mL)* firmly packed brown sugar
1 c.	*(250 mL)* butter
½ c.	*(125 mL)* dark corn syrup

½ tsp.	*(2 mL)* salt
½ tsp.	*(2 mL)* baking soda
1 c.	*(250 mL)* mixed salted nuts

Heat oven to 200°F *(93°C)*. In roasting pan place popcorn; set aside. In 2-qt. *(2-L)* saucepan combine brown sugar, butter, corn syrup and salt. Cook over med. heat, stirring occasionally, until mixture comes to a full boil (12 to 14 min.). Continue cooking, stirring occasionally, until candy thermometer reaches 238°F *(114°C)* or small amount of mixture dropped in ice water forms a soft ball (4 to 6 min.). Remove from heat; stir in baking soda. Pour over popcorn; sprinkle nuts over caramel mixture. Stir until all popcorn is coated. Bake for 20 min.; stir. Continue baking for 25 min. Remove from oven; immediately place caramel corn on waxed paper. Cool completely. Break into pieces. Store in tightly covered container.

Orange Spiced Gingerbread Cookies

6 dozen
3 hours 30 minutes

Aunt Emily's Soft Caramels

This buttery caramel recipe has been enjoyed for generations.

2 c.   *(500 mL)* sugar
1 c.   *(250 mL)* firmly packed brown sugar
1 c.   *(250 mL)* butter, softened
1 c.   *(250 mL)* milk

1 c.   *(250 mL)* whipping cream
1 c.   *(250 mL)* light corn syrup
1 tsp. *(5 mL)* vanilla

In 4-qt. *(4-L)* saucepan combine all ingredients *except* vanilla. Cook over low heat, stirring occasionally, until sugar is dissolved and butter is melted (20 to 25 min.). Continue cooking, without stirring, until candy thermometer reaches 248°F *(120°C)* or small amount of mixture dropped into ice water forms a firm ball (about 2 hr.). Remove from heat; stir in vanilla. Pour into buttered 13 × 9" *(33 × 23 cm)* pan. Cool completely; cut into 1 × 1½" *(2,5 × 3 cm)* pieces.

Tip: After cutting, wrap each caramel in plastic wrap.

10 to 14 apples
60 minutes

Carnival Caramel Apples

Reminiscent of carnivals and county fairs, these chewy treats are sure to please.

½ c.   *(125 mL)* butter
2 c.   *(500 mL)* firmly packed brown sugar
1 c.   *(250 mL)* light corn syrup
         Dash salt
14-oz.   *(385-mL)* can sweetened condensed milk

1 tsp.   *(5 mL)* vanilla

10 to 14 tart apples, washed, dried
1 c.   *(250 mL)* chopped salted peanuts

In 2-qt. *(2-L)* saucepan melt butter. Add brown sugar, corn syrup and salt. Cook over med. heat, stirring occasionally, until mixture comes to a full boil (10 to 12 min.). Stir in sweetened condensed milk. Continue cooking, stirring occasionally, until candy thermometer reaches 245°F *(118°C)* or small amount of mixture dropped into ice water forms a firm ball (20 to 25 min.). Remove from heat; stir in vanilla. Dip apples in caramel mixture. Dip end of apples in chopped peanuts; place on greased waxed paper. Refrigerate until firm (10 min.).

Carnival Caramel Apples

Old-Fashioned Peanut Brittle

2 pounds *(900 g)*
2 hours 30 minutes

A favorite during the holidays, this candy brings back memories.

2 c.	*(500 mL)* sugar		1 c.	*(250 mL)* butter, cut into pieces
1 c.	*(250 mL)* light corn syrup		2 c.	*(500 mL)* raw peanuts
½ c.	*(125 mL)* water		1 tsp.	*(5 mL)* baking soda

In 3-qt. *(3-L)* saucepan combine sugar, corn syrup and water. Cook over low heat, stirring occasionally, until sugar is dissolved and mixture comes to a full boil (20 to 30 min.). Add butter; continue cooking, stirring occasionally, until candy thermometer reaches 280°F *(138°C)* or small amount of mixture dropped into ice water forms a pliable strand (80 to 90 min.). Stir in peanuts; continue cooking, stirring constantly, until candy thermometer reaches 305°F *(152°C)* or small amount of mixture dropped into ice water forms brittle strands (12 to 14 min.). Remove from heat; stir in baking soda. Pour mixture onto 2 buttered cookie sheets; spread about ¼" *(0,5 cm)* thick. Cool completely; break into pieces.

Microwave Directions: In 3-qt. *(3-L)* casserole combine sugar, corn syrup and water. Microwave on HIGH, stirring after half the time, until sugar is dissolved and mixture comes to a full boil (5 to 8 min.). Add butter; microwave on HIGH, stirring after half the time, until microwave candy thermometer reaches 280°F *(152°C)* or small amount of mixture dropped into ice water forms a pliable strand (15 to 20 min.). Stir in peanuts. Microwave on HIGH, stirring after half the time, until microwave candy thermometer reaches 305°F *(152°C)* or small amount of mixture dropped into ice water forms brittle strands (6 to 8 min.). Stir in baking soda. Pour mixture onto 2 buttered cookie sheets; spread about ¼" *(0,5 cm)* thick. Cool completely; break into pieces.

Buttery Chocolate Nut Toffee

1¼ pounds *(565 g)*
45 minutes

One taste of this old-time favorite and you'll be back for more!

1 c.	*(250 mL)* sugar		6-oz.	*(175-g)* pkg. semi-sweet chocolate chips
1 c.	*(250 mL)* butter, cut into pieces		¼ c.	*(50 mL)* chopped walnuts

In 2-qt. *(2-L)* saucepan combine sugar and butter. Cook over low heat, stirring occasionally, until candy thermometer reaches 300°F *(149°C)* or small amount of mixture dropped into ice water forms brittle strands (25 to 30 min.). Spread on waxed paper-lined 15 × 10 × 1" *(38 × 25 × 2,5 cm)* jelly roll pan. Sprinkle chocolate chips over hot candy; let stand 5 min. Spread melted chocolate evenly over candy; sprinkle with nuts. Cool completely; break into pieces.

Microwave Directions: In 2-qt. *(2-L)* casserole combine sugar and butter. Microwave on HIGH, stirring occasionally, until microwave candy thermometer reaches 300°F *(149°C)* or small amount of mixture dropped into ice water forms brittle strands (12 to 18 min.). Spread on waxed paper-lined 15 × 10 × 1" *(38 × 25 × 2,5 cm)* jelly roll pan. Sprinkle chocolate chips over hot candy; let stand 5 min. Spread melted chocolate evenly over candy; sprinkle with nuts. Cool completely; break into pieces.

Old-Fashioned Peanut Brittle (top)
Buttery Chocolate Nut Toffee (bottom)

To Store Cookies for Short Term (1 Week):

1. Cool cookies completely.

2. Do not mix soft and crisp varieties in the same container or the crisp cookies will soon become soft.

3. Store soft cookies in a container with a tight-fitting lid.

4. Store crisp cookies in a container with a loose-fitting lid.

5. Store bar cookies in the pan in which they were baked; cover pan tightly with aluminum foil or plastic wrap.

To Store Cookies for Long-Term (6 Months):

1. Both frosted and unfrosted cookies can be frozen and stored up to six months.

2. Arrange cookies in a container lined with plastic wrap or aluminum foil. Separate with layers of aluminum foil or plastic wrap.

3. Tightly seal container, label and freeze.

4. Thaw cookies by allowing them to stand loosely covered on a serving plate for about twenty minutes.

For Mailing:

1. Bar, drop or fruit cookies can best withstand mailing. Tender, fragile cookies are apt to crumble when mailed.

2. Use a heavy cardboard box or empty coffee can as mailing container.

3. Line container with aluminum foil or plastic wrap.

4. Wrap four to six cookies of the same size together in aluminum foil, plastic wrap or plastic bags and seal securely with freezer tape.

5. Place the heaviest cookies in the bottom of the container and layer the wrapped cookies with crumpled paper toweling around them.

6. Seal container with freezer, plastic or adhesive tape.

7. Wrap container with an outer paper wrapper.

8. Print mailing address and return address on the package in ink. Mark the package "Perishable Food" to ensure more rapid transit and careful handling.

To Make Candies:

1. Follow directions carefully.

2. Use the recommended size heavy cooking pan to prevent candy from boiling over.

3. Use a dependable candy thermometer! Stand it upright in the candy mixture, making sure the bulb is completely covered with liquid while not resting on the bottom of the pan.

4. If you do not have a candy thermometer, use the cold water test. Drop a small amount of the candy mixture into a cupful of very cold water. Remove candy drop from water and form into a ball with fingers. The firmness of the ball determines the candy temperature and is an indication of doneness.

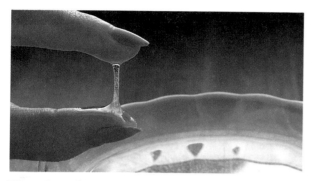

Thread: 223° to 234°F *(106° to 112°C)*: Forms a 2" *(5 cm)* soft thread.

Soft Ball: 234° to 240°F *(112° to 115°C)*: Forms a soft ball which flattens when removed from water.

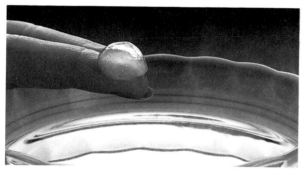

Firm Ball: 242° to 248°F *(117° to 120°C)*: Forms a firm ball which does not flatten when removed from water.

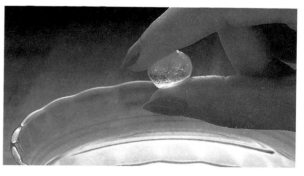

Hard Ball: 250° to 268°F *(121° to 131°C)*: Forms a hard, but pliable ball.

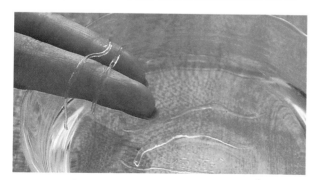

Soft Crack: 270° to 290°F *(132° to 143°C)*: Separates into hard, but pliable strands.

Hard Crack: 300° to 310°F *(149° to 154°C)*: Separates into hard, brittle strands.